Social Media Communication

This updated third edition presents a wide-scale, interdisciplinary guide to social media. Examining platforms like Facebook, Instagram, LinkedIn, Snapchat, TikTok, Twitter and YouTube, the book analyzes social media's use in journalism, broadcasting, public relations, advertising and marketing.

Lipschultz focuses on key concepts, best practices, data analyses, law and ethics – all promoting the critical thinking that is needed to use new, evolving and maturing networking tools effectively within social and mobile media spaces. Featuring historical markers and contemporary case studies, essays from some of the industry's leading social media innovators and a comprehensive glossary, this practical, multipurpose textbook gives readers the resources they will need to both evaluate and utilize current and future forms of social media communication.

Among other changes, updates to the third edition include a deep dive into new approaches to analytics, as well as greater discussion of law and ethics in light of the Facebook Cambridge Analytica scandal, the roll-out of GDPR and new case law relating to social media. *Social Media Communication* is the perfect social media primer for students and professionals, and, with a dedicated teaching guide, ideal for instructors, too.

Jeremy Harris Lipschultz is Peter Kiewit Distinguished Professor in the UNO Social Media Lab, and School of Communication, University of Nebraska at Omaha. Lipschultz is an international media source and frequently speaks on industry and social trends. He has been a blogger for *The Huffington Post*, and currently writes for LinkedIn. He has authored or co-authored six previous books and dozens of articles.

For more information about the book, supplementary updates and teaching materials, follow the Social Media Communication, Professor Jeremy Harris Lipschultz and UNO Social Media Lab Facebook pages, @JeremyHL on Twitter, Jeremy Harris Lipschultz on LinkedIn, and the UNO Social Media Lab on SlideShare.

Facebook:
www.facebook.com/SocialMediaCommunication
www.facebook.com/ProfessorJeremy/
www.facebook.com/UNOSML/

Twitter:
@JeremyHL @unosml1 #UNOSML #SMC2021 #SMProfs

LinkedIn and SlideShare:
www.linkedin.com/in/jeremyharrislipschultz/
www.slideshare.net/jeremylipschultz

Social Media Communication

Concepts, Practices, Data, Law and Ethics

Third Edition

Jeremy Harris Lipschultz

Routledge
Taylor & Francis Group

NEW YORK AND LONDON

Third edition published 2021
by Routledge
52 Vanderbilt Avenue, New York, NY 10017

and by Routledge
2 Park Square, Milton Park, Abingdon, Oxon, OX14 4RN

Routledge is an imprint of the Taylor & Francis Group, an informa business

© 2021 Taylor & Francis

The right of Jeremy Harris Lipschultz to be identified as author of this work has been asserted by him in accordance with sections 77 and 78 of the Copyright, Designs and Patents Act 1988.

All rights reserved. No part of this book may be reprinted or reproduced or utilised in any form or by any electronic, mechanical, or other means, now known or hereafter invented, including photocopying and recording, or in any information storage or retrieval system, without permission in writing from the publishers.

Trademark notice: Product or corporate names may be trademarks or registered trademarks, and are used only for identification and explanation without intent to infringe.

First edition published by Routledge 2015

Second edition published by Routledge 2018

Library of Congress Cataloging-in-Publication Data
A catalog record has been requested for this book

ISBN: 978-0-367-19495-6 (hbk)
ISBN: 978-0-367-19500-7 (pbk)
ISBN: 978-0-429-20283-4 (ebk)

Typeset in Warnock Pro
by Swales & Willis, Exeter, Devon, UK

Visit the eResources: www.routledge.com/9780367195007

Contents

1 Introduction to Social Media Concepts   1

2 CMC, Diffusion, and Social Theories   39

7 New and Mobile Media Technologies, Innovation, and Investment — 183

8 Big Data and Privacy — 205

9 Law and Regulation — 223

Tables and Boxes

Preface

Social media went from being used by a relatively small number of college students at the beginning of the century, to a common way for most Americans to spend their free time. The 2020 Covid-19 Coronavirus global pandemic raised the stakes on the importance of social media communication. Confined to our homes, we turned to social media for news, information, entertainment and work functions. Social media communication matured and evolved in the six years since the first edition of this book. At the time of this writing, global online universities have begun developing degree programs, concentrations and certificates focused on how to become a social media influencer on Instagram and other sites. The CEO of the world's largest public relations (PR) firm, Richard Edelman, estimates that this form of influence is six times more powerful than that coming from celebrities: "People are saying, 'I want to hear it from someone who I identify with, not somebody who is just famous."[1] Social media companies, such as Twitter, have hired large PR agencies to manage branding and storytelling strategies. Golin was managing communication about Twitter's decision to ban political advertising, as well as its "guidelines" that limited "how cause-based advertisers can target their ads."[2] Change is happening as Facebook and other sites venture into augmented reality (AR) and virtual reality (VR) technologies popular on gaming sites. The activity is driving a significant slice of growth in the US and global economy, as people click and buy online products and services.

In the three years since the second edition of this book, Instagram, YouTube and TikTok apps have soared in popularity. Instagram had an estimated 1 billion active users, and it offered dramatically higher engagement than Facebook, Twitter and other sites. As we entered 2020, there were an estimated 3.5 billion social media users worldwide. YouTube channels tend to be less social, but they attract smartphone viewers and generate advertising revenue. TikTok burst onto the scene, and parent company ByteDance was developing a competitor to Spotify for streaming music. In a surprise, a Vine co-founder revived the six-second video concept in an app called Byte, which quickly soared in its first weekend to the top of iPhone free downloads. Facebook and its more than 2 billion users were ahead of other social media companies in the Western world. The majority of Facebook's users are now outside of the US and Canada. AR, such as Pokémon Go, also offered a glimpse into how the world of social media communication continues to change.

The importance of the Internet also cannot be ignored within the broader context of political strife. In Iran, for example, about 80 million people were isolated in 2019 when the government blocked access during gasoline price increase protests – a practice of censorship common from Ethiopia to Russia.[3] By sheer numbers China's social media platforms rapidly grew and challenged the global dominance of Facebook. At the same time, younger social media users loved Snap, Inc.'s Snapchat and its filters, lenses and dynamic involvement for storytelling, as Instagram rushed to be more like it. Still, the fickle nature of social media use and new applications assures a frontier of constant change.

Mobile software applications ("apps"), such as Whisper, promoted posting "anonymous" memes and other content – confessions or secrets. However, location-based YikYak closed in 2017 after raising $73.5 million in funding, but sold its engineers for only $1 million.[4]

Because of the technical nature of the Internet, no message is truly anonymous, yet the idea of it has a following. Regardless of which specific platforms grow or wane, social media communication ushered in a fundamental shift from one-way mass media to interactivity of engagement within media audiences. Social media companies also exert power through algorithms that determine what we see or not in news feeds. Comedian and actor Sacha Baron Cohen suggested that Facebook (Instagram, Messenger and WhatsApp) and two other companies – Google (YouTube) and Twitter have created "the greatest propaganda machine in history," in the spread of lies and hate. "The ultimate aim of society should be to make sure that people are not targeted, not harassed and not murdered because of who they are, where they come from, who they love or how they pray."[5]

This book explores the emerging field of social media communication, as practitioners use new tools to communicate with the public through mass media or directly via social networking. The field of PR informs many of the best practices and new rules of social media. At the same time, social media concepts, tools and practices are useful for those studying and working in journalism, advertising and marketing. Social media, collectively, flourish under a broad umbrella for understanding the diffusion of social and technological change. In 2012, Barack Obama's @BarackObama Twitter account tweeted a "four more years" photograph of the president and Michelle Obama embracing.

The image was retweeted more than 500,000 times and liked by more than 3.5 million Facebook users on election night, briefly becoming the most popular social media communication ever. Ellen DeGeneres engineered a selfie with Bradley Cooper, Jennifer Lawrence, Brad Pitt and Meryl Streep at the 2014 Oscars and sparked more than 3.3 million retweets. Six years later, Ellen (@TheEllenShow) had more than 79.2 million Twitter followers. Obama's January 2017 farewell tweet ("Thank you for everything. My last ask is the same as my first. I'm asking you to believe – not in my ability to create change, but in yours.") on the official @POTUS account had more than 1.7 million retweets, and he left office with his personal @BarackObama account having more than 80.5 million followers. In early 2020, the account had more than 111 million followers – more than any other on Twitter.

FIGURE 0.1 *This 2012 election night photo was the most popular social media image ever at that time on Twitter and Facebook.*

The 2016 presidential election winner Donald Trump (@realDonaldTrump) credited his growing Twitter following, as well as nearly twice that number, including Facebook and Instagram. After the election, Trump told CBS *60 Minutes* Correspondent Lesley Stahl that he would continue using Twitter as president:

> I'm going to be very restrained, if I use it at all, I'm going to be very restrained. I find it tremendous … It's a modern form of communication. There should be nothing we should be ashamed of … It's where it's at … I do believe this, I really believe that the fact that I have such power in terms of numbers with Facebook, Twitter, Instagram, et cetera – I think it helped me win all of these races where they're spending much more money than I spent … social media has more power than the money they spent, and I think maybe to a certain extent, I proved that … It's a great form of communication. … I'm not saying I love it, but it does get the word out. When you give me a bad story or when you give me an inaccurate story or when somebody other than you … I have a method of fighting back
>
> (Flores, 2016, paras. 1–6)[6]

President Trump was anything but *very restrained* in his first term, and he frequently launched personal attacks in regular tweet storms. He grew his Twitter following from about 20 million to more than 71 million in early 2020. He broke new ground by using Twitter as a channel for official presidential notice about possible attacks on Iran:

FIGURE 0.2 *This 2020 @realDonaldTrump tweet was criticized for using social media instead of traditional congressional notice.*

One commentator wrote, "Apparently if Congress wants to stay informed on President Donald Trump's efforts to goad Iran into war, they'll have to check his Twitter feed."[7] As his impeachment trial began in the US Senate, Trump broke a personal record by tweeting and retweeting 143 times on January 22, 2020, while attending the World Economic Summit in Davos, Switzerland.

While the president also repeatedly blasted journalists as producing "fake news," Twitter and Facebook cracked down on the spread of fake accounts that may have influenced the close election, as well as the use of data. Following the Cambridge Analytica scandal, Facebook ended most third-party access to personal data on the site. Social media companies responded with new rules limiting candidate ability to target and reach key demographic groups, such as undecided voters. As NPR's Michel Martin put it, "One of the effects of microtargeting is that you can tailor a lie to the people most likely to believe that lie."[8] So-called "deepfake" videos that manipulate and purposely alter reality were banned by Facebook in 2020:

> Manipulations can be made through simple technology like Photoshop or through sophisticated tools that use artificial intelligence or 'deep learning' techniques ... While these videos are still rare on the Internet, they present a significant challenge for our industry and society as their use increases.[9]

From YouTube stars ("YouTubers") to Snapchat celebrity influencers and less famous micro-influencers with 1,000 to 100,000 followers, social media were established as entertainment and brand spaces. As a group, the Kardashian family had an astounding more than half a billion followers across social media sites, and they were dominant on Instagram. Celebrity world football (soccer) star Cristiano Ronaldo and entertainers Ariana Grande, Selena Gomez and Dwayne "The Rock" Johnson were ahead of Kim Kardashian West and Kylie Jenner in the rankings. Still, the Kardashian family managed to turn reality TV into a highly profitable social media genre of oversharing. It came at a price for Kim Kardashian West when she reported being robbed at gunpoint following a post in Paris showing her jewelry, went into hiding, and then sought ways to retain personal privacy while returning as a social media star. The Kardashians ushered in an era in which anyone could become an influencer or micro-influencer receiving free gifts (gifting) from brands or earning income through sponsored posts as contracted promoters. This led the Federal Trade Commission (FTC) to demand transparency in paid posts. Fines and court cases followed.

It is a complex media world in which online personal branding may also be seen in some contexts (i.e., "selfies") as addictive narcissism. Regardless, social media communication now represents big business. Global issues have sprouted, as new media tools are used for political and economic purposes. Journalists, broadcasters, PR practitioners, advertisers, marketers and others in business and non-profit sectors explore the effectiveness of developing social network sites, social media and longer-term business plans. Some universities, such as ours, have developed social media labs for research and community engagement.

At universities, social media are being studied in the development of communication theory, research methodology and best practices. Academic programs continue to revise curricula. In some cases, new online journalism and digital media courses have been developed and offered. Others have grounded social media use within traditional foundations of media storytelling. While it is possible to incorporate social media skills into journalism, public relations and other writing courses, an interdisciplinary approach to social media is needed. While newspapers sharply reduced newsroom staffing through buyouts and layoffs that worsened during the Covid-19 crisis, Internet media employment, including social media jobs, tripled since 2009 to 277,000 jobs.[10]

Many concentrations in new media were developed prior to the proliferation of social media, and these tend to be grounded in production techniques. Social media practices, however, extend interpersonal communication skills into mediated, online social spaces. This book is designed to promote the critical thinking and media literacy skills needed to effectively use new tools and navigate social media spaces.

It is clear that the media marketplace – from local newspapers to international television channels – is in a state of flux. This book seeks to make a contribution to those academics and professionals exploring curriculum revision, industry convergence and impact on the broad field, which now includes communication studies and media communication.

Social Media Communication is grounded in a wide set of theories and research methods. The author believes readers benefit from the application of traditional media and communication studies concepts, Internet studies, computer-mediated communication (CMC), social networks, electronic word-of-mouth (eWOM) marketing and other research. Some scholars bristle at the idea that we can move beyond the traditional academic silos of fields such as journalism, broadcasting and electronic media, public relations, advertising and marketing. However, social media tools such as Instagram promote interaction rather than disciplinary boundaries. Social networks and so-called social media "tribes" form around opinion leaders, influencers and their common topical interests found within social networks and clustered sub-networks.

While many newer books describe online media and recent texts focus on social media for journalists, public relations practitioners or marketers, the author seeks to engage all fields in an important dialogue. We will address specific "best practices" but also move toward a larger framework for understanding social media. In this regard, developing research exploring virtual teams and collaboration in information technology (IT) offers promising paths. This book will assume that readers have basic experience with tools such as Facebook, Instagram, LinkedIn, Twitter, Reddit, YouTube, Snapchat, TikTok, Byte and Pinterest. Additionally, the text and online companion sites will track apps such as Slack and Microsoft Yammer that focused on smaller, more private communication. Even here, though, Facebook exerted influence with its Messenger and WhatsApp apps. Meanwhile, blog sites, such as Tumblr, Medium, WordPress and LinkedIn, challenge professional news sites. Through research findings and case studies, the book will guide the reader toward a greater understanding of what is at stake for social media professionals. BeTheMedia.com's David Mathison was among the first to say that everyone online essentially has the power to be a personal, organization or business media brand. The re-definition of journalism and public relations within a social media context requires deeper thinking about the nature of "tweets," "wall posts," "pins" and social media behavior that favors amplified communication.

The book sees an ever-growing array of social media tools as defining an emerging era of communication, as we move from largely one-way mass communication for large audiences to social networked media communication. The #BlackLivesMatter social movement, police #BlueLivesMatter response, and Donald Trump's #MAGA (Make America Great Again) hashtags reflected how social media are now central in a wide range of *polarized* social and political movements. Social network analysis also revealed that partisans prefer to remain in "polarized crowds." When they interact, online anger and bullying may be present. So, social media communication may be at the center of the discussion on the future of democracies. While journalists, public relations practitioners, marketers and others will continue to sometimes communicate with large, mass audiences, the perspective of this book is that *influence and trust* are key concepts and will depend, in part, on the strength and character of an individual's or organization's social networks and branding.

Trust is a necessary but not sufficient requirement for communication to be influential through source and message credibility. Pew data have painted a troubling picture: three-fourths of the audience in 2005 said news organizations were more concerned with attracting the largest audience, while less than one-fourth said they cared about informing the public. No wonder that so-called "fake news," spread on social media, became perhaps *the* issue in the 2016 election cycle. One of the challenges in the 21st century is to find a balance between individual interests and the greater public interest or good. Trust binds us into social units, and there is a need for trusted information, as well as the individuals and institutions behind narrative storytelling. Trusted stories connect us within social media communication and across social networks. Influencers establish social rules and are leaders when it comes to social media participation. Social concepts, such as trust, are important in understanding the development of best practices and the use of data within boundaries of law and normative ethics.

The audience for new forms of social media needs a media and information literacy framework that critically examines new tools and social norms – whether or not the user engages in social media because of her or his career or for general interest. Taken together with concerns about audience fragmentation and the future of democratic consensus, trust is a key to the future. Through theory-based concepts, we should be able to measure networked data and understand communication patterns of social influence. We want to know why people participate in social networks, how they become influential, and what role trust may play in online user engagement. Ultimately, we should see the emergence of reliable predictive analytics. In some ways, a fundamental shift began before the launch of Facebook and other successful social media sites. As theorists Steven Chaffee and Miriam Metzger observed in 2001, the Internet appeared to bring a decline in traditional media agenda-setting, a fragmented world view, a shift away from elite power, increased access and greater choice. These developments suggested an evolution from "mass" to "media" communication. While this book recognizes that power is a struggle in play across channels, the social media communication perspective accepts that there are many new questions – from government surveillance to new laws and regulation.

Of course, these issues are of interest to those in journalism, public relations, advertising and marketing. Every business seeks return on investment (ROI) from time and money spent on social media communication. At the same time, fields such as information technology, political science, sociology, criminal justice, education and gerontology also recognize the importance of social media. As social media use continues to rise across the world, this book will be of increasing interest to the general public. The book will clearly define concepts in a way that will be useful to libraries and their readers.

This book, *Social Media Communication: Concepts, Practices, Data, Law and Ethics, Third Edition*, uses the idea of the social network as a heuristic and pedagogical device for understanding social media. It takes the reader beyond a cursory understanding of social media tools toward the development of a framework for assessing social media goals, objectives and possible new rules. By applying communication theory, research and understanding, the reader will be prepared to assess each new tool that enters the social media marketplace.

Three editions of this book could not have happened without the ongoing ideas, insights, editing suggestions and love of my spouse Sandy Shepherd Lipschultz. For nearly four decades, she has been my most important discussion partner on the teaching and research of media. We have been blessed to have two wonderful children, Jeff and Elizabeth, who grew up as "digital natives" experimenting with evolving social network sites. We learned a lot from parenting during this time. Daughter-in-law Holly also helped cultivate our understanding of how younger people communicate online. Our newest personal experience comes from watching granddaughter Catherine grow up in this social media world.

Aging increases my appreciation of the contributions from those who came before us: my parents, Hank and Maxine; Sandy's parents, Don and Faye; and our grandparents. All of them shared a love for learning and exploring, and in a later time no doubt would have been intrigued by the rapid spread of social media communication.

My colleagues at the University of Nebraska at Omaha are knowledgeable, insightful and wonderful. College of Communication, Fine Arts and Media (CFAM) Dean Michael L. Hilt (and Gail F. Baker before him), School of Communication Director Hugh Reilly, Associate Vice Chancellor and Graduate Dean Deborah Smith-Howell and the UNO administration have supported my social media communication work, and for this I am extremely thankful. Likewise, AEJMC has been a constant source of enrichment through the Law & Policy, Public Relations, Electronic News, and Communication Technology divisions, as well as our high-quality journals.

My students in Computer-Mediated Communication, Social Media Measurement and Management, Communication Law and Policy, and Communication & Technology courses continue to be early adopters of new iterations of social media communication, and they also continue to challenge our field to offer stronger conceptualization, data and research findings.

At Routledge in 2013, former Senior Editor Erica Wetter quickly grasped the vision for the original project and moved to advance it to publication. Editorial assistants provided careful review, editing and processing. Former UNO CFAM colleague Avery Mazor offered early technical help on images. The second edition was skillfully guided by Editorial Assistant Mia Moran. Emma Sherriff, who also collaborated on *Social Media Measurement and Management: Entrepreneurial Digital Analytics*, shepherded both books through the editorial processes.

Finally, from my "tweeps" on Twitter to friends, fans and followers on Facebook, Instagram and other sites, I appreciate our daily social media online activity. Some of my strongest connections are found within these pages as "thought leaders" or sources for important quotation. I hope this book contributes an important piece of our continuing conversation.

Jeremy Harris Lipschultz
February 2020

NOTES

1 Cerullo, M. (October 17, 2019, para. 5). Italian University Offers Degree In How To Become An Online Influencer. *CBS News.* https://www.cbsnews.com/amp/news/influencer-marketing-degree-italian-university-e-campus-offering-three-year-influencer-degree/

2 Bradley, D. (November 21, 2019, para. 5). Twitter Names Golin US Consumer Comms AOR. *PR Week.* https://www.prweek.com/article/1666569/twitter-names-golin-us-consumer-comms-aor

3 Bajak, F. (November 21, 2019). Iran Net Outage First To Effectively Isolate a Whole Nation. *Associated Press.* https://apnews.com/adbef9e66f3d4911b7486f84a090d292

4 Statt, N. (April 28, 2017). Yik Yak, Once Valued at $400 million, Shuts Down and Sells Off Engineers for $1 Million. *The Verge.* https://www.theverge.com/2017/4/28/15480052/yik-yak-shutdown-anonymous-messaging-app-square

5 Novak, M. (November 22, 2019, paras. 1, 15). Sacha Baron Cohen Says Social Media Companies Have Created the "Greatest Propaganda Machine in History." *Gizmodo.* https://gizmodo.com/sacha-baron-cohen-says-social-media-companies-have-crea-1839994830

6 Flores, R. (November 12, 2016). In "60 Minutes" Interview, Donald Trump Weighs Twitter Use as President. http://www.cbsnews.com/news/donald-trump-60-minutes-interview-weighs-twitter-use-as-president/

7 Cabrera, C. (January 5, 2020). Trump Declares His Tweets to be Official Notice to Congress on Attacks Against Iran. Talking Points Memo (TPM). https://talkingpointsmemo.com/news/trump-declares-his-tweets-to-be-official-notice-to-congress-on-attacks-against-iran

8 NPR (November 23, 2019, para. 11). Social Media Platforms Roll Out New Rules For Political Ads. *National Public Radio.* https://www.npr.org/2019/11/23/782335377/social-media-platforms-roll-out-new-rules-for-political-ads

9 Bickert, M. (January 6, 2020, para. 2). Enforcing Against Manipulated Media. *Facebook.* https://about.fb.com/news/2020/01/enforcing-against-manipulated-media/

10 Johnson, B. (January 3, 2020). Internet Media Employment Has Tripled Over the Past Decade. *Ad Age.* https://adage.com/article/year-end-lists-2019/internet-media-employment-has-tripled-over-past-decade/2221941

Introduction to
Social Media Concepts

In the next decade, will public discourse online become more or less shaped by bad actors, harassment, trolls, and an overall tone of griping, distrust, and disgust?
– Pew Research Center (@pewinternet, 2019)

I think anyone on the internet with eyeballs at this time and place is a bargain. Because it's so new, no one really knows what they're worth.
– Logan Paul (@LoganPaul, 2016)

We live in a time where brands are people and people are brands.
– Brian Solis (@briansolis, 2013)

In early 2019, an Internet phenomenon called "The Momo Challenge" began to spread, and data suggest that it spiked in early March before disappearing that summer. NBC called it "a global social media hoax about a paranormal threat to kids" that "morphed into a U.S. viral phenomenon" (Collins & Wodinsky, 2019, para. 1). As social media posts from celebrity Kim Kardashian, local police departments, school principals and others infected Momo with source and message credibility that the YouTube video could lead to suicide attempts, there was acceptance of the threat before it subsided. While the idea that a suicide "dare" edited into an otherwise normal video would be against site rules, the **meme** appeared to be a hoax launched earlier in Argentina and Mexico (paras. 3–6):

> "Momo" itself is an innocuous sculpture created by the artist Keisuke Aisawa for the Japanese special-effects company Link Factory. The real title of the artwork is *Mother Bird*, and it was on display at Tokyo's horror-art Vanilla Gallery … in 2016. After some Instagram photos of the exhibit were posted to the subreddit Creepy, it spread, and the "Momo challenge" urban legend was born
>
> (Lorenz, 2019, para. 6)

1

Binder (2019) discovered that the origin of Momo was a July 2018 YouTube upload by the AL3XEITOR account to his audience at the time of nearly 1 million subscribers, and this generated more than 5 million initial views (paras. 1–2). Fear is a powerful communication tool that can drive attention toward false or truthful social media communication. Frequently, for example, reports of school or other shootings, true or false, have led to panic in a community. Social media and traditional news media, such as local and national television news, may drive a fear of crime that can rise to the level of panic. In a sense, social media serve to amplify audiences consuming traditional news stories, and these have not changed very much over the years.

On a cool mid-April day in 2013, tragedy struck at the finish line of the Boston Marathon. Two bombs were detonated, injuring dozens of runners and spectators. As journalists scrambled to learn what happened and event organizers worked with emergency responders, Twitter immediately lit up with a burst of information, images and video. Some of the initial reports by eyewitnesses and media were accurate, but there was also a stream of false information spreading across users' **social networks**. At Golin, their real-time public relations newsroom The Bridge immediately alerted marketing client Cisco, which pulled content to avoid appearing disconnected from unfolding events (PR News, 2013). The chaotic scene generated massive amounts of information, including numerous factual errors.

Meanwhile, the Twitter **social network site (SNS) hashtag (#)** #BostonMarathon had been used for **live-tweeting** photographs and positive news about the annual event, but now it was the online space to track responses to the attack. Unfortunately, even mainstream news media, such as CNN and ESPN, reported inaccurate information in the early hours and days of the coverage, as in this tweet: "@SportsCenter: An arrest has been made in the Boston Marathon bombings, CNN reports" (April 17, 2013). The incorrect tweet was retweeted 13,930 times and made a favorite 2,476 times. A 2015 documentary, *The Thread*, later revealed the role that the social media site Reddit and its "Redditors" played curating content during the manhunt, and the "fake news" problem foreshadowed a rise in false information during the 2016 election – from a bizarre "Pizzagate" conspiracy theory about Hillary Clinton to claims of paid protesters of President-elect Donald Trump (Maheshwari, 2016; Silverman, 2016). Massanari (2015) through Reddit's upvoting and downvoting aggregated stories is about culture, community and play: "Voting is intended to show others what material deserves more (or less) attention from the community" (p. 3, 47). In the case of the Boston bombing investigation, Reddit was seen as having "potential for enabling collective action, whether for good or for ill" (p. 6). The use of social networking for "collective intelligence" (p. 47), though, may devolve into "mob justice" or a vehicle for "underlying distrust of law enforcement" (p. 49).

As the Boston Marathon bombing investigation continued, social media also shared a graphic YouTube video of the explosions and aftermath. Six months later, the bombing event continued to attract social media attention – from the Boston Red Sox World Series parade stop at the marathon finish line, to the photograph posted online of an inappropriate Halloween costume. A 22-year-old from Michigan dressed as a Boston Marathon bombing victim, and she sparked a large negative reaction from her Instagram photo that was also shared on Twitter.

The online publication *BuzzFeed* reported on the story of Alicia Ann Lynch, who received thousands of negative tweets and even death threats. One called Lynch "an absolutely disgusting human being." Clearly, Lynch's dress was insensitive, but Twitter users went so far as to identify her by sharing a photo of her Michigan driver's license. After deleting social media accounts, Lynch briefly returned on Twitter before having her account suspended. Lynch claimed that this online apology reported by media came from someone else: "@SomeSKANKinMI: Plz stop with the death threats towards my parents. They did nothing wrong. I was the one in the wrong and I am paying for being insensitive" (November 1, 2013). Lynch apologized with a simple "I'm sorry" on Twitter, but the attacks continued. Eventually, some on Twitter accepted the apology and called the continuing online "rage" an example of cyber-bullying and online mob behavior (Zarrell, 2013).

A practitioner of journalism, public relations (PR), advertising or marketing needs to understand how to effectively operate within social media. There is no single way because social media communication can be political and cultural (Chaffee & Metzger, 2001). For example, Shezanne Cassim, 29, spent nearly one year in a Dubai prison for posting a parody YouTube video before the Minnesotan was released in late 2013 (Gumuchian & Sidner, 2013). What might have been considered harmless in the US – poking fun at suburban teens liking hip-hop music culture – was found to be criminal in the United Arab Emirates. However, by developing strategies through planning and creating tactics, it is possible to avoid social media pitfalls and serve many goals within media and other organizations.

For many performers in social media communication, it has been an amazing decade. Felix "PewDiePie" Kjellberg, for example, launched a YouTube channel, dropped out of school the next year and became the first individual to reach 100 million subscribers (Webb, 2019). His video game and cultural content was second only to a record label in India: "PewDiePie spent months recruiting new fans to try to beat T-Series to 90 million subscribers, but was ultimately overtaken by T-Series' array of musical talent and YouTube's rapidly expanding user base in India" (para. 5). PewDiePie's rise to fame, however, also has been marked by controversies. Kjellberg's early videos included rape jokes, but he responded to media coverage of criticism and stopped. In 2017, he offered to pay for someone to post "DEATH TO ALL JEWS," but again apologized by explaining that he wanted to show how far people would go to make money online. Nevertheless, some brands distanced themselves from his ongoing anti-Semitic and racist jokes. In 2019, dozens were killed in the Christchurch, New Zealand, mosque shootings in which the shooter said "subscribe to PewDiePie" during a livestream of the horrific events. Kjellberg tweeted that he felt "absolutely sickened having my name uttered by this person." Some critics have argued that PewDiePie's use of racist humor may incite some young people inclined toward extremism, radicalization and violence. As PewDiePie aged with YouTube, he remained one of their key celebrities that attracted audiences larger than late-night television (Roose, 2019). However, at age 30 the vlogger abruptly announced plans to take a break from his 102 million subscribers and 24 billion video views: "I'm tired. I'm feeling very tired. I don't know if you can tell. Just so you know, early next year I'll be a way for a little while. I'll explain that later but I wanted to give a heads up" (Sky News, 2019, paras. 2, 5). From the beginning of YouTube, the lack of media gatekeeping and filtering exposed audiences to raw content. This became a serious misinformation problem during the 2020 Covid-19 Coronavirus pandemic.

When Hurricane Sandy hit the East Coast in late October 2012, it marked what the technology site *Mashable* later called a "Social Storm." The storm, tracked on Twitter with the **hashtag** #Sandy, was perhaps the first large-scale natural disaster in which officials coordinated to "disseminate emergency information to residents and provide emergency services in response to residents' posts" (Berkman, 2013, para. 6). On the one hand, citizens were urged to stay indoors and remain safe. On the other hand, the city monitored social media for reports from those venturing outside. One official said, "At no point, did we actively ask the public to collect media."

> "You see an enormous number of people who are using social media and consuming social media, both producing and discovering information, to a much higher extent than you would at any other point," Rachel Haot (@rachelhaot), chief digital officer for New York City, told *Mashable*.
>
> (Berkman, 2013, para. 7)

Natural disasters tend to draw traditional media attention that feeds social media communication. The path of Hurricane Dorian in 2019 also highlighted the news value of conflict. President Trump tweeted that Alabama was in the path of the storm, but meteorologists disputed the claim. A #Sharpiegate social storm followed over a doctored map that penned in the state when *The Washington Post* reported that the National Oceanic and Atmospheric Administration (NOAA) staff had been pressured to not challenge the president's false information, even as the storm spun up the Atlantic coast. The rapid growth of social media use has also disrupted the careful curation of all forms of breaking news.

☐ BOX 1.1

Air Berlin's Failed Customer Online Engagement

In a less dramatic but very early example of social media engagement, Air Berlin found out the hard way that engaging customers on Twitter might produce unintended results. When the airline lost a business traveler's luggage, the exchange between a social media content manager and customer turned into a very public branding #fail.

@_5foot1: Arrived in Dusseldorf without my bag. @airberlin are useless. No apology, no idea. What happened to German efficiency?

@airberlin – @_5foot1: We're sorry for the inconvenience caused. Did you contact the Lost & Found at Düsseldorf airport?

@_5foot1 – @airberlin: of course. Bag left in LDN. No assurance it will be on the next flight. I'm here for business meetings with no clothes.

@airberlin – @_5foot1: We understand how annoying this is and apologise! Unfortunately we can't help you right now, the Lost & Found will contact you

The next day:

@_5foot1 – @airberlin: Do you have a number i can call and speak to a human being. The tracking number is giving me no info

@airberlin – @_5foot1: Unfortunately there is no number I can give you, the Lost & Found will get in touch as soon as they found your bag.

While Air Berlin was correct to engage the customer, the conversation probably should have been taken off Twitter and onto a telephone with an eye toward solving the problem through traditional customer service. Perhaps the airline could have offered to buy the customer a set of clothes for the business meeting. The poor experience could also have been converted into positive social media message **engagement**. Best practices a decade later included the development of customer care programs that systematically address complaints through rapid response.

Source: Waldman, K. (September 4, 2013). I'm Here for Business Meetings with No Clothes. *Slate*. www.slate.com/articles/business/moneybox/2013/09/ air_ber lin_lost_luggage_the_german_airline_melts_down_on_social_media. single.html

In 2005 only about 5% of people in the US used social media, but Pew Research Center has found that about seven in ten were active (Pew Research Center, 2019) – in just 14 years we moved from a relatively small band of college student users to presidents and world leaders tweeting policy to hundreds of millions. Current data suggest that about two-thirds of American adults respond to surveys that they at least occasionally obtain news from social media sites: YouTube (73%), Facebook (69%), Instagram (37%), Pinterest (28%), LinkedIn (27%), Snapchat (24%), Twitter (22%), WhatsApp (20%) and Reddit (11%). The most recent statistics show about 430 million Reddit users, 21 billion monthly screen views, with 26% of its audience in the young Gen Z user group (Bump, 2019, paras. 7–12).

One could argue that social media were at the center of political change that included the rise of the "alt-right" movement, promotion of racism, spread of fake news and even a potential contributor in the election of Donald Trump (Romano, 2016). Aja Romano (@ ajaromano) at Vox.com concluded that: "All of this happened, to a large degree, because of the internet – specifically because of social media, and the convergence of elements that played out across social media" (para. 5). Pew data found that "20% of social media users say they've modified their stance on a social or political issue because of material they saw on social media, and 17% say social media ... helped to change their views about a specific candidate" (Anderson, 2016, para. 3) – more than enough to impact an election outcome. Among content choices was Russian-funded RT America television. It had more YouTube subscribers than BBC World, CNN/CNN International and Al Jazeera English, even though RT had comparatively fewer Twitter followers (Drum, 2017). The 2016 US presidential election year was clearly a complex mix, as reflected in Twitter's top hashtag list that included the Olympics, politics and entertainment:

1. #Rio2016

2. #Election2016

3. #PokemonGo

4. #Euro2016

5. #Oscars

6. #Brexit

7. #BlackLivesMatter

8. #Trump

9. #RIP

10. #GameofThrones

(Kottasova, 2016)

The rise in use of #BlackLivesMatter during protests in Ferguson, Missouri and Baltimore reflected political change (Cobbina, 2019). "The depth of anger and frustration among protesters was palpable, as they roused a sleeping nation and urged it to come to terms with the many, largely Black civilians who are murdered by police" (p. 73). Twitter was key in mobilizing protests. For example, #Ferguson appeared in more than 6 million tweets (p. 95). The use of mobile phone video "played a key role in prompting public outcry," as tweets "created a sense of urgency and immediacy, which galvanized thousands to mobilize against police violence" (p. 96).

From the user desire to filter content to the need for social media literacy skills, global media encompass the most important aspects of private and public life. The desire of individuals to engage and participate has its roots in technological developments more than five decades ago. The origins of this social media revolution can be found in the development of Internet structures, beginning with a 1960s military project called ARPANET. Early personal computer users' interest in local bulletin board systems (BBS) in the 1980s was a harbinger of interest in networked communication. The explosive growth of email, which remains the leading online function, and the World Wide Web in the 1990s sparked scholarly interest in the study of **computer-mediated communication (CMC)**.

The early site LiveJournal demonstrated that individuals like to share personal information with friends. The popular social sites Friendster, LinkedIn and MySpace launched in 2002–2003. LinkedIn was purchased by Microsoft in 2016, pivoted to a focus on professional networks through the sharing of business-oriented content, and experienced huge growth to more than 500 million users. LinkedIn data showed 90 million senior-level influencers and millions with the power to make business decisions.

MySpace remained very active within the music industry, and other targeted areas. There was a lot of early 21st-century interest in "participatory media, online community newspapers, and citizen journalism" (Mathison, 2009, p. 311). During a subway bombing in London in 2005, for example, the BBC used camera phone video for the first time, along with information from thousands of emails and photographs.

YouTube's first video, "Me at the zoo" had 4 million views at a time when video streaming was slow and cumbersome. The brief San Diego Zoo video demonstrated that there was audience interest in non-professional video content.

YouTube emerged as a primary video site with 1.3 billion users. An estimated 300 hours of video were uploaded in one minute, and every day users watch an estimated 5 billion videos. YouTube reports that more than 80% of adults in the coveted 18 to 49-year-old demographic are at least occasional viewers.

FIGURE 1.1 *The first YouTube video was not very dramatic.*

FIGURE 1.2 *@jkrums: "There's a plane in the Hudson. I'm on the ferry going to pick up the people. Crazy."*

Source: https://twitter.com/jkrums, posted at: *Los Angeles Times* (January 15, 2009). Citizen Photo of Hudson River Plane Crash Shows Web's Reporting Power. http://latimesblogs.latimes.com/technology/2009/01/citizen-photo-o.html#sthash.X2PUIScJ.dpuf

At about the same time, the Craigslist site grew from an email list developed in the mid-1990s to nearly 2 billion pageviews. Wikipedia also was growing in online popularity. Facebook in 2006 evolved from a university student platform to a public site. Twitter was about to burst onto the scene, ushering in communication brevity with its original 140-character limitation that doubled to 280-characters for each **tweet**. One of the early defining moments of the social media era in the US happened more than a decade ago. A US Airways jet made a crash landing in New York's Hudson River, and entrepreneur Janis Krums (@jkrums) posted a dramatic photograph on Twitter before news media could arrive at the scene.

The news value of the photograph came to symbolize the powerful combination of millions of citizens and their mobile phones. Other top moments in the development of social media include:

- TMZ reported the death of entertainer Michael Jackson in 2009 (http://latimes blogs.latimes.com/technology/2009/12/top-10-social-media-events.html).

- The Library of Congress decided in 2010 to archive all tweets since the Twitter 2006 launch (www.huffingtonpost.com/2010/12/29/social-media-moments-2010_n_802024.html).

- Wyclef Jean's Yele Haiti Foundation raised $1 million through $5 donations on Twitter and mobile following the 2010 earthquake (www.huffingtonpost.com/2010/12/29/social-media-moments-2010_n_802024.html).

- Rebecca Black uploaded a music video to YouTube in 2011, and it went **viral** with more than 160 million views in its first few days (http://mashable.com/2011/12/15/social-media-moments-2011/).

- The **meme** became popular in 2011. After University of California campus police pepper-sprayed student protesters who posted a video, the event was mocked through a series of viral images (http://gawker.com/5861431/uc-davis-pepper-spray-cop-is-now-a-meme/).

- LinkedIn skyrocketed to 90 million registered users by 2011, and then grew to more than 500 million by the end of 2019.

- Vine became the hot app of 2013. By limiting users to six-second looping mobile video, it created Twitter-like communication boundaries (www.youtube.com/watch?v=0wRUDazRh9I). It had been sold to Twitter, but closed in 2016 after entertainers wanted profits earned from their creative work. Some of that type of video moved to TikTok. Then, Vine co-founder Dom Hoffman launched Byte as "essentially the second coming of Vine, with updated features" (Hutchinson, 2020, para. 1). Byte quickly rose to the top of the iPhone free download list, perhaps because of its Vine-like potential (Savav, 2020). "It was where controversial YouTube star Logan Paul, whose channel now has more than 20 million subscribers, got his start" (para. 2).

- Instagram, purchased by Facebook, grew from more than 150 million users in 2013, as Facebook grew to more than 2 billion across the globe. Hubspot reported in 2019 that Instagram was atop social media sites for brands with over 500 million active daily users from more than 1 billion accounts. Facebook remains a giant platform, but it appears to have reached a plateau in comparison to Instagram.

- In August 2014, the ALS Ice Bucket Challenge that encouraged social media users to record videos of themselves having ice dumped upon them raised $220 million for research. The campaign could not duplicate viral results in subsequent years. Peter Frates (Team Frate Train), who championed the challenge, died from the disease in 2019 (www.bc.edu/bc-web/bcnews/campus-community/alumni/frates-family-statement.html).

- Snapchat had been the fastest-growing social media site among young users, with more than 200 million active daily users, 3.5 billion daily Snaps and 90% of 13 to 24-year-olds (https://zephoria.com/top-10-valuable-snapchat-statistics/). However, Instagram and TikTok quickly captured younger users. For example, Maris Jones used her DSLR camera and Final Cut editing to produce a series of videos that imitated the Beatles. "Occasionally, she'll add animation as well, like the psychedelic flowers that surround Harrison and the sitar" (Martoccio, 2019, para. 7). TikTok was the fastest-growing app and quickly monetized through social commerce links (Singh, 2019). One issue was the need for negotiating a deal with major record labels

FIGURE 1.3 *This University of California Pepper Spray Meme spread as a viral social media image.*

(Reuters, 2019). Nevertheless, Snap, Inc. (Snapchat) CEO Evan Spiegel suggested that TikTok, and its more than 400 million daily active users (DAUs), was near to passing Instagram's amazing popularity (Sydow, 2020; Waller, 2020). TikTok and Disney+ in 2019 quickly nudged into the list of top video streaming sites (p. 33).

- About seven in ten Americans now get news from social media, and more get their news from social media sites than newspapers (www.pewresearch.org/fact-tank/2018/12/10/social-media-outpaces-print-newspapers-in-the-u-s-as-a-news-source/).

- Instagram cat videos by @smudge_lord received millions of views, as the TikTok short style spread to other sites (www.instagram.com/p/B45wmw-nVl9/). Cat video and photo popularity was reminiscent of the late Grumpy Cat, which captured public attention and popularity on Twitter.

Social media are distinguished by a high level of interactivity, user identity formation and an openness to share content across developing communities: "the overall dynamics of online social networks can be tied to centrifugal forces of globalization that are gradually bridging cultural divides ..." (Kurylo & Dumova, 2016, p. 2). Social networks are technical infrastructures, interactive, increasingly mobile, yet ambiguous and paradoxical in terms of power, control and emerging social movements. In part, this is because the use of networking and social media as tools of social change typically are met with harsh responses. In Turkey, for example, about 1,656 social media users were arrested "for allegedly supporting terrorist organizations or insulting officials on social media" after a failed coup (AP, 2016, para. 1). Thousands more were investigated. Turkey's highest court, though, later ruled that the banning of Wikipedia for two years was a free expression violation (AP, 2019).

Definitions vary, but the fundamental character of SNS engagement is the linkage of individuals through online technology as a way to communicate using a variety of media forms. Social media also are characterized by the creation of new sites. Many of the newest are focused on **mobile communication**. This dynamic and evolving nature of technology has helped social media spread in popularity to most of the world. Less is known about decisions to use or not use social media, leaving a site but returning later, addiction urges ("withdrawal, sudden urges, limited self-control, etc.") and negotiation of boundaries through perception of "surveillance and impression management" (Baumer et al., 2015, p. 10). Beyond individuals being watched by government, Facebook and Google surveillance is considered so extensive that Amnesty International (2019) has called it a human rights threat.

> To increase their revenue from advertisers, Google and Facebook compete to offer the best predictions about the most people. To achieve this, they need to expand their data vaults and refine their predictive algorithms. This incentivizes the companies to seek more data on more people to expand their operations across the internet, into physical space and, ultimately, across the globe.
>
> (p. 12)

The global Internet is huge. China blocked sites such as Facebook and Twitter but hosts government-sponsored social media services. China grew to 829 million Internet users in 2019, or about 58% of its population. India was second in the world with 560 million users and 41% of its people. The US is third with 312 million users, and 96% of the population. The developing world continues to catch up with the digital revolution that began in the United States in the 1990s. China and India mirror international trends of rapidly growing mobile Internet use projected to grow to more than half the global population.

This book focuses on the emergence of social media communication as a primary source of information for people across the world. Drawing from the historical Edelman PR **media cloverleaf** and its more recent iteration, social media are among four overlapping environments, which also include traditional media, owned media and hybrid media. Print and broadcast media were once the leaders of most public discussion and some public opinion. With the development of the Internet and Web in the 1990s, companies began to develop websites. These owned media, along with application software (**apps**), turned all of those with online identities into media companies. In this century, hybrid media emerged from blogging. *The Huffington Post* was one of the earliest hybrid media to take advantage of the shift by commercializing it and activating a network of citizen bloggers. Medium, LinkedIn Articles, Tumblr, Blogger and WordPress fuel interest in directly reaching targeted audiences through blogging. Social media, through early popular sites, such as Facebook, Twitter and YouTube, empowered individuals to interact as media, promote content and engage new people across social networks.

The rapid **diffusion** of social media over a few short years changed job **roles** for news reporters, PR people, marketers and others in a wide variety of positions. At the same time, social media are transforming the fields of advertising and marketing through a focus on reaching and engaging social networks.

This book examines social media from a communication perspective that focuses on important concepts and practices. For example, some of what we now study as social networking within social media can be examined through Katz and Lazarsfeld's filter hypothesis of personal influence (Katz & Lazarsfeld, 1955, as cited in Schmitt-Beck, 2003). People form social groups, sometimes seek out influencers and gauge social trends: "personal communication mediates the influence of mass communication ... reinforcing or blocking the impact of media information, depending on the evaluative implications of that information and on the political composition of voters' discussant networks" (p. 233). Influence extends well beyond politics and elections. As Katz (1957) observed about the nature of studying leaders and influencers: "It began to seem desirable to take account of chains of influence longer than those involved in the dyad; and hence to view the adviser-advisee dyad as one component of a more elaborately structured social group" (Katz, 1957, p. 5). In other words, personal influence happens within a context of networked groups. Decades later, Katz (1994) observed that, although we may be able to observe influence, "to activate this knowledge is not as easy ... (and) tends to be more expensive and more complicated than simply reaching everybody" (p. x). Social media, however, ushered in an era of visualizing human communication, tracking it within large amounts of data – big data – and sometimes placing activation within reach. It is clear that the amount and quality of social media research continues to grow, aligning with the growth in "use of social media for sharing various forms of user-generated content" (Khang, Ki, & Ye, 2012, p. 279).

The nature of influence, as well as the contemporary examination of social networks and social media, raises legal and ethical issues. For example, a restaurant or small business review on Yelp, whether or not it is accurate, might cause economic harm, if left to stand without response. Despite the challenges of breadth, social media became a force – perhaps the most important communication source – in the 21st century. Despite awareness of potential influence, individual users, including those working for media and corporations, continue to make huge mistakes on social media platforms, such as Twitter. Particularly when it comes to **breaking news** events and **real-time social engagement**, split-second decisions made by professionals frequently miss the mark. In order to better understand the challenges of social networking and social media communication, it is important to develop concepts built upon social research.

SOCIAL MEDIA CONCEPTS AND THEORIES

Participants in social media are networked individuals engaging in interpersonal, yet mediated, communication. Through CMC, users create online identities, interact and engage with others, participate in online communities, and may activate groups to respond. Communication behavior may involve politics, power and culture – even when it originates as consumer behavior.

The communication within social media sites, such as Twitter, may trigger **crowdsourcing** and even funding, in which an audience pieces together bits of information into a larger narrative for **storytelling**. The crowdsourcing question-and-answer program called Jelly, created by Twitter co-founder Biz Stone, was a 2014 mobile media response to user desire to leverage information and rich media images available within personal social network sites. After this failed to have enough interest, in late 2016 Stone announced in an email that Jelly was "totally reinvented" as "a search engine and a social network with a purpose," through "anonymous" questions. It was acquired by Pinterest in 2017, but the name became associated with game apps. The Twitter "Search" window became a new way to search for trending and other social conversations.

Effective distribution of stories, images and videos requires an understanding of specific online **platforms** and context. In marketing, for example, messages must connect with audiences: "With the instant access to social media made possible by mobile devices, there's no such thing as undivided attention anymore" (Vaynerchuk, 2013, p. 4). In this sense, social media content involves human storytelling that has a foundation within informational and persuasive communication. SNSs offer different tools to facilitate storytelling: Facebook "walls," Twitter feeds, Instagram and Snapchat "stories," Pinterest "pins," and LinkedIn "posts" or endorsements. For example, Microsoft also acquired Slideshare to integrate presentation sharing across social media sites, especially LinkedIn. Each new SNS diffuses into the marketplace, but only some are widely adopted by a mass audience.

---

t⊼ BOX 1.2

Thought Leader James Spann

The most important role that social media play in my business is audience engagement during life-threatening weather events. More than a decade ago, before social media communication, I could not buy a valid storm report from many rural parts of my state; now with one simple tweet, or request via Facebook, Snapchat, or Instagram, I not only have good reports, but pictures and video, as well. Most of these people have not gone through spotter training, but by sending a photo to us, they allow professional meteorologists to evaluate the storm, making the warning process more effective.

FIGURE 1.4 *@Spann.*
Courtesy of James Spann

In addition, we are able to push critical severe weather information to many who would not consider using television, especially younger people (18–24-year-olds). Social media served as a lifeline during our generational tornado outbreak on April 27, 2011, including a deadly one that struck near the University of

Alabama campus in Tuscaloosa. I think it is interesting that, on many days, I reach more people via social media than on television. Times are changing.

Time management is a big issue for us. We are working on social media very hard around the clock, seven days a week, with the same number of people we had many years ago. People expect us to be there via social media to answer their questions and provide weather information on demand. Our job has morphed into a 24/7 kind of thing, which can lead to fatigue and strains on family relationships. You have to maintain a rigid priority table when it comes to managing time.

Another challenge is sorting through bogus weather reports; there are always some people who want to damage the warning process with false information. We have to make decisions "on the fly" concerning the validity of the reports we receive during winter storms and severe weather. Also, for some reason, some people begin circulating old pictures, claiming they are current and related to an ongoing weather event. This is problematic, but we do our best to sort out the bad images and not use them on the air.

For our audience, one of the biggest issues is the reliance on Facebook for severe weather information. Facebook is simply a horrible platform for severe weather warning dissemination because only a small percentage of followers/fans actually see the posted warnings on their timeline. Facebook, Twitter, Snapchat and Instagram are crucial in our communication plan, but with so many on Facebook we have to do a better job of educating them. We prefer people get severe weather warnings via smartphone apps, such as WeatherRadio by WDT, and not rely on social media as their primary source.

We are using the live video capabilities on social networks, and they are becoming more important in reaching a large number of people during severe weather events. We stream our "wall-to-wall" tornado coverage on Facebook Live. The number of people watching live on Facebook rivals the audience we have through conventional television and our live stream, available on the station's mobile app and the Web.

During life-threatening weather, I simply want to reach the largest number of people. I don't care if they watch via television, an app, or Facebook. I just want them watching and paying attention.

In recent years, Instagram has become an increasingly important platform for us. Many have left Facebook due to a number of reasons, including privacy concerns and constant political rhetoric. I use Instagram Live (IGTV) even on routine weather days; during our nightly 10 pm Alabama newscast, I start an Instagram Live session for "Song of the Night." Those watching get to see some "behind the scenes" television, and during the final commercial break of the show we play a song (we have weekly themes, like "Best of the 80s," or "Songs from the year you were born"). We talk about the song, and let those watching give a thumbs up or down to the song. The real reason for this is to help us become familiar with the various social media live platforms, so we have great knowledge of how they work and who they reach, and also to allow those not watching conventional TV news to get to know us. They will seek us out when tornadoes start touching down because of our "Song of the Night" family.

James Spann, CBM, is Chief Meteorologist at ABC 33/40 in Birmingham, Alabama, where he has worked since 1996. Spann is author of the book, *Weathering Life* (2019). He also hosts Weather Brains, reports on two-dozen radio stations, is heard on the Rick and Bubba Network, and is a partner in Big Brains Media and The Weather Factory. He was educated at Mississippi State University. www/alabamawx.com. In 2019, when President Trump incorrectly tweeted that Alabama would be impacted by Hurricane Dorian, Spann quickly corrected: "Alabama will not be impacted by Dorian in any way." Spann's colleagues at the National Weather Service (NWS) in Birmingham were reportedly pressured by the Trump Administration to not contradict the president.

The fragmented environment means that content increasingly competes within a sea of clutter. We know from the **uses and gratifications** communication perspective that media users select content and use it with expectations in mind. Satisfaction and expectation drive future media consumption. At the same time, users will tend to avoid content that does not provide psychological rewards. Media run the risk of losing followers if they fail to consistently reward readers, listeners and viewers. Over time, then, media user behavior falls into habits built upon stimuli, responses and a set of expectations that may reflect positive, neutral or negative views. These dimensions are particularly important in social media because it is possible to identify user feelings through **sentiment analysis**, which codes media content along a positive–negative continuum.

In a broad sense, social media have the potential to redefine the culture. Voices can be heard through social media that have tended to be ignored by traditional media **gatekeepers**. During most of the 20th century, newspaper and wire service editors, radio news directors and television assignment editors (among others) selected a relatively small number of stories as news, and most events fell through the gatekeeping process. Social media offer opportunities for sharing events and news, but SNSs may also spread content that is capable of amplifying and manipulating public opinion and behavior. In this way, traditional media and social media may interact across ideological boundaries, impacting debate and participation (Soo-bum & Youn-gon, 2013).

Advertisers and marketers were some of the first to discover social media as a way to inexpensively reach large numbers of people with their messages. Social media content, like its predecessors, may be fair or not. At first, merely having a Facebook page or Twitter feed was enough to generate some interest. Fairly soon, however, these spaces opened brands to public criticism and required content managers to engage in customer relations. Product and service campaigns have evolved and grown to feature strategic plans that include social media **tactics**. Planning creates real-time opportunities to engage in social media during large events, such as the Super Bowl or Academy Awards live television broadcasts. At the same time, brand managers may jump in at any moment when there is an unexpected event. For example, when *Today* show weatherman Al Roker overslept for the first time in nearly four decades of work, a Twitter conversation followed.

Golin, an integrated agency with PR and digital content, operated one of the firm's global real-time engagement spaces called The Bridge, which has collaborated with longtime client McDonald's. The Chicago office was among more than a dozen global real-time centers, and is the global headquarters. In 2012, former journalists built a team of experienced engagement analysts. They provided clients with a variety of real-time services – insights, relationship building, hyper-relevant media relations, customer engagement and content creation. By late 2019, the global firm had integrated social media data analytics within the broader agency services of content creation, production, management, amplification, influence marketing, public affairs and social purpose.

FIGURE 1.5 *A major brand successfully engaged the **Today Show** by using Twitter to reach out to them.*

McDonald's
@McDonalds

Stick with us @AlRoker, we'll help you wake up for the next 39 years #McCafe

8:07 AM - 6 Aug 2013

37 RETWEETS 54 FAVORITES

As part of the show making fun of Roker, an early tweet was featured during on-air anchor conversation. The **earned media** cost only the time to engage, in contrast to the more expensive price of advertising within the show, plus it was more valuable coming from TV talent. Roker also yawned in a Vine video that poked fun at missing his early broadcast. While the event was brief, it demonstrated how social media conversation may shift and move quickly from one topic to another.

The emergence of a complex social media landscape may seem overwhelming to students and the general public. A social media communication perspective can help. Individuals need to actively develop and use media literacy skills. These can be used to understand how brands make plays within social media. At the same time, open dissemination of information requires all of us to learn how to discern truths from falsehoods.

SOCIAL MEDIA IN JOURNALISM

Decades ago, journalism was defined by its gatekeeping process, through which editors carefully selected news for distribution. The Associated Press (AP) and United Press International (UPI) maintained a news wire system with local newsroom partners. The wire provided a means to identify, edit and share news to newsrooms. Journalists then shared their selections with audience members. By the early 1980s, journalists were beginning to experiment with portable computers to write and send news reports from a location, such as a courtroom. This Tandy Radio Shack 100 laptop was one of the first mobile devices.

FIGURE 1.6 *This TRS-100, an early laptop for journalists, was on display in 2009 at the Newseum's former building in Washington, DC.*

By June of 2009, major news organizations had evolved to begin using Twitter feeds and YouTube videos to report on an Iranian uprising that led to street protests covered by citizen journalists using portable video recording devices. Journalists today are expected to use social media sites, monitoring content and participating in discussions. For example, the AP is a primary news distribution company and has issued specific social media guidelines for its employees and journalism practitioners working in "sensitive situations" (AP, 2013). These are based upon news values and journalistic principles:

> The Social Media Guidelines are designed to advance the AP's brand and staffers' personal brands on social networks. They encourage staffers to be active participants in social networks while upholding our fundamental value that staffers should not express personal opinions on controversial issues of the day.
>
> (AP, 2013, para. 1)

The AP encourages all journalists to have social media accounts, but this is not universal across journalism. While reporters may not post confidential information, they are urged to use a profile photograph and required to identify themselves as AP reporters. They cannot disclose political affiliations or "express political views." The AP (2013) also restricts online opinions, as "AP employees must refrain from declaring their views on contentious public issues in any public forum ..." (para. 20). Even in the areas of sports and entertainment, the AP (2013) guidelines declared:

- "trash-talking about anyone (including a team, company or celebrity) reflects badly on staffers and the AP" (para. 10)

- "you have a special obligation to be even-handed in your tweets" (para. 11)

- "posts and tweets aimed at gathering opinions for a story must make clear that we are looking for voices on all sides of an issue" (para. 12)

- "a retweet with no comment of your own can easily be seen as a sign of approval of what you're relaying" (para. 29)

In general, AP (2013) applied its traditional rules of journalism with regard to accuracy and corrections to social media spaces. While journalists were encouraged to promote their stories, they are also warned to be careful online. The guidelines are sound advice in a current news environment compromised by fake news, political propaganda and other noise (Benkler, Faris & Roberts, 2018). The researchers found that social network analysis offers a method for creating visual maps that identify disinformation campaigns:

> The consistent pattern that emerges from our data is that, ... there is no right-left division, but rather ... the right wing of the media ecosystem behaves precisely as the echo-chamber models predict exhibiting high insularity, susceptibility to information cascades, rumor and conspiracy theory ...
>
> (p. 73)

Journalism, as a profession, is being challenged by the open access and publication nature of the Internet. The WikiLeaks site, for example, initially challenged traditional journalistic methods of sourcing and official verification: "Its use of new technologies and the way it puts information into the public domain forces us to reconsider what journalism is and its moral purpose in contemporary global politics" (Beckett, with Ball, 2012, pp. 2–3). Everyone seems to agree that social media have changed journalism. "Regardless of how people get news from the web, this medium has become a dominant channel of communication and has passed newspapers as a primary source of public affairs news and information" (McCombs et al., 2011, p. 16). The Arab Spring, the Occupy movement and more recent election manipulation through social media posts suggest that trust is a variable given physical and technological barriers (Haci-yakupoglu & Zhang, 2015). As younger social media users, even those with high education, distrust traditional sources of political power: "The concept of *system trust*" is that "people are likely to trust a digital platform, such as a website, if they can denote structural elements that increase perceived credibility, reduce perceived risks, and make usage easy" (p. 452).

In Turkey, for example, following an apparent terrorist attack on a nightclub, the nation's deputy prime minister announced from Istanbul that the government would monitor 347 "provocative" social media accounts that "sow seeds of enmity among the public" (AP, 2017, paras. 3–4). Turkish law enforcement worked with Facebook and Twitter to shut down "suspect accounts" (para. 5): "We are not going to sit by and watch as three to five social media trolls spread discord among the people" (para. 6). Turkey, though, went further by prosecuting a journalist and other government critics following an earlier failed coup. In general, as there is more political instability in a nation, we tend to see increased levels of media and social media restrictions. Hong Kong protesters in 2019 attempted to similarly leverage social media in their fight with the Chinese government, but a protest ended in campus arrests. Nevertheless, in much of the world the pace of technological change remains brisk.

Growth in digital content usage pushed journalism education to broaden and emphasize visual storytelling (Green et al., 2012). Storytelling will continue to evolve because of technological change. For example, **augmented reality (AR)** mobile tools offer the evolution of storytelling, as it is "transformed into a more interactive, first-person participatory form utilizing the location-based, geographically anchored nature of AR" (Pavlik & Bridges, 2013, p. 41). Pokémon Go caused a brief media flurry, as social media users rushed to find geo-locations. At the same time, 3-dimensional (3D) storytelling by *The Guardian* and others ushered in new media storytelling possibilities to allow viewers to experience a place.

Mobile media tool availability appears to predict news consumption among younger users (Chan-Olmsted, Rim & Zerba, 2013). Perceived relative content advantages, utility and ease of use were all predictors of news consumption, suggesting that the younger news user may be driven, in part, by the availability of mobile apps. Mobile news users may be some of the first to document news events.

Breaking news reports frequently begin with eyewitness accounts, which may be followed up on as journalists seek facts. Journalism tends to be defined by its key elements:

the search for truth, "loyalty" to citizens, verification of information, practitioner independence and "monitor of power" (Craft & Davis, 2013, p. 41). The #BlackLives-Matter protests in many cities across the United States represented new political voices through "black Twitter" and other examples (Adams, 2015, para. 3). Social unrest presents difficult challenges for news organizations seeking business success, which also requires attracting and retaining large audiences through engaging and entertaining content.

Journalists are often urged to develop a personal brand by publishing a **blog**, which tends to be short and frequent posts of information and analysis. Best practices for blogging include:

- Frequently updated entries in reverse chronological order,

- Write effective headlines post with links, photos or graphics and

- Participate in the community by encouraging comments.

(Briggs, 2020, p. 51)

Digital journalism quickly expanded beyond blogging to micro-blogging on Twitter. As the publishing industry was disrupted, journalists found value in the continuous use of mobile devices, crowdsourced media storytelling, increased use of photography and video, and new forms of data-driven reporting. "Building social capital is an increasingly important strategy for journalists and news companies" (Briggs, 2020, p. 291). Instant polling, for example, is considered a direct audience connection. "We are now a full decade into using social media for journalism and this is still a vastly underused tool and tactic" (p. 296).

Blogging, however, blurs the lines between news and opinion. While reputable journalists maintain popular blogs, so too do paid bloggers working for corporate clients. At the heart of the emerging conflict between traditional news values practices and online media are the rules of engagement and use of opinion. "This open dialog is one of the hallmarks of digital journalism along with interactivity and collaboration" (Luckie, 2011, p. 51).

Internet news is "more horizontal" because its orientation places journalists within large and diverse social networks (Tewksbury & Rittenberg, 2012, p. 5). While traditional journalism informed citizens in order to aid in democratic decision-making through voting, **citizen journalism** has transformed the audience for news, as scholar Jay Rosen observes, through important online discussion. The interaction and **conversation monitoring** itself may be a driver for social change, even as voter apathy has grown. So-called "participatory journalism" features "open gates" that help explain "fundamental change currently underway" and sometimes "transcends national boundaries" (Singer et al., 2011, p. 5).

In such a journalism environment, traditional norms of **objectivity** through balanced opinions and the search for facts has been questioned and studied. Maras (2013) observed that objective journalism is a complex professional ideal in which journalists seek to report "reality," obtain "facts" and avoid "personal opinion" by "[s]eparating facts from opinion," exercising emotional detachment and promoting "fairness and balance" (pp. 7–8). Obviously, these news values directly smash into the openness of the Internet.

While journalism was once defined by elite news organizations competing within a fairly narrow range of media, Internet users are no longer restricted by choices offered within the context of media economics and regulation.

> With developments in media technology it is becoming even less clear in which sense it is meaningful to speak of media pluralism, if the media landscape is characterized more by abundance and limitless choice than by scarcity or lack of options.
>
> (Karppinen, in Hesmondhalgh & Toynbee, 2008, p. 40)

Journalism, then, is likely to be redefined by emerging SNSs and their business practices. Albarran (2013), for example, observed that social media are defined by a "lack of significant barriers to entry," since almost anyone is free to create social media accounts and user profiles (p. 6). As such, media economists think of social media as a "disruptive communications industry" (p. 14). One emerging model is non-profit journalism. For example, *The Salt Lake Tribune* was among major local newspapers to become a non-profit news organization: "While all cash donations will be tax deductible, there will be no immediate changes to digital or print subscriptions, though it is possible that digital subscriptions will become tax deductible in the future" (Canham, 2019, para. 15).

Researchers have found variables that differentiate the social media landscape. Content dissemination, for example, has been related to news reception, friend behavior and partisanship (Weeks & Holbert, 2013): "both reception and friending are highly predictive of dissemination of news within social media" (p. 226). At its core, social media frequently involve the distribution of unfiltered news and even rumors. Former National Public Radio's (NPR) senior strategist Andy Carvin (@acarvin) described in his book *Distant Witness* how he has cultivated sources on the ground in Egypt, Syria and other Middle East countries to attempt to verify information circulating on Twitter. Because of the nature of revolutions since the "Arab Spring" uprisings beginning in 2009, anonymous sources frequently shared videos to YouTube of what appeared to be atrocities. Supporters shared links on Twitter, but it may be difficult to determine authenticity through crowdsourcing. Still, the technique offers promise for journalists seeking news from dangerous locations. Storyful, a Dublin-based company, has worked with Yahoo News, Reuters, ABC News and brands to verify social media content by monitoring for social media "spikes" in traffic and conducting "360 (degree) forensic verification of video" as an extension of newsrooms (Rieder, 2013, paras. 12–13).

The nature of communication on Twitter is that online communication also generates social networks, which can be observed in real-time but also visualized using data analysis tools. Most users tend to form a passive audience, but the center of the social network often reveals news media, PR and community boosters – not dissimilar from offline and traditional media interaction. In a sporting event, for example, it is rare for Twitter users to be faced with trying to confirm facts. However, crowdsourcing usually emerges in the early moments of breaking news stories. Before journalists can do their traditional work of verifying facts, Twitter and other social media sites can be a forum for conflicting eyewitness accounts, as well as attempts by some to spread false and malicious information.

Social media Twitter users have also been called micro bloggers because tweets are limited to 280 characters of space, including links to images, video or other websites. Media storytelling, however, can be expanded through the use of blogs and tools, such as Twitter Moments, which organizes multiple tweets into a running narrative.

While some have treated the Internet and social media as a sort of Wild West without rules and norms, this approach is not recommended. Similar to their mainstream and traditional media predecessors, social media journalists are constrained by rapidly developing law and regulation (Stewart, 2017). This also applies to those social media users who do not identify themselves as journalists, and those considering themselves PR professionals. In an age of so-called "big data," information access, control and privacy protection are among the central concerns (Carter & Lee, 2016; Youm & Park, 2016). Data insights create targeting opportunities, and media storytelling research has found that narrative structure and free choices enhance content interest and memory: "a narrative structure may be considered more 'effective' if measured in its ability to immerse readers or increase reader enjoyment ..." (DeAngelo & Yegiyan, 2019, p. 401). The complex emotional spread of social media communication ultimately involves a host of issues explored in later chapters of this book.

SOCIAL MEDIA IN PR

Public relations organizations use social media sites to represent brands and engage with consumers. Coombs and Holladay (2007) suggested that academics and practitioners share the frustration that PR "activities are often equated with spin, stonewalling, distortion, manipulation, or lying" (p. 1). In response, modern definitions emphasize "public interest," a "management function," "mutually beneficial relationships," and "relationships with stakeholders" (pp. 22–23). PR discourse may focus on identity and branding. A user "packages himself in the language of his relationship to the dominant medium" (p. 12).

Data suggest that social media are gaining traction compared to traditional email as the best way to target through influence and identify pain points to address with a marketing solution (Chen, 2018). The blending of this with 21st-century public relations and advertising begins with raising awareness. Digital PR appears to be focused on branding and its impact. Integrated marketing, PR and advertising plans reflect the need for varied content across social channels. The key is to measure outcomes and respond. Crestodina (2018) noted the shift over about 25 years from Web-based traditional marketing to a focus on credible branded content that can move a consumer to buy. However, US-based social marketing models frequently do not work across cultures.

Global PR efforts face challenges, including being able to communicate and work across cultures. Reid and Spencer-Oatey (2012) identified a "global people competency framework" of knowledge and ideas, communication, relationships and personal qualities involving "communicate management," "shared knowledge and mutual trust" (p. 19,

21). Trust is a relational dimension that may be connected with social interaction and shared values that motivate site usage (Lin & Lu, 2011). Public relations, as a field, has been concerned with the ability of PR practitioners to influence decisions within their organizations. Smith and Place (2013), building upon Grunig's 1992 work, found that integrated structure may have an impact on "the expertise of the individual practitioner *and the use of social media*, which yields tangible evidence for the organization to assess the value of the public relations function" (p. 179, emphasis added). Smith and Place (2013) related this to forms of power – expert, legitimate, structural and discursive.

In this book, we use three overarching concepts – **trust**, **influence** and engagement – to understand the power of social media. Source and message **credibility** may evoke audience trust, which is a driver of influence through strategic engagement. Interactive communication may or may not promote identity and community within social media settings. PR involves many functions, including copywriting, media relations, event planning, crisis communication, corporate communication, reputation management and strategic planning. Each of these may incorporate social media tactics for clients, events, messages and branding.

TRUST

Journalism researchers began to study what was called source and message credibility. For example, Slater and Rouner (1996) found that message quality may have an effect on the assessment of source credibility. Eastin's (2006) experiments manipulated source expertise and knowledge about health information online content. Perceptions may be impacted by variation in source and message credibility.

While trust has long been assumed to be important for journalists in their relationship with readers, listeners and viewers, it is only recently becoming central to public relations practitioners. Edelman PR (2020) for many years has produced an annual Trust Barometer, which highlights the need for corporate and governmental leaders to "practice radical transparency," establish clear goals for operating, and take note of employee credibility. By doing so, each employee may "spread messages to their networks, which helps build and support trust company-wide."

> The 2020 Edelman Trust Barometer reveals that despite a strong global economy and near full employment, none of the four societal institutions that the study measures – government, business, NGOs and media – is trusted. The cause of this paradox can be found in people's fears about the future and their role in it, which are a wake-up call for our institutions to embrace a new way of effectively building trust: balancing competence with ethical behaviour
>
> (Edelman, 2020, para. 1)

A year earlier, Edelman found that "people have shifted their trust to the relationships within their control, most notably their employers" (Edelman, 2019, para. 1).

Media audiences usually value trustworthy information found within peer-to-peer networks. We want to be able to trust our leaders and the information they share. In a democracy, the availability of accurate information is valued as one way for voters to make decisions. In a world driven by social media content, disclosure of new facts can rapidly change public opinion and policy. By 2009 and 2010, social media contributed to growing **Arab Spring** protests, public awareness and revolution. In Egypt and Libya, longtime leaders were overthrown. In Syria, social media contributed to a spreading civil war, as the ISIS terrorist group gained prominence. They shared videos of beheadings on social media channels. In Iran, public demonstrations were captured on portable video cameras and uploaded to YouTube. In countries ruled by dictators, social media made it more difficult to control **propaganda** and rule by force.

While US reporting by news organizations such as *The New York Times* and NBC News historically has been seen as very trusted, social media are bringing a new global perspective for consumers. For example, when US Special Forces killed Osama Bin Laden, Al Jazeera had early and accurate reporting. Some watched an Internet livestream of the broadcast and shared it to social networks more than an hour before former President Barack Obama made an official statement.

Trust also is important for consumer brands. Traditionally, trust was seen as "the critical component in credibility," but new media have redefined these key concepts: "Trust, we come to find, tends to evolve from audience perceptions of the source's expertise on the topic at hand ... and is a critical aspect of the advertising persuasion process" (Stafford, in Stafford and Faber, 2005, pp. 286–287). One of the credibility challenges is the nature of online sources (Sundar & Nass, 2011). Cues and context are particularly important in evaluating source and message credibility within a broadening social media sphere.

INFLUENCE AND ENGAGEMENT

Social media sites are often the battleground for the influence to determine who we consider to be a **thought leader** or **idea starter**. Engagement is defined as "the collective experiences that readers or viewers have with a media brand" (Mersey, Malthouse, & Calder, 2012, p. 698, quoting Mersey, Malthouse, & Calder, 2010). Engagement can be understood through consumer beliefs about brands and brand experiences. Engagement has been connected through research to satisfaction and media use, as expectation and evaluation may influence "gratification-seeking behavior" and ultimately includes reading (p. 699).

In social media, reading is an important behavior, but it is not the only behavior. Users process photographs, charts and other visual communication, such as video. These stimuli are consumed and sometimes result in reactions. For example, Facebook "likes" and "shares," Twitter "favorites" and "re-tweets," and Pinterest **board** "pins" follow consumption. At the same time, a user decision to post new content or share content from others may result in additional responses from others. Frequently, a social media campaign goal is to increase engagement to grow reach and build fan loyalty – asking questions and commenting help to build social media relationships (Tappin, 2016).

SOCIAL MEDIA IN ADVERTISING AND MARKETING

Early in the development of social media, **marketing** became an important function. This has impacted the fields of **advertising** and PR. Online advertising spending grew across all areas – paid search advertising, display advertising, classified advertising, rich media, referrals of sales leads, sponsorship and email (Tuten, 2008). eMarketer estimated that the growth rate for global digital advertising spending would slow from a whopping 21% in 2018 to about 8% by 2023 – $517 billion (Enberg, 2019, para. 4). The industry born in 1996 grew to $2 billion by 2000, and then soared to $10 billion in 2013. The Interactive Advertising Bureau (IAB) pegged an average growth rate of nearly 16%. In 2020, digital now accounts for more than half of all media advertising dollars.

As early as 2012, a study by Adobe reported that a majority of consumers found online advertising annoying (68%) and distracting (51%), and that marketers underestimated these responses. Product reviews, for example, appeared credible for most – but not all – online users. Likewise, individuals varied in response to different media approaches (Adobe, 2012). The data supported a social media perspective, as follow-up studies suggested the need to use online data to improve customer experiences. Tuten (2008) viewed social media as "an umbrella phrase" for understanding "online communities that are participatory, conversational, and fluid," and emphasize "an individual's relationship to the community, the rights of the members to collaborate and be heard within a protective space, which welcomes the opinions and contributions of participants" (p. 20).

In this sense, social media have begun to move the discussion of online advertising and marketing beyond the historically favored practice of sponsored search and keyword advertising that has made Google so successful (Jansen, 2011). The online structure allows advertisers to measure **click-through rates (CTR)** for early banner advertising, but sponsored search helped advertisers to pay "only when a potential customer clicks on a sponsored result," which allowed for measurement accountability (Jansen, 2011, p. 12). Social media, within this context, empower potential customers to "share an ad, comment on an ad, and give feedback on an ad" (p. 225). Social media advertising, then, may use a **cost per click (CPC)** pricing structure instead of the traditional audience size estimates.

This helps explain why **word-of-mouth (WOM)** and the marketing extension of **electronic word-of-mouth (eWOM)** have become important marketing phrases for brands wanting to spread the word through a growing group of followers and **fans**. So-called "brand ambassadors" may be activated by company and product messages. Through conversation monitoring, brand community managers can assess awareness, spark popularity and even convert followers and fans to loyal customers. They can become part of an earned media strategy that leverages customer passion for a product or service. Social media WOM and "customer evangelism," as some marketing gurus have labeled it, amounts to free advertising by authentic customers who engage with others as trusted spokespeople. Somewhat related are those buyers and purchasers who rate products on sites, such as Amazon.com. These ratings and subsequent conversations may reflect brand loyalty or even competitor attacks.

Community managers are paid to monitor conversation and activity and to engage, as needed. For example, if online conversation turns unfairly negative on Twitter, then a company representative may need to engage and participate by providing additional information or offering assistance. Failure to engage when competitors do could be a competitive disadvantage. Some customers may determine product choice based, at least in part, on the quantity and quality of company online engagement. Here, advertising, marketing and PR may converge based upon strategic goals. The cost of online engagement may be considered by a **return on investment** analysis, although some professionals suggest that this does not make sense for social media. Analogous to ROI for a receptionist, social media may be a cost for doing business in a professional manner. An alternative is the so-called **Cost of Ignoring (COI)** social media (MacLean, 2013). With more than two-thirds of consumers on Facebook, Twitter and other social media, the argument is that businesses must be present in order to be listening and engaging in five areas: 1) customer service, 2) reputation management, 3) crowdsourcing to build loyalty, 4) collaboration and 5) recruitment of job candidates (MacLean, 2013).

The WOM process involves everything from generating conversation through business blogs to hiring paid bloggers (a controversial ethical issue), offering customer relations, triggering viral media content, handling a crisis, managing individual and organizational reputations, and monitoring conversation **buzz**. One of the earliest social media measurement techniques was to track buzz for individual brands and compare it to others. Measurement quickly became more sophisticated.

All online activities are open to measuring **benchmark data**, which may establish beginning points for measuring future growth and effects of strategic campaign tactics. Quantitative goals may be set for future growth. Further, qualitative analyses of key conversations may yield clues to marketing and sales successes and failures. Best practices for social media involve the development of strategies and tactics for setting specific new media goals. Later in this book, we will explore new models for building social media plans (Luttrell, 2016; Quesenberry, 2019). These generally begin with social media audits of current activity, and then carefully proceed to clear objectives, definitions, strategies and tactics over time and within a budget. Social media have come to be viewed as tools that may raise awareness, help spark new engagement, support customer relations and prod behavior change within a campaign structure (Lipschultz, 2020).

NEW MEDIA

Drawing upon the seminal work of Lievrouw and Livingstone (2006), Cheong, Martin and Macfayden (2012) "position new media as information and communication technologies *and* their social contexts" (p. 2). The study of changing technological devices – **hardware** and **software** – is dynamic and driven by continuous change over time. For example, the development and proliferation of smartphones has driven interest in mobile devices and media. Ling and Campbell (2011) concluded that mobile technologies "rearranged the social scene" by enhancing "some interactions" yet straining others (p. 329).

Consider the apps downloaded and located on a smartphone screen. These represent priorities for the users.

FIGURE 1.7 *This book author's iPhone home screen, as seen in early 2020, reflects his most important personal apps.*

However, we live in a multi-screen world in which user attention is split between many screens – sometimes with more than one active in a given moment. Beyond desktop and laptop computers, tablets and smartphones, television screens and place-based screens in public places may each offer engaging content. Social media appear to follow the findings of early Internet studies that concluded that user motivations matter. Media may group people into "interpretive communities," which "are neither homogeneous nor monolithic" (Mankekar, in Hesmondhalgh & Toynbee, 2008, p. 149). Instead, demographic differences among social media users may produce content that mirrors or departs from existing offline power structures. The growing US Latinx population, for example, represented one-fifth of consumers, with a median age of only 28 (Nielsen, 2019). "Latinx consumers are digitally savvy, highly social and exerting an outsized influence on every aspect of American life," and "the Latinx consumer journey can reveal important implications for brands looking to drive growth in a multicultural market" (paras. 1, 14). As such, the Latinx sector is seen as an emerging force in politics and culture (Morales, 2018). It is suggested that the Latinx are "streaming into newly developing digital and social media," such as YouTube, to find voice and identity, "rallying the community," and "immortal evidence of our endlessly diverse experiences" (pp. 239–240). While social media offer an alternative to traditional media gatekeeping, however, access to large audiences must be considered within the context of credibility and trust.

One key difference within social media is the rapid spreading of information, even when it is false. When the normally credible @AP Twitter account was hacked with incorrect information in 2013, crowdsourcing was important in users correcting through a variety of other news sources. Eventually, AP had to suspend its account and restart it. Within one month, AP again had more than 2 million followers – they followed the trusted news source after the brief incident.

The emergence of social media within PR coincides with convergence of traditional practices with advertising and marketing.

t📡 BOX 1.3

Thought Leader Melanie James

PR education and consultancy has become less linear. The planning landscape has changed completely over the last five years. This is, in large part, driven by the fact that social media are integral to all work that I do. That it's "social" means practitioners have to expect and often even encourage interaction, and this by its nature increases both risk and opportunity.

I'm no longer developing campaign plans that outline intended activities in detail stretching over weeks or months, which were approved by clients before implementation. The emergence of agile approaches to communication and PR work is clearly better suited to today's business and societal needs.
This means developing advanced

FIGURE 1.8 *@melanie_james*
Photograph by George Hyde

skills and insights beyond what has traditionally been used in strategic planning processes, such as mainly relying on hard facts and past trend data. I know I'm using more skills that center on sensemaking and pattern recognition, often of real-time data, such as social media analytics and audience/user engagement content.

No longer do I spend much time writing lengthy press statements, although these still have a place. My time is more likely spent with clients to help them shape their story, and then working out ways across all media to tell that story. We work on scenario planning, predicting possible responses to such efforts so that ways of leveraging audience or user engagement to meet strategic goals can be worked through. Based on this, I work to "pre-load" social media posts across platforms that align with other initiatives in the wider campaign. The cycle of "scrumming" with clients, daily check-ins and agreed upon "sprints," such as designed by Betteke van Ruler (2015) works well. It aligns with contemporary management practices.

The days of being able to rely on the organic reach of social media have gone in PR and the rise of the "media placement specialist" is evident. With new platforms emerging, and audience segments moving across to them, or further fragmenting, the budget for paid social campaigns is being increasingly stretched.

Defining what appropriate return on investment in social media looks like for organizations remains challenging, as this can vary widely depending on the nature of the entity's mission. Much of the data used to measure success needs practitioners to have analytical skills. This is hard for a profession that traditionally has attracted people from liberal arts rather than from mathematics or information systems backgrounds. Those with marketing analytics skills can be seen getting ahead of traditionally trained workers. Organizations continue to struggle with how best to structure communication and PR functions, with many still going through the "trial and error" stage.

The way success is viewed in public relations continues to change, with many viewing successes as not having been achieved until target publics have both changed their attitude or behavior, and propagated the idea that others do the same through social media networks. People are increasingly "wising up" to the way their social sharing benefits business and are being in some cases generously rewarded for this "work." Now called "influencers," those with social media followings on specific platforms can offer these audiences to PR and advertising agencies, either directly or through agents. Already this has posed headaches for regulators who are increasingly requiring that "influencers" fully disclose any "cash for comment" to followers.

The divide between social media and other media has for the most broken down and now many argue there is just "media." It is more important than ever to know why your client is in the space, how success will be measured, and, what ROI looks like. Practitioners who demonstrate excellent pattern recognition and analytical skills, and the ability to translate these into agile emergent strategy, will be greatly sought after. Such skills will be essential to adapt to the ever-increasing pace and fragmentation that continues to unfold.

Melanie James (@melanie_james), Ph.D., retired in 2018 as Senior Lecturer in Communication and Media, School of Creative Industries, University of Newcastle, Sydney area, Australia. Her research on new media, PR and positioning has been widely cited. James joined the university in 2006 after working in senior management roles in PR – strategic, government and marketing communication. She was an early adopter of social media in PR practice and education and continues to work as a strategic communication consultant.

Source: van Ruler, B. (2015). Agile Public Relations Planning: The Reflective Communication Scrum. *Public Relations Review*, 41(2), 187–194 (https://bettekevanruler.nl/agile-working/).

Engaging consumers – within the context of PR, advertising or marketing – appears to be "more about conversations, connections, and shared control and less about passive consumption of packaged content" (Tuten, 2008, p. 3). It is a fundamental shift that will continue to have an effect on PR and other professionals for years to come. While personal branding has become popular, the new mobile-social media may be best reflected by singer Taylor Swift as an "UnBrand" – "a symbol or emblem to a group of people" that begins as "blank space, allowing various groups of fans to identify with her and project their ideal self" (Honjo, 2016, para. 6). In a digital age with a "marketplace of attention," this makes sense: "Although public attention is often indispensable to the exercise of economic, political, or social influence, it's harder to come by" (Webster, 2014, p. 6). Social media may facilitate a form of social bonding: "Generally, strong ties seem to promote 'complex contagions' that can affect people's beliefs and behaviors, not just what they know" (p. 40). Social media company Facebook and its Messenger, WhatsApp and Instagram apps are among the most popular smartphone uses along with Google, Apple and Amazon. These data suggest the central importance of social media communication in how people use time.

Communicating, social sharing, searching and shopping, then, make up a sort of mobile core of user behavior that may help explain the future direction of social media.

AHEAD

In the next chapter, computer-mediated communication will be used to explore the importance of **identity**, **interaction** and **community** within social media spaces. As new ideas and technologies spread, online communication may influence cultural

TABLE 1.1 *Most Popular Multi-Platform Sites*

	Sites	2019 Unique Visitors	2016 (App Rank)
1.	**Google (YouTube)**	**254 million**	**113 million (3–7)**
2.	**Facebook (Instagram)**	**219 million**	**146 million (1–2, 8)**
3.	Microsoft Sites	216 million	
4.	Verizon Media	213 million	
5.	Amazon Sites	211 million	
6.	ComcastNBC	177 million	
7.	CBS Interactive	169 million	
8.	Apple, Inc.	161 million	68 million (9)
9.	PayPal	159 million	
10.	Hearst	159 million	
11.	**Twitter**	**157 million**	
19.	**Snapchat**	**123 million**	
22.	**Pinterest**	**110 million**	
25.	**LinkedIn**	**103 million**	
28.	**Yelp**	**98 million**	
38.	**Reddit**	**83 million**	

In 2016, the top ten apps by average unique uses and annual growth were: 1. Facebook, 146.0 million (+14); 2. Facebook Messenger, 129.7 million (+28); 3. YouTube, 113.7 million (+20); 4. Google Maps, 105.7 million (+22); 5. Google Search, 104.0 million (+9), 6. Google Play, 99.8 million (+8); 7. Gmail, 88.6 million (+18); 8. Instagram, 74.7 million (+36); 9. Apple Music, 68.4 million (+20); and 10. Amazon, 65.5 million (+43).

Sources: comScore (August 2019). Top 50 Multi-Platform Properties (Desktop and Mobile) August 2019. www.comscore.com/Insights/Rankings; Ng, A. (December 29, 2016). Facebook, Google, Top Out Most Popular Apps in 2016. *CNet.* www.cnet.com/news/facebook-google-top-out-uss-most-popular-apps-in-2016/.

change in powerful ways. A large number of social media tools are now in use within journalism and public relations. These occupations now borrow **branding** techniques from advertising and marketing, as **convergence** continues to take hold across many media industries.

Entrepreneurs creating new businesses, investing in **start-ups** and constantly creating new media industries are driving some of the change. The **innovation** culture often ignores old media organizations and practices in favor of fundamental change. The new media landscape is not without challenges. As we will learn in this book, "big data" collection and analyses raise concerns about personal **privacy**. There are legal and ethical issues surrounding social media technologies, and there are calls for global regulation. Perhaps the best we can hope for right now is the development of **best practices** by journalists, PR practitioners and others that are informed by guidelines and a general set of policies. We can learn from case studies that expose social media successes and failures. More can be learned through the use of social media **metrics** and **analytics**.

For example, **search engine optimization (SEO)** rules affect the words we should use in effectively spreading online content. At the same time, popular measurement tools – Google Analytics, Hootsuite, SproutSocial and others – offer new intelligence about communication behavior. As we will see in this book, SEO may be positively or negatively impacted by social media conversation, from online engagement to product and service sales. The quality of those sites linking to a story, conversation or site may raise or lower the prominence of content at any given moment. This can be important for story placement on search engines, such as Google, but it also has implications within social media conversation over time. Likewise, Facebook insights data help community brand managers select and promote social media storytelling. Knowing which stories are liked, shared and commented upon offers important explanations about why content is moving through social networks.

Some are turning to **media literacy** as a way to explore best practices of journalists and PR people. In order to effectively engage within a social network, strategies and tactics must constantly return to concerns about online trust and influence.

DISCUSSION QUESTIONS: STRATEGIES AND TACTICS

1. How has the presence of false information, or "fake news," impacted who or what you trust? How could social media communication users do a better job of critically thinking about online information? What challenges exist for journalists, PR practitioners, advertisers and marketers? What legal and ethical concerns exist? How should social media users judge source and message credibility?

2. What are the similarities and differences in roles and functions for journalists, PR practitioners, advertisers and marketers? How do social media blur the lines between these fields? What are the challenges for practitioners moving from journalism to PR? What about moving from PR to journalism? What is an example you recall of social media engagement that did not seem to be authentic?

3. How do you determine whether or not to trust a social media voice? How do social media change the nature of influencing others compared to traditional word-of-mouth sharing? How do you influence others within social media spaces? How will your influence evolve as a social media professional? How was your view of social media influence and trust impacted during the 2016, 2018 and 2020 US elections?

REFERENCES

Adams, G. M. (2015, March 13). SXSW: How Black Twitter is Changing the Narrative of Black Stories. *The Root.* www.theroot.com/articles/culture/2015/03/sxsw_how_black_twitter_is_changing_the_narrative_of_black_stories/

Adobe. (2012, October). *Click Here: The State of Online Advertising.* www.adobe.com/aboutadobe/pressroom/pdfs/Adobe_State_of_Online_Advertising_Study.pdf

Albarran, A. B. (Ed.) (2013). *The Social Media Industries.* New York, NY: Routledge.

Amnesty International. (2019). Surveillance Giants: How the Business Model of Google and Facebook Threatens Human Rights. *Amnesty International.* www.amnesty.org/download/Documents/POL3014042019ENGLISH.PDF

Anderson, M. (2016, November 7). Social Media Causes Some Users to Rethink Their Views on an Issue. *Pew Research Center.* www.pewresearch.org/fact-tank/2016/11/07/social-media-causes-some-users-to-rethink-their-views-on-an-issue/

AP. (2013, May). *Social Media Guidelines for AP Employees.* www.ap.org/Images/Social-Media-Guidelines_tcm28–9832.pdf

AP. (2016, December 24). Turkey Arrests 1,656 Social Media Users Since Summer. http://abcnews.go.com/Technology/wireStory/turkey-arrests-1656-social-media-users-summer-44383595

AP. (2017, January 2). The Latest: Turkey Monitoring Social Media Accounts. http://bigstory.ap.org/b6d1abe1a2b248e0b71a3ac516134db6

AP. (2019, December 29). Court Rules Turkey Violated Freedoms By Banning Wikipedia. https://apnews.com/3dc4b3da93ba67f728b27608badb7d93

Baumer, E. P. S., Guha, S., Quan, E., Mimno, D., & Gay, G. K. (2015, July-December). Missing Photos, Suffering Withdrawal, or Finding Freedom? How Experiences of Social Media Non-Use Influence the Likelihood of Reversion. *Social Media + Society,* 1–14.

Beckett, C., with Ball, J. (2012). *Wikileaks, News in the Networked Era.* Cambridge, UK: Polity Press.

Benkler, Y., Faris, R., & Roberts, H. (2018). *Network Propaganda: Manipulation, Disinformation, and Radicalization in American Politics.* New York: Oxford University Press.

Berkman, F. (2013, October 29). Sandy was Our Social Storm. But at What Cost? *Mashable.* http://mashable.com/2013/10/29/sandy-social-media-storm-safety/

Binder, M. (2019, February 27). Why Momo Challenge Panic Won't Go Away. *Mashable.* https://mashable.com/article/momo-challenge-youtube-urban-legends/

Briggs, M. (2020). *Journalism Next,* fourth edition. Los Angeles: SAGE.

Bump, P. (2019, December 5). 33 Reddit Stats and Facts to Know in 2020. *HubSpot.* https://blog.hubspot.com/marketing/reddit-stats

Canham, M. (2019, November 6). In Historic Shift, *The Salt Lake Tribune* Gets IRS Approval to Become a Nonprofit. *The New York Times.* www.sltrib.com/news/2019/11/04/historic-shift-salt-lake/

Carter, E. L., & Lee, L. T. (2016, Summer). Information Access in an Age of Big Data. *Journalism & Mass Communication Quarterly 93*(2), 269–272.

Chaffee, S. H., & Metzger, M. J. (2001). The End of Mass Communication? *Mass Communication & Society 4*(4), 365–379.

Chan-Olmsted, S., Rim, H., & Zerba, A. (2013). Mobile News Adoption among Young Adults: Examining the Roles of Perceptions, News Consumption, and Media Usage. *Journalism & Mass Communication Quarterly 90*(1), 126–147.

Chen, J. (2018, October 30). How to Get Started on Your Content Marketing Strategy. *Sprout Social.* https://sproutsocial.ocm/insights/content-marketing-strategy/

Cheong, P. H., Martin, J. N., & Macfadyen, L. P. (Eds.) (2012). *New Media and Intercultural Communication, Identity, Community and Politics.* New York, NY: Peter Lang.

Cobbina, J. E. (2019). *Hands up Don't Shoot, Why the Protests in Ferguson and Baltimore Matter, and How They Changed America.* New York: New York University Press.

Collins, B., & Wodinsky, S. (2019, February 28). How 'Momo,' a Global Social Media Hoax about a Paranormal Threat to Kids, Morphed into a U.S. Viral Phenomenon. *NBC News.* www.nbcnews.com/tech/tech-news/how-momo-global-social-media-hoax-about-paranormal-threat-kids-n977961

Coombs, W. T., & Holladay, S. J. (2007). *It's Not Just PR, Public Relations in Society*. Malden, MA: Blackwell.

Craft, S., & Davis, C. N. (2013). *Principles of American Journalism, an Introduction*. New York, NY: Routledge.

Crestodina, A. (2018). *Content Chemistry, the Illustrated Handbook for Content Marketing*, fifth. Chicago, IL: Orbit Media.

DeAngelo, I. I., & Yegiyan, N. S. (2019, Summer). Looking for Efficiency: How Online News Structure and Emotional Tone Influence Processing Time and Memory. *Journalism & Mass Communication Quarterly 96*(2), 385–405.

Drum, K. (2017, January 7). Maybe RT has a Bigger Influence on American Politics than We Think. *Mother Jones*. www.motherjones.com/kevin-drum/2017/01/maybe-rt-has-bigger-influence-american-politics-we-think

Eastin, M. S. (2006). Credibility Assessments of Online Health Information: The Effects of Source Expertise and Knowledge of Content. *Journal of Computer-Mediated Communication 6*(4), http://onlinelibrary.wiley.com/doi/10.1111/j.1083-6101.2001.tb00126.x/full.

Edelman, P. R. (2014). *TweetLevel*. http://tweetlevel.edelman.com/

Edelman, P. R. (2020, 2019). *2019 Edelman Trust Barometer*. www.edelman.com/trustbarometer

Enberg, J. (2019, March 28). Global Digital Ad Spending 2019: Digital Accounts for Half of Total Media Ad Spending Worldwide. *eMarketer*. www.emarketer.com/content/global-digital-ad-spending-2019

Green, S. C., Lodato, M. J., Schwalbe, C. B., & Silcock, B. W. (2012). *News Now, Visual Storytelling in the Digital Age*. Boston, MA: Pearson.

Gumuchian, M. L., & Sidner, S. (2013, December 23). American Gets 1-Year Prison Sentence for Parody Video. *CNN*. www.cnn.com/2013/12/23/world/meast/uae-american-sentence/index.html

Haciyakupoglu, G., & Zhang, W. (2015). Social Media Trust during the Gezi Protests in Turkey. *Journal of Computer-Mediated Communication 20*, 450–466.

Hesmondhalgh, D., & Toynbee, J. (Eds.) (2008). *The Media and Social Theory*. London, UK: Routledge.

Honjo, K. (2016, July 25). Haters Gonna Hate: Taylor Swift Is Revolutionizing Marketing (No Really). *Salesforce Blog*. www.salesforce.com/blog/2016/07/taylor-swift-revolutionize-marketing-unbrand.html

Hutchinson, A. (2020, January 25). Byte, the Second-Coming of Vine, is Now Available on iOS and Android. *Social Media Today*. www.socialmediatoday.com/news/byte-the-second-coming-of-vine-is-now-available-on-ios-and-android/571091/

Jansen, J. (2011). *Understanding Sponsored Search, Core Elements of Keyword Advertising*. New York, NY: Cambridge University Press.

Katz, E. (1957). The Two-Step Flow of Communication: An Up-To-Date Report on an Hypothesis. Departmental Papers (ASC). *Annenberg School for Communication*. http://repository.upenn.edu/cgi/viewcontent.cgi?article=1279&context=asc_papers

Katz, E. (1994). Forward. In G. Weimann (Ed.), *The Influentials, People Who Influence People*, pp. ix–xi. Albany: State University of New York Press.

Khang, H., Ki, E. J., & Ye, L. (2012). Social Media Research in Advertising, Communication, Marketing, and Public Relations. *Journalism & Mass Communication Quarterly 89*(2), 279–298.

Kottasova, I. (2016, December 6). The Top Hashtag of the Year Had Nothing to Do with Donald Trump. *CNN Money*. http://money.cnn.com/2016/12/06/technology/twitter-top-events-hashtags-2016/

Kurylo, A., & Dumova, T. (2016). Introduction: Social Networking Without Walls. In A. Kurylo and T. Dumova (Eds.), *Social Networking: Redefining Communication in a Digital Age*, Lanham, MD: Rowman & Littlefield.

Lievrouw, L. A., & Livingstone, S. (Eds.) (2006). *Handbook of New Media (Updated Student Edition)*. London: Sage.

Lin, K. Y., & Lu, H. P. (2011). Intention to Continue Using Facebook Fan Pages from the Perspective of Social Capital Theory. *Cyberpsychology, Behavior, and Social Networking 14*(10), 565–570.

Ling, R., & Campbell, S. W. (Eds.) (2011). *Mobile Communication, Bringing us Together and Tearing us Apart*. New Brunswick, NJ: Transaction.

Lipschultz, J. H. (2020). *Social Media Measurement and Management: Entrepreneurial Digital Analytics*. New York and London: Routledge.

Lorenz, T. (2019, February 28). Momo is Not Trying to Kill Children. *The Atlantic*. www.theatlantic.com/technology/archive/2019/02/momo-challenge-hoax/583825/

Luckie, M. S. (2011). *The Digital Journalist's Handbook*. Lexington, KY: Mark S. Luckie.

Luttrell, R. (2016). *Social Media: How to Engage, Share, and Connect*, second edition. Lanham, MD: Rowman & Littlefield.

MacLean, H. (2013, May 28). The Cost of Ignoring Social Media. *Sales Force Marketing Cloud*. www.salesforcemarketingcloud.com/blog/2013/05/cost-of-ignoring-social-media/

Maheshwari, S. (2016, November 20). How Fake News Goes Viral. *The New York Times*. www.nytimes.com/2016/11/20/business/media/how-fake-news-spreads.html

Maras, S. (2013). *Objectivity in Journalism*. Malden, MA: Polity Press.

Martoccio, A. (2019, November 21). This Beatles Fan Does Pitch-Perfect Imitations of the Fab Four on TikTok. *Rolling Stone*. www.rollingstone.com/music/music-features/beatles-superfan-tiktok-videos-914662/

Massanari, A. L. (2015). *Participatory Culture, Community, and Play*. New York: Peter Lang.

Mathison, D. (2009). *Be the Media*. New York, NY: natural E creative.

McCombs, M., Holbert, R. L., Kiousis, S., & Wanta, W. (2011). *The News and Public Opinion, Media Effects on Civic Life*. Malden, MA: Polity Press.

Mersey, R. D., Malthouse, E. C., & Calder, B. J. (2012). Focusing on the Reader: Engagement Trumps Satisfaction. *Journalism & Mass Communication Quarterly 89*(4), 695–709.

Morales, E. (2018). *Latinx, the New Force in American Politics and Culture*. London and New York: Verso.

Nielsen. (2019, September 19). La Oportunidad Latinx: Meeting U.S. Hispanics on the Path to Purchase. *Nielsen*. www.nielsen.com/us/en/insights/article/2019/la-oportunidad-latinx-2/

Pavlik, J. V., & Bridges, F. (2013, Spring). The Emergence of Augmented Reality (AR) as a Storytelling Medium in Journalism. *Journalism & Communication Monographs 15*(1), 1–59.

Pew Research Center. (2019, April 10). Share of U.S. Adults Using Social Media, Including Facebook, is Mostly Unchanged since 2018. www.pewresearch.org/fact-tank/2019/04/10/share-of-u-s-adults-using-social-media-including-facebook-is-mostly-unchanged-since-2018/

PR News. (2013, October 21). PR Teams Build Internal Newsrooms as Communications Strategies Shift. www.prnewsonline.com/topics/media-relations/2013/10/21/pr-teams-buildinternal-newsrooms-as-communications-strategies-shift

Quesenberry, K. (2019). *Social Media Strategy: Marketing, Advertising, and Public Relations in the Consumer Revolution*, second. Lanham, MD: Rowman & Littlefield.

Reid, S., & Spencer-Oatey, H. (2012). Beyond Stereotypes: Utilising a Generic Competency Approach to Develop Intercultural Effectiveness. In V. Carayol and A. Frame (Eds.),

Communication and PR from a Cross-Cultural Standpoint, Practical and Methodological Issues, pp. 15–26. Bruxelles: P.I.E. Peter Lang.

Reuters (2019, November 17). The Owner of TikTok Is Reportedly in Talks with Major Record Labels to Launch A Music Streaming Service. *Business Insider*. www.businessinsider.com/tiktok-owner-bytedance-plans-to-launch-music-streaming-ft-2019-11

Rieder, R. (2013, September 5). Storyful Verifies Social Media Video from Syria. *USA Today*. www.usatoday.com/story/money/columnist/rieder/2013/09/05/storyful-verifying-video-on-socialmedia-from-syria/2771029/

Romano, A. (2016, December 31). The Year Social Media Changed Everything. *Vox*. www.vox.com/2016/12/31/13869676/social-media-influence-alt-right

Roose, K. (2019, October 9). What Does PewDiePie Really Believe? *The New York Times*. www.nytimes.com/interactive/2019/10/09/magazine/PewDiePie-interview.html

Savav, V. (2020, January 27). The New Vine Successor Byte is Already Beating TikTok in the App Store, *Time*. https://time.com/5772227/vine-creator-tiktok/

Schmitt-Beck, R. (2003). Mass Communication, Personal Communication and Vote Choice: The Filter Hypothesis of Media Influence in Comparative Perspective. *British Journal of Political Science 33*(2), 233–260.

Silverman, C. (2016, December 4 Update, November 4). How The Bizarre Conspiracy Theory Behind "Pizzagate" Was Spread. *Buzzfeed*. www.buzzfeed.com/craigsilverman/fever-swamp-election

Singer, J. B., Hermida, A., Domingo, D., Heinhonen, A., Paulussen, S., Quandt, T., Reich, Z., & Vojnovic, M. (2011). *Participatory Journalism, Guarding Open Gates at Online Newspapers*. Malden, MA: Wiley-Blackwell.

Singh, M. (2019, November 15). TikTok Tests Social Commerce. *TechCrunch*. https://techcrunch.com/2019/11/15/tiktok-link-bio-social-commerce/

Sky News. (2019, December 16). PewDiePie Announces Break from YouTube because He's 'Very Tired'. *Sky News*. https://news.sky.com/story/pewdiepie-announces-break-from-youtube-because-hes-very-tired-11887823

Slater, M. D., & Rouner, D. (1996). Value-affirmative and Value-Protective Processing of Alcohol Education Messages that Include Statistical Evidence or Anecdotes. *Communication Research 23*(2), 210–235.

Smith, B. G., & Place, K. R. (2013). Integrating Power? Evaluating Public Relations Influence in an Integrated Communication Structure. *Public Relations Research 25*(2), 168–187.

Soo-bum, L., & Youn-gon, K. (2013). A Frame Analysis on Korean Daily Newspapers' Coverage of Twitter: Focusing on the Perspective of Political Communication and Formation of Public Opinion. *Korean Journalism Review 7*(2), 51–77.

Stafford, T. (2005). Mobile Promotional Communication and Machine Persuasion: A New Paradigm for Source Effects? In M. R. Stafford and R. J. Faber (Eds.), *Advertising, Promotion, and New Media*, pp. 278–297. Armonk, NY: M.E. Sharpe.

Stewart, D. R. (Ed.) (2017). *Social Media and the Law, A Guidebook for Communication Students and Professionals*, second. New York, NY: Routledge.

Sundar, S. S., & Nass, C. (2001). Conceptualizing Sources in Online News. *Journal of Communication 51*(1), 52–72.

Sydow, L. (2020, January 15). The State of Mobile in 2020. *App Annie*. www.appannie.com/en/insights/market-data/state-of-mobile-2020/

Tappin, S. (2016, December 5). Using Social Media in 2017. *Pulse*. https://www.linkedin.com/pulse/ultimate-business-guide-using-social-media-2017-steve-tappin

Tewksbury, D., & Rittenberg, J. (2012). *News on the Internet, Information and Citizenship in the 21st Century*. Oxford, UK: Oxford University Press.

Tuten, T. L. (2008). *Advertising 2.0, Social Media Marketing in a Web 2.0 World*. Westport, CT: Praeger.

Vaynerchuk, G. (2013). *Jab, Jab, Jab, Right Hook*. New York, NY: HarperCollins.

Waldman, K. (2013, September 4). I'm Here for Business Meetings with No Clothes. *Slate*. www.slate.com/articles/business/moneybox/2013/09/air_berlin_lost_luggage_the_german_airline_melts_down_on_social_media.single.html

Waller, H. (2020, January 19). Snap CEO Spiegel Says TikTok Could Grow Bigger than Instagram. *Bloomberg*. www.bloomberg.com/news/articles/2020-01-19/snap-ceo-spiegel-says-tiktok-could-grow-bigger-than-instagram

Webb, K. (2019, August 26). PewDiePie Just Became the First Solo YouTuber to Reach 100 Million Subscribers. *Business Insider*. www.businessinsider.com/youtube-star-pewdiepie-100-million-subscribers-2019-8

Webster, J. G. (2014). *The Marketplace of Attention: How Audiences Take Shape in a Digital Age*. Cambridge, MA: The MIT Press.

Weeks, B. E., & Holbert, R. L. (2013, Summer). Predicting Dissemination of News Content in Social Media: A Focus on Reception, Friending, and Partisanship. *Journalism & Mass Communication Quarterly 90*(2), 212–232.

Youm, K. H., & Park, A. (2016, Summer). The "Right to Be Forgotten" in European Law: Data Protection Balanced with Free Speech? *Journalism & Mass Communication Quarterly 93*(2), 273–295.

Zarrell, R. (2013, November 2). What Happens When You Dress as a Boston Marathon Victim and Post it on Twitter. *Buzzfeed*. www.buzzfeed.com/rachelzarrell/what-happens-when-you-dress-as-a-boston-marathon-victim

CMC, Diffusion, and Social Theories

This connected mobility changes not only our communication ability but our relational expectations as well.

— John C. Sherblom (@Cognella, 2020, p. xv)

Some users enjoy the opportunities for political debate and engagement that social media facilitates, but many more express resignation, frustration over the tone and content of social media platforms.

— Meave Duggan (@maeveyd, 2016)

One of the most devastating relational developments in the world of social media is the "status" bar on Facebook.

— Tammy Nelson (@drtammynelson, 2012)

You might not think that Chinese-owned video app TikTok would be a social media space for global political controversy, but it is. A teenager in the US was blocked and later un-blocked for TikTok posts about the mistreatment of Muslims (AP, 2019b). "TikTok is popular with millions of U.S. teens and young adults but several US senators have raised concerns about data collection and censorship on the site of content not in line with the Chinese government" (para. 3). National security concerns have been raised by US officials (Togoh, 2019).

> A bulletin issued by the Navy … showed up on a Facebook page serving military members, saying users of government issued mobile devices who had TikTok and did not remove the app would be blocked from the Navy Marine Corps Intranet.
>
> (Pell & Wang, 2019, para. 2)

TikTok also was accused of hiding videos that featured people with disabilities (Köver & Reuter, 2019). Documents revealed that moderators were instructed to mark users at risk of bullying, such as those who are overweight or openly gay, and this limited the reach for the posts. However, the paradox of social media communication is that Tik-Tok also was praised for raising awareness about the novel Coronavirus (Meisenzahl, 2020), at the same time that Coronavirus misinformation quickly spread during the outbreak. "It plays to our worst fears" (Miller, 2020, para. 11).

Meanwhile, in the United Arab Emirates (UAE), the government appeared to use similarly named app ToTok as a spy tool to track conversations, location and images by promoting it as an alternative to WhatsApp and FaceTime, which have been blocked by censors (AP, 2019a). The app co-creator claimed no knowledge of government spying: "Its surge in popularity was likely driven by the fact that it allowed users to make internet calls that have long been banned in the UAE, a US-allied nation where the largest city is Dubai" (Gambrel, 2020, para. 3). Clearly, there are intended and unintended uses for all social media tools. While sites sometimes intervene, more frequently, online difficulties arise via conflicts between users.

Another emerging problem is the connection between social media screen time and mental health issues (Boers et al., 2019). For adolescents, anxiety symptoms have been observed in relation to lack of physical activity and symptoms of depression (Teychenne, Costigan, & Parker, 2015; Twenge et al., 2018). When social media users are isolated in online worlds and limit face-to-face communication, they may be more susceptible to suicide-related outcomes, identity theft and other deception.

Former Notre Dame linebacker Manti Te'o, who went on to play in the National Football League (NFL), told a story about a dead girlfriend, allowed it to spread across traditional and social media during the 2013 college football bowl season ahead of the NFL draft and then had to deal with the fallout (Sonderman, 2013). The online publication *Deadspin* titled their report, "Manti Te'o's Dead Girlfriend, The Most Heartbreaking and Inspirational Story of the College Football Season, Is a Hoax." People "were taken in" by what sounded like a great story. Te'o then released a statement, which read, in part:

> This is incredibly embarrassing to talk about, but over an extended period of time, I developed an emotional relationship with a woman I met online. We maintained what I thought to be an authentic relationship by communicating frequently online and on the phone ... To realize that I was the victim of what was apparently someone's sick joke and constant lies was, and is, painful and humiliating ...
> ... To think that I shared with them my happiness about my relationship and details that I thought to be true about her just makes me sick ... In retrospect, I obviously should have been much more cautious. If anything good comes of this, I hope it is that others will be far more guarded when they engage with people online than I was.
>
> (Burke & Dickey, 2013)

Te'o had apparently accepted the identity of a girlfriend named "Lennay Kekua." In the story, they met after a game and talked by telephone every night until she was in a car crash and later died of leukemia. National sports media latched onto the lie, and they repeatedly distributed it without checking. The university called it a "troubling matter" that appeared to be "a sad and very cruel deception to entertain its perpetrators." The "**catfishing**" incident is hardly unusual, as online communication has been increasingly compromised by a lack of authentic identity (Burke & Dickey, 2013).

IDENTITY

Interpersonal communication researchers developed CMC as a way to describe the digital nature of mediated online communication as it developed in the 1980s and 1990s (Barnes, 2001; Negroponte, 1995; Turkle, 1995). In general, CMC addressed identity formation, presentation, distribution and other issues. Each of us has an online presence expressed by what we choose to share about others and ourselves. This happens through continuous and ongoing interaction with others. Self-presentation may be accurate in depiction or reflect virtual transportation to another "place" or ideal.

CMC examines how identities and interactions sometimes produce online communities. CMC may offer a voice to groups seeking social change, cultural shifts and even political power. In this sense, CMC is connected to the historical development of the Internet as a revolutionary infrastructure that quickly spawned numerous useful communication tools. CMC began as message bulletin board systems (BBS) and email, and quickly grew through the development of the World Wide Web (WWW) in the 1990s.

FIGURE 2.1 *This book's author held virtual classes in Second Life in 2008.*

Barnes (2003) was among those categorizing CMC as interpersonal communication: "Internet interactivity occurs as interpersonal interactivity, informational interactivity, and **human–computer interaction (HCI)**" (p. 1). This approach includes everything from email to Web pages, and interactivity "supports message interest and involvement," as it "plays a central role in online social dynamics and group communication" (pp. 20–21). What we consider as social is a function of individual psychological development. "It's the natural consequence of having brains that were built to make sense of other brains and to understand everyone's place in the pecking order" (Lieberman, 2013, p. 302). CMC also may assist individuals in presenting identity in a way that seeks to be truthful (Bargh, 2002; Bargh & McKenna, 2004; Bargh, McKenna, & Fitzsimons, 2002). The social process of human–Internet interaction is found within social media communication.

INTERNET HISTORY

More than 50 years ago, Silicon Valley development began at Stanford University's electrical engineering program and Frederick Terman's experiences at MIT (Williams, 2018). Electronics came to be seen as an enhancement of "machine-age civilization" (p. 311). A 1960s military project called the Advanced Research Projects Agency Network (ARPANET) by the United States Department of Defense had a goal of connecting the east and west coasts of the United States with instantaneous computer communication. The earliest mainframe computers were at the Pentagon and on university campuses across the nation, but the computer networks did not connect. ARPANET demonstrated that data could be divided into labeled packets, sent and then re-assembled, and this **packet switching** model also was adopted as an efficient way to move messages on the Internet.

Early public systems, such as CompuServe, Prodigy, America Online and The WELL began to connect non-military users across the country during the 1980s and 1990s to telephone line dial-up chat rooms, information services and online games. At the same time, **early adopters** began to develop simple Web pages. Some of the first online communities, such as Classmates.com, LiveJournal, Friendster, MySpace and LinkedIn, developed the concept of **user profiles** that contained personal information going beyond sharing an email address.

The concept of the SNS (Social Network Site) reflected the idea of extending interpersonal and face-to-face (f2f) networks into online spaces through creation of a personal profile and development of connection lists on a platform that offered the capability to view the activities of others and interact (Albarran, 2013; boyd & Ellison, 2008). Within this broad framework, numerous functions emerged – from **tagging** and sharing content to shopping and product reviews.

The basic idea was that people would have an interest in finding friends, communicating with them and sharing information. By the time Facebook, Twitter, Google+, Pinterest and other social networking sites had become popular, social networking was a mainstream form of online communication. The concept became more flexible and fluid with the development and success of mobile sites Instagram and Snapchat.

Software programs became mobile apps providing a wide array of functions that replaced stand-alone devices, such as music players, cameras and video hardware.

SOCIAL NETWORK SITE (SNS) DEFINITIONS

CMC happens within the broad context of SNS. These are defined as:

> web-based services that allow individuals to (1) construct a public or semipublic profile within a bounded system, (2) articulate a list of other users with whom they share a connection, and (3) view and traverse their list of connections and those made by others within the system. The nature and nomenclature of these connections may vary from site to site.
>
> (boyd & Ellison, 2008, p. 211)

This SNS definition avoids the word "networking," which may imply meeting strangers through online interaction. Instead, "frequently" the emphasis is on activating pre-existing offline "latent" social "ties" (p. 211). For example, Google's Gmail is a SNS that connects usually identifiable users with others across the Internet. Similarly, LinkedIn reconnects business contacts by offering current work status and other information. Of course, new connections are made, but they tend to reflect nearby mutual associations with other contacts. Professional and personal interests, as well as geography, may be important.

☐ BOX 2.1

Social Media Functions and Sites

Form	Functions	Examples
Blogging: Personal Blogs	Storytelling and Commentary	Medium, WordPress, LinkedIn, Blogger, Facebook Wall, Tumblr
Blogging: Professional	Storytelling and Commentary	Huffington Post, Slate, Salon, Daily Kos, LinkedIn, Medium, Vice
Blogging: Micro-blogs	Content Sharing	Twitter, Pinterest, Tumblr, Weibo
Blogging: Aggregator	Content Aggregator	Twitter Moments, Instagram Stories, Facebook Stories, Snapchat Stories
Traditional News	Content Sharing	*The New York Times*, CBS, Fox News, AP, ESPN
Social News	Curating and Tagging	Reddit, Fark, Flipboard

Form	Functions	Examples
Technology News	Tech Trends	Mashable, TechCrunch, The Verge, CNET, Gizmodo, Wired
Social Cultural	Culture Sharing and Humor	Buzzfeed, Cracked
Social Entertainment	Celebrity Sharing	TMZ, KnowYourMeme, LOLCATS
Wikis	Collaborative	Wikipedia, Fandom (Wikia), Encyclopedia
Shopping and Reviews	Consumer Purchase	Amazon, Yelp, Viewpoints
Social SNS	Social Networking	Twitter, Facebook, Snapchat, TikTok (Douyin China)
Business SNS	Social Networking	LinkedIn, MySpace, Slack, Yammer
SNS Search	Crowdsourcing	Reddit
Photographs	Photograph Sharing	Instagram, Flickr, Imgur, 9gag
Audio: Podcasts	RSS and Apps	Apple Podcasts, etc.
Audio: Voice	Audio Sharing	Soundcloud, BlogTalkRadio, Voxer
Audio: Music	Music Listening	Spotify, Tidal, Apple Music
Video	Video Sharing	YouTube, TikTok, Vimeo, Byte (Vine 2)
Video Streaming	Live Video	Instagram Live, Facebook Live, Zoom, Skype, Google Hangouts
Geolocation	Location Based Services (LBS)	Snap Maps, Apple Find My Friends, Grindr, Tinder, Waze
Games	Social Gaming	Words With Friends, Fortnite, Nintendo Online, Xbox Live
Virtual Reality (VR)	Avatar Interaction	Second Life, VirBELA, VR-Chat
Augmented Reality (AR)	Vision Enhancement	Minecraft Earth, Pokémon GO!, Snapchat Spectacles
Dashboards	Management and Measurement	Google Analytics, Hootsuite, Sprout Social, Twitter Analytics, Facebook Insights, Dasheroo, NUVI, Union Metrics

What we call social networking happens within a cybercultural context (Bell, 2001; Benedikt, 1991). It is understood to frequently involve existing interpersonal friendships that move into somewhat fluid online spaces (Berger, 2005; Gasser, 2008). These global communities have varying levels of media richness (Williams, Caplan & Xiong,

2007), and potential ambiguity in terms of self-disclosure and other psychological variables (Bernie & Horvath, 2006; Ramirez, 2007). It is not that the Internet is anonymous, but rather that identity can be altered. Some social media communication sites, such as Twitter, make it easier for a user to maintain an anonymous profile. Discussion boards, messaging and video conferencing sites offer highly interactive opportunities for user communication. At the same time, a user may broadcast produced messages through blogs, video blogs (**vlogs**), podcasts and other means.

Some of these are incredibly popular. The "vlogbrothers," created by brothers John (@realjohngreen) and Hank (@HankGreen) Green, began as a way to talk to each other and grew to over 3.3 million YouTube subscribers. It is about "nothing in particular, but the brothers share humorous exchanges to their followers, known as 'Nerdfighters.'" Their regular video posts attract millions of views.

Online users also enter virtual spaces through graphical or gaming environments hosted on SNS platforms. Of particular importance, an online user may have a virtual connection with others that mimics the feeling of travel to another location, such as with the Second Life or more recent VirBELA site that calls itself "The Open Campus." Within virtual environments, teams may be able to collaborate online and need only limited face-to-face interaction. Common SNS characteristics include:

- Profile user pages, which may include demographic and psychographic descriptions

- Relationships displayed as friends, followers, fans, contacts or other labels

- Public connection displays, which are a form of "impression management"

- Types of "self-presentation" that serve as "identity markers"

- Varying degrees of privacy through site and user settings.

(boyd & Ellison, 2008, pp. 211–221)

Beyond privacy settings, the nature of social media sharing leads to loss of control of personal data. Clearview AI developed a facial recognition app built upon public social media photographs and video from Facebook, YouTube and millions of other sites:

> Federal and state law enforcement officers said that while they had only limited knowledge of how Clearview works and who is behind it, they had used its app to help solve shoplifting, identity theft, credit card fraud, murder and child sexual exploitation cases.
>
> (Hill, 2020, para. 4)

More than 600 law enforcement agencies have used the app (para. 6).

The early adoption of online communication tools was a foundation for the development of social networks and broader use of social media. The study of how individuals interact in social settings has been the focus of research for more than 50 years.

Tubbs and Moss (1983), for example, traced investigations in the nature of "popular" or "overchosen" and "unpopular" or isolated people (pp. 108–109). In describing social interaction between popular and unpopular people, they diagrammed through the "sociogram" how positive traits, such as enthusiasm and maturity, may be related to judgments about "sincerity" of another's conversation (p. 110). Information theory and models emphasize the flow of messages through channels. The perception of communication depends upon situations, context and social conditions (Bourdieu & Coleman, 1991; Cole, 2003; Severin & Tankard, 2001). Heider's balance theory and Festinger's cognitive dissonance theory from the 1950s have been related to social judgment (Milburn, 1991). Burnett and Marshall (2003) linked communication models to Internet discussion:

> At the very core of the meaning of the Web is linkage and connection: it is fundamentally about modes of communication and presenting possibilities about how those modes might intersect. Thus, the Web is simultaneously a mass-mediated *and* one-to-one form of communication. It is a site of incredible cultural consumption *and* cultural production and makes it harder to establish the boundary between these two activities.
>
> (p. 59)

Rheingold (2014), an online community pioneer, has emphasized the need to produce content, and not simply be a consumer of it. CMC, then, depends upon online identity. Burnett and Marshall (2003) contend that "shifting boundaries" are moved by such factors as anonymity, language, narcissism and gender (pp. 78–80). Although users sometimes may assume they are anonymous, as with memes posted on the mobile Whisper app, packet switching and **Internet Protocol (IP)** addresses guarantee that the original source of a message can be tracked and traced by government entities and others.

Within these contexts, social media communication may be observed and represented through visual graphs. Twitter users, for example, may be analyzed to identify "visual patterns found within linked entities" (Hansen, Shneiderman & Smith, 2011, p. 32). Researchers have proposed and developed methods for analysis of structure and grouping of categories and clusters within a social network. One model is called Group-In-A-Box (GIB):

> One particularly important aspect of social network analysis is the detection of *communities*, i.e., sub-groups of individuals or entities that exhibit tight interconnectivity among the other, wider population. For example, Twitter users who regularly re-tweet each other's messages may form cohesive groups within the Twitter social network. In a network visualization they would appear as clusters or sub-graphs, often colored distinctly or represented by a different vertex shape in order to convey their group identity.
>
> (Rodrigues et al., 2011, para. 2)

Some researchers call the network graph that is produced by analysis software a "socio-gram," which has "vertices (also called nodes or agents) and edges (also called ties or connections)" (Hansen, Shneiderman & Smith, 2011, p. 33). In social network analyses, lines in social space may connect active Twitter users. The maps represent the center of a group of people and the core of a network.

Network analyses are grounded in nearly 300 years of study in graph theory. In modern terms, "It is often useful to consider social networks from an individual member's point of view" (Hansen, Shneiderman & Smith, 2011, p. 36). News and information diffuse either from one point to another, or from one point to many other points, and these may be visually displayed through computer-generated mapping. As early as the 1930s, researchers were developing hand-drawn "pictures of patterns of people and their partners" (p. 38). This theoretical perspective has influenced the modern study of relationships. For example, Heaney and McClurg (2009) applied social networks to the study of American politics. They found these useful in understanding information flow, as well as collaboration within political organizations.

Garton, Haythornthwaite, and Wellman (1997) describe social network analysts as examining relations:

> They treat the description of relational patterns as interesting in its own right – e.g., is there a core and periphery? – and examine how involvement in such *social networks* helps to explain the behavior and attitudes of *network members* ... They use a variety of techniques to discover a network's densely-knit clusters and to look for similar role relations.
>
> (para. 3)

Communication theory has also been concerned with how networks relate to personal influence. Cooley (1909/1966) identified four factors: expressiveness, permanence, swiftness and diffusion of communication; he viewed the extension of messages as "enlargement" and "animation" (pp. 149–159).

> Social contacts are extended in space and quickened in time, and in the same degree the mental unity they imply becomes wider and more alert. The individual is broadened by coming into relation with a larger and more various life, and he is kept stirred up, sometimes to express, by the multitude of changing suggestions which this life brings to him.
>
> (p. 150)

Rogers (1995) connected his expansive diffusion theory to "direct" and "indirect collaboration" in opinion leadership toward change through networked "cliques" (pp. 201–203). Baran and Davis (2006) suggested that the influence of opinion leaders may be understood through similar interests and social stratification of leaders and their followers. At the same time, however, the shift from interpersonal to mediated communication is likely to reduce feedback as people orient within a social network

(Westley & MacLean, 1957). Influence may disperse from the center of a social network. This influence often accelerates when a leader is "stimulating" what have been called "**virtual communities**" (Koh et al., 2007, p. 70). In order to be sustainable, the researchers contend that four principles must exist: clear purpose/vision, clear member role definition, moderator leadership and online/offline events (pp. 70–71). Events, in fact, play a key role in strengthening member identification within a social network. Within a large social network, there tend to be user clusters. The existence of social relationships may produce a social network map that resembles a smaller version of an online community. Social network analyses continued to evolve as scholars refine methods (Butts, 2008). In particular, the methods used to define social network centrality and boundaries are open to discussion. Petronio (2002) explored the importance of boundaries of privacy and disclosure. Communication privacy management, in this view, begins with "the paradox of managing a public persona while maintaining the dignity of one's private life" (p. 1). The model suggested that "because people consider private information something they own, and over which they desire control, they both reveal and conceal information" (p. 9). She argues that boundaries are rules that are developed based upon "cultural expectations," as well as gender and psychological motivation (p. 24). In recent research the work has been applied to family communication (Child, Pearson & Petronio, 2009). Social media communication sharing or concealment, then, may be modeled. As additional events are analyzed, it should be possible to begin to predict participation behavior (Howard, 2008; Wright, 2011).

Early communication studies demonstrated an understanding of group behavior, sharing, socialization, entertainment, and following (Schramm, 1972). Social networks have introduced new communication questions about leadership, behavior, and online social influence (Greenhow & Robelia, 2009; Huffaker, 2010). Researchers need to extend existing communication theories to the social networking landscape. By performing future systematic content analyses of the language used in online interaction, it may be possible to discover emerging patterns of interaction and engagement. Such research should strengthen understanding about the nature of popularity, social isolation, opinion diffusion and social network leadership.

INTERACTION

At the heart of the social media communication shift is the desire to use the online network to connect with others and broaden social networks. Since the beginning of the digital shift and disruption of analog media in the 1990s, there has been tension between the desire of governments to regulate online interaction and those that see the Internet as fundamentally different. John Perry Barlow (@JPBarlow), who once wrote music lyrics for the Grateful Dead and joined The WELL (an early online community in the 1980s), helped define the independent attitude of users through his writings. Following passage of the *Communications Decency Act of 1996*, Barlow responded with *A Declaration of the Independence of Cyberspace*, distributed via email.

📱 **BOX 2.2**

A Declaration of the Independence of Cyberspace

Date: Fri, February 9, 1996 17:16:35 +0100
To: barlow@eff.org
From: John Perry Barlow <barlow@eff.org>
Subject: A Cyberspace Independence Declaration

Yesterday, that great invertebrate in the White House signed into the law the Telecom "Reform" Act of 1996, while Tipper Gore took digital photographs of the proceedings to be included in a book called "24 Hours in Cyberspace."

I had also been asked to participate in the creation of this book by writing something appropriate to the moment. Given the atrocity that this legislation would seek to inflict on the Net, I decided it was as good a time as any to dump some tea in the virtual harbor.

After all, the Telecom "Reform" Act, passed in the Senate with only five dissenting votes, makes it unlawful, and punishable by a $250,000 to say "shit" online. Or, for that matter, to say any of the other seven dirty words prohibited in broadcast media. Or to discuss abortion openly. Or to talk about any bodily function in any but the most clinical terms.

It attempts to place more restrictive constraints on the conversation in Cyberspace than presently exist in the Senate cafeteria, where I have dined and heard colorful indecencies spoken by United States senators on every occasion I did.

This bill was enacted upon us by people who haven't the slightest idea who we are or where our conversation is being conducted. It is, as my good friend and Wired Editor Louis Rossetto put it, as though "the illiterate could tell you what to read."

Well, fuck them.

Or, more to the point, let us now take our leave of them. They have declared war on Cyberspace. Let us show them how cunning, baffling, and powerful we can be in our own defense.

I have written something (with characteristic grandiosity) that I hope will become one of many means to this end. If you find it useful, I hope you will pass it on as widely as possible. You can leave my name off it if you like, because I don't care about the credit. I really don't.

But I do hope this cry will echo across Cyberspace, changing and growing and self-replicating, until it becomes a great shout equal to the idiocy they have just inflicted upon us.

I give you ...

A Declaration of the Independence of Cyberspace Governments of the Industrial World, you weary giants of flesh and steel, I come from Cyberspace, the new home of Mind. On behalf of the future, I ask you of the past to leave us alone. You are not welcome among us. You have no sovereignty where we gather.

We have no elected government, nor are we likely to have one, so I address you with no greater authority than that with which liberty itself always speaks. I declare the global social space we are building to be naturally independent of the tyrannies you seek to impose on us. You have no moral right to rule us nor do you possess any methods of enforcement we have true reason to fear.

Governments derive their just powers from the consent of the governed. You have neither solicited nor received ours. We did not invite you. You do not know us, nor do you know our world. Cyberspace does not lie within your borders. Do not think that you can build it, as though it were a public construction project. You cannot. It is an act of nature and it grows itself through our collective actions.

You have not engaged in our great and gathering conversation, nor did you create the wealth of our marketplaces. You do not know our culture, our ethics, or the unwritten codes that already provide our society more order than could be obtained by any of your impositions.

You claim there are problems among us that you need to solve. You use this claim as an excuse to invade our precincts. Many of these problems don't exist. Where there are real conflicts, where there are wrongs, we will identify them and address them by our means. We are forming our own Social Contract. This governance will arise according to the conditions of our world, not yours. Our world is different.

Cyberspace consists of transactions, relationships, and thought itself, arrayed like a standing wave in the Web of our communications.

Ours is a world that is both everywhere and nowhere, but it is not where bodies live. We are creating a world that all may enter without privilege or prejudice accorded by race, economic power, military force, or station of birth. We are creating a world where anyone, anywhere may express his or her beliefs, no matter how singular, without fear of being coerced into silence or conformity.

Your legal concepts of property, expression, identity, movement, and context do not apply to us. They are based on matter, there is no matter here.

Our identities have no bodies, so, unlike you, we cannot obtain order by physical coercion. We believe that from ethics, enlightened self-interest, and the commonweal, our governance will emerge. Our identities may be distributed across many of your jurisdictions. The only law that all our constituent cultures would generally recognize is the Golden Rule. We hope we will be able to build our particular solutions on that basis. But we cannot accept the solutions you are attempting to impose.

In the United States, you have today created a law, the Telecommunications Reform Act, which repudiates your own Constitution and insults the dreams of Jefferson, Washington, Mill, Madison, DeToqueville, and Brandeis. These dreams must now be born anew in us.

You are terrified of your own children, since they are natives in a world where you will always be immigrants. Because you fear them, you entrust your bureaucracies with the parental responsibilities you are too cowardly to confront yourselves. In our world, all the sentiments and expressions of humanity, from the debasing to the angelic, are parts of a seamless whole, the global conversation of bits. We cannot separate the air that chokes from the air upon which wings beat.

In China, Germany, France, Russia, Singapore, Italy and the United States, you are trying to ward off the virus of liberty by erecting guard posts at the frontiers of Cyberspace. These may keep out the contagion for a small time, but they will not work in a world that will soon be blanketed in bit-bearing media.

Your increasingly obsolete information industries would perpetuate themselves by proposing laws, in America and elsewhere, that claim to own speech itself throughout the world. These laws would declare ideas to be another industrial product, no more noble than pig iron. In our world, whatever the human mind may create can be reproduced and distributed infinitely at no cost. The global conveyance of thought no longer requires your factories to accomplish.

These increasingly hostile and colonial measures place us in the same position as those previous lovers of freedom and self-determination who had to reject the authorities of distant, uninformed powers. We must declare our virtual selves immune to your sovereignty, even as we continue to consent to your rule over our bodies. We will spread ourselves across the Planet so that no one can arrest our thoughts.

We will create a civilization of the Mind in Cyberspace. May it be more humane and fair than the world your governments have made before.

Davos, Switzerland
February 8, 1996
****
John Perry Barlow, Cognitive Dissident Co-Founder, Electronic Frontier Foundation
Home(stead) Page: www.eff.org/~barlow
Message Service: 800/634–3542
Barlow in Meatspace Today (until Feb 12): Cannes, France
Hotel Martinez: (33) 92 98 73 00, Fax: (33) 93 39 67 82
Coming soon to: Amsterdam 2/13–14, Winston-Salem 2/15, San Francisco 2/16–20, San Jose 2/21, San Francisco 2/21–23, Pinedale, Wyoming
In Memoriam, Dr. Cynthia Horner and Jerry Garcia
****
It is error alone which needs the support of government. Truth can stand by itself.

– Thomas Jefferson, Notes on Virginia

Source: Barlow, J. P. (1996). A Cyberspace Independence Declaration. http://w2.eff.org/Censorship/Internet_censorship_bills/barlow_0296.declaration

Barlow, who died in 2018, had suggested that governments should have "no sovereignty" over "cyberspace" and its users: "On behalf of the future, I ask you of the past to leave us alone." This idealistic view of online life attempted to separate it from the physical world and its limitations. Still, Barlow's **Electronic Frontier Foundation (EFF)** since the idealistic 1990s has remained active in fighting government regulation and intrusion, such as the National Security Agency (NSA) collection of online and telephone data. The hacking of Clinton campaign emails during the 2016 presidential election became a large issue, as there was some evidence that the Russian government collaborated with Wikileaks on the release of sensitive information. Freedom of information and privacy remain in conflict, and we continue to negotiate the future of the Internet and social media.

Another CMC pioneer, Howard Rheingold (@HRheingold), observed that virtual communities involve creation of social groups and relationships over time: "You can't kiss anybody and nobody can punch you in the nose, but a lot can happen within those boundaries" (Rheingold, 1993, p. 3). Rheingold, also an early member of The WELL, imported 1960s hippie culture into online, Web and social media communication.

CMC involves social experimentation: "Social isolation becomes a difficult proposition for any contemporary community" (Jones, 1998, p. 17). It is often assumed that computers "break down boundaries" or "break down hierarchies" in Cyberspace: "And yet computers can just as easily create boundaries and hierarchies" (p. 27). When it comes to social media communication, individuals present themselves online, and use a constructed identity for impression management in relationships. "Social networking sites, such as Facebook, are particularly interesting to communication researchers because they are dedicated specifically to forming and managing impressions, as well as engaging in relational maintenance and relationship-seeking behaviors" (Rosenberg & Egbert, 2011, p. 2).

COMMUNITY

Online community emerges from the development of individual social identities and realistic relationships between people (Bugeja, 2005; Lindlof & Taylor, 2002; Raacke & Bonds-Raacke, 2008). Chen and Persson (2002) found that older Internet users tended to score higher on measures of personal growth and life purpose. "In a sense, older Internet users were more like young adults than non-users" (p. 741). That is, people spending time online share common characteristics that separate them from those less likely to participate. Social media communication platforms create symbolic environments in which metaphors, such as the Facebook "wall" or the Pinterest "board," construct shared meaning and understanding. Mediated interpersonal communication develops when online communication begins to function as it would in a face-to-face environment. Individual relationships are unique, interdependent and rich with sharing and disclosure. Social media tend to emphasize sharing more than disclosure. When people say that there is a need for more engagement within social media, they may not understand that stronger relationships are built upon trust and transparency.

DIFFUSION OF NEW IDEAS

The adoption and spread of new ideas, new technologies and new practices follow somewhat predictable patterns. Although the United States has experienced dramatic growth of Internet and social media communication technologies over two decades, diffusion is uneven, and much of the world was slower to change (Bargh & McKenna, 2004). At the same time, however, in India, China and other rapidly developing countries, adoption of computers, mobile media and social media communication has advanced quickly in recent years. Rogers' (1995) model has been used to study change within a variety of contexts. It labels types of adopters within categories and allows us to track diffusion using a S-shaped curve over time. Social media communication began with the adoption of personal, home computers that were relatively simple to use, offered increasing computing power and were priced less expensively over time: "home computers became more user friendly, and their rate of adoption rose gradually" (Rogers, 1995, p. 243).

Internet and social media users tend to be early adopters of an innovative communication technology. The adoption process involves five major stages: awareness, interest, evaluation, trial and then adoption (Lowery & DeFleur, 1995, p. 128). Rogers' model proposed five groups that roughly fit a normal curve distribution.

📱 **BOX 2.3**

The Diffusion Model

- *Innovators*: the earliest people experimenting with the change (2.5%).
- *Early adopters*: those swayed by the innovators to jump on board of what is obviously a new trend (13.5%).
- *Early majority*: the first wave of mass appeal (34%).
- *Late majority*: the last wave of mass appeal (34%).
- *Laggards*: the remaining people who are either slow to come to the change, or resist it entirely (16%)

Source: Lowery, S. A., & DeFleur, M. L. (1995). *Milestones in Mass Communication Research, Media Effects, third edition.* White Plains, NY: Longman, p. 130.

USES AND GRATIFICATIONS

Social media offer a nearly unlimited range of potential uses, and these may or may not meet user expectations for new need gratification (Sundar & Limperos, 2013). Large amounts of time online have been shown to increase overall satisfaction: "For those individuals who spend less time on the Internet, the supportive relationships may be perceived as too insignificant to exhibit costs or rewards" (Wright, 2000, p. 115). While social media may offer the hope of breaking down traditional social barriers, communication theory suggests that this was not the case with uses of traditional mass media: "Open and easy communication as a basis for social solidarity between people becomes *more difficult* because of social differentiation, impersonality and distrust due to psychological alienation, the breakdown of meaningful social ties, and increasing anomie among the members" (Lowery & DeFleur, 1995, p. 12). In a sense, social media are the current test for our ability to create meaningful online communities, relationships and social movements (Mohammad, 2020).

Online communication also follows traditional media use patterns in terms of motivation. People use CMC for information about the world around them, relaxation, entertainment, excitement, and as an escape from the stresses of daily life (Perse & Dunn, 1995). Early research offered clues as to why social media have emerged, as national surveys found that computer use was connected with friends and family activities, a vehicle to avoid loneliness and development of new habits. A 2011 Edelman US national survey also confirmed that a majority viewed social media as entertainment, with a whopping 70% doing so among 18 to 29-year-olds.

One concern is the willingness of people to speak out about issues while online. Yun and Park (2011) considered the potential for there to be fear of isolation, as suggested by the spiral of silence (Noelle-Neumann, 1984) media theory:

Since online forums technically guarantee anonymity, there is no reason for participants to experience the fear of isolation. However, it appears that it is inevitable for human beings to have a certain degree of fear of isolation whether online or offline. It is possible that people may bring their norms and habits of offline social interaction to their online communications. A difference in the level of the trait fear of isolation was also observed between message posters and lurkers. People with low fear of isolation were more likely to post a message than people with high fear of isolation.

(p. 216)

CMC has explored the influence of media technology in creating interaction, online communities and a sense of identity for various groups (Barnes, 2001). Personal and family Web usage allows people to share information over great distances (Barnes, 2003). Ferguson and Perse (2000) suggested that the Web was becoming a functional alternative to TV for many.

Media technology uses (Pavlik, 1996) and gratifications (Lin, 1993), address the cultural importance (Stevenson, 1995) of cyberculture, online communities and individual identities (Bell, 2001; Du Gay, Evans, & Redman, 2000). Social media communication represents an evolution of individual, social and cultural desires to connect with new people.

⚡ BOX 2.4

Thought Leader Lili Bosse

Social media played a significant role when I ran for office, as it was a fabulous no-cost method of reaching my constituents with my message. I have used it as a way to let residents know what was happening in our city on a daily basis. It allowed me to be accessible, which has been very important to me as an elected official.

The biggest issue ahead is the balance of private and public life as an elected official. With social media now, everything is public. The challenge will be how to be an effective leader by being very transparent and open; however balancing the importance of one's personal and private life will be the challenge.

FIGURE 2.2 *@LiliBosse1*

Photograph by Vince Bucci, courtesy of Lili Bosse

The largest opportunity will be reaching more and more people by providing an easy way to be an accessible and open communicator. Social media is the most effective tool to reach a whole new younger voting demographic and allows for transparency and the ability to create back-and-forth dialog between the constituents and public officials.

Lili Bosse was the 73rd (2014–2015) and 76th (2017–2018) mayor of Beverly Hills, California and ran and won city council election in 2020. She was mayor of Beverly Hills during the city's 2014–2015 Centennial year. She previously served as vice mayor and city council member since 2011. She also served on the Beverly Hills Planning Commission, Fine Art Commission and Traffic and Parking Commission. Bosse, a Rotary Club member, has been active on community education and religious boards. Bosse, a philanthropist, is the daughter of Holocaust survivors. She has supported many Jewish causes in the United States and Israel.

ONLINE CULTURE AND POWER

Social media communication happens within a cultural context of values, ritual and even "chaos" (Carey, 1992, p. 34). Carey theorized that words *reshape* "our common culture" (p. 35), and the emerging social media culture is full of new words and developing social relationships. While some use social media in an effort to maintain existing power, others use it to try to grab new power. Social media extend the shifting emphasis toward the importance of communication "through which experience is described, shared, modified, and preserved" (Williams, 1966, p. 18).

⚡ BOX 2.5

Thought Leader Tunette Powell

From Rags to Reach
There are arguably three things that can level the playing field of success – money, a strong network and education. Having grown up in poverty, I did not have access to the first two. While I have been fortunate enough to earn a bachelor's degree and work toward a doctoral degree, it has been a nontraditional style of education that has contributed to my success – that is a vivid understanding of how to navigate social media.

In 2010, in an attempt to give us, including our toddler son, a better life, my husband enlisted in the United States Air Force. That same year, we were relocated from our hometown of San Antonio, Texas, and stationed at Offutt Air Force Base in Bellevue, Nebraska. My husband was making about $25,000 a year, and we did not know anyone near the base. With very little money and no local network, I decided to use Google – a search engine that I could access for free at any local library – to search for local nonprofit organizations. From there, via Facebook and Twitter, I reached out to the leaders of these organizations in hopes of developing a local network. It was through these social media sites that I met a then 16-year-old high school student living in a small town in Nebraska who would eventually design my first professional website. It was through these social media sites that I landed my first job in Nebraska as the program director of a youth-serving nonprofit. Even before obtaining my bachelor's degree, as long as I had access to the Internet, these media were free and provided a form of cultural capital. Social media gave me direct access to people I would have never come into contact with and also gave me an audience. With this new-found audience, in 2012, I published a memoir about growing up with a father addicted to drugs and saw public speaking success at the intercollegiate level. My first TEDx Talk in 2013 stemmed from a tweet to me from the curator.

FIGURE 2.3 *@TunettePowell*
Photograph by Brenda Lopez, courtesy of Tunette Powell

Most of my time on social media has been spent reaching out to successful people in the fields of education, social justice and journalism. Some days, I have reached out to as many as 20 people and have only heard back from one of them. But I have a rule: every week, I vow to reach out to at least ten people to request video conference calls or in-person meetings at coffee shops or at their place of business. Depending on the platform, video conference calls are free and coffee shops are great regardless, but especially if you're networking on a budget.

This form of engagement has been the greatest strategy for reaching people – both locally and nationally. Through social media platforms, including blogging and sites such as Instagram, I have been able to tell and share my story with people everywhere. Because of this, I transitioned from blogging on my own site to a paid blogger for the *Omaha World-Herald*. I published two books – one of which was a collection of stories generated from making requests on social media. I have served on nearly a dozen nonprofit boards, all because of my online interaction. Nationally, my social media presence helped land an appearance on *Oprah* and features with CNN, MSNBC and NPR's *This American Life* and *The Takeway*. In the six years that I spent in Nebraska; I was known as the transplant that had more network connections than most of the hometown people.

In 2016, my husband and I – now the parents of three children – transitioned out of the military and moved to Los Angeles – once again with very little money and no local network. But this time, unlike before, we had another form of capital – social media. Right before moving to Los Angeles, one of the first things I did was use Instagram, LinkedIn, Twitter and Facebook to connect with people in Los Angeles. Just one month into our move to Los Angeles, I received a flyer via snail mail about an upcoming election for my community's neighborhood council. At that time, I only knew of two people who would actually vote for me – my husband and I. Still, I decided to run, and officially announced my decision to run on social media. From there, people began connecting me to people who lived in my neighborhood. I joined Facebook groups that were specific to the area that I was running in and used social media to engage with area residents about the issues that were important to them.

Over the course of my three-month campaign, my new community only saw me speak in public once. But I was available and *active every day* on social media. I posted videos and regularly shared my hopes for our community. In June 2016, just four months after moving to Los Angeles, I was elected to the Central San Pedro Neighborhood Council and appointed as the Chair of the Homeless Committee. I spent about $75 on my campaign, which was all I could afford. My campaign was not about money; it was about meeting people where they were at and they were on social media.

Just a few months later, a woman – someone I had only known through social media – suggested I reach out to a friend of hers who had a consulting contract with the Los Angeles Unified School District – the second-largest school district in the United States. That woman – someone I did not even realize I was social media friends with – gave me a glowing recommendation despite never having met me in person. Because of her, without ever interviewing, I was offered a consulting position with the district. Since then, I have settled into Los Angeles – purchased a home – and continue to use social media as a way to build relationships with people who would otherwise be untouchable. I have landed multiple opportunities in Los Angeles due to my social media engagement, including being asked by parents and community members to run for the school board of the Los Angeles Unified School District – a campaign that has primarily been run through social media. The level of engagement and interaction has allowed me to develop meaningful relationships and to do so with very little money. As social media continue to evolve and change, so does this story. It is easy to look at the success I have had and call it the ultimate rags to riches story. But for me, it has been from rags to reach – that is being able to reach out to anyone in the world through social media – a new form of cultural capital.

Tunette Powell is an author, nationally recognized public speaker, program director of the UCLA Parent Project and an Urban Schooling doctoral candidate at the University of California, Los Angeles.

Hunsinger and Senft (2014) explored the capacity of social media "to support and extend in-depth social interactions" in that they "are increasingly seen as an ideal way to help communities engage in outreach" (pp. 1–2). While online political campaigning has been viewed as positive, researchers also fear the negative effects of so-called "imagined communities" within social network sites:

> in other words, the interfaces are places that we inhabit and that inhabit us as we imagine ourselves in them and using them … This social imagination varies … it is the interfaces and infrastructures of social media that now enable significant parts of our social imagination and with that significant parts of our social memory.
>
> (Hunsinger, 2014, p. 9)

The paradox of social media, then, are related to the blending of realities and social reproduction. Media technologies use narrative storytelling techniques to make sense of practices within communities. Within this context, Stevenson (1995) suspected that new communication tools functioned in the service of socially reproducing the status quo rather than *real* change. In the context of social media communication, there is an ongoing fear that virtual spaces confuse reality, representing myth and ritual as truth. However, this may be no more the case than what may be observed in socially constructed face-to-face communication. The use of computers to communicate, however, may create mediated online spaces offering a variety of unique properties.

CMC AND SOCIAL MEDIA

Computer-mediated communication began decades ago with interest in discussion boards and email communication. The earliest concerns related to CMC as a tool able to recreate communities of interest online, as well as its limitations. CMC did not offer communication that was as rich as face-to-face communication, and the lack of understanding resulted in negative experiences, such as "flame war" online fights. CMC, though, also allowed people to overcome physical and psychological limitations (Amichai-Hamburger, Wainapel & Fox, 2002). Some negative communication consequences, however, have been related to a preference for online social interaction, psychosocial depression, loneliness and problematic Internet use (Caplan, 2003). Research has supported the idea that "preference for online socialization is a key contributor to the development of problematic Internet use," and there appeared to be "a significant relationship between psychosocial health and preference for online socialization" (p. 638). In other words, CMC is a tool that may lead people with problems to take these into online environments, rather than, as is often assumed, the negative effects being caused by online usage.

In the case of so-called massively multiplayer online (MMOs) games, research has studied the boundaries between gameplay and life in the formation and maintenance of relationships and romance (Huynh, Lim & Skoric, 2013): "The typology of players differentiated by their construction of the play/life boundary indicates that they are active participants in creating and appraising the play experience and determining how it should be transformed" (p. 261).

CMC also helps us understand the spread of Internet memes, which are "commonly applied to describe the propagation of content items such as jokes, rumors, videos, or websites from one person to others" and "may spread in its original form, but it often also spawns user-created derivatives" (Shifman, 2013, p. 362). Readers may be familiar with the use of memes on social media sites, such as Facebook. Shifman (2013), drawing from Richard Dawkins' 1976 invention of the term as linked to "melodies" and "catch-phrases," sees memes as "abstract beliefs" (p. 363). In a process similar to genetic evolution, memes are thought to compete for attention through imitation and iteration:

1. Memes are "understood as cultural information that passes along from person to person, yet gradually scales into a shared social phenomenon."

2. They "reproduce by various means of imitation."

3. They are interesting because of "their diffusion through competition and selection."
(pp. 364–365)

Although online users have freedom, research indicates the existence of cultural boundaries. "This pattern suggests that the ostensibly chaotic world (wide web) may in fact follow more organized cultural trajectories than meets the eye" (p. 372). For example, the Cheeky Nando's meme refers to a British expression about going to a South African restaurant chain, often after drinking (KnowYourMeme, 2020). It appears to have been first used in 2011, spread on Twitter in 2012 and then was used across a variety of social and news media channels. Use peeked in 2015 and has been in decline ever since. Some memes last only a day, such as the Twitter #fartgate meme launched when a MSNBC host appeared to release gas during a broadcast (Welsh, 2019).

A paradox may be found within social media that they may both have a tendency to trigger silence on controversial issues, but users may also feel liberated to express opinions (Gearhart & Zhang, 2014). Spiral of silence theory, which suggests people assess the climate of opinion before responding, appears to be active within online public opinion. Gearhart and Zhang (2014) discovered that on social media sites – Facebook, Twitter, LinkedIn and YouTube – experiments reveal monitoring behavior:

> Practitioners should note that seemingly non-active users are actively engaged in this medium by observing the SNS opinion climate. SNS users in the current study demonstrate this by indicating that although they may not publicly comment themselves, they would read the comments in both conditions and some indicate they would tell others offline about the situation. Further, no groups are more likely to ignore the story and comments completely. Practitioners should consider this form of engagement when developing new methods of interaction and/or methods of user tracking in this medium.
>
> (p. 16)

The Pew Research Center conducted an exhaustive study of #BlackLivesMatter and other social media conversations about race (Anderson & Hitlin, 2016). Black users were twice as likely as white users to see racial content on social media sites. Over the course of 15 months – from January 2015 through March 2016 – Pew found 995 million tweets about race; an average of 2.1 million tweets per day represented 0.04% of a total of about 500 million tweets each day (para. 5). Nearly two-thirds of tweets mentioning race "were directly related to news events, like the church shooting in Charleston, South Carolina, or the Grammy performance of rapper Kendrick Lamar" (para. 6). Crimson Hexagon software was used to code the massive number of tweets (para. 9): Among 60% of current event tweets, 10% were about the 2016 election, 7% police or the judicial system, 7% celebrities or entertainment and 35% other events (para. 4).

Coban (2016) and his colleagues have viewed this form of social movement as a social media revolution that functions through activists in content sharing designed to expose corruption, exploitation and criminal behavior. Global anarchists found social media, such as Twitter, to be new utopian tools of influence, collaboration and education. Social media practices during protests seem to treat Twitter and other platforms as contested spaces in a struggle to mobilize social movements in the face of government power and control (Dencik & Leistert, 2015).

Sherblom (2020) focuses CMC on relational communication, media richness, naturalness and experiences. Social media sites have constraints, and this may have an impact upon "social presence" (p. 65). "Through CMC, members of a social network are able to stay in touch even as they change locations in time and space" (p. 191). Still, critical concerns of race and gender must be considered. For example, "The fact that advertisers are targeting predominantly white women bloggers in the United States has global implications" (Daniels, 2012, p. 53). Digital media offer CMC identity formation that may be made legitimate through reach.

Current CMC research has one focus on the problem of psychological addiction and well-being when it comes to the social pressures of smartphone use at any hour, as well as the expectation of immediate response (French & Bazarova, 2017; Halfmann & Rieger, 2019). Social media and CMC challenge the traditional concept of mass communication. For Chaffee and Metzger (2001), the Internet age turned the term into an oxymoron, "as a set of media institutions, as a societal problem, or as an academic field of study" (p. 366). Drawing upon the classic work of Bauer (1964, p. 319), communication is seen as "transactional" instead of "one-way influence" (p. 368). Clearly, Chaffee and Metzger (2001) were among the first to understand the importance of "users' ability to become content producers" and create and disseminate "material that is fairly sophisticated at low cost" (p. 369). CMC helps us to better understand online communication and the foundations of social media. It also is a framework for understanding social media application in fields, such as journalism, public relations, advertising and marketing.

DISCUSSION QUESTIONS: STRATEGIES AND TACTICS

1. How has CMC influenced the way we form relationships? How may it blur the lines between reality and fantasy? In what ways have you felt addicted to social media, and how do you control this? What are the best ways to cultivate healthy online relational communication?

2. How would a visualization of your social networks depict communication patterns and relationships? How could this be used to influence future online behavior?

3. Describe your favorite Internet meme: Why do you like it? How does it transfer cultural understandings from one person to another?

4. Think about a time when you felt as though too much time was spent using social media sites: How did you become aware of this? What did you do about it?

REFERENCES

Albarran, A. B. (2013). Introduction. In A. B. Albarran (Ed.), *The Social Media Industries*, pp. 1–15. New York, NY: Routledge.

Amichai-Hamburger, A., Wainapel, G., & Fox, S. (2002). On the Internet No One Knows I'm an Introvert: Extroversion, Neuroticism, and Internet Interaction. *CyberPsychology & Behavior* 5(2), 125–128.

Anderson, M., & Hitlin, P. (2016, August 15). Social Media Conversations About Race. *Pew Research Center*. www.pewinternet.org/2016/08/15/social-media-conversations-about-race/

AP. (2019a, December 28). Report: Popular UAE Chat App TikTok A Government Spy Tool. *Associated Press*. https://apnews.com/02291ff7e07d173153b1af3c9ead67bb

AP. (2019b, November 30). Video App TikTok Unblocks Teen Who Posted on China's Muslims. *Associated Press*. https://apnews.com/e68090cebc8944abbf8aad5aaa976032

Baran, S. J., & Davis, D. (2006). *Mass Communication Theory*, Fourth edition. Belmont, CA: Thomson Wadsworth.

Bargh, J. (2002). Beyond Simple Truths: The Human-Internet Interaction. *Journal of Social Issues* 58(1), 1–8.

Bargh, J., & McKenna, K. (2004). The Internet and Social Life. *Annual Review of Psychology 55*(1), 573–590.

Bargh, J., McKenna, K., & Fitzsimons, G. (2002). Can You See the Real Me? Activation and Expression of the "True Self" on the Internet. *Journal of Social Issues 58*(1), 33–48.

Barlow, J. P. (1996). A Cyberspace Independence Declaration. http://w2.eff.org/Censorship/Internet_censorship_bills/barlow_0296.declaration

Barnes, S. B. (2001). *Online Connections: Internet Interpersonal Relationship*. Cresskill, NJ: Hampton Press.

Barnes, S. B. (2003). *Computer-Mediated Communication, Human-to-Human Communication across the Internet*. Boston, MA: Allyn and Bacon.

Bauer, R. A. (1964). The Obstinate Audience. *American Psychologist, 19*, 319–328.

Bell, D. (2001). *An Introduction to Cybercultures*. London, UK: Routledge.

Benedikt, M. (1991). Cyberspace: Some Proposals. In M. Benedikt (Ed.), *Cyberspace: First Steps*, pp. 119–124. Cambridge: Massachusetts Institute of Technology Press.

Berger, C. (2005). Interpersonal Communication: Theoretical Perspectives, Future Prospects. *Journal of Communication 55*(3), 415–447.

Bernie, S., & Horvath, P. (2006, June). Psychological Predictors of Internet Social Communication. *Journal of Computer Mediated Communication 7*(4).

Boers, E., Afzali, M. H., Newton, N., & Conrod, P. (2019). The Association of Screen Time and Depression Adolescence. *JAMA Pediatrics 173*(9), 853–859.

Bourdieu, P., & Coleman, J. S. (1991). *Social Theory for a Changing Society*. Boulder, CO: Westview Press.

boyd, d. m., & Ellison, N. B. (2008). Social Network Sites: Definition, History and Scholarship. *Journal of Computer-Mediated Communication 13*(1), 210–230.

Bugeja, M. (2005). *Interpersonal Divide*. New York, NY: Oxford University Press.

Burke, T., & Dickey, J. (2013, January 16). Manti Te'o's Dead Girlfriend, the Most Heartbreaking and Inspirational Story of the College Football Season, Is a Hoax. *Deadspin*. http://deadspin.com/manti-teos-dead-girlfriend-the-most-heartbreaking-an-5976517

Burnett, R., & Marshall, P. D. (2003). *Web Theory: An Introduction*. London, UK: Routledge.

Butts, C. T. (2008). Social Network Analysis: A Methodological Introduction. *Asian Journal of Social Psychology 11*, 13–41.

Caplan, S. (2003). Preference for Online Social Interaction: A Theory of Problematic Internet Use and Psychosocial Well-Being. *Communication Research 30*(6), 625–648.

Carey, J. W. (1992). *Communication as Culture, Essays on Media and Society*. New York, NY: Routledge.

Chaffee, S. H., & Metzger, M. J. (2001). The End of Mass Communication? *Mass Communication & Society 4*(4), 365–379.

Chen, Y., & Persson, A. (2002). Internet Use among Young and Older Adults: Relation to Psychological Well-Being. *Educational Gerontology 28*(9), 731–744.

Child, J. T., Pearson, J. C., & Petronio, S. (2009). Blogging, Communication, and Privacy Management: Development of the Blogging Privacy Management Measure. *Journal of the American Society for Information Science and Technology 60*(10), 2079–2094.

Coban, B. (2016). Social Media R/evolution, an Introduction. In B. Coban (Ed.), *Social Media and Social Movements, The Transformation of Communication Patterns*, pp. vii–xix. Lanham, MD: Lexington Books.

Cole, J. I. (2003). *The UCLA Internet Report, Surveying the Digital Future, Year Three.* Los Angeles, CA: UCLA Center for Communication Policy. www.ccpa.ucla.edu.

Cooley, C. H. (1909/1966). The Significance of Communication. In B. Berelson and M. Janowitz (Eds.), *Reader in Public Opinion and Communication,* second edition, pp. 147–155. New York: Free Press.

Daniels, J. (2012). BlogHer and Blogalicious: Gender, Race and Political Economy of Women's Blogging Conferences. In R. Gajjala and Y. J. Oh (Eds.), *Cyberfeminism 2.0,* pp. 29–60. New York: Peter Lang.

Dencik, L., & Leistert, O. (Eds.) (2015). *Critical Perspectives on Social Media and Protest: Between Control and Emancipation.* London: Rowman & Littlefield.

du Gay, P., Evans, J., & Redman, P. (Eds.) (2000). *Identity: A Reader.* London, UK: Sage.

Ferguson, D. A., & Perse, E. M. (2000). The World Wide Web as a Functional Alternative to Television. *Journal of Broadcasting & Electronic Media 44*(2), 155–174.

French, M., & Bazarova, N. N. (2017, November). Is Anybody Out There? Understanding Mass-personal Communication through Expectations for Response across Social Media Platforms. *Journal of Computer-Mediated Communication 22,* 303–319.

Gambrel, J. (2020, January 2). Co-creator Defends Suspected UAE Spying App Call ToTok. *Associated Press.* https://apnews.com/67165c626c35ab0cca1ef9cbf6cea274

Garton, L., Haythornthwaite, C., & Wellman, B. (1997, June). Studying Online Social Networks. *Journal of Computer-Mediated Communication 3*(1). 10.1111/j.1083–6101.1997.tb00062.x/full.

Gasser, H. (2008). Being Multiracial in a Wired Society: Using the Internet to Define Identity and Community on Campus. *New Direction for Student Services, 23,* 63–71.

Gearhart, S., & Zhang, W. (2014). Gay Bullying and Online Opinion Expression: Testing Spiral of Silence in the Social Media Environment. *Social Science Computer Review 32*(1), 18–36.

Greenhow, C., & Robelia, B. (2009, July). Old Communication, New Literacies: Social Network Sites as Social Learning Resources. *Journal of Computer-Mediated Communication 14*(4), 1130–1161.

Halfmann, A., & Rieger, D. (2019, May). Permanently on Call: The Effects of Social Pressure on Smartphone Users' Self-Control, Need Satisfaction, and Well-Being. *Journal of Computer-Mediated Communication 24*(4), 165–181.

Hansen, D. L., Shneiderman, B., & Smith, M. A. (2011). *Analyzing Social Media Networks with NodeXL.* Burlington, MA: Elsevier.

Heaney, M. T., & McClurg, S. D. (2009, September). Social Networks and American Politics. *American Politics Research 37*(5), 727–741.

Hill, K. (2020, January 18). The Secretive Company that Might End Privacy as We Know It. *The New York Times.* www.nytimes.com/2020/01/18/technology/clearview-privacy-facial-recognition.html

Howard, B. (2008, November). Analyzing Online Social Networks. *Communications of the ACM 51*(11), 14–16.

Huffaker, D. (2010, October). Dimensions of Leadership and Social Influence in Online Communities. *Human Communication Research 36*(4), 593–617.

Hunsinger, J. (2014). Interface and Infrastructure in Social Media. In J. Hunsinger and T. Senft (Eds.), *The Social Media Handbook,* pp. 5–17. New York: Routledge.

Hunsinger, J., & Senft, T. (2014). Introduction. In J. Hunsinger and T. Senft (Eds.), *The Social Media Handbook,* pp. 1–4. New York: Routledge.

Huynh, K. P., Lim, S. W., & Skoric, M. M. (2013). Stepping Out of the Magic Circle: Regulation of Play/Life Boundary in MMO-Mediated Romantic Relationship. *Journal of Computer-Mediated Communication 18*(3), 251–264.

Jones, S. G. (1998). *Cybersociety 2.0, Revisiting Computer-Mediated Communication and Community*. Thousand Oaks, CA: Sage.

KnowYourMeme. (2020). Cheeky Nando's. https://knowyourmeme.com/memes/cheeky-nandos

Koh, J., Kim, Y.-G., Butler, B., & Bock, G.-W. (2007, February). Encouraging Participation in Virtual Communities. *Communications of the ACM 50*(2), 69–73.

Köver, C., & Reuter, M. (2019, December 2). TikTok Curbed Reach for People with Disabilities. *Netzpolitik*. https://netzpolitik.org/2019/discrimination-tiktok-curbed-reach-for-people-with-disabilities/

Lieberman, M. D. (2013). *Social, Why Our Brains are Wired to Connect*. New York, NY: Crown Publishers.

Lin, C. A. (1993). Adolescent Viewing and Gratifications in a New Media Environment. *Mass Communication Review 20*(1–2), 39–50.

Lindlof, T., & Taylor, B. (2002). *Qualitative Communication Research Methods*. Thousand Oaks, CA: Sage.

Lowery, S. A., & DeFleur, M. L. (1995). *Milestones in Mass Communication Research, Media Effects*, Third edition. White Plains, NY: Longman.

Meisenzahl, M. (2020, January 24). China's Version of TikTok Launches Feature to Spread Awareness and Fight Wuhan Coronavirus. *Business Insider*. www.businessinsider.com/wuhan-coronavirus-douyin-tiktok-launches-feature-to-help-fight-virus-2020-1

Milburn, M. A. (1991). *Persuasion and Politics*. Belmont, CA: Wadsworth.

Miller, A. (2020, January 25). 'It Plays To Our Worst Fears': Coronavirus Misinformation Fueled By Social Media. *CBC*. www.cbc.ca/news/health/coronavirus-canada-social-media-misinformation-1.5440334

Mohammad, M. (2020). *Social Media and Democratization in Iraqi Kurdistan*. Lanham, MD: Lexington Books.

Negroponte, N. (1995). *Being Digital*. New York, NY: Alfred A. Knopf.

Noelle-Neumann, E. (1984). *The Spiral of Silence, Public Opinion – Our Social Skin*. Chicago, IL: University of Chicago Press.

Pavlik, J. V. (1996). *New Media Technology, Cultural and Commercial Perspectives*. Boston, MA: Allyn and Bacon.

Pell, M. B., & Wang, E. (2019, December 20). The US Navy Banned TikTok from Government-Issued Mobile Devices, Citing a 'Cybersecurity Threat'. *Reuters, Business Insider*. www.businessinsider.com/us-navy-bans-tiktok-from-government-issued-mobile-devices-2019-12

Perse, E. M., & Dunn, D. G. (1995). The Utility of Home Computers: Impact of Multimedia and Connectivity. *Paper presented to the Association for Education in Journalism and Mass Communication*, Washington, DC, August.

Petronio, S. (2002). *Boundaries of Privacy, Dialectics of Disclosure*. Albany, NY: State University of New York Press.

Raacke, J., & Bonds-Raacke, J. (2008). Myspace and Facebook: Applying the Uses and Gratifications Theory to Exploring Friend-Networking Sites. *CyberPsychology & Behavior 11*(2), 169–174.

Ramirez, A. (2007). The Effect of Anticipated Future Interaction and Initial Impression Valence on Relational Communication in Computer-Mediated Interaction. *Communication Studies 58*(1), 53–70.

Rheingold, H. (1993). *The Virtual Community*. Ontario: Addison-Wesley.

Rheingold, H. (2014). Howard Rheingold. *YouTube*. www.youtube.com/watch?v=661xiu6LidQ

Rodrigues, E. M., Milic-Frayling, N., Smith, M., Shneiderman, B., & Hansen, D. (2011). *Group-In-A-Box Layout for Multi-Faceted Analysis of Communities*. http://hcil.cs.umd.edu/trs/2011–24/2011–24.pdf

Rogers, E. M. (1995). *Diffusion of Innovations*, fourth edition. New York, NY: Free Press.

Rosenberg, J., & Egbert, N. (2011). Online Impression Management: Personality Traits and Concerns for Secondary Goals as Predictors of Self-Presentation Tactics on Facebook. *Journal of Computer-Mediated Communication 17*(1), 1–18.

Schramm, W. (1972). Nature of Communication between Humans. In W. Schramm and D. F. Roberts. (Eds.), *The Process and Effects of Mass Communication*, revised edition, pp. 8–32.Urbana: University of Illinois Press.

Severin, W. J., & Tankard, J. W., Jr. (2001). *Communication Theories*, fifth edition. New York, NY: Longman.

Sherblom, J. C. (2020). *Computer-Mediated Communication, Approaches and Perspectives*. San Diego, CA: Cognella.

Shifman, L. (2013). Memes in a Digital World: Reconciling with a Conceptual Troublemaker. *Journal of Computer-Mediated Communication 18*(3), 362–377.

Sonderman, J. (2013, January 17). Notre Dame Football Player Te'o Girlfriend Hoax "Became Truth through the Media." *Poynter*. www.poynter.org/latest-news/mediawire/200919/notredame-football-player-teo-girlfriend-hoax-became-truth-through-the-media/

Stevenson, N. (1995). *Understanding Media Cultures, Social Theory and Mass Communication*. London, UK: Sage.

Sundar, S. S., & Limperos, A. M. (2013). Uses and Grats 2.0: New Gratifications for New Media. *Journal of Broadcasting & Electronic Media 57*(4), 504–525.

Teychenne, M., Costigan, S. A., & Parker, K. (2015). The Association between Sedentary Behaviour and Risk of Anxiety: A Systematic Review. *BMC Public Health*, *15*, 530.

Togoh, I. (2019, November 22). U.S. Army to Review TikTok Security after Warning from Schumer. *Forbes*. www.forbes.com/sites/isabeltogoh/2019/11/22/army-to-review-tiktok-security-after-warning-from-schumer/#73c6ebad1225

Tubbs, S. T., & Moss, S. (1983). *Human Communication*, fourth edition. New York, NY: Random House.

Turkle, S. (1995). *Life on the Screen: Identity in the Age of the Internet*. New York: Simon and Schuster.

Twenge, J. M., Joiner, T. E., Rogers, M. L., & Martin, G. N. (2018). Increases in Depressive Symptoms, Suicide-related Outcomes, and Suicide Rates among U.S. Adolescents After 2010 and Links to Increased New Media Screen Time. *Clinical Psychological Science 6*(1), 3–17.

Welsh, C. (2019, November 19). For One Beautiful Night, #fartgate Actually United All of Twitter. *Mashable*. https://mashable.com/article/eric-swalwell-chris-matthews-fartgate-memes/

Westley, B. H., & MacLean, M. S., Jr. (1957). A Conceptual Model for Communications Research. *Journalism Quarterly 34*(1), 31–38.

Williams, D., Caplan, S., & Xiong, L. (2007). Can You Hear Me Now? The Impact of Voice in an Online Gaming Community. *Human Communication Research 33*(4), 427–499.

Williams, J. C. (2018). Frederick E. Terman and the Rise of Silicon Valley. In C. Pursell (Ed.), *Technology in America, A History of Individuals and Ideas*, third edition, pp. 297–311. Cambridge: The MIT Press.

Williams, R. (1966). *Communications*. London: Chatto & Windus.

Wright, A. (2011, May). Web Science Meets Network Science. *Communications of the ACM 54*(5), 23.

Wright, K. (2000). Computer-Mediated Social Support, Older Adults, and Coping. *Journal of Communication 50*(3), 100–118.

Yun, G. W., & Park, S.-Y. (2011). Selective Posting: Willingness to Post a Message Online. *Journal of Computer-Mediated Communication. 16*(2), 201–227.

Social Media in Journalism

3

Spoiler alert: TikTok's probably not going to save journalism. But ... when the video-based service adds the ability to include links in video descriptions, it could be a funnel for new Post subscribers – and for news consumers everywhere.
— Alex Mahadevan (@Poynter, 2019)

While journalists increasingly use social media for self-promotion and information seeking purposes ... college students are more apt to use social media for personal networking.
— Ammina Kothari & Andrea Hickerson (@abkothari & @aehickerson, 2016)

If engagement is to be effective and meaningful, journalists must earn their audiences' attention, build loyalty, and deepen trust while finding new revenue streams to subsidize the public-interest journalism that market forces have never supported anyway.
— Jake Batsell (@jbatsell, Batsell, 2015)

Every new social media site offers the potential to be the next rising star, and TikTok captured public and news industry attention because of its rapidly growing, youthful audience. Mahadevan (2019) followed Dave Jorgensen, as he became *The Washington Post*'s point person for millions of TikTok views. The app quickly had more than 16 million users opening it numerous times per day for an average of more than 45 minutes (para. 5). The *Post* used short and funny videos for its strategy to engage potential future subscribers. TikTok is the latest iteration of the online disruption of journalism. The allure of shiny new tools fits within a larger and disturbing context of news aggregation. As Coddington (2019) puts it: "I define news aggregation as *taking news from published sources, reshaping it, and republishing it in an abbreviated form within a single place*" (p. 5). Social media expand the reach of stories through this process, but:

It is the process of information accretion, a practice through which published news is added onto, reshaped, or stripped down, and its meanings reinterpreted or reinforced ... This is the peril of aggregation as productive circulation

(pp. 206–207)

Coddington (2019) identifies the paradox of aggregation. It may be used either in the service of "haphazard fabrication," or repackaging that is "defined by the meanings" – perhaps clarification, as news "evolves along a path through various audiences and platforms" (p. 207). Increasingly, the process will be automated by computer programmers writing algorithms, as well as "hybrid journalism" that also continues to involve human interaction (Diakopoulos, 2019, p. 245).

It is unclear if news organizations can compete with the audience attraction of young stars on YouTube and TikTok. Ryan Kaji, for example, was 8 years old when his Ryan's World YouTube review of new toys earned millions of dollars from a rapidly growing brand that spread to a Nickelodeon television show (Perelli, 2019, para. 5). Once young social media influencers attract millions of followers, they can leverage a following through traditional talent agencies. "Since the rise of YouTube influencers, Hollywood's top talent agencies have developed digital-focused departments, and now work with popular YouTube stars like Emma Chamberlain (8.5 million subscribers) and Shane Dawson (23 million subscribers) in developing multi-platform businesses" (para. 10). However, most of the viral celebrities have little to do with journalism.

The journalism industry continues to develop and apply a set of best practices, including those that Ken Doctor at Newsonomics packaged into a venture called Lookout: "digital-only," "mobile-first," and at "scale" for local newsrooms (Doctor, 2020, 4:04). Journalism struggled in a social media communication age to identify its "value proposition" through an entrepreneurial process (7:14). In late 2020, Lookout planned to incubate the ideas in one local news market based upon community engagement, customer focus, and spending more money on creating content. Online journalism continues to disrupt traditional media business models.

Even some of the disruptive online publications found themselves disrupted by economic and legal forces. Deadspin, for example, was gobbled up by **private equity (PE)** firm G/O Media during bankruptcy and following the successful Gawker lawsuit and sale of Univision (Kalaf, 2020). PE firms targeted many news organizations "to make those companies more efficient, with the aim of profiting from a sale" (para. 4). Alden Capital, for example, acquired 32% of the *Chicago Tribune*, and it also bought shares of other major daily newspapers (Jackson & Marx, 2020, para. 5). "Unless Alden reverses course – perhaps in repentance for the avaricious destruction it has wrought in Denver and elsewhere – we need a civic-minded local owner or group of owners" (para. 15). However, few local newspapers appeared to be prepared to survive the digital disruption that began more than two decades ago. At the national level, collaboration is an important element for publications, such as ProPublica, that thrive by using data and software in enterprise journalism projects (Tornoe, 2020).

As president and editor in chief of *The Huffington Post* and its media group, Arianna Huffington was at the forefront of redefining journalism through an online business model. When asked to define journalism by *Columbia Journalism Review* (CJR), Huffington was not alone in moving beyond the traditional who, what, when, where, why, and how listing of questions. Alexander Jutkowitz (@GroupSJR), Group SJR managing partner, said that the digital age affords people and organizations a way to share: "A tongue-in-cheek essay, an infographic that makes a complicated topic instantly accessible, or an in-depth piece of reporting that teaches, inspires, or reveals – all of these things make people smarter and better able to navigate the world" (CJR, 2013, para. 2).

The changes sparked industry interest in what has been called "engaged journalism" (Batsell, 2015; DeJarnette, 2017). Facebook formed news partnerships to promote the use of Facebook Live video and other tools by journalists and news organizations (Mullin, 2017). At the same time, Facebook struggled to remain neutral in the news dissemination and filtering process. After a strained relationship with news organizations, Facebook launched Facebook News to share some revenue. CEO Mark Zuckerberg seemed to want to deflect criticism of his site and its contribution to battering American newspapers: "We feel acute responsibility because there's obviously an awareness that the internet has disrupted the news industry business model. We've figured out a different way to do this that we think is going to be better and more sustainable" (Isaac & Tracy, 2019, para. 4).

Journalism is changing because of the use of social media and rapid mobile media adoption. Much of what happens within SNS (social networking sites) in terms of news sharing behavior may be contextualized as "internalizing" browsing and personalization or "externalizing" re-contextualization or endorsement, as "news sharing is now transforming news culture" (Choi, 2016, pp. 816, 831). The social media shift is impacting all aspects of the industry – from the newsroom to advertising and management. For content managers at newspapers, for example, **content management systems (CMS)** made it easier to share news content across traditional and social media platforms. Facebook has been a popular tool for news sharing, but Twitter continues to be important for news. News managers, armed with the latest industry data, urge reporters to not only share links to their stories, but also to engage with audience members using interesting and useful content. Twitter also remains a source for journalists. As Donald Trump (@realDonaldTrump) successfully ran for president in 2016, he grew his followers to more than 20 million by engaging nearly every day on the site – even during the transition team's work after the election. By early 2020, President Trump's Twitter handle tripled to about 70 million followers. It became clear that Twitter could be used as a tool in the direct advancement of policy and diplomacy, though the airing of political statements directly to the public by going around *and* through following journalists was criticized by some. Trump's frequently incorrect tweets were fact-checked by *The Washington Post* in its weekly feature (Lee, 2017). As president, Trump frequently attacked journalism, and he used Twitter to go around the press and directly to his millions of followers.

Meanwhile, BuzzFeed's decision to publish and share on Twitter a dossier of unsubstantiated reports about Trump's private life generated debate among journalists (Burneko, 2017). BuzzFeed's editor Ben Smith defended the controversial decision based upon a "presumption to be transparent," erring "on the side of publishing," and "how we see the job of reporters in 2017" (Ember & Grynbaum, 2017, paras. 7–8). Some called that a "ridiculous rationale" (Wemple, 2017). The document was in the hands of numerous news organizations for months, and *Mother Jones* mentioned it three months before the BuzzFeed release (Bogle, 2017; Corn, 2016). When one considers the nature of news, it is easy to see why reporters and editors may interpret journalistic ethics and differ on a decision to publish. Journalism is a distinct type of content. Craft and Davis (2013) identified five foundational democratic needs:

1. Journalism informs, analyzes, interprets, and explains.

2. Journalism investigates.

3. Journalism creates public conversation.

4. Journalism helps generate social empathy.

5. Journalism encourages accountability.

(p. 11)

Within a social media context, journalism is often, though not exclusively, the first to "break" news on sites, such as Twitter. Shared links lead readers to more in-depth stories that may provide analysis, interpretation, and explanation. A less common but important function of journalism is independent investigation of the political system. We sometimes speak of journalists playing a watchdog role over public officials. Increasingly, the sharing of news through social media is a spark for public conversation in online spaces. The idea of "vertical" accountability through journalism is perhaps the most difficult, as "horizontal" checks and balances within government provide the most formal accountability (Craft & Davis, 2013, pp. 19–20). Still, it is fair to say that by initiating online public conversation that often includes public officials, journalists and the public have the potential to press for a measure of accountability in government.

⚡ BOX 3.1

Thought Leader Amy Guth

What has changed? Reader behavior, really. Nobody waits around loyally to get a story from the local paper; people want immediate information, regardless of the medium.

Even six or seven years ago in newsrooms, we began to see shifts to support and recognize this, such as in an emphasis on breaking news desks monitoring social media to help surface information as it's happening in real-time, or soon after. Quite simply, we began to see user behavior shifting; fewer and fewer were going to pick up a phone and call a breaking news editor; people began to just whip out a phone, take a photo and post it. Done.

Granted, with this amazing era of access to information, we also have to be hyper-vigilant about fact-checking, too. There's immense pressure to be "first" and report information at Twitter-speed, but it's more important than ever to meticulously verify information.

That said, the smartphone has also revolutionized the role of the eyewitness – accounts of natural disasters, crime, protests, and police-involved shootings. We've even seen citizen live-streaming fill in gaps of news media coverage (Ferguson, Hong Kong protests) and serve to make all of us witnesses (Philando Castille shooting).

Within the industry as a journalist, one of the most significant changes

FIGURE 3.1 *@amyguth.*
Photo courtesy of WGN Radio

has been that it's not enough to simply file your story anymore. We must all be proactive and use digital tools available to us, both to build networks and to make data-driven decisions. Some have bemoaned that shift and been reluctant, but personally, I think the shift has been exciting to watch. It's always better to be able to steer your own ship, so to speak.

It is my hope that media literacy takes a bigger share of the spotlight in the years to come, and a large part of that is on us, in the industry, to explain how newsrooms operate – that editorial boards are separate from newsrooms, that reporters are to share verified facts while columnists are supposed to have an opinion while still sharing facts. I think we haven't done the best job of educating the public about how it all works and about how we verify information, and, in my opinion, we must do that in order to survive as an industry.

While our access to information is greater than ever before, the importance of being able to discern between a story reported by a trained journalist (regardless of medium of delivery) and conjecture or speculation will hopefully become more of an area of discussion.

What I predict is a move to follow individuals as sources of content, rather than the publications of their employers. So, for journalists, building a personal "brand" will be essential and an exciting way to take an internal locus of control approach to one's career.

Amy Guth hosts Crain's Daily Gist for *Crain's Chicago Business* and the daily business podcast. She also is developing an independent podcast. Guth has hosted talk radio on WGN Radio. Recently, Guth has been recognized on the NewCity 2019 Film50 list. Guth produced and directed the episodic documentary film project about online harassment and suppression, "Din," and associate produced, "La Mitad Del Mundo," a Spanish-language documentary film about sex trafficking in Ecuador. Guth is also author of the novel *Three Fallen Women*, and has contributed work to *Los Angeles Review of Books*, *Los Angeles Times*, WGN-TV, WBEZ, WCIU-TV, *Chicago Tribune*, *Orlando Sentinel*, *Hartford Courant*, *Sun-Sentinel*, Rivet Radio, *The Nosher*, Monkeybicycle, Bookslut, Jewcy, and *The Believer*, among others. Previously, Guth was general manager/publisher and oversaw operations of RedEye and Metromix at Tribune Publishing Company, and managed social media and search engine optimization at the *Chicago Tribune*. She also serves as immediate past president of Association for Women Journalists Chicago.

McCombs et al. (2011) described a "changing environment" for news and public opinion because of the online shift and emphasis on entertainment within media:

> The age of media convergence has brought together media genres that used to be seen as quite disparate. Diana Mutz has argued that it is futile to speak of a distinction between news and entertainment within the present media landscape because it is increasingly difficult to tell where the news begins and the entertainment ends and vice versa … This will become all the more the case in the coming years.
>
> (p. 25)

The psychological need to be entertained through emotionally arousing content has been related to social sharing, including the spread of inspirational news content (Qihao et al., 2019). "The presence of terms associated with the specific emotions of hope and elevation, as well as with general inspiration, strongly predicted whether an article would be judged to be inspirational or not …" (p. 885). More than one in five online stories from *The New York Times* were found to be inspirational, including 36% of the top 50 shared items (p. 884).

Journalists have learned to become generalists by writing for the Web, blogging, developing digital photography skills, audio/video techniques, programming, and social networking (Luckie, 2011): "Many social networkers use the sites to share and comment on news stories and by doing so have transformed the way journalism is distributed on the web" (p. 169). Twitter, for example, can also involve either a "back-and-forth exchange" or private **direct message (DM)** between two followers (p. 172). Journalists must make decisions about how much audience engagement serves the goals of their personal and company brands.

Among the issues for newsrooms is the power that Facebook, owner of Instagram, now holds over the publishing industry through Facebook Live and content sharing with Facebook and Instagram Stories. Snapchat remains a relatively small news site (Fitts, 2015; Tompkins, 2016). Beyond business concerns of publishing traffic within these sites instead of owned digital properties, the pressure to use live video raised legal and ethical concerns. In St. Louis, for example, a Fox 2 reporter made a joke about the killing of Mike Brown during a Facebook Live broadcast and was quickly fired (Rivas, 2016). The pressure to attract eyeballs has an impact on news judgment. Buzzfeed, for example, had more than 10 million views by exploding a watermelon during a Facebook Live event (Rutenberg, 2016): "Traditional journalists everywhere saw themselves as the seeds, flying out of the frame" (para. 2). *The New York Times* was one of the first major news organizations to accept the new model of news economics: "Mobile *can* be harnessed to share the day's news, and works far better to keep us informed than newsprint ever could" (Doctor, 2016, para. 6). Still, the continued news layoffs, importance of site clicks, and ownership turnover all threaten investigative journalism (Hare, 2016). While millennials value keeping up with news, data suggest they are less likely than older people to pay (Lichterman, 2015). At the same time, it may be a mistake to lump this group with younger social media users from Gen Z. One young adult marketer wrote: "While my sister, born in 2001, is always posting on her Finsta and TikTok profiles, I'm still sharing early-2000s memes on Facebook. And, while she's just starting college, I'm budgeting to pay off my student loans" (Bump, 2019, para. 12). Facebook for Business (2019) emphasizes authenticity and personal communication for both groups through the use of Facebook Stories and Messenger. Generalizations about any group should be made with caution – especially when it comes to generational differences. Still, news people continue to explore and use a variety of social media tools to try to reach audiences of all ages and backgrounds.

Journalists are very active on Twitter, especially during breaking news events. They are being encouraged to not only share story links, but also rich media – photographs, videos, and source links. Media groups, though, face unique circumstances in each market. In smaller towns, for example, Twitter may not be as popular as in larger cities. Another problem is that female journalists frequently face social media harassment by online trolls (Hepworth, 2016). As news managers become more sophisticated about social media, they want to be able to demonstrate ROI of time and resources. Some news organizations have used Facebook groups to reach out to Asian-Americans, Latinx, African-Americans, Muslims, LGBTQ+, and others with interest in specialized news content (Clark, 2016). Of course, this also can lead to fragmentation and polarization of audiences. What began as a digital media revolution two decades ago has morphed into a social media landscape in which journalists have been required to adopt new tools in order to participate in a developing form that places value on interactivity and is transparent and "collaborative" (Briggs, 2020, p. 120).

Although social media are seen as a path to news content once dominated by Google searches, SEO remains an important concern. CMS tools now prompt the user to use SEO-friendly **keywords** for headlines and tags. Google Analytics allows news organizations to track site visitors coming from social media platforms. In a highly competitive news environment, any advantage to attract potential audience members is seen as important. The issue for many newsrooms is how to identify important local social media conversation. By practicing effective conversation monitoring, it is possible for newsrooms to attempt to "capture" engagement topics and participate as opinion leaders. Every local community has influencers, and newsrooms must engage them and offer valuable content within their social networks.

At newspapers, one important tactic has been to add videos to their websites. Unlike local TV news, most newspapers now have a **paywall** that limits reader access to subscriber use. As video compression and Internet speeds have made it easier to view and share videos, it has become a way to increase the amount of time users spend on specific news pages. So-called "content verticals" in key topic areas – sports, arts and entertainment, men, women, lifestyles, home décor, business and technology, and news and politics – can be sold to advertisers and generate needed revenue. The struggling newspaper industry remains desperate to slow newsroom layoffs, as offline subscription revenues dwindle. Social media content sharing is one way to expand reach and leverage pre-roll video advertising. Traditional media **cost per thousand (CPM)** pricing has been used.

Nevertheless, between 2009 and 2019, US newspapers cut about 52% of staff, or 144,000 jobs (Johnson, 2020, para. 7). During the same period, the number of Internet jobs tripled to 277,000 (para. 4). The newspaper industry could not change quickly enough to respond to digital disruption. During the same decade the number of broadcast television, cable, and radio jobs declined by about 1%. It is fair to conclude that Internet media, including social media communication, effectively won a head-to-head battle with print newspapers. They continue to pivot to become online media companies.

As such, media companies seek to measure all activity on their sites. They have attempted to move beyond page views and unique viewers to use advanced Google Analytics that track the traffic coming from social media sites, as well as engagement reflected by the amount of time on sites. Social media influencers are increasingly seen as important because their sharing and discussion of news media content may trigger additional interest. In this sense, news media are now interested more than ever in what audience members and their friends are talking about.

The steady decline of most US newspapers can be attributed to the digital shift. Pew (2019) documented key data: Print and digital circulation declined about 9% to 28.6 million during the week and 30.8 million on Sunday (para. 2). The peak was 63 million in 1973 (para. 5). At the current rate of decline, many newspapers will disappear during the decade ahead.

JOURNALISM THEORIES

The introduction of social networking sites and social media continued to fundamentally change journalism. Tewksbury and Rittenberg (2012) concluded: "The shift from a top-down media system to one that features more horizontal interaction of people and news represents a change in the relationship that citizens and others in a nation have with information" (p. 5), and:

> Private citizens creating content online ... are redefining the nature of news. They are adding to the flow of information online – be it opinion, links to related concepts, images, or other content – and they are contributing to the social and political lives of nations ... The trend of information control shifting away from a few powerful entities toward smaller outlets and even citizens is a type of information democratization.
>
> (p. 11)

The historical paradigm that news agenda-setting influences what people think about (McCombs & Shaw, 1972) may be weakened by the increasing importance of social media effects on media and public discussion (Jacobson, 2013). A Pew Research Center and Knight Foundation study in 2012 found that nearly half of Facebook users, or about one-third of the population, consume news on the largest social media platform (Mitchell et al., 2013). The major conclusion was that "news is a common but incidental experience" (para. 1). While users went on the social network for other purposes, they often found news (Pew, 2012).

Pew reported that by 2016, 86% of Americans were Internet users, and half of the public turned to social media sites (Facebook, Instagram, Pinterest, LinkedIn, and Twitter) for election news. Facebook was the clear leader of older and female users, while younger audiences preferred messaging apps (Greenwood, Perrin, & Duggan, 2016).

Social media reflect the convergence of media content, as social networking sites attract professional journalists from around the globe. The growing appetite for mobile news content also may encourage engagement between journalists and their international readers (Westlund, 2008): "These people are always connected and appreciate access to news independent of time and space" (p. 460). Journalists may be pressured to post rapid news updates, and this could damage long-term credibility with audience members (Johnson & Kaye, 2010). However, the perceived credibility of information increases when writer information and a hyperlink are part of the post (Johnson & Wiedenbeck, 2009).

News organizations see social media, in part, as new tools for promotion and even profit. Kerrigan and Graham (2010) treat social media spaces as settings for buyer and seller interaction. If news people are selling their stories, then social marketing comes into play. The relationships also may foster the selling of story ideas to journalists participating in social media interaction.

CITIZEN JOURNALISM

Journalism shifted from being largely one-way mass communication to participatory work that includes some **user-generated content (UGC)**. Paulussen and Ugille (2008) examined UGC influence on mainstream media and identified a shift in interest toward professional collaboration with audience members. (Domingo, 2008; Wardle & Williams, 2010.) The organizational context, including editorial staff and information technology (IT) staff cultures, may reflect either tension or conditions more favorable to IT collaboration. In the end, deadline pressures and the need for reliable and trusted sources may limit use of UGC: "Therefore, it can be expected that professional journalists will make rather limited use of user generated content, because they somewhat routinely and passively rely on a number of official suppliers of information" (Paulussen & Ugille, 2008, p. 34). When their content is ignored, as might be expected, citizen journalists express frustration about editorial content decisions that favor traditional routines: "Their gate-keeping skills are among the major traits through which professionals distinguish themselves from amateur journalists" (p. 38). The assessment, based upon observations in Europe, reflected a degree of realism about the historic sociology within newsrooms. There has been interest in and enthusiasm for the idea of citizen journalism with stronger social ties to communities and access to publishing via blogs and other online methods (Matheson, 2004). News can be seen as a product that is in need of re-articulation based upon the creation of online blogs and other points of digital destination.

CROWDSOURCING

During a breaking news event, users may provide information not yet available to professional journalists. In an era in which most people carry smartphones with high-quality cameras with them almost everywhere, photographs appear almost instantaneously on Twitter from the sites of most breaking news events.

☐ BOX 3.2

The Andy Carvin Method

Andy Carvin was a journalism innovator at National Public Radio (NPR) during the Arab Spring uprisings in the Middle East beginning in 2009 until he was offered a contract buy-out at the end of 2013. He participated in newsroom startups and blogging.

At NPR, Carvin used the live tweet method during several Middle East political revolutions, including Libya, Egypt and Syria. Carvin told *The Guardian* in 2011 that his work is "a form of situational awareness." During the Libyan uprising, Carvin tweeted 1,200 times over a two-day period. He told *The Guardian* that by using known sources or observing online behavior, he filtered those messages that may be credible. His followers helped verify information. Carvin called this "open source journalism," even though his "Real-time Informational DJ & occasional journalist" approach included private communication. His work was grounded in activism and technology, rather than extensive, formal journalism training.

In Carvin's book *Distant Witness*, he described how social media helped loosen control over news. Carvin told NPR's program *On the Media* that he differentiated what was happening on Twitter from traditional news practices.

"Instead, if I just share more openly what I know and what I don't know, someone out there will probably come out and have an answer," Carvin said. "I made a decision early on that I wasn't going to censor myself simply because it was graphic, and I had a lot of people complain about that," Carvin said. "My Twitter followers and I, just by talking to each other," figure things out.

"I'm trying to capture their stories," he said. The live-tweeting method is to ask sources for assertions and confirmation. Media critic Michael Wolff challenged Carvin's "overreach" during live-tweeting of the Newtown shootings. The crowdsourcing on Twitter generated false reports about a purple van, a second shooter, and a fake letter. "While the guise is to re-tweet in order to verify," Wolff wrote, "the effect is to propagate."

Carvin's methods were particularly shaky when applied to reporting within other cultural contexts. Sarar Mohamed Khamis, University of

FIGURE 3.2 *National Public Radio (NPR) headquarters in Washington, DC, as seen in this 2013.*

Photograph by Jeremy Harris Lipschultz

Maryland professor and Arab media expert, explained that a YouTube video may be viewed as blasphemy in the Middle East, which produces violent reactions in the Muslim world. "There is a very, very high level of respect to all religious symbols and all the messages of God," she said. "This is a very, very sensitive topic for any Muslim."

"Freedom of expression is a fundamental human right," University of Minnesota Professor Jane Kirtley said. "It's not uniquely American – we like to think that we've been moving toward perfecting it, but this is not an example of America trying to impose its values."

The "borderless Internet" across languages, cultures and religions is seen as a problem because of anonymity, hate speech, attacks, and lack of representation of religious leaders. "If it is not really somehow 'regulated' … somehow put in the right perspective, it can go out of hand," Khamis said.

Carvin, however, echoed the decidedly Western view on free speech.

> Social media has the word "social" in front of it for a reason because you have human beings interacting with each other … everything from talking about the news to sharing their latest cat videos, and I think all of it is valid and all of it is important.

In 2019, Carvin became a Senior Fellow at the Atlantic Council in Washington, DC.

Sources: Lipschultz, J. H. (August 20, 2013). Live Tweets, Journalism, Middle East Culture and NPR Branding. Media. *The Huffington Post.* www.huffingtonpost.com/jeremy-harris-lipschultz/live-tweets-journalism-mi_b_3779940.html

Ingram, M. (February 4, 2014). Andy Carvin, A Pioneer in Using Twitter for Real-Time Journalism, Joins Omidyar's First Look Media. *Gigaom.* http://gigaom.com/2014/02/04/andy-carvin-a-pioneer-in-using-twitter-for-real-time-journalism-joins-omidyars-first-look-media/

MICRO-BLOGGING AND CURATION

Most newsrooms are happy to have journalists using micro-blog sites, such as Twitter, to push out links to stories and engage with audience members. Some sensational stories, however, may be seen as "click-bait" (designed to simply drive user traffic to a site), as was the case when publicity for a book featured a claim that President Obama once told staff that he was "really good at killing people" (Cantor, 2013, para. 1).

The micro-blogging influence of Twitter goes beyond early adopters to news media that use it for content sharing (Schmierbach & Oeldorf-Hirsch, 2012). The research suggested that journalists used Twitter more for sharing than engagement and interaction with followers. An ongoing issue is that information on Twitter is generally viewed as less credible and trustworthy than the mainstream sites. This may help explain why journalists remain cautious in using social media for engagement:

> In contrast to many studies of online credibility, this study shows that even somewhat regular users of Twitter do not see it as providing more credible information, and the population as a whole is unusually skeptical of Twitter relative to other means of distribution. ... The exact mechanisms are unclear. ... On the surface, however, it is noteworthy simply because unlike traditional blogs, Twitter here is not serving as a selective source. ... Yet participants still viewed the content on Twitter differently ... Perhaps the positive responses to other selecting sources are also due to cues, and not to reasoned evaluations about the benefits of custom-selected material. At an applied level, this study suggests the need for caution in the use of Twitter as a way to distribute news.
>
> (Schmierbach & Oeldorf-Hirsch, 2012, p. 333)

Even when the news distributor was a large organization, such as *The New York Times*, the research found less trust attached to tweets. The "trust of news information" is theoretically distinct from "trust of those who deliver the news" and "trust of media corporations" (Williams, 2012, p. 117). These can be seen as "informational," "interpersonal," and "institutional" trust (p. 119). News is "increasingly produced and disseminated by individuals and agencies that act outside of traditional media establishments," and "it is particularly important for media practitioners to remain attentive to changes in news audiences' attention patterns and assessments of media trustworthiness" (p. 127). However, it is not clear what happens to trust when journalists release editorial control through social media.

Park and Kaye (2018) found that, among South Korean adults, the news may be reconstructed. "Curatorial news" involves evaluation prior to reconstructing and sharing on social media sites: "News curation via social media is a strong predictor of three key dimensions of democratic engagement – political knowledge, political efficacy, and political participation" (p. 1119).

User-generated content, also called participatory journalism, is one way to reflect "the idea of collaborative and collective – not simply parallel – action" (Singer et al., 2011, p. 2). In this view, social networking sites are seen as one of many online forms (including blogs, comments, and polls) that allow for great participation (p. 17). The active audience selects, filters, and even creates content through what has been called citizen journalism. To the extent that audience members take on this quasi-journalist role, they challenge the traditional professional journalism news gatekeepers who sifted and edited for them. The public may serve as "eyewitnesses," "experts" through their comments, "commentators," "pulse-takers," "guardians of quality," "ancillary reporters," or independent journalists (pp. 38–44). The level of audience activity varies widely, and it is most often the case that audience members remain passive consumers. CMC theorizes a desire to create and participate in online communities, though these tend to exist within specialized interest areas.

JOURNALISM CASE STUDIES

The WikiLeaks site represented the most dramatic example of participatory journalism, by becoming "networked into mainstream media across the globe as it shifted from isolated whistle-blower to collaborative investigator and publisher" (Beckett, with Ball, 2012, p. 9). By publishing raw material that publicly accuses wrongdoing, the site has worked both with news organizations and independently. Here, too, we see signs of a fundamental redefinition of journalism and political power: "WikiLeaks is a network exploit that uses the Internet in a radical way to gather material, protect itself and to tap into other networks, including mainstream media" (p. 13). That said, WikiLeaks has not been entirely protected in recent years from responses by formal governmental powers. Australian Julian Assange, founder and editor-in-chief of WikiLeaks, was facing extradition to the United States on charges that "he conspired to break into a classified Pentagon computer and could receive a 175-year jail sentence if convicted" (Busby, 2019, para. 10). Chelsea (previously Bradley) Manning, a US Army private who provided information to WikiLeaks, was convicted of violating the Espionage Act and faces up to 35 years in prison at the maximum-security Fort Leavenworth, Kansas. Wikileaks, meanwhile, faced a political backlash in the wake of its role in sharing Hillary Clinton campaign emails just before the 2016 US presidential election. Social media "democracy of distribution" has changed the news-making process (Ingram, 2011, para. 1). During the 2011 Tunisian and Egyptian revolutions, for example, groups included a number of key actors, including activists, mainstream newsrooms and journalists.

ᵗ⚡ BOX 3.3

Case Study: Young Journalist Loses Job Over Old Posts

Des Moines Register trending news reporter Aaron Calvin lost the job he had for seven months because of social media. Calvin was covering Carson King – a University of Iowa alum who held up a sign shown on ESPN's College GameDay show. The sign asking for beer money raised more than $1 million through TV and social media, and he pledged to donate it all to a local children's hospital.

Calvin conducted a pre-publication background check that revealed King had posted offensive tweets years before when he was in high school. After the news story ran, Calvin was the target of verbal attacks on Twitter. During the social media storm, Calvin says he also was targeted:

> In the hours after [Carson] King's [apology] statement, people on Twitter found material that they used to discredit me, instead. They shared offensive tweets that I'd posted when I was younger, including statements that were meant sarcastically but that employed homophobic and misogynistic language and could be read as such if taken at face value. I also tweeted, verbatim, a Kanye West lyric that used the N-word.
>
> Tweeting these things was a mistake, and I apologize for them. I would not tweet the same things now. Like many people as they mature, I've come to understand that such language can cause real harm, and I've learned to better represent my values
>
> (Calvin, 2019, paras. 13–14)

Calvin received death threats, even though his story had downplayed the social media aspect. Publisher Gannett decided to fire Calvin because his "tweets had compromised ... credibility as a reporter" (para. 20). For his part, Calvin was disappointed: "I wish Gannett would have taken into further consideration how I'd represented myself as an employee ... they vindicated bad-faith attacks and allowed disingenuous arguments to influence their decisions" (para. 30). The case is a warning to journalists that they cannot hold news sources to a higher standard than their own social media behavior.

Source: Calvin, A. (November 4, 2019). Twitter Hates Me. The *Des Moines Register* Fired Me. Here's What Really Happened. *CJR*. www.cjr.org/first_person/aaron-calvin-viral-story-tweets.php

BLOGGERS

Blogging became popular online early in the new century. Independent bloggers were able to use new tools to reach large audiences. Commercial sites, such as *The Huffington Post*, were launched and became successful challengers to traditional media. Most local and national media now have active bloggers offering opinions and interpretations.

> ## □ BOX 3.4
> ### *Huffpost* Blogger Terms and Guidelines
>
> There was an early example of a contractual agreement that *The Huffington Post* used with its now-defunct Contributor program. In 2018, the site ended its unpaid blogger participation that had grown readership. Editor Lydia Polgreen told *TechCrunch* that there were many other open blogging sites, from WordPress to LinkedIn:
>
> > One of the biggest challenges we all face, in an era where everyone has a platform, is figuring out whom to listen to. Open platforms that once seemed radically democratizing now threaten, with the tsunami of false information we all face daily, to undermine democracy. When everyone has a megaphone, no one can be heard. Our hope is that by listening carefully through all the noise, we can find the voices that need to be heard and elevate them for all of you.
> >
> > (Lunden, 2018, paras. 3–4)
>
> In its day, though, *The Huffington Post* walked a tightrope between being an edited publication and a space for free speech:
>
> "By submitting blog posts for publication on the HuffingtonPost.com website or on any other site owned or operated by The Huffington Post .com," bloggers were told not to submit posts if they did not agree.
>
> *The Huffington Post* specified that bloggers did not receive any pay or benefits, and each was treated as "an independent contractor." Bloggers instead were offered "a large, diverse audience." The author of *Social Media Communication* was a contributor for six years.
>
> As an independent contractor, a blogger was not "under the direction or control" of the site. *The Huffington Post* could remove content that violates rules. An important aspect that will be discussed later in the book is disclosure, and *HuffPost* urged bloggers to be transparent: "*HuffPost* bloggers should disclose any financial conflicts of interest." Where there may be an issue, "that information should be disclosed at the bottom of the applicable blog post."
>
> While bloggers retained content copyright, *The Huffington Post* retained "a non-exclusive, worldwide, royalty-free, irrevocable, perpetual license to exercise all rights under copyright law."
>
> The 2016 contributor terms told writers "don't submit," if they did not agree to the terms. "You cannot hold yourself out as our agent or representative or attempt to bind us to any obligations."
>
> Importantly, *Huffington Post* may sell the content to "business partners, as well as for marketing and promotional purposes, online or offline, in any

medium and mode of delivery." As the site focuses now on paid blogger content, writers were governed under "work for hire" contracts.

Sources: *HuffPost* Contributor Platform (2016), *The Huffington Post.* Contributor.huffingtonpost.com/cms/blog-docs/terms; Terms and Conditions (2014). *The Huffington Post.* www.huffingtonpost.com/terms.html; and Blogger Guidelines. (2010). *The Huffington Post.*

Lunden, I. (January 18, 2018). Farewell Unpaid Blogger. *HuffPost* Drops Free Contributor Platform That Drove Its Growth. *TechCrunch.* https://techcrunch.com/2018/01/18/farewell-unpaid-blogger-huffpost-drops-free-contributor-platform-that-drove-its-growth/

Most blog posts tend to be 500 to 1,500 words, as online readers are more likely to consume short rather than long reads. At the same time, online sites tend to have fewer editors than traditional publications. Longer posts may not be edited as quickly. Sites vary in terms of style rules, such as capitalization, use of SEO keywords and phrases, and quotation style. Blogging sites tend to encourage the use of **hyperlinks** as references to content that is discussed, as shorthand for those interested in reading more about the topic.

Use of images and video links varies across blog sites. Most editors want stories that are visually appealing and keep readers at the site for as long as possible. Some CMS systems, though, are easier to use than others for sizing images and embedding video links. From an SEO standpoint, the Google algorithm rules keep changing, but bloggers use tags and keywords entered on the CMS system to make it easier to find the post through an online search. Social media communication has impacted this, as authors are encouraged to push their content out on the social Web. This is encouraged through email lists, Facebook and Twitter posts, contacting other bloggers, responding to all comments at the blog and social sites, leveraging friends and online fans, and generally engaging within social networks.

Copyright issues abound for those interested in re-publishing work. For example, a University of Toronto psychology professor maintained a website featuring his academic work published by the American Psychological Association (APA). However, he (and many colleagues) were hit with a copyright take-down notice and WordPress warning. Professors responded with a petition that APA should pay $300 per article:

> We engage in practices like voluntary reviewing for APA because we feel a commitment to producing a public good that others can use to promote scientific progress … By using these profits to restrict us from sharing our own work, you have privatized a public good and made our relationship transactional.
>
> (Flaherty, 2019, paras. 3–5)

In a sense, public intellectuals were becoming micro-celebrities facing the problems and concerns of life in the public eye.

SOCIAL MEDIA CELEBRITY

There has been a blurring of the lines, as some of those active on Twitter cut across these traditional categories. For example, Jillian York (@jilliancyork), director for International Freedom of Expression at the Electronic Frontier Foundation, is also a blogger who was active during the Arab Spring. Visualization of social networking revealed that she was an important hub for information. She now has more than 146,000 tweets and nearly 53,500 Twitter followers.

Social media also were an influential place for conversation about gun laws following the 2012 school shooting in Newtown. Pew (2012) found that 64% of Twitter assertions were calls for stricter gun control (p. 1):

> From the news of the shooting on Friday afternoon through noon on Monday, the discussion on blogs and Twitter paralleled each other closely. The discussion about our country's gun laws ranked first on each platform, accounting for 28% of the overall conversation about the tragedy. And, the focus remained remarkably steady over the course of the three days, already registering at a quarter of the conversation on each platform by midnight on Friday.
>
> (p. 2)

The gun reform discussion was slightly higher than the expression of sympathy and prayers (25%) on Twitter. So-called "straight news" represented only 13% of the Twitter talk during the period.

The "Kony 2012" viral video (www.youtube.com/watch?v=Y4MnpzG5Sqc) is an example of media content becoming its own media event: "The next 27 minutes are an experiment, but in order for it to work you *have* to pay attention." The YouTube video about Ugandan warlord Joseph Kony rapidly attracted the attention of young adults, which is a group that does not tend to pay as much attention to traditional news as older groups. The 30-minute video, though, had nearly 80 million views in just 10 days (Choney, 2012). A year later, it had more than 98 million views worldwide. Unlike a typical entertainment video that goes viral, such as the "Gangnam Style" music video (with more than 2 billion views), Kony 2012 was a **Non-Governmental Organization (NGO)** Invisible Children advocacy video (Harsin, 2013). To begin with, no theory has so far convincingly explained the video's virality yet failure to mobilize people to "cover the night." Roughly, theories emphasize production quality and narrative to explain its popularity; then, credibility problems, filmmaker (Jason) Russell's breakdown, and lazy "clicktivism" (p. 265) to explain its failure to prompt action. So-called clicktivism is a way to explain how simple it is to click in support of an online cause without doing anything else. One explanation for the video's simultaneous success and failure is the role celebrities played in using social media to spread the video. "Oprah's tweet alone spiked its visibility by 15 percent" (p. 266).

It would seem that opinion leadership and interest in entertainment came together to help push the media content. Oprah is trustworthy, and the promotion of a video essentially manufactures a news event. From celebrities to micro-influencer "YouTubers," who may command monetized audiences in the hundreds of thousands; journalism continues to be an increasingly fragmented set of voices, issues and politics.

In an international context, breaking news events present both mainstream journalism and social media challenges. Trust in content often comes down to judging media source credibility, which can be a product of media bias, gatekeeping bias, coverage bias, and statement bias (Tian & Chao, 2012). Social media content may have a life of its own online, but there is no guarantee that engagement and conversation translate to offline action. The Kony 2012 project raised awareness, but the warlord remained on the run from an international criminal indictment, as interest faded.

The most significant challenge facing journalism in the social media age is paying for the enterprise. Major newspapers responded to declining subscriptions, revenue loss due to online competition, and new technologies with waves of layoffs. Traditional journalists have been replaced with younger, online-experienced employees. Some are journalists, but others are computer programmers and social media specialists. The timing of the 2008–2009 global economic recession further impacted the direction of all mainstream media toward a "leaner" business model. College media also faced financial difficulties with the decline in advertising revenue. As those in government and business use the Internet to directly communicate with the public, there is "a continued erosion of news reporting resources" for quality journalism: "This adds up to a news industry that is more undermanned and unprepared to uncover stories, dig deep into emerging ones or to question information put in its hands" (Pew, 2013, p. 3). Advertorials and native content were among newsroom issues, as downsizing and use of social media sources further eroded credibility (pp. 5–6). Most adults talk with friends and family as a common way to receive news through word-of-mouth (WOM), and there are growing numbers using social networking sites to get news from friends and family (Greenwood, Perrin, & Duggan, 2016). All of this adds up to both a challenge to and opportunity for professional journalists and news organizations.

Once the dream of every journalism student was to someday write for *The New York Times*, but social media have helped change the landscape. Former *Times* technology columnist David Pogue (2013), who wrote a book full of Twitter tweets, left the newspaper after 13 years to join Yahoo, became self-employed, and then rejoined *The New York Times* in 2018 as a "Crowdwise" columnist. While technological innovation drives change, social uses of new technology products surprised even the inventors and innovators.

US journalists trained in the last century were infused with the ideal of objectivity. It was sometimes suggested that journalism should strive for balance and fairness by telling two or more sides to a story and letting audience members be the judge. The norm of objectivity, which has spread globally to many cultural contexts, remains a topic of contentious debate (Maras, 2013). The search for truth or reality, at least one devoid of personal opinion, is nearly impossible within a social media world that is flooded with bloggers and tweets. Maras (2013) observed that a group of gate-watching bloggers monitors mainstream media: "The concept serves as a 'pretence' for quality journalism at a time when social media is opening up new possibilities for collaborative news creation" (p. 190, citing Rettberg, 2008, p. 310). In fact, as mentioned early in this chapter, social media have challenged the very definition of journalism:

> This is not to suggest this is a zone without issues, and media organizations are faced with new decisions around working with citizen journalists and online communities … a different but no less serious set of reputational issues arise from staff reporters using social media such as Twitter, which demands a style of writing and opinion very different from that encountered in most news articles.
>
> (Maras, 2013, pp. 191–192)

This suggests that by engaging in collaborative communities, journalists must release some editorial control and enter into a state of negotiation with the public over facts and opinions. In this sense, news organizations that "face their critics" through social media engagement may encourage fairness through an ongoing listening process (Nunnelley, 2006, p. 53). This transformation of journalism is a work in process.

The art of storytelling, across a variety of media platforms, is transforming journalism and media education. Hart (2011) has focused upon "**narrative** possibilities" within passionate storytelling:

> Story makes sense out of a confusing universe by showing us how one action leads to another. It teaches us how to live by discovering how our fellow human beings overcome the challenges in their lives. And it helps us discover the universals that bind us to everything around us.
>
> (p. 5)

Story, to Hart, is universal because a good story has no print and broadcast division. In this sense, there are essential principles – a sequence of actions, a sympathetic character, a complication, and a resolution. Hart (2011) challenges the reader to consider decisions about stance, distance, and the ladder of abstraction, which he sees as "one of the most useful concepts for any writer" (p. 55). Thornburg (2011) views online news as working through traditional news values, but "you'll also take advantage of the three attributes of online communication that make reporting, producing and distributing your stories via the Internet fundamentally different from working in any other medium" (p. 8). Thornburg (2011) divides the terrain into multimedia ("a variety of choices about how to combine storytelling techniques"), interactive and on-demand. Journalists within a social media environment are audience-centered, conscious of keywords and SEO, unafraid of marketing and ready for continuous engagement:

> Politicians, businesspeople and celebrities are now speaking directly to the audience, without a reporter as an intermediary. And the audience is now demanding explanations, both from reporters and directly from sources. It is getting harder to tell who is the reporter, who is the source and who is the audience.
>
> (pp. 306–307)

The *conversation* of journalism today leads Thornburg (2011) to argue for "Remixing the News" (p. 333). He describes a type of journalism filled with data distribution, nonlinear narratives, chunks, links and filters.

Batsell's (2015) *Engaged Journalism* textbook explores industry case studies through face-to-face communication, social media, hyper-localism, interactivity and measurement. For example, KTVK, Phoenix "calculates an engagement rate for each of the station's more than forty Twitter accounts and twenty Facebook pages" and produces a "Social Media Score-

FIGURE 3.3 *@DaVonteMcKenith*.
Photograph courtesy DaVonte McKenith

card" (p. xix). DeJarnette (2017) found engaged journalism progress through social listening, hosting events, trustworthy source identification, new conferences, and communities of practice. In 2016, and Engagement Manifesto argued for newsrooms to care about their audiences, management to embrace engaged audiences, and to use improved metrics that value quality engaged journalism (Haeg, 2016).

Broadcast journalists, such as Winston-Salem, North Carolina TV news anchor DaVonté McKenith, used Twitter as "more in the minute and up-to-the-minute."

McKenith says trained journalists provide the valuable role of verifying information, as they engaged with audience members:

> I think Facebook allows you to be more of a person as well because that opportunity for engagement is there … you're able to keep a thread with your viewers able to let that thread be shared with the other viewers on your page … I think you're able to show more personality… Facebook Live is using that as a conversation driver … and allows for more engagement down the road.
>
> (3:14–4:39)

McKenith uses Facebook, Twitter, Instagram, and Snapchat as top social media platforms for different types of viewer engagement. Going forward, he predicts that mobile media channels will ultimately be more important than traditionally licensed broadcast station channels.

Some journalists remain skeptical of the long-term value of social media. They point, for example, to a study showing that the average Twitter account has only one follower (Reuters, 2013). On the other side of the argument, however, *The New York Times* continues to build the size of its social media team to cater to millions of followers

(Roston, 2014). Twitter followers who track breaking news in the moment expect speed, but newspapers' social media desks have also learned that some enterprise stories are worthy of repeating multiple times during the week. As experience grows, a set of journalism best practices is emerging.

The Wall Street Journal has been among the leaders in the introduction of machine learning and artificial intelligence into the media storytelling process. *WSJ* used **natural language generation (NLG)** to create 968 college rankings stories, or about 250,000 words of copy, "a volume that would've been untenable within the timeframe had the stories been compiled by humans alone" (McAllister, 2019, para. 12):

> Looking at the reach, engagement, and ability to drive habit we saw audience engagement that beat our expectations. We found that more than 60% of the visits were from new users. These visitors also over-indexed in *WSJ*'s internally-calculated engagement metrics and generated subscriptions that outpaced similar projects. Of those who interacted with the automated stories, the average tool user expanded nearly 5 college descriptions.
>
> (para. 13)

These positive results may lead to new pressures within journalism organizations to emphasize data science methods. Journalists must continue to respond to younger users growing up "in the age of likes, lols and longing" (Contrera, 2016, para. 1). At a deeper level, "experiential news" is an evolutionary shift away from linear and toward interaction:

> Across a variety of media environments, news content places an increasing emphasis on engaging users in an experiential environment where they are interactive participants in a narrative that is navigated through an increasingly natural user interface such as voice command, gesture, or touch.
>
> (Pavlik, 2019, p. 22)

Against a virtual reality context, words sometimes appear out of context from immersive experiences.

The constant tweeting claims of "fake news" by President Donald Trump (@realDonaldTrump) appeared to validate censorship by governments around the globe. In Singapore, for example, the government enacted a new law attacking "false statements of fact," and applied it to "an opposition politician that questioned the governance of the city-state's sovereign wealth funds" in a Facebook post (Griffiths, 2019, paras. 2–4). The law was also applied to a blog post from Australia. In both posts, the government ordered that their rebuttal of allegations be placed at the top of the content: "The government announcements were accompanied by screenshots of the original posts with the word 'FALSE' stamped in giant letters across them" (para. 4). Partisan social media posts are very important because research has found a link between exposure and voting behavior (Ksiazek, Kim, & Malthouse, 2019). News organizations, as well as Facebook and other social media site content distributors, face a need to take responsibility for the potential effects from polarized coverage. It remains to be seen how the journalism industry will evolve into sustainable business models that fully take advantage of social media without being swallowed by these popular sites.

DISCUSSION QUESTIONS: STRATEGIES AND TACTICS

1. How do you define journalism? How do you think traditional definitions of the work of journalists are being altered through participation in social media? What can working journalists do to respond to inaccurate "fake news" claims by politicians and governments?

2. What must journalists do to be relevant to young people? What role should entertaining videos play in attracting new audiences to journalism? Are there other tactics journalists can use to have a positive effect on business economics?

3. Does the norm of objectivity remain important within your definition of journalism? Are there other strategies journalists need to adopt to be considered as a trusted source for fair information within their communities?

REFERENCES

Batsell, J. (2015). *Engaged Journalism, Connecting with Digitally Empowered News Audiences.* New York, NY: Columbia University Press.

Beckett, C., with Ball, J. (2012). *WikiLeaks, News in the Networked Era.* Cambridge, UK: Polity Press.

Bogle, A. (2017, January 10). Ben Smith Reveals Why BuzzFeed Published the 'Explosive' Trump Reports. *Mashable.* http://mashable.com/2017/01/10/ben-smith-donald-trump-allegations/

Briggs, M. (2020). *Journalism Next, A Practical Guide to Digital Reporting and Publishing,* Fourth edition. Los Angeles: SAGE.

Bump, P. (2019). Millennials vs. Gen Z: Why Marketers Need to Know the Difference. *HubSpot.* https://blog.hubspot.com/marketing/millennials-vs-gen-z

Burneko, A. (2017, January 11). Craven Reporters Scold BuzzFeed for Reporting News. *Deadspin.* http://theconcourse.deadspin.com/craven-reporters-scold-buzzfeed-for-reporting-news-1791071084

Busby, M. (2019, October 21). Julian Assange Extradition Judge Refuses Request for Delay. *The Guardian.* www.theguardian.com/media/2019/oct/21/julian-assange-extradition-judge-refuses-request-for-delay-wikileaks

Cantor, M. (2013, November 3). Book: Obama Claimed to Be 'Really Good at Killing People.' *Newser.* www.newser.com/story/176961/book-obama-claimed-to-be-really-good-at-killing-people.html?utm_source=twitterfeed&utm_medium=twitter

Choi, J. (2016). News Internalizing and Externalizing: The Dimensions of News Sharing on Online Social Network Sites. *Journalism & Mass Communication Quarterly* 93(4), 816–835.

Choney, S. (2012, March 15). Kony Video Proves Social Media's Role as Youth News Source: Pew. *TECHNOLOGY. NBC News.* www.nbcnews.com/technology/kony-video-proves-social-medias-role-youth-news-source-pew-455365

CJR. (2013, September 3). Who, What, When, Where, Why, and How. CJR Asks the Question: What is Journalism For? *Columbia Journalism Review.* www.cjr.org/cover_story/who_whatwhen.php

Clark, M. D. (2016, June 27). It's Time for a New Set of News Values. Here's Where We Should Start. *Poynter*. www.poynter.org/2016/its-time-for-a-new-set-of-news-values-heres-where-we-should-start/418952/

Coddington, M. (2019). *Aggregating the News, Secondhand Knowledge and the Erosion of Journalistic Authority*. New York: Columbia University Press.

Contrera, J. (2016, May 25). 13, Right Now. This is What It's like to Grow up in the Age of Likes, LOLs and Longing. *Washington Post*. www.washingtonpost.com/sf/style/2016/05/25/13-right-now-this-is-what-its-like-to-grow-up-in-the-age-of-likes-lols-and-longing/

Corn, D. (2016, October 31). A Veteran Spy Has Given the FBI Information Alleging a Russian Operation to Cultivate Donald Trump. *Mother Jones*. https://www.motherjones.com/politics/2016/10/veteran-spy-gave-fbi-info-alleging-russian-operation-cultivate-donald-trump/

Craft, S., & Davis, C. N. (2013). *Principles of American Journalism: An Introduction*. New York, NY: Routledge.

DeJarnette, B. (2017, January 2). 5 Ways 'Engaged Journalism' Made Progress in 2016. *MediaShift*. http://mediashift.org/2016/12/5-ways-engaged-journalism-movement-made-progress-2016/

Diakopoulos, N. (2019). *Automating the News, How Algorithms are Rewriting the Media*. Cambridge, MA: Harvard University Press.

Doctor, K. (2016, March 7). Newsonomics: The New York Times Re-invents Page One – And It's Better than Print Ever Was. *Nieman Lab*. www.niemanlab.org/2016/03/newsonomics-the-new-york-times-re-invents-page-one-and-its-better-than-print-ever-was/

Doctor, K. (2020, January 15). Lookout: A New Newsroom Business Model. Ken Doctor Is 1-on-1 with Mike Blinder. *YouTube*. https://youtu.be/K73jc-UV6I0

Domingo, D. (2008). Interactivity in the Daily Routines of Online Newsrooms: Dealing with an Uncomfortable Myth. *Journal of Computer-Mediated Communication 13*, 680–704.

Ember, S., & Grynbaum, M. M. (2017, January 10). BuzzFeed Posts Unverified Claims on Trump, Stirring Debate. *The New York Times*. www.nytimes.com/2017/01/10/business/buzzfeed-donald-trump-russia.html

Facebook for Business. (2019, November 14). Building Better Brand Connections with Gen Zers and Millennials. www.facebook.com/business/news/insights/build-better-brand-connections-with-gen-zers-and-millennials

Fitts, A. S. (2015, March 28). What Happens When Platforms Turn Into Publishers? *Columbia Journalism Review*. www.cjr.org/analysis/platforms_as_publishers_facebook_snapchat.php

Flaherty, C. (2019, October 23). Where Research Meets Profits. *Inside Higher Ed*. www.insidehighered.com/news/2019/10/23/what-happened-when-professor-was-accused-sharing-his-own-work-his-website

Greenwood, S., Perrin, A., & Duggan, M. (2016, November 11). Social Media Update 2016. *Pew Internet*. www.pewinternet.org/2016/11/11/social-media-update-2016/

Griffiths, J. (2019, November 30). Singapore Just Used its Fake News Law. Critics Say It's Just What They Feared. *CNN*. www.cnn.com/2019/11/29/media/singapore-fake-news-facebook-intl-hnk/index.html

Haeg, A. (2016, February 25). The Engagement Manifesto: Part I. *Medium*. https://medium.com/groundsource-notes/the-engagement-manifesto-part-i-9c348b34200f#.b04y33s4v

Hare, K. (2016, August 8). John Oliver: 'The Media is a Food Chain Which Would Fall Apart without Local Newspapers.' www.poynter.org/2016/john-oliver-the-media-is-a-food-chain-which-would-fall-apart-without-local-newspapers/425319/

Harsin, J. (2013). WTF Was Kony 2012? Considerations for Communication and Critical/Cultural Studies (CCCS). *Communication and Critical/Cultural Studies 10*(2–3), 265–272.

Hart, J. (2011). *Story Craft: The Complete Guide to Writing Narrative Nonfiction*. Chicago, IL: University of Chicago Press.

Hepworth, S. (2016, September 14). Trollbusters Enlisting Frustrated Journalists Targeted by Online Harassment. *Columbia Journalism Review*. www.cjr.org/b-roll/trollbusters_women_journalist_online_harassment.php

Ingram, M. (2011, December 21). News as a Process: How Journalism Works in the Age of Twitter. *GIGAOM*. http://gigaom.com/2011/12/21/news-as-a-process-how-journalism-works-in-the-age-of-twitter/

Ingram, M. (2014, February 4). Andy Carvin, A Pioneer in Using Twitter for Real-Time Journalism, Joins Omidyar's First Look Media. *Gigaom*. http://gigaom.com/2014/02/04/andycarvin-a-pioneer-in-using-twitter-for-real-time-journalism-joins-omidyars-first-look-media

Isaac, M., & Tracy, M. (2019, October 25). Facebook Calls Truce with Publishers, as it Unveils Facebook News. www.nytimes.com/2019/10/25/technology/facebook-publishers-news.html

Jackson, D., & Marx, G. (2020, January 19). Opinion: Will the Chicago Tribune Be the Next Newspaper Picked to the Bone? *The New York Times*. www.nytimes.com/2020/01/19/opinion/chicago-tribune-alden-capital.html

Jacobson, S. (2013). Does Audience Participation on Facebook Influence the News Agenda? A Case Study of *The Rachel Maddow Show*. *Journal of Broadcasting & Electronic Media 57*(3), 338–355.

Johnson, B. (2020, January 3). Internet Media Employment Has Tripled over the past Decade. *Ad Age*. https://adage.com/article/year-end-lists-2019/internet-media-employment-has-tripled-over-past-decade/2221941

Johnson, K. A., & Wiedenbeck, S. (2009). Enhancing Perceived Credibility of Citizen Journalism Web Sites. *Journalism & Mass Communication Quarterly 86*(2), 332–348.

Johnson, T. J., & Kaye, B. K. (2010). Choosing is Believing? How Web Gratifications and Reliance Affect Internet Credibility among Politically Interested Users. *Atlantic Journal of Communication 18*(1), 1–21.

Kalaf, S. (2020, January 22). Dead and Spun: A Story in Three Meetings. *CJR*. www.cjr.org/special_report/deadspin-gawker-gomedia.php

Kerrigan, F., & Graham, G. (2010). Interaction of Regional News-media Production and Consumption through the Social Space. *Journal of Marketing Management 26*(3/4), 302–320.

Kothari, A., & Hickerson, A. (2016). Social Media Use in Journalism Education: Faculty and Student Expectations. *Journalism & Mass Communication Educator 71*(4), 413–424.

Ksiazek, T. B., Kim, S. J., & Malthouse, E. C. (2019, Winter). Television News Repertoires, Exposure Diversity, and Voting Behavior in the 2016 U.S. Election. *Journalism & Mass Communication Quarterly 96*(4), 1120–1144.

Lee, M. Y. H. (2017, January 13). What Trump Got Wrong on Twitter This Week (#2). *The Washington Post*. www.washingtonpost.com/news/fact-checker/wp/2017/01/13/what-trump-got-wrong-on-twitter-this-week-2/

Lichterman, J. (2015, March 16). Millennials Say Keeping up with the News is Important to Them – But Good Luck Getting Them to Pay for It. *Nieman Lab*. www.niemanlab.org/2015/03/millennials-say-keeping-up-with-the-news-is-important-to-them-but-good-luck-getting-them-to-pay-for-it/

Lipschultz, J. H. (2013, August 20). Live Tweets, Journalism, Middle East Culture and NPR Branding. Media. *The Huffington Post*. www.huffingtonpost.com/jeremy-harris-lipschultz/live-tweets-journalism-mi_b_3779940.html

Luckie, M. S. (2011). *The Digital Journalist's Handbook*. Lexington, KY: Mark S. Luckie.

Lunden, I. (2018, January 18). Farewell, Unpaid Blogger: HuffPost Drops Free Contributor Platform that Drove Its Growth. *TechCrunch*. https://techcrunch.com/2018/01/18/farewell-unpaid-blogger-huffpost-drops-free-contributor-platform-that-drove-its-growth/

Mahadevan, A. (2019, October 2). How The Washington Post's TikTok Guy Dave Jorgenson Gets Millions of Views by Being Uncool. *Poynter*. https://www.poynter.org/reporting-editing/2019/how-the-washington-posts-tiktok-guy-dave-jorgenson-gets-millions-of-views-by-being-uncool/

Maras, S. (2013). *Objectivity in Journalism*. Cambridge, UK: Polity Press.

Matheson, D. (2004). Weblogs and the Epistemology of the News: Some Trends in Online Journalism. *New Media & Society 6*(4), 443–468.

McAllister, K. (2019, October 11). How We Turned the WSJ/THE College Rankings into a Tool for Readers. *Medium: WSJ Momentum*. https://medium.com/the-wall-street-journal/turning-the-wsj-the-college-rankings-into-a-student-first-resource-1fbbc43f43ee

McCombs, M., Holbert, R. L., Kiousis, S., & Wanta, W. (2011). *The News and Public Opinion, Media Effects on Civic Life*. Cambridge, UK: Polity Press.

McCombs, M., & Shaw, D. (1972). The Agenda-Setting Function of Mass Media. *Public Opinion Quarterly 36*(2), 176–187.

McKenith, M. (2016, November 16). *YouTube JeremyHL58*. www.youtube.com/watch?v=e-McLNCXGWk

Mitchell, A., Kiley, J., Gottfried, J., & Guskin, E. (2013, October 24). The Role of News on Facebook, Common yet Incidental. *Pew Research Center*. www.journalism.org/2013/10/24/the-role-of-news-on-facebook/

Mullin, B. (2017, January 6). Facebook Names Campbell Brown Head of News Partnerships. *Poynter*. www.poynter.org/2017/facebook-names-campbell-brown-head-of-news-partnerships/444531/

Nunnelley, C. (2006). *Building Trust in the News, 101+ Good Ideas for Editors from Editors*. New York, NY: Associated Press Managing Editors.

Park, S. P., & Kaye, B. K. (2018, Winter). News Engagement on Social Media and Democratic Citizenship: Direct and Moderating Roles of Curatorial News Use in Political Involvement. *Journalism & Mass Communication Quarterly 95*(4), 1103–1127.

Paulussen, S., & Ugille, P. (2008). User Generated Content in the Newsroom: Professional and Organisational Constraints on Participatory Journalism. *Westminster Papers in Communication and Culture 5*(2), 24–41.

Pavlik, J. (2019). *Journalism and Virtual Reality, How Experiential Media are Transforming News*. New York: Columbia University Press.

Perelli, A. (2019, November 21). Introducing Influencer Dashboard, A Weekly Newsletter on the Business of YouTube, Instagram and Influencers. *Business Insider*. www.businessinsider.com/youtube-and-influencer-business-trends-newsletter-for-november-21-2019-11

Pew. (2012). *In Social Media and Opinion Pages, Newtown Sparks Calls for Gun Reform*. Washington, DC: Pew Research Center's Project for Journalism Excellence.

Pew. (2013). *The State of the News Media, an Annual Report on American Journalism*. Washington, DC: Pew Research Center's Project for Journalism Excellence. http://StateOfTheMedia.org

Pew. (2019). Newspapers Fact Sheet: State of the News Media. *Pew Research Center*. www.journalism.org/fact-sheet/newspapers/

Pogue, D. (2013, October 21). Goodbye – and Hello. *Tumblr*. http://pogueman.tumblr.com/post/64682813641/goodbye-and-hello

Qihao, J., Ramey, A. A., Janick-Bowles, S., Dale, K. R., Oliver, M. B., Reed, A., Seibert, J., & Raney, A. A., II. (2019, Autumn). Spreading the Good News: Analyzing Socially Shared Inspirational News Content. *Journalism & Mass Communication Quarterly 96*(3), 872–893.

Rettberg, J. W. (2008). *Blogging*. Cambridge, UK: Polity Press.

Reuters. (2013). Study Shows Average Twitter Account Has Only 1 Follower. *Circa*. http://cir.ca/news/average-followers-on-twitter

Rivas, R. (2016, July 28). Black Cops Call for Dismissal of Fox 2 Reporter Bobby Hughes after 'Lead Diet' Joke about Killing of Mike Brown. *The St. Louis American*. www.stlamerican.com/news/local_news/black-cops-call-for-dismissal-of-fox-reporter-bobby-hughes/article_18c73814-538e-11e6-80ab-23a8ebd2e6ec.html

Roston, M. (2014, January 6). If a Tweet Worked Once, Send It Again – and Other Lessons from *The New York Times*' Social Media Desk. *Nieman Journalism Lab*. www.niemanlab.org/2014/01/if-a-tweet-worked-once-send-it-again-and-other-lessons-from-the-new-yorktimes-social-media-desk/

Rutenberg, J. (2016, April 17). For News Outlets Squeezed from the Middle, It's Bend or Bust. *The New York Times*. www.stlamerican.com/news/local_news/black-cops-call-for-dismissal-of-fox-reporter-bobby-hughes/article_18c73814-538e-11e6-80ab-23a8ebd2e6ec.html

Schmierbach, M., & Oeldorf-Hirsch, A. (2012). A Little Bird Told Me, so I Didn't Believe It: Twitter, Credibility, and Issue Perceptions. *Communication Quarterly 60*(3), 317–337.

Singer, J. B., et al. (2011). *Participatory Journalism, Guarding Open Gates at Online Newspapers*. Malden, MA: Wiley-Blackwell.

Terms and Conditions. (2014). *The Huffington Post*. www.huffingtonpost.com/terms.html

Tewksbury, D., & Rittenberg, J. (2012). *News on the Internet: Information and Citizenship in the 21st Century*. New York, NY: Oxford University Press.

Thornburg, R. M. (2011). *Producing Online News: Digital Skills, Stronger Stories*. Washington, DC: CQ Press, p. 405.

Tian, D., & Chao, C. C. (2012). Testing News Trustworthiness in an Online Public Sphere: A Case Study of *the Economist*'s News Report Covering the Riots in Xinjiang, China. *Chinese Journal of Communication 5*(4), 455–474.

Tompkins, A. (2016, July 8). 10 Questions Journalists Should Ask Themselves before Going Live on Facebook. *Poynter*. www.poynter.org/2016/10-questions-journalists-should-ask-themselves-before-going-live-on-facebook/420594/

Tornoe, R. (2020, January 23). Digital Publishing: How ProPublica is Harnessing the Power of Collaboration. *Editor & Publisher*. www.editorandpublisher.com/columns/digital-publishing-how-propublica-is-harnessing-the-power-of-collaboration/

Wardle, C., & Williams, A. (2010). Beyond User-Generated Content: A Production Study Examining the Ways in Which UGC Is Used at the BBC. *Media, Culture & Society 32*(5), 781–799. http://mediaeducation.org.mt/wp-content/uploads/2013/05/User_gnerated_content_journalism_BBC1.pdf

Wemple, E. (2017, January 10). BuzzFeed's Ridiculous Rationale for Publishing the Trump-Russia Dossier. *The Washington Post*. www.washingtonpost.com/blogs/erik-wemple/wp/2017/01/10/buzzfeeds-ridiculous-rationale-for-publishing-the-trump-russia-dossier/

Westlund, O. (2008). From Mobile Phone to Mobile Device: News Consumption on the Go. *Canadian Journal of Communication 33*(3), 443–463.

Williams, A. E. (2012). Trust or Bust? Questioning the Relationship between Media Trust and News Attention. *Journal of Broadcasting & Electronic Media 56*(1), 116–131.

Social Media in Public Relations

Regardless of how you define it, good public relations require excellent manage-ment ... publics are ready to call you on it if you try to promote your organization in ways inconsistent with how your organization is managed.
— Tom Kelleher (@tkell, 2018, p. 6)

The desire of public relations practitioners to both better understand and measure engagement is not surprising, given the emphasis on the strategic use of social media technologies and other digital platforms.
— Toby Hopp & Tiffany Gallicano (@tm_hopp & @Gallicano, 2016)

We try to amass followers and likes as if it's a "thing." We try to get views because that's how we justify and substantiate our work. But why? What's it all for? What does it mean? What does it matter?
— Brian Solis (@briansolis, 2013)

When Brian Solis, former principal analyst at the Altimeter Group, took the stage at the PRSA (2013) International Conference in Philadelphia, he challenged public relations professionals to re-focus PR on relationships and influence:

> We go through this journey and that journey is a mess. Why? Because the people who own mobile don't talk to people who own the website. The people who own the website don't talk to the people who are running Facebook ... It's the same problem over and over again. So you see multiple brands, multiple voices instead of one company. That is PR's opportunity – redefine the whole journey, the entire experience
> (PRSA, 2013, para. 10)

Solis' social media PR formula centers on ART – actions, reactions and transactions – that can impact outcomes, behaviors and actions (paras. 11–12).

The Public Relations Society of America (PRSA) uses a four-step PR process in its APR accreditation: Research, Planning, Implementation, and Evaluation (RPIE). The path aligns with what the field has called the "management process," which is divided as: Step One: Defining Public Relations Problems; Step 2: Planning and Programming; Step 3: Taking Action and Communicating; and Step 4: Evaluating the Program (Broom & Sha, 2013, pp. 261–359). As we will see later in this book, social media marketers have focused a process on conducting rigorous social media audits, developing goals and objectives, and measuring outcomes.

The PRSA (2019) International Conference foci reflected a field that is blending with advertising and marketing: marketing communication; digital communication; leadership and management; data, analytics and measurement; reputation and crisis management; skills, tools, and techniques; and special interests. PR measurement systems that focus on leadership business strategy, measurable goals, and useful reporting of data (Volz, 2019). One survey found that executives favor spreadsheets over analytics (PRSA, 2019). Another approach is to connect PR to behavioral communication, such as social norms, salience and framing in client communication (Gils, 2019).

The flood of daily emails announcing public PR webinars, white papers, and other resources suggests that the field is experiencing a fundamental transformation. This book is about how social media are shifting the work in many fields, including PR. The emphasis is moving from press releases and traditional media relations to "shareable online content" (including online press releases, but also media storytelling) with a relatively new interest in the direct reach of a message.

Traditional print and broadcast media, from *The New York Times* and CBS News to your local radio stations and newspapers, once were *the* leaders of most public discussion. The media gatekeepers have been weakened, and PR people have an opportunity to offer digital content in traditional media relations, along with direct audience engagement. It is no secret that US newsroom staffing continues to decline, as digital revenue growth fails to replace traditional advertising dollars. The newspaper industry response is to harness online data and leverage remaining "assets." Enter the new offers from digital PR experts pitching client stories through packaged content.

By 2016, the landscape again was redefined by rapid technological and social change. Data, metrics, platform knowledge, and story flow all are important, Porter told educators. Porter said a driving factor is

> incredible de-population of certainly our U.S. media environment mirrored in most of the developed world ... the tremendous shrinkage of that world and what it means ... The idea of owned-to-earned is also something that we're seeing (that) is incredibly important and powerful in programming

Porter added. "What is that piece of content based around a great story that is the first domino to fall, and to set off a great groundswell of coverage?"

Data are used to convince media, such as *USA Today* and *CNN*, that publishing a story will "drive a tremendous amount of social sharing." Edelman's "collaborative journalism" was designed "to help journalists be successful" (Lipschultz, 2016) in this new environment. The question remains: Will journalists be able to maintain a degree of independence and objectivity at the hand of paid advocates? Aron Pilhofer, former executive editor for digital at *The Guardian*, told AEJMC professors that his internal digital teamwork included visuals (photo, interactive, graphics, multimedia, and design), data projects, and virtual reality (VR) studio. The journalistic goal is to "try to build a community" and reach a targeted interest group. "This is why marketing is so important to the future of journalism." Data analytics show that social media engagement does sometimes lead to subscribing to a site and paying for news stories and other digital content. The data analytics are not trade secrets: "That is work we could be doing as an industry or as a collaboration."

Pilhofer says engaged citizens are leading the field toward "participatory journalism that is interactive, collaborative and experiential." For example, The Guardian's "witness" page offered readers "current assignments" that encourage them to create and share on the site. The future of participatory journalism might include having readers vote on story assignments. Between 2014 and 2016 traditional print news advertising revenue declined faster than predicted. Pilhofer urged new business models that should include shared services and collaboration with universities. By producing "relevant, distinctive and timely" journalism, the goal is to cultivate site visitors that return, increase their levels of participation, and grow a sense of community. A "deeper relationship" opens the door to paying for news, which is one way to increase revenue and stay in business. PR, meanwhile, has been successfully pitching news stories for decades, but the rules seem to be changing when it comes to digital. Struggling newsrooms will be tempted to use and share expensive digital content in exchange for online clicks and engagement. It remains uncertain, however, whether US journalism has a sustainable business model.

Within PR, there has been a developing interest in influencing the **C-suite**, which refers to top senior-level executives at a corporation. The terminology is used to identify chief executive officers (CEO), chief operating officers (COO), chief information officers (CIO), and, most recently, chief digital officers (CDO). From a business perspective, PR seeks to influence the influencers who make key decisions and have the power to spend money hiring outside the company for social media services. Often, large corporations have a vice president of corporate communications with responsibilities to develop in-house PR offices, as well as outside services. Depending upon corporate structure, the C-suite may or may not be interested in social media decision-making. PR firms wanting to land new clients or grow existing businesses must keep an eye on the C-suite, which has the power to hire and fire agencies representing them as clients.

PR MANAGEMENT

PR stakeholders are no longer impressed with simply including social media within a campaign. Increasingly, clients want a return on investment (ROI) for dollars spent on advertising, public relations and marketing efforts. In the **eCommerce** environment, the use of Google Analytics and other social media data dashboards allow businesses to link social media efforts to results that go beyond Facebook likes and shares.

A company may be trying to increase website traffic, generate sales leads, increase conversions to online purchases, reduce company expenses, and improve customer awareness and relations.

So-called **key performance indicators** focus on continuous monitoring of social media and sales activity data. In other words, businesses want social media to be connected to their larger goals and strategies for maintaining and growing business. This is what some thought leaders have termed "social business." It places social media within the more traditional context of word-of-mouth (WOM) activity related to brands. Social media conversation can assist with ongoing branding activities, which are crucial to developing, maintaining, and generating customer brand loyalty.

In social media, influence is important. While data suggest that actual friends are most influential, PR seeks to tap into the influence of social networks. By creating content within social networks and mobile social platforms, such as Instagram, Snapchat, or TikTok, it may be possible to increase measured influence. Klout, which closed its business in 2018, used an algorithm to create a score between 1 and 100 based upon social media followers. By identifying influencers, even in a rough sense, a brand may seek to engage with people or brands that can move toward a larger set of strategic goals.

Whether or not you place much trust in influence scores, these offer data that enable a user to identify influencers connecting with previous social media content and perceived brand influence. However, an inability to defend the reliability and validity of influence measurement led academics to focus on social network analysis (SNA) because it demonstrated scientific, statistically reliable measures. At the same time, the media industry frequently equated subscriber numbers with influence levels, but this macro-level observation fails to recognize important granular data.

In contrast to unscientific measures, the NodeXL tool applies scientific measures to identify influence using social network analysis. Top influencers are found at the center

TABLE 4.1 *Top Influencers in the UK (2019)*

	Name	Site	Genre	Subscribers
1.	Felix Kjellberg (PewDiePie)	YouTube	Gaming	101 million
2.	Olajide William Olatunji (KSIOlajidebtHD)	YouTube	Gaming, Music	7.3 million
3.	Craig Thompson (MiniLadd)	YouTube	Gaming	5.7 million
4.	Billy Wingrove & Jeremy Lynch	YouTube	Football	10.6 million
5.	Saffron Barker	YouTube	Lifestyle	2.2 million

Source: Williams, Laura (September 9, 2019). These Are the Top 100 Influencers in the UK, According to *The Sunday Times*. https://thetab.com/uk/2019/09/09/these-are-the-top-100-influencers-in-the-uk-according-to-the-sunday-times-124476

of visualized social media conversation. By doing this, the strategy might be to reach out to specific influencers with targeted content that would drive an increase in future influence. Tracking data over time allows the user to observe whether the influence tactics have any measurable effect.

While mainstream or traditional media continue to be opinion leaders, they now share the spotlight with three other overlapping media environments, as depicted in the original Edelman PR cloverleaf. Richard Edelman spoke to media professors at a 2012 Academic Summit in Palo Alto, California, and urged that PR embrace the shift to integrating tradition and social media into campaigns. The development of the Internet and Web in the 1990s led companies, organizations, and individuals to create websites. These **owned media**, along with apps, turned all of those with online identities essentially into media companies. In this century, **hybrid media** (also called "new media" or "tra-digital"), emerged from blogging. Technology sites, such as Mashable, political sites like Politico, and other specialized niche markets flourished in this new space. Social media, through early popular sites, such as Facebook, Twitter, and YouTube, empowered individuals to interact as media producers. The rapidly growing mobile media market driven by smartphones and tablets created a need for newer apps and platforms, Instagram for photographs and video, and Yelp for geo-location services.

The evolving model identified three publishers: **Media** (traditional news), **Brands**, and **Influencers** (YouTube, Linkedin, etc.). These were surrounded by three platforms:

FIGURE 4.1 *Edelman CEO and President Richard Edelman frequently uses the Cloverleaf to place social media within the context of other media forms.*

Social (SNS), **Curators** (Medium, Flipboard, etc.), and **Search** (Google, Yahoo!, etc.). The model highlights the integrated nature of Internet searches and social media that may be measured and observed within Google Analytics and other social media measurement tools.

The blending of PR functions with "paid amplification" through social media led to a degree of chaos in the field. Edelman PR (@EdelmanPR) gathered top leaders in Hamburg, Germany, in 2013 to develop company strategy for responding to rapid industry change (Sudhaman, 2013). Edelman's share of $14 billion in global 2015 revenues were not enough to keep them from worrying about challenges from the world's top ten global leaders. Current data reflect how the top five firms closed in on digital PR leadership. Weber Shandwick, BCW, FleishmanHillard, and Ketchum all emphasized social media importance.

Edelman's "Hamburg Principles" urged a PR focus that utilizes digital media, research, and partners with advertising agencies when working for large clients. PR work may be considered as a "reference point for how smart marketers are playing the game" (Sudhaman, 2013, para. 46). The brand-building function of "PR is actually an attitude" – one that enters the business conversation amid dramatic social media shifts (para. 47). David Armano (2013, @armano) has classified five content archetypes that offer examples of how PR advice now flows to large clients. Armano describes curated,

TABLE 4.2 *PR Top Firm Growth 2015–2019.*

	Firm	2019 Income (millions), Growth	2015 Data
1.	Edelman (@EdelmanPR)	$888, −0.6%	$850, +5.2%
2.	Weber Shandwick (@WeberShandwick)	$840, +5.0%	$775, 7.2%
3.	BCW (Burson, Cohn & Wolfe, @BCWGlobal)	$723, +2.0%	$480, +0.6%
4.	FleishmanHillard (@FleishmanHilliard)	$605, +6.1%	$530, −1.7%
5.	Ketchum (@KetchumPR)	$545, −0.9%	$530, 2.9%
6.	MSL (@msl_group France)	$450, −2.2%	$480, −0.6%
7.	Hill+Knowlton Strategies (@HKStrategies)	$400, +0.0%	$385, +1.3%
8.	Ogilvy PR (@ogilvypr)	$388, +9.6%	$347, 8.1%
9.	BlueFocus (China)	$336, +10.8	$245, 36.7%
10.	Brunswick (UK)	$280, +7.7	N/A

Source: The Holmes Report (2016, 2019). www.holmesreport.com/ranking-and-data/global-pr-agency-rankings/2019-pr-agency-rankings/top-10. Note that Golin (@GOLINglobal) dropped out of the top ten list to eleventh since the last edition of this textbook in 2018.

co-created, original, consumer-generated, and sponsored content amid the new mobile publishing environment:

1. *Curated content* is managed by brands determining "highest value to consumers" (para. 1).

2. *Co-created content* "is co-produced either peer to peer or brand to participant" (para. 2).

3. *Original content* is exclusive brand messages (para. 3).

4. *Consumer-generated content* happens "without the brand's involvement" (para. 4).

5. *Sponsored content* is "paid" promotion (para. 5).

From Facebook's feed to other mobile platforms, such as Instagram, "dominated by content and sharing" that "is only a button tap or click away" (Armano, 2013, para. 7). Perhaps the most volatile area for PR is sponsored content. A brand may purchase **promoted posts** on Facebook, which function similar to **paid search** by appearing atop a feed. At the same time, though, sponsored content refers to paid content that mimics organic efforts or boosts them.

From small stores to global brands, social media triggered a shift in resources toward communicating directly with potential and existing customers through the use of online content. At the same time, valued content was created to raise awareness, inform consumers, strengthen brand loyalty, build trust, and manage reputation. This has resulted in a focus on branded content, content marketing, strategy, and planning. What started as text-based information quickly shifted to rich media campaigns complete with photographs, info-graphics, memes, viral videos, new media channels, and a push toward precise measurement of results through web analytics. The purpose of online content marketing is often to drive traffic to a commercial website, which may be a link for the rapid sharing of content. Platforms, such as Twitter, Facebook, or Pinterest, allow users to gain earned media without the high cost of national advertising. Branded storytelling through employee advocates, for example, may treat social crowds as targets for what Brito (2018) calls "participation marketing" (p. 14). Mobile app Dynamic Signal developed a model in which relevant employees are encouraged to function as **brand evangelists** and collaborate in sharing engaging content. **Word-of-mouth** marketing techniques are integrated with SEO "visibility" in an integrated approach that aligns with organization social media policies and governance (p. 42). **Paid, earned, shared, and owned (PESO)** media are advanced through the efforts of "social employees" (pp. 46–54). This appears to align with an approach that places less emphasis on content, and more on social influence. LinkedIn Pages was merged with Elevate to help "organizations to interact at scale" and "help their employees be brand advocates" (Hutchinson, 2020, para. 2).

Steve Rubel (2017, @SteveRubel), Edelman chief media ecologist, has shifted focus away from content and toward faces, franchises, and platforms. Rubel tracked the "inversion" of influence "through peer individuals," attention "earned" by "relationships over reach," and the conclusion that "content is no longer king" because Facebook and other powerful platform algorithms "now prioritize peers over professional creators" (paras. 3–5). We trust and may advocate for brands through loyalty that begins with awareness and engagement, grows stronger during evaluation and purchasing, and is psychologically reinforced afterwards (Kosaka, 2018). In other words, social media communication is an important form of frequently compelling visual and emotional advocacy, such as happens in more than 400 million daily Instagram Stories (Barnhart, 2018). An Instagram photo, for example, of a happy consumer showing off her new car is a credible organic sales pitch within a social network that is likely to reach and activate others beginning to consider buying. Marketers may overlay a sales funnel onto Instagram Stories content by: identification of warm leads, relationship building through educational stories, lifestyle branded content, production of highlights, and optimization with analytics (Tayenaka, 2019).

At the beginning and end of online PR is evaluation in the general sense, as opposed to the specific formula, of return on investment. In other words, was the effort worth our valuable resources and time? PR's largest firm emphasizes global trust data in the 2019 Edelman Trust Barometer. it makes sense that source and message credibility depend upon trusted online relationships.

PR HISTORY AND TACTICS

PR was not always the way we see it now. Message management began with the church and political propaganda centuries ago, and it was fueled by 20th-century technological and social change. From P. T. Barnum's circus to early practitioner Edward Bernays, PR began to shift from wild and false claims to "professionals as comparable to attorneys, counseling clients" (Smith, Kaufman, & Martinez, 2012, p. 20). In the 1940s, PR featured traditional tactics, such as traveling publicity tours. A company selling home hair permanents in a radio and print advertising campaign that featured store visits across the country, for example, used the Toni Twins. The 75-city media tour was the idea of Dan Edelman, who went on to found his global PR firm:

> Politicians and celebrities had long toured America, going from one speaking engagement to the next. What if, Dan thought, a company organized a tour geared not toward events, but aimed at local media? A media tour would ignite conversation everywhere it touched down. They could easily cobble together a reason to be in town, but the real purpose would be to generate coverage in the local newspapers, magazines, and on local radio.
>
> (Wisner, 2012, p. 13)

Amid lobbying by beauticians against home hair treatments, the Toni Twins were arrested in Tulsa, Oklahoma, for "practicing salon procedures without a license" (p. 10). Crisis communication was born. Edelman turned the arrest into a photo opportunity and national press coverage by the AP and other news organizations. The events spawned Edelman's first 60-page PR plan, a large corporate budget, and eventually the launching of his own firm based upon a simple philosophy: "Do good. Tell other people about it" (p. 18).

At the same time, Harold Burson also was building one of the largest global firms by merging his PR firm with Bill Marsteller's large advertising agency in 1953. During the 1970s, Berson-Marsteller grew to 50 offices, 2,500 employees, and $64 million in revenue (PR Week, 2020, para. 7). After Burson's retirement in 1988, he remained active and was named the most influential PR person of the 20th century (para. 1). The firm merged with Cohn & Wolf to become BCW in 2018 two years before Burson's death in early 2020. Burson's style of PR that reached the post-World War II consumer redefined all forms of campaigns (Burson, 2017).

Harry Truman in 1948 had conducted a nationwide "whistle-stop" train tour designed to obtain live local radio coverage (Carroll, 1987). It would be called the last radio campaign. Between 1949 and 1952, when Edelman launched his small PR firm, post-war America had quickly adopted the new technology of television with millions watching *I Love Lucy* and other popular shows. News and politics also drew large audiences. Early television did not have a clear separation between programming and advertising, and celebrity scandals generated a need for reputation management.

PR today is managed within social media as planned and interactive communication. Practitioners focus on reputation management and crisis communication. It may function as internal communication within organizations, but it also serves external communication needs for publicity, government and community relations, and even fundraising. During Hurricane Dorian, for example, a Charleston hospital responded by activating its command center for "essential" staffing (Donovan, 2019, p. 16). Increasingly, the practice of PR includes real-time monitoring and response.

Published academic PR studies fall into three general categories – "introspective" articles about PR as a profession, "practice/application" of PR, and development of theory (Fussell Sisco, Pressgrove, & Collins, 2013, p. 286). Among these studies, important areas include excellence theory, organizational-public relationships, framing, dialogic communication, situational theory, role theory, and diffusion of innovation (p. 290).

Within this context, it appears that both the industry and academic researchers identify the growing importance of nonprofit public relations. This sector typically works with small budgets, and social media are seen as a way to generate awareness and interest through direct communication and engagement with the public.

PR THEORIES

The field of public relations tends to have a focus on communication strategies and tactics, organizational practices, and management. For example, common PR tactics include the use of news releases, press conferences, events, and publications. All of these may be connected to a social media campaign, which pushes content to media and the public. As with the broader communication industry, there is debate about the value of theory versus practice. Most agree that critical thinking abilities of students, interns, and professionals are key. Measurement of social media data, for example, challenges the traditional conception of research sites and tools (McIntosh, 2019). The ability to continuously track human behavior, collect streaming data, and target with precision requires that social media managers and consumers study and understand what is happening.

Among the most commonly mentioned theoretical perspectives are agenda-setting, cultivation, ethics, issues management, organizational communication, and persuasion (Miller & Kernisky, 1999). These theories may be applied to communication message strategies (Toth, 2006). Social media are closely related to mediated communication, which is built upon interpersonal communication theories. Tactics alone, without strategies, are not enough to manage complex issues (Elliott & Koper, 2002).

Grunig (1989) contended that PR "practice is dominated by the presupposition that the purpose of public relations is to manipulate the behavior of publics for the assumed, if not actual, benefit of the manipulated publics as well as the organization" (p. 29). He identified four models:

- Press agentry/publicity – "propagandistic" PR seeking "media attention in almost any way possible"

- Public information – "journalists-in-residence" disseminating "generally accurate information," but "do not volunteer negative information"

- Two-way asymmetrical – the Bernays approach uses research and sophisticated manipulation methods "to identify the messages most likely to produce support of publics without having to change the behavior of the organization"

- Two-way symmetrical – has "effects that a neutral observer would describe as benefitting both organization and publics" through "bargaining, negotiating, and strategies of conflict resolution to bring about symbiotic changes."

(p. 29)

Grunig (1989) found through research that "the models function as situational strategies that organizations use for different publics and public relations problems," and "presuppositions of the models function as part of an organization's ideology" (p. 31). Grunig also articulated the importance of organizational "orientation," which described such characteristics as closed-mindedness, elitism, and traditionalism (pp. 32–33). There is no reason to believe that social media participation would change fundamental organizational viewpoints, but these should impact the manner of communication and degree of engagement with the public. If old PR rules apply in social media spaces, then organizations may be overestimating the value of message distribution in raising awareness, as opposed to employing Grunig's symmetrical approach. On the other hand, public social media communication also may create opportunities to discuss, engage, and even negotiate social change. It may be that social media communication reflects traditional persuasion constraints of behavior reinforcement, cognitive beliefs and evaluation intention of future behavior, and involvement (Hamilton, 1989).

An early study of Twitter references to "public relations" and "PR" by Xifra and Grau (2010) found eight specific categories:

Labour introspective 15.2% (N = 99): All direct references to the vacancies and applications for positions in public relations.

Academic introspective 2.3% (N = 15): Both references clearly issued by students and lecturers, as well as information in the university public relations universe.

Practice 10.9% (N = 71): All information sent out by public relations practitioners, either as members of a company or the press agent of an organization ... It also comprises tweets that refer to work by firms.

Press release references 4.3% (N = 28): Announcements of the issue of press releases and links to read and/or download the press release.

General information on the public relations sector 14.4% (N = 94): General information on the public relations sector. It comprises the group of tweets that deal with the industry, on the state of the art or references to public relations as a concept, economic sector or important part of organisations' communication strategies.

The sender of the tweet and their dialogue with the community 18.7% (N = 122): It groups opinions and thoughts on the sector, heavily marked by the sender's viewpoint. Also @replies (answers) to other users involving the existence of a dialogue with them on public relations.

Research 5.6% (N = 37): It includes all requests and invitations to answer or to involve all users that read or capture a question or questionnaire issued to the community. *Announcements, reviews, agenda, followfriday, and retweets* 28.6% (N = 187): This group includes all tweets that facilitate acceleration, transmission and expansion of communication between the members of the community.

(pp. 171–172)

The study confirmed that Twitter was seen as an alternative channel for presenting a positive company image. Twitter often was used as a tool for professional information, including listings for jobs.

Curtis et al. (2010) found gender and other differences in the perception of Twitter. While Twitter use was ubiquitous, practitioners with "defined public relations departments are more likely to adopt social media technologies and use them to achieve ... organizational goals" (p. 92). Social media use was related to perceived credibility, strategic message targeting, client relationships, and an ability to reach the public.

CREDIBILITY

The potential for attitude and behavior change through social media communication requires an understanding of credibility. It has been related to believability, leadership, warmth, salience, trustworthiness, expertise, attractiveness, skills, accuracy, and sincerity (Hwang, 2013). In a study of Twitter use by Korean politicians, attitudes about Twitter use influenced the perceived credibility of the politicians using Twitter.

Politicians were perceived as "attractive and classy" by "challenging themselves" to use the new tool:

> Social media makes it possible for organizations to fully engage in dialogic communication with stakeholders … the word *dialogue* indicates open-minded, specific message content and a sincere listening attitude … When politicians actively share their candid opinions through the open public sphere of Twitter, this can cultivate an open-minded image that leads members of the public to perceive politician users as sincere and reliable.
>
> (p. 254)

Donald Trump has continued to use his Twitter, Facebook, and Instagram accounts to speak directly to followers and the press in a sometimes blunt and unfiltered style. By provoking strong opinions, the content tends to be widely shared across individuals' social networks. At the same time, however, there are numerous examples of US politicians speaking their minds on Twitter, only later having to retract or apologize for saying something that was perceived by media and the public as beyond normative boundaries.

SOCIAL CAPITAL, CONFLICT, AND COLLABORATION

Social capital is a popular idea within the social sciences and has been related to social interaction, trust, shared value, and social media use (Lin & Lu, 2011). It refers to the ability of individuals and organizations to benefit from communication behavior. In the context of social media, "Gaining social capital really means becoming a strong, consistent member of the online community" (Solomon, 2013, p. 35). A Save Ohio Libraries 2009 campaign on Twitter was unable to leverage social capital because it was primarily one-way, outbound communication. Librarians have since learned the importance of regularly engaging with their communities by providing helpful information and links. Solomon (2013) urges libraries to make social capital deposits within their social media sites:

> Every time your library promotes something or asks for a favor, it is making a withdrawal. If your withdrawals exceed your deposits, your library effectively becomes a community leech – and in some cases, a pariah. Spend social capital wisely.
>
> (p. 37)

Conceptually, Robert Putnum popularized social capital in the mid-1990s, as he argued for declining American social relationships. "This is a shorthand way of saying learning, motivation, best practice, problem solving and access to resources, among other factors, can often be better facilitated through networks – the social contacts made with professional colleagues – than individually" (Taylor, 2013, p. 34). Individual and organizational social capital may have value in economic terms, and it also may offer benefits for professional development and working culture. Across a wide variety of fields, social capital is seen as a way to understand intangibles that are important within prospering communities. Taylor (2013) listed important benefits:

- Trust – "information, knowledge and skills" sharing, as well as "support."

- Shared norms and values – "understanding" of others' "perspectives," and "shared language and common goals" with "a particular context."

- Shared resources and knowledge – "wider access to resources and knowledge" for "taking forward good practice."

- Reciprocity – "it is likely that others in the network will reciprocate and give to that relationship."

- Resilience within relationships – "Strong networks are resilient in the face of challenges," and are accepting of "constructive conversations around difficult areas."

- Coordination and cooperation for the achievement of common goals – as "best professional practice extends beyond traditional organisational boundaries."

(p. 35)

In other words, using social networking and media to cultivate social capital should generate opportunities to collaborate beyond organizational boundaries. Twitter, for example, can be seen as valuable individual career support through sustained relationship building while serving in "complex roles" (Taylor, 2013, p. 37). Beyond the obvious value to individual workers, collaboration may grow into "strategic business alliances" that cut costs by sharing the need to keep pace with rapid industry change (Harper & Norelli, 2007, p. 15). In PR, there are potentially a large number of opportunities within most communities to utilize virtual collaboration through social media.

SOCIAL MEDIA TACTICS

Historically, PR people had a heavy reliance on the simple press release or news release. The idea was that, if the writing and ideas were attention-getting to news gatekeepers, a story about an event, product, or service would follow. Enter the digital era and the Internet. Every release of information today should be designed for online consumption by news media and the general public. PR people are in search of "traction" amid the noisy and cluttered world of social media. One way to break through the clutter is to use SEO keywords and structure them in order to move the information toward the top of a Google search. At the same time, social media demand more.

Phil Gomes, a PR executive who now focuses on blockchain technologies, examined buzz in the early days of Twitter and researched how online chatter could be monitored through social media measurement techniques, which are much more sophisticated now. There is a need to share rich media content – photographs, audio, video, infographics, and links – across social platforms, such as Facebook, Twitter, and Pinterest. Developing tactics can create buzz, if the content is engaging and truly employs media storytelling techniques.

The PR professional in search of earned media and social sharing, even viral distribution, must be strategic by offering timely information. Increasingly, PR content is integrated into the news cycle, which is very fast. As news breaks, Twitter content may light up the social network with activity. Real-time PR professionals, often working from "war rooms" ready to respond, link the strategic goals of their clients with relatable **organic** content. Still, there are so many people now trying to take advantage of the moment in social media spaces that it has become increasingly difficult to be clever enough to break through the noise with valuable content.

t⚡ BOX 4.1

Thought Leader Phil Gomes

With the advent of social media, PR people suddenly became part of the story, which was always a kind of "fourth wall" that was never to be breached. This is both good *and* bad.

It's good in that PR is a largely distrusted profession, and I'm a big proponent of earning that trust by "open sourcing" PR's "operating system," to some degree. Social media offer ways to do that. Increasingly, blockchain technology – that which supports cryptocurrencies like Bitcoin – will serve as another layer of trust by providing a tamper-resistant digital audit trail.

FIGURE 4.2 *@philgomes.*

However, it's bad because there are an awful lot of PR people who want to insert themselves into the conversation to such a degree that it 1) actually *adds* to the distrust, and 2) produces further confusion as to what PR is. Having moved from 22 years of PR agency life to an in-house role, I'm very careful to ensure that I never put myself ahead of our executives and founders. After all, would you rather hear from my CEO (one of the key figures in the early days of Bitcoin) or the communications person? That said, we do aim to use both conventional social channels (e.g., blogs, Twitter) and emerging ones (e.g., Telegram) to full advantage. When appropriate, I step out front, usually to discuss matters related to media or community engagement in our industry.

All media are social and, despite what many legislators and marketing-discipline partisans might say, all social are media. "Digital" departments will be a company's core group of innovators and trend spotters, while basic social media and digital skills will be just as much a part of communications as, say, media relations. The distinctions will evaporate over time. As for me, that integration is already here.

Phil Gomes is chief communications and marketing officer at Bloq and director of communication for the Chicago Blockchain Center. He previously served as senior vice president (SVP) at Edelman Chicago, where he explored areas of communications well outside conventional PR practice. He holds a B.A. from St. Mary's College of California and an MBA from Purdue University Northwest. He is primarily known for starting the first PR blog (2001) and first articulating the potential for blockchain technology in communications and media (2015).

Social media tend to blur the lines between PR, advertising, and marketing. Vaynerchuk (2013), a disruptive voice within the industry, instructs brands to do storytelling within the context of a particular social media platform. He calls this type of social media marketing "native," in that it understands a platform and is fluent within it (p. 16). This rule also applies to PR. The difference is that while PR may emphasize brand awareness, influence, or positive sentiment, marketing ultimately seeks conversion from interaction to sales: "Successful social media marketing requires throwing many jabs before converting the sale with a right hook" (pp. 17–18). Vaynerchuk narrowed social media to the nine most important platforms at that time. Six of them – Twitter, Facebook, Instagram, LinkedIn, Pinterest, and Snapchat – remain important six years later, while TikTok and other new sites emerged. While marketers jab, PR professionals seek new ways to engage in timely and relevant exchanges.

PR NEWSROOMS AND MESSAGE TARGETING

One idea to address the need for real-time social media monitoring, response and strategy was to hire former journalists to staff the newsroom:

> Edelman built the Creative Newsroom, to provide clients with an agile and integrated platform for storytelling, for both planned and real-time marketing. We partner with clients to produce relevant content and real-time creative assets that support traditional, hybrid, social, and owned strategies and align with longer-term brand and corporate narratives.
>
> (Edelman, 2014)

The focus on client media storytelling for engaging audiences may build upon "trend spotters", identify trends and events, collaborate with account leaders, and design creative concepts. Ideas are shared with clients, and then decisions are made about posting or not.

Real-time social media are transforming marketing and public relations. Golin created The Bridge two years earlier than Edelman's Creative Newsroom. Golin hired professional journalists, but also created "a holistic engagement network" to offer businesses "a front-row seat to the most important conversations, broadcast and news headlines tied to your industry" (GolinHarris, 2014). The firm has had journalists in Chicago and Dallas running The Bridge in 2012. Golin constructed 13 global "command centers" for this form of industry collaboration. The Bridge won a *PR Week* award for innovative design of "holistic engagement" that connected business insights, engaged influencers and customers, and purposely created content with a goal of *shaping* "news and conversations" (para. 4). The basic idea was to provide 24/7 conversation monitoring for clients and offer a rapid response within social media. When Al Roker overslept his *Today Show* shift for the first time ever, for example, the McDonald's account tweeted at him:

> @McDonalds: Stick with us @AlRoker, we'll help you wake up for the next 39 years #McCafe.
>
> (August 6, 2013)

The tweet was read on the air, which is earned media from social media engagement with traditional media. Traditional media – television, radio, newspapers, and

FIGURE 4.3 *The Bridge in Chicago utilized real-time social media monitoring, strategy and response.*

magazines – are blending with real-time PR and marketing content. News organizations are now in the business of conversation monitoring and engaging. In this sense, the news model shares with PR the goal of creating viral videos, flashy graphics, photographs, memes, and other popular social media content. Everyone is competing for measurable engagement that may translate into new revenue.

The integration of digital requires that PR newsrooms "keep brands' names alive on the **trending** charts as well as the daily zeitgeist" (PR News, 2013b, para. 3). Ogilvy, which came to social media from an advertising agency perspective, strategized about real-time events but urged their clients to *create their own newsrooms* through earned media. Golin's vision was to place conversation at the center of idea creation for clients.

PR BLOGGING AND CASE STUDIES

Public relations blogging has been used to give personal and company brands voice within new social media spaces. More generally, bloggers may be social media influencers. While companies pay some bloggers, the vast majority is unpaid and fairly independent. In some cases, bloggers seek to build their personal brand and promote products, such as books.

☐ BOX 4.2

The Chicago Cubs and A Wrigley Field Pearl Jam Concert

The Chicago Cubs used social media to help promote a summer Pearl Jam concert at Wrigley Field – the first of many rock concerts over the years. The summer concerts became a new way to generate revenue while the baseball team was on the road for weeks at a time. Former Cubs manager of communications Kevin Saghy (@CredibleKev) utilized existing relationships. Pearl Jam musician Edder Vedder (@PearlJam) is a huge Cubs fan, and Cubs president of baseball operations Theo Epstein (@Cubs) also is a Pearl Jam fan. Saghy told a Cision (@Cision) marketing webinar (Denten & Saghy, 2013), "We executed a social media leak strategy." It began one morning with cryptic Facebook and Twitter posts using #StayTuned to heighten interest. "Over the course of the day, people following both accounts started to pick up on this, and the buzz just built throughout the day."

The announcement of the forthcoming concert attracted traditional local media coverage and morning television the next day. The Cubs also received attention in music industry publications, such as *Rolling Stone*. Saghy told PRSA that the Cubs "relied upon 'traditional' PR tactics to attract attention to our social media outlets" by securing "quite a bit of coverage" for the Pearl Jam concert and a Social Media Night at Wrigley Field (Jacques, 2013, para. 18).

The PR function aligns with baseball operations on the release of personnel information, roster moves and updates during games. The Cubs connect "memorable" offline experiences to social media; "fans remember these interactions for life, and the positive stories spread organically" (para. 10). The Cubs went on to win the #World Series in 2016, the team's first in 108 years. A variety of influencers – entertainers, current players, and former players – helped spread the Cubs social media messaging on their Twitter, Instagram, Facebook, and Snapchat accounts. Paid Twitter **hashflags** #WorldSeries and #FlyTheW during the season automatically generated trophy and W flag icons when users posted content with them. Current stars, such as Javy Baez, have large Instagram followings and an active presence.

FIGURE 4.4 *The Chicago Cubs used social and mass media to promote a Pearl Jam concert at Wrigley Field.*

Social media have become PR tools that offer many unique ways to be creative and generate customer brand interest. There are many examples frequently mentioned by PR professionals, including:

- The video camera @gopro on Instagram features customer video and photos from around the world and grew from more than 6 million in 2019 to 16.7 million in early 2020.

- The Old Spice Guy, a brand representative, created hundreds of personalized videos for fans.

- Microsoft and Bing announced a partnership during a Twitter chat.

- Hershey's launched its Simple Pleasures candy with a Sweet Independence Facebook page that encouraged follower posts and generated more than 200 million media impressions.

PR people can reward loyal customers by making simultaneous Facebook page and media release announcements. Using social media to cover press conferences and national launch tours can help coordinate the integration of traditional and social media. By inventing new hashtags or hijacking ("hashjacking") an existing trending topic, a brand can connect with new potential customers. During NBC's live "Sound of Music" broadcast with singer Carrie Underwood, pizza brand DiGiorno capitalized on the highest TV ratings since the E.R. finale to live tweet using the official tag:

@DiGiorno: #TheSoundOfMusicLive Can't believe pizza isn't one of her favorite things smh.

(December 5, 2013)

"Now of course DiGiorno got a ton of pizza references in there by seamlessly incorporating their brand with the conversation, but they were not pushing products" (Quintana, 2013, para. 6). The increase in this type of live tweet, however, runs a risk of turning off fans who see this as too opportunistic. Nevertheless, fast-food brands Wendy's and Burger King are among those using edgy humor to connect and engage.

@BurgerKing: GOOD THING IT WILL ONLY BE AVAILABLE IN SELECT MARKETS FOR A LIMITED TIME

Ashleigh Court @piglct: OF COURSE WHEN I DECIDE TO CUT OUT FAST FOOD THEY DECIDE TO MAKE AN IMPOSSIBLE CROISSANWICH. I AM GONNA SCREAM.

(January 8, 2020)

The connection between PR events and social media may produce numerous positive outcomes. PR influence now extends to blogger and VIP influencers by creating experiences that lend themselves to social media content creation. Traditional news media increasingly are active on social media, and social media engagement may cut across traditional and new media. Many brands have incorporated prize packages and scavenger hunts into their social media plans.

Companies also need to consider the role that employees play within social media. Their employees may be connected to very active social networks, and they are brand ambassadors. Employees also may be able to help a social media brand manager by taking photographs and having their posts featured on a blog or social media site. Employees are increasingly seen as stakeholders with a voice inside and outside the company. Hilton, for example, has five prongs in its employee advocacy strategies:

1. Develop a shortlist of employees always wanting to do more.

2. Train team members by teaching them new knowledge and skills.

3. Create a solid social media policy that offers guidance, yet makes it fun.

4. Leverage existing programs.

5. Frequently thank team members.

(Sain-Dieguez, 2019)

The integrated approach to PR and digital marketing may be positive for brand visibility, customer loyalty and even sales. An earned media management (EMM) model emphasizes positive sentiment through the systematic use of data to map influencers, content and audiences in a way that demonstrates outcomes (Cision, 2018). Social media may generate new business through use of new platforms and engagement with fans and followers – ideally within a responsible business framework.

CORPORATE SOCIAL RESPONSIBILITY (CSR)

With so much attention being paid to seemingly self-serving company and brand efforts within social media, there has been renewed interest in looking beyond sales and profits. Perhaps driven by an era of government deregulation that began in the late 1970s in the United States, CSR asks companies to consider the effects of their businesses on social and environmental conditions. Corporate citizens operating within a CSR model would consider long-term social interests, not just quarterly profits. Clearly, social media engagement can be related to CSR by emphasizing social responsibility for individuals, groups and companies. CSR also can be seen as a way to develop legal, ethical, and global best practices within a large corporation. Freeman (1984/2010) influenced thinking about the need for multinational corporations, including the move beyond narrow stockholder interests and toward the broader interests of stakeholders. Freeman's book was published at a time when US manufacturing, particularly the automobile industry, was being overtaken by imports from Japan. As such, CSR was framed within a strategic management perspective that considered suppliers, owners, employees, and customers as stakeholders within an environment of "internal and external change" (p. 12). Most notably, companies were receiving media scrutiny based on the emergence of consumer protection and employee rights and responsibilities. If a company moved away from top-down management practices, then it should involve employees at all levels in decision-making and listen to customer wants and needs. In other words, CSR emphasized self-regulation within companies as a more effective way to achieve social good over previous efforts of "big government" regulation. The CSR message resonated in the 1980s US political environment, which saw President Ronald Reagan pushing for aggressive deregulation of "bureaucracy" in all sectors (p. 15).

> Let us consider the customer of a firm, and suppose that for whatever reason, the customer is unhappy with the product. He or she can exit, simply take the business elsewhere and buy from another producer, given that there is a reasonable number of competing firms. Exit is the paradigm of the "economic" strategy. When enough customers exit, the firm gets the message that the product is no longer viable, that it is not producing at the "efficient frontier."
>
> (pp. 18–19)

An alternative approach is the use of customer "voice." Freeman (1984/2010) saw customer feedback to management as "more immediate" (p. 19). Brand loyalty in the marketplace, then, is a combination of consumer decisions and voice. Traditional, mainstream media might identify a particular consumer complaint or problem, but social media allow consumers to voice immediate dissatisfaction and engage with others having similar issues. Yelp, for example, is driven by consumer reviews. If a number of people report a similar problem at a restaurant, the social media content may affect business. Social media amplify and accelerate consumer voice, not only forcing company response, but also nudging interest in CSR.

The CSR approach suggests that responsible behavior may also be good for business, but it is not clear that social good always has a positive economic impact (McWilliams & Siegel, 2001). As early as 1970, it had been argued (via "agency theory") that "managers who use" shareholder and "corporate resources to further some social good are doing so only to advance a personal agenda such as promoting their self image" (McWilliams, Siegel, & Wright, 2006b, p. 4). Corporate Social Performance (CSP) instead emphasized the need to test CSR against traditional financial outcomes (Carroll, 1979). One view of CSR emphasizes stakeholders, ethical behavior, "trust and cooperation" (McWilliams, Siegel, & Wright, 2006b, p. 3). This approach has been shown to "demonstrate that the returns to socially responsible behavior are captured through the reputation of the firm" (McWilliams, Siegel, & Wright, 2006a, p. 6). Particularly on the international stage, communicating CSR may result in positive effects, such as increased brand loyalty for those customers in search of socially responsible products and company behavior. Communicating brand differentiation through CSR may be part of a broader engagement strategy. However, CSR may be co-opted as a PR strategy that fails to back up communication with action: "As a discipline, PR more often has incorporated CSR as a 'reactive communication tactic' for generating publicity rather than organically acting as *corporate conscience* across the organization ..." (Pompper, 2018, p. 12). The idea is that PR and human relations (HR) offices could collaborate to promote responsible behavior throughout large organizations, but smaller non-profits also need strategies for utilizing social media to advance worthy goals.

NON-PROFITS

Non-profits have perhaps the most to gain from the social media communication PR shift. They are typically faced with low or non-existent media budgets and hope to benefit through earned media. While it is still possible to place stories in the local newspaper or on radio and television stations to gain community awareness, there are greater possibilities within social media. Non-profits may cultivate social friends and fans, drive traffic to fundraising campaign sites, and generate interest in community events. Stewardship, non-profits, and donor relationships have been extensively studied, but research is just beginning to understand the organization-public relationship or OPR (Pressgrove & McKeever, 2016). Loyalty, behavioral intention and related strategies suggest that there is a complex model: relationship nurturing, reciprocity (recognition and appreciation), responsibility and reporting related to stewardship; trust, satisfaction, and commitment related to affect; cognitive, affective, and behavioral aspects of loyalty; and behavioral intents (p. 205). "The viability and longevity of a nonprofit is often dependent not only on fiscal gifts, but also on the support of volunteers who contribute their time and talents" (p. 205). Social media may be valuable in the long-term cultivation of stakeholder interest – the donation of money or their time.

Chief executive officers may play an important role in developing social media PR success stories. *PR News* reported that CEO sociability may have a positive impact on company reputation, and CEO blogging magnifies effect. When a CEO becomes a thought leader, she or he has the potential to influence conversation and followers. As blog posts spread across social media spaces, the CEO and company brands should grow. Among benefits listed in an Intel chart are those shown in Table 4.2.

CEO social media use has the potential to increase perceptions of credibility, when strategic and careful. By establishing a presence within social media, a CEO should be

TABLE 4.3 *Top Five Benefits of CEO Blogging and Social Media Use*

Benefits	Social Media Use	CEO Blogging
1. Shows innovation	76%	85%
2. Build media relations	75%	84%
3. Human face/personality	75%	80%
4. Business results	70%	76%
5. Workplace perception	69%	76%

Source: PR News (June 7, 2013a). Benefits of CEO Participation in Social Media. PR News. www.prnewsonline.com/topics/research/2013/06/10/social-media-and-mobile-video-equal-more-web-sharingdeath-of-newspapers-greatly-exaggerated-for-a-change/attachment/chart2-2/

more ready to handle media and public backlashes during times of crisis. There are, however, no guarantees. Participating in social media also opens brands to potential criticism and attack.

The most common problem for individuals and companies is the distribution of a social media message without thinking it through and filtering it in terms of PR strategic planning and goals. The online site *Mental Floss* reported 16 cases in which people had been fired from their jobs because of a tweet (Conradt, 2013). Among the examples, an employee tweeting for Chrysler thought he was on his own private account:

> @ChryslerAutos: I find it ironic that Detroit is known as #motorcity and yet no one here knows how to fucking drive.
>
> (March 9, 2011)

While this firing was immediate, sometimes an old tweet comes back to haunt an employee. This 2011 tweet was discovered and reported by the *Milwaukee Journal Sentinel* after Taylor Palmisano was hired as deputy finance director for Wisconsin Governor Scott Walker's campaign.

> @itstaytime: This bus is the worst fucking nightmare Nobody speaks English & these ppl don't know how 2 control their kids #only3morehours #illegalaliens.
>
> (January 2, 2011)

Nearly a decade later, social media fails continue to haunt employees that may be punished or fired based upon the formal language within social media policies at a company or other organization.

Most employers clearly will not tolerate racist rants. Another problem is the disclosure of confidential information. *Glee* extra Nicole Crowther "tweeted a spoiler of a pivotal scene" (para. 4) of the popular primetime television show. She was banned from future work through her casting agency (Conradt, 2013). More recently, a winner of The Great British Bake Off was accidentally revealed before the television show aired when Prue Leith, a judge, prematurely tweeted the winner (Westbrook, 2018). Apparently, she had become confused while traveling because of the time zone difference. She also apologized in a tweet:

> @PrueLeith: I am so sorry to the fans of the show for my mistake this morning, I am in a different time zone and mortified by my error #GBBO (October 31, 2017).
>
> (para. 12)

Westbrook (2018) recounted how Leith also apologized in the press: "I'm in Bhutan. The time difference is massive. I thought that they got it six hours ago. I'm in too much of a state to talk about it. I fucked up" (para. 10). The key point here is that she publicly acknowledged the error, and the show also responded with humor at the start of the next season. A "Back to the Future" parody made a joke out of the problem tweet, and everyone was able to go on working at the show. The responses showed that messaging was audience-centered.

PR practitioners can use social media communication content in the promotion of client products and services. Ogilvy's director of media influence calls this "the age of content" (Risi, 2013):

> Media relations has undergone a sea change in recent times with the proliferation of platforms, fusion of formats, and blurring of the lines between traditional and social media. What has persisted is the potency of media exposure – it can make or break your PR campaign and thereby, your client's brand. It can establish newbies, transform dogged perceptions, and restore tarnished brands. Companies are increasingly turning to PR agencies for brand building and reputation management, and agencies must navigate their clients through an increasingly muddled media landscape.
>
> (para. 1)

Risi (2013) offered a summary of traditional, social, and earned media focused on business results.

1. **Measure what matters** … Impressions and ad equivalency are moot points if your media efforts aren't impacting the company's bottom line.

2. **Re-think media placements** … social sharing, online pieces are often driving conversation better than print coverage.

3. **Adopt a channel-agnostic approach** … by connecting content across earned, owned, and paid media, brands can tell a cohesive story that resonates with discerning consumers today.

(paras. 4–6)

---

t📡 BOX 4.3

Thought Leader Karen Freberg

The Importance of Emojis

Emojis have been used to express a feeling, reaction, or even as part of a branding campaign. Emojis were originated in Japan a few decades ago by Shigetaka Kurita, who was an employee of the Japanese telecom company NTT Docomo (Sternberg, 2014). They made their mark in the current communication and marketing landscape thanks to integration with mobile devices, such as iPhones and Androids. In 2015, Oxford Dictionaries named "emoji" the word of the year (Oxford Dictionaries Blog, 2015). Emojis have not only been integrated into mainstream society, but in our overall business communication functions. In October 2016, Apple added a feature of the touch screen menu bar on their to incorporate an emoji option, making them even more of a dominant form of communication for people across all devices and platforms.

Emojis, in many ways, are able to help people re-energize or even reestablish some of the personality, emotion, and communication nuances we are not able to comprehend with simple text messages. While emojis do not replace face-to-face communication (facial expressions and nonverbal corre-

FIGURE 4.5 *@kfreberg*

spondence), they do add a bit of context and an additional layer of information while tapping into the emotion of the receiver or audience for which the message was intended. Communication professionals have embraced emojis because they are able to get on the same communication stream as their key audiences (fans, customers, potential audience members, etc.) to help build a stronger connection with them on a level of which they are familiar. Emojis, and understanding the meaning behind specific emojis is important for PR and marketing professionals.

Emojis have been actively used in various campaigns – from those that are sponsored and paid for by a company for an event (i.e., Coca-Cola and #ShareACoke or StarWars and their character hashtag emojis) to education (GE and Emoji Science), transactions made just with emojis (Domino's with the pizza emoji), promoting team spirit among fans virtually (NFL and NBA), integrating emojis as part of a brand (Clemson Tigers), and raising awareness of a cause or partnership (World Wildlife Fund).

While emojis are prominent in personal communications and marketing campaigns, they are also a topic of conversation when it comes to email and business communication etiquette. In an article in *Public Relations Tactics*, public relations professionals were advised to limit their use of emojis in their professional correspondence and evaluate the situation to determine if these would be appropriate to use in this particular arena. While the meanings of certain emojis are quite apparent to the individual receiving the emoji in a message, there are others which could be interpreted mean something completely different than originally intended.

FIGURE 4.6 *Apple iPhone Emoji*

Sources: Sternberg, A. (November 16, 2014). Smile, You're Speaking Emoji: The Rapid Evolution of a Wordless Tongue. *NY Magazine*. http://nymag.com/daily/intelligencer/2014/11/emojis-rapid-evolution.html; Oxford Dictionaries. (2015). Word of the Year. http://blog.oxforddictionaries.com/2015/11/word-of-the-year-2015-emoji/.

Karen Freberg is an Associate Professor in Strategic Communications at the University of Louisville. She also is an adjunct faculty member for the West Virginia University IMC Graduate Online program. Freberg is also a research consultant in social media and crisis communications and has worked with several organizations and agencies such as Firestorm Solutions, Hootsuite, General Motors, Kentucky Derby Festival, DHS, CDC, National Center for Food Protection and Defense (NCFPD), Kentucky Organ Donor Affiliates, and the Colorado Ski Association. Freberg's research has been published in several book chapters and in academic journals such as *Public Relations Review*, *Media Psychology Review*, *Journal of Contingencies and Crisis Management*, and *Health Communication*. She also serves on the editorial board for *Psychology for Popular Media Culture*, *Corporate Communication*, *Marketing Education Review*, *Journal of Public Relations Research*, and *Case Studies in Strategic Communication* (CSSC).

Unintended use of a branded emoji can cause a stir and social media engagement. In 2019, the Pope used #Saints in a TweetDeck tweet, and it automatically added the New Orleans Saints football team Fleur-de-Lis branded hashflag emoji logo. There were more than 100,000 retweets. The team added the tweet image into a Facebook post and responded that they were, "Blessed and highly favored." This was shared on Facebook more than 5,000 times. While the original post may have been a mistake, it resulted in positive sentiment.

Beyond users, the sites themselves have a large impact on PR professionals seeking to use social media for strategic communication. Freberg (2019) points out that,

> Unlike other channels of communication, social media professionals are at the mercy of what these platforms decided to do (or not do) for their users … This is the nature of social media as we are operating in rented space … We will have to be agile, adaptive, and willing to learn on the go when it comes to social media.
>
> (p. 275)

The ever-changing social media landscape requires an openness in the way PR people work going forward. That includes the introduction of artificial intelligence and machine learning. McCorkindale (2019) worried about the impact of automation: "The curve of adoption and innovation will continue to move faster, and I don't want our profession to be unprepared" (p. 5). The emphasis is away from traditional press releases and media relations tactics and toward engaging content that is timely and contextual. By producing the right content at the right time, and on the right social media platform, it is possible to meet ROI business objectives that can be measured. A social media policy may be developed through clear definition and purpose, organizational support, disclosure, and individual consequences (Convince & Convert, 2019). At the same time, as we will see later in this book, development of company social media policies and use of employees as brand ambassadors may run into legal and ethical issues.

PR is converging and blending with advertising and marketing. Social media engagement calls for customer focus and a clear content strategy (Edelman, 2013). In the next chapter, the attention turns to social media for advertising and marketing purposes.

DISCUSSION QUESTIONS: STRATEGIES AND TACTICS

1. How is PR changing because of social media use? What are the positives and negatives of the shift? How do you believe the blending of PR, advertising, and marketing will influence your career?

2. How is it possible to integrate the different media forms described by the Edelman cloverleaf? How can strategic PR be used to identify KPI's that can be measured over time? What are the most important limitations to integrated PR?

3. What do you see as the most important corporate social responsibility issues related to social media? How might these change in the future?

REFERENCES

Armano, D. (2013, October 28). The Five Content Archetypes. *Edelman*. http://darmano.type-pad.com/logic_emotion/2013/10/content.html

Barnhart, B. (2018, August 21). The Ultimate Guide on How to Use Instagram Stories. *Sprout Social*. https://sproutsocial.com/insights/how-to-use-instagram-stories/

Brito, M. (2018). *Participation Marketing*. London: Kogan Page.

Broom, G. M., & Sha, B. L. (2013). *Cutlip and Center's Effective Public Relations*, eleventh edition. Boston, MA: Pearson.

Burson, H. (2017). *The Business of Persuasion, Harold Burson on Public Relations*. New York: RosettaBooks.

Carroll, A. (1979). A Three-Dimensional Model of Corporate Performance. *Academy of Management Review 4*, 497–505.

Carroll, R. L. (1987, Spring). Harry S. Truman's 1948 Election: The Inadvertent Broadcast Campaign. *Journal of Broadcasting & Electronic Media 31*(2), 119–132.

Cision. (2018). Earned Media Management: The Evolution of PR and Comms. *Cision*. www.cision.com/content/dam/cision/Resources/white-papers/Cision_earned_media_management.pdf

Conradt, S. (2013, December). 16 People Who Tweeted Themselves into Unemployment. *Mental Floss*. http://mentalfloss.com/article/54068/16-people-who-tweeted-themselves-unemployment

Convince & Convert. (2019, October 21). Social Media Policy Template, Your Company Social Media Checklist. www.convinceandconvert.com/social-media-marketing/how-to-create-a-social-media-policy-for-employees/

Curtis, L., Edwards, C., Fraser, K. L., Gudelsky, S., Holmquist, J., Thornton, K., & Sweetser, K. D. (2010). Adoption of Social Media for Public Relations by Nonprofit Organizations. *Public Relations Review 36*, 90–92.

Denten, L. L., & Saghy, K. (2013, October 24). Bridging Social to Traditional PR. *Cision*. http://us.cision.com/events/on-demand-webinars/Bridging-the-Gap-to-Traditional-PR.asp

Donovan, B. (2019, November). Crisis Management: A Charleston Hospital's Crisis Response to Hurricane Dorian. *PRSA Strategies & Tactics*. p. 16.

Edelman, D. (2013, October 30). Say Hi to the Social Media Elephant in the Room. *LinkedIn*. www.linkedin.com/today/post/article/20131030130324–1816165-say-hi-to-the-social-media-elephant-in-the-room

Edelman, P. R. (2014). Creative Newsroom. www.edelman.com/expertise/creative-newsroom/

Elliott, G., & Koper, E. (2002). Public Relations Education from an Editor's Perspective. *Journal of Communication Management 7*, 21–23.

Freberg, K. (2019). *Social Media Strategic Communication, Creative Strategies and Research-Based Applications*. Los Angeles: SAGE.

Freeman, R. E. (1984/2010). *Strategic Management: A Stakeholder Approach*. Cambridge, UK: Cambridge University Press.

Fussell Sisco, H., Pressgrove, G., & Collins, E. L. (2013). Paralleling the Practice: An Analysis of the Scholarly Literature in Nonprofit Public Relations. *Journal of Public Relations Research 25*(4), 282–306.

Gils, A. (2019, December). The Role of Behavioral Science in Communications. *PRSA Strategies & Tactics*. p. 6.

GolinHarris. (2014). The Bridge: Holistic Engagement Centers. http://golinharris.com/#!/approach/the-bridge/

Grunig, J. E. (1989). Symmetrical Presuppositions as a Framework for Public Relations Theory. In C. H. Botan and V. Hazleton, Jr. (Eds.), *Public Relations Theory*, pp. 17–44. Hillsdale, NJ: Lawrence Erlbaum.

Hamilton, P. K. (1989). Application of a Generalized Persuasion Model to Public Relations Research. In C. H. Botan and V. Hazleton, Jr. (Eds.), *Public Relations Theory*, pp. 323–334. Hillsdale, NJ: Lawrence Erlbaum.

Harper, T., & Norelli, B. P. (2007). The Business of Collaboration and Electronic Collection Development. *Collection Building 26*(1), 15–19.

Hopp, T., & Gallicano, T. D. (2016). Development and Test of a Multidimensional Scale of Blog Engagement. *Journal of Public Relations Research 28*(3–4), 127–145.

Hutchinson, A. (2020, January 26). LinkedIn Announces Merger of Elevate Functionality with Company Pages. *Social Media Today*. www.socialmediatoday.com/news/linkedin-announces-merger-of-elevate-functionality-with-company-pages/571087/

Hwang, S. (2013). The Effect of Twitter Use on Politicians' Credibility and Attitudes toward Politicians. *Journal of Public Relations Research 25*(3), 246–258.

Jacques, A. (2013, August 1). Take Me Out to the Ball Game: Kevin Saghy on Managing Communications for the Chicago Cubs. *PRSA Tactics*. www.prsa.org/Intelligence/Tactics/Articles/view/10277/1081/Take_me_out_to_the_ball_game_Kevin_Saghy_on_managi

Kelleher, T. (2018). *Public Relations: Engagement, Conversation, Influence, Transparency, Trust.* New York: Oxford University Press.

Kosaka, K. (2018). Customer Lifecycle Marketing: The Complete Guide. *Alexa Blog.* https://blog.alexa.com/customer-lifecycle-marketing/

Lin, K. Y., & Lu, H.-P. (2011). Intention to Continue Using Facebook Fan Pages from the Perspective of Social Capital Theory. *Cyberpsychology, Behavior, and Social Networking 14*(10), 565–570.

Lipschultz, J. (2016, August 8). PR Pitches Client "Collaborative Journalism." *The Huffington Post.* www.huffingtonpost.com/entry/pr-pitches-digital-client-collaborative-journalism_us_57a8d7fde4b08f5371f1c2b9

McCorkindale, T. (2019, May). #TheWayWeWork. *PRSA Strategies & Tactics.* p. 5.

McIntosh, H. (2019). Social Media and Research Methods. In S. M. Croucher and D. Cronn-Mills *Understanding Communication Research Methods*, second edition, pp. 147–159. New York and London: Routledge.

McWilliams, A., & Siegel, D. (2001). Corporate Social Responsibility: A Theory of the Firm Perspective. *Academy of Management Review 26*, 117–127.

McWilliams, A., Siegel, D. S., & Wright, P. M. (2006a). Corporate Social Responsibility: International Perspectives. *Rensselaer Working Papers in Economics.* Troy, NY: Rensselaer Polytechnic Institute Press.

McWilliams, A., Siegel, D. S., & Wright, P. M. (2006b). Corporate Social Responsibility: Strategic Implications. *Journal of Management Studies 43*(1), 1–18.

Miller, D. P., & Kernisky, D. A. (1999). Opportunities Realized: Undergraduate Education within Departments of Communication. *Public Relations Review 25*(1), 87–100.

Pompper, D. (2018). Picking at an Old Scab in a New Era: Public Relations and Human Resources Boundary Spanning for a Socially Responsible and Sustainable World. In D. Pompper (Ed.), *Corporate Social Responsibility, Sustainability and Ethical Public Relations: Strengthening Synergies with Human Resources*, pp. 1–34. Bingley, UK: Emerald Publishing Limited.

PR News. (2013a, June 7). Benefits of CEO Participation in Social Media. *PR News.* www.prnewsonline.com/topics/research/2013/06/10/social-media-and-mobile-video-equal-more-web-sharing-death-of-newspapers-greatly-exaggerated-for-a-change/attachment/chart2-2/

PR News. (2013b, October 21). PR Teams Build Internal Newsrooms as Communications Strategies Shift. *PR News.* www.prnewsonline.com/topics/media-relations/2013/10/21/pr-teams-build-internal-newsrooms-as-communications-strategies-shift/

PR Week. (2020, January 10). Burson-Marsetller Founder Harold Burson Dead at 98. www.prweek.com/article/1670474/burson-marsteller-founder-harold-burson-dead-98

Pressgrove, G. N., & McKeever, B. W. (2016). Nonprofit Relationship Management: Extending the Organization-Public Relationship to Loyalty and Behaviors. *Journal of Public Relations Research 28*(3–4), 193–211.

PRSA. (2013, October 27). Conference Recap: Brian Solis on the Future of Public Relations. *PRSA Tactics.* www.prsa.org/SearchResults/view/10397/105/Conference_Recap_Brian_Solis_On_the_Future_of_Publ

PRSA. (2019, September). Survey Finds Executives Prefer Spreadsheets Over Analytics Platforms. *PRSA Strategies & Tactics*, p. 4.

Quintana, J. (2013, December 5). Real-Time Marketing Lessons from DiGiorno. *Lonelybrand.* http://lonelybrand.com/blog/real-time-marketing-digiorno/

Risi, J. (2013, November 4). Three Ways to Maximize PR in the Age of Content. *PR Week.* www.prweekus.com/three-ways-to-maximize-pr-in-the-age-of-content/article/319180/

Rubel, S. (2017, January 3). Why Brands Need Faces and Franchises in the Platform Age. *AdAge.* http://adage.com/article/steve-rubel/brands-invest-faces-franchises-platform-age/307272/

Sain-Dieguez, V. (2019, November 27). Hilton's 5-Prong Approach to Employee Advocacy on Social. *The Social Shake-Up.* www.socialshakeupshow.com/hilton-employee-advocacy-social/

Smith, B. L., Kaufman, C. O., & Martinez, G. D. (2012). *Engaging Public Relations: A Creative Approach*, third edition. Dubuque, IA: Kendall Hunt.

Solomon, L. (2013, May). Understanding Social Capital. *American Librarian Magazine 44*(5), 34–37.

Sudhaman, A. (2013, December 1). The 'Organized Chaos' of the World's Largest PR Agency. *The Holmes Report.* www.holmesreport.com/featurestories-info/14285/The-Organized-Chaos-Of-The-Worlds-Largest-PR-Agency.aspx

Tayenaka, T. (2019, December 24). How to Use Instagram Stories in Your Sales Funnel, *Social Media Examiner.* www.socialmediaexaminer.com/how-to-use-instagram-stories-sales-funnel/

Taylor, R. (2013). Networking in Primary Health Care: How Connections Can Increase Social Capital. *Primary Health Care 23*(10), 34–40.

The Holmes Report. (2016, 2019). Global Top 250 PR Agency Ranking 2016. www.holmesreport.com/ranking-and-data/global-communications-report/2016-pr-agency-rankings/top-250

Toth, E. L. (2006). On the Challenge of Practice Informed by Theory. *Journal of Communication Management 10*(1), 110–111.

Vaynerchuk, G. (2013). *Jab, Jab, Jab, Right Hook: How to Tell Your Story in a Noisy Social World.* New York, NY: HarperCollins.

Volz, K. (2019, July). How to Set up a PR Measurement System. *PRSA Strategies & Tactics.* p. 20.

Westbrook, C. (2018, August 28). What Did Prue Leith Tweet Ahead of Last Year's Bake off Final? *Metro.* https://metro.co.uk/2018/08/28/what-did-prue-leith-tweet-ahead-of-last-years-bake-off-final-7889345/

Wisner, F. (2012). *Edelman and the Rise of Public Relations.* Chicago, IL: Daniel J. Edelman.

Xifra, J., & Grau, F. (2010). Nanoblogging PR: The Discourse on Public Relations in Twitter. *Public Relations Review 36*, 171–174.

Social Media in Advertising and Marketing

The heavy spending on Facebook comes even as leading party officials have raised alarms about the site's role in American democracy.
– Shane Goldmacher & Quoctrung Bui (@nytimes, 2019)

Facebook stands tall as the largest recipient of social media advertising dollars in the world – by a long shot.
– eMarketer (@eMarketer, 2016)

Social media marketing has always been a peculiar animal ... we're now witnesses to an era with rock-solid platforms, useful advertising options, and plenty of free opportunities to make our content public.
– Jayson DeMers (@jaysondemers, 2015)

The ability of advertisers to precisely target demographic, geographic, and psychographic variables offered Facebook an advantage during the 2020 presidential election. *The New York Times* reported that former Vice President Joe Biden went after older prospective voters while others emphasized younger ones. Goldmacher and Bui (2019) found that in the year before the election, Democrats had spent nearly $32 million on Facebook ads, which was higher than television. This was considered "a striking measure of the social network's ever-rising influence on politics" (para. 3). While Facebook data showed that the social network allowed candidates to target age and gender, the site was not selling race and ethnicity targeting campaigns, as it had done earlier. At the same time, however, the algorithm allowed candidates to optimize an action, such as a donation. The general shift toward paid and promoted social media posts reflects an industry interest in demonstrating direct outcomes.

"Advertising is commonly defined as paid, one-way promotional communication in any mass media" (Tuten, 2008, p. 2). Social media, however, are interactive two-way consumer and brand communication. "Online, advertising becomes more about conversations, connections, and shared control and less about passive consumption of packaged content" (p. 3). Online advertising also blurs the traditional line between it and marketing functions, and it offers key advantages. "Because of the networked nature of online computers, the Internet has proven to be highly measurable" (Kelley, Jugenheimer, & Sheehan, 2012, p. 253).

Context, including the level of consumer involvement with media, has become increasingly important:

> Media should be thought of more from the consumers' viewpoint, and it is no longer enough to know basic media usage figures … Rather consumers' relationships with the media can be critical to the way they respond to the brand message.
>
> (Katz, 2007, p. 29)

Social media are maturing into an industry that aligns with traditional media advertising and marketing plans designed to reach large audiences (Miller, 2013). Beyond offering additional marketing channels, social media are unique because of relationship building. **Earned exposure** is defined as when customers "relay their positive experiences" to others "via social media sites for reviews and ratings" (p. 89). In fact, early research found that three-fourths of comments to retailer sites were positive. Still, potential customers "want to see negative reviews to be able to accurately assess the degree of product risk they face when purchasing" (Tuten, 2008, p. 121). The ultimate goal in most advertising and marketing campaigns is to convert people, through a **conversion** process, from having an initial interest into completing a sale for products or services:

> The basis of social media is informal conversation. Prospects want to be involved in a dialogue, not subjected to a stream of sales pitches. Even when no back-and-forth conversation is taking place, a company's posts need to sound like human speech.
>
> (P. Miller, 2013, p. 92)

David Edelman (2013), now chief marketing officer at Aetna (CVS), wrote that social media began as an unstructured, spontaneous activity, but organic development generated little strategy and may have inflated company fears – sometimes leading to a denial of its importance. Four foundations were explained:

1. *Customer care* must address complaints: "Having a formal social care team that peels off those posts and handles them in a structured way, with real case management tools to resolve problems is essential" (para. 3). Cost per case is a fraction of telephone customer service.

2. *Risk management* involves careful use of filters and disclaimers: "Few have a formal triage system laid out for which types of posts can simply adhere to some basic guidelines and go out, which ones need legal review, and what just cannot be sent" (para. 4).

3. *Content maximization* relates to leveraging conversation monitoring and content repurposing: "Stepping back and rethinking how to unlock more vectors of content and then funneling access to it to those on the front line of posting can amortize the value of content investments, and open up more ways to get engagement" (para. 5)

4. *Analytics* are important "to get ahead of the sentiment of the market" and amplify content in it: "[W]e have seen enormous value from social analytics that enable spotting new innovation ideas, building social lead flows, and testing marketing messages before going big."

(para. 6)

Because of the nature of the more subtle social media conversion process, advertising and marketing content have been adapted to blend with editorial content.

Digital native advertising, which looks like online journalism, rapidly increased at Forbes' Media, and it reached over 40% of direct revenue with profits up 42% in 2019 (Fletcher, 2016; Mickey, 2013; Willens, 2019). The Federal Trade Commission developed native advertising disclosure guidelines for clarity between editorial and paid content. A label, such as "paid advertisement" or "sponsored content," is reasonable in terms of transparency (Fletcher, 2016, para. 5). Despite the possibility of reader confusion, paid content was a popular method for generating needed revenue. David Carr, who was a reporter at *The New York Times*, prior to his death worried that native advertising might diminish the credibility of journalism because of its proximity to news content:

> Now the new rage is "native advertising," which is to say advertising wearing the uniform of journalism, mimicking the storytelling aesthetic of the host site. Buzzfeed, Forbes, The Atlantic and, more recently, *The New Yorker*, have all developed a version of native advertising, also known as sponsored content; if you are on Buzzfeed, World of Warcraft might have a sponsored post on, say, 10 reasons your virtual friends are better than your real ones.
>
> (Carr, 2013, para. 3)

Carr wrote that Wonderfactory founder Joe McCambley, one of the pioneers of banner advertising in 1994, is among those raising issues about native ads. Among the questions about sponsored content is clear disclosure through labeling for the reader. McCambley told Carr that it is a mistake for publishers to offer PR and advertising firms direct access to content management systems. *The Atlantic* made one of the earliest mistakes when it allowed the Church of Scientology to publish a sponsored story within the site's content stream. The publication quickly issued a simple apology: "We screwed up" (Stelter & Haughney, 2013, para. 1).

Online publications, anxious to grow revenue, are tempted to allow sponsored posts that may look much like editorial content – even using similar design and art standards. Forbes' online site features a mixture of content types, which may add to the confusion by diminishing traditional advertising separation from news. Forbes incubated "this whole notion of giving marketers a seat at the table" (Sebastian, 2013, para. 4). Concerns about website content, though, seemed to quiet as social media took center stage.

For example, Facebook banned an Israeli app named The Spinner for posting paid Facebook and Instagram posts that were "disguised as editorial content" designed to "subconsciously influence" targeted audiences (Nunis, 2020, para. 2). The sketchy start-up claimed to be able to "brainwash" people into losing weight, end smoking, have more sex or other behaviors (para. 6). The program spread content over months, but Facebook claimed it used "fake accounts and fake Facebook pages to 'strategically bombard' Facebook users with advertisements" (para. 9). Facebook's self-regulation of commercial speech may avoid further scrutiny by government regulators.

The US FTC (2019), however, offered disclosure guidelines for online influencers working "with brands to recommend or endorse products" (p. 2). This includes tags, likes, pins and other support. "Disclose when you have any financial, employment, personal, or family relationship with a brand" (p. 3). The FTC urged superimposing a disclosure on Snapchat and Instagram Stories photos. The use of "simple and clear" language, such as "sponsor" or "advertisement," is better than "vague or confusing terms" (p. 5). The FTC emphasized that post claiming personal "experience" or "scientific proof" must be truthful (p. 6). In this sense, the trends return us to the early issues faced with media advertising.

ADVERTISING AND MARKETING THEORIES

The advertising and marketing industries experienced explosive growth, as products were marketed through commercial mass media, such as radio and television. We are now experiencing an important online shift. As the book *Youtility* described it, consumers now expect trustworthy online information and answers: "Success flows to organizations that inform, not organizations that promote" (Baer, 2013, p. xi):

> Youtility is marketing upside down. Instead of marketing that's needed by companies, Youtility is marketing that's wanted by customers. Youtility is massively useful information, provided for free, that creates long-term trust and kinship between your company and your customers.
>
> (p. 3)

Baer (2013) related this fundamental shift to traditional marketing ideas:

- Top-of-Mind Awareness – branding through "a sustained level of marketing and messaging" that influences customers at the time of purchase.

- Frame-of-Mind Awareness – "reaching potential customers when they are in an active shopping and buying mode."

- Friend-of-Mine Awareness – "your prospective customers must consider you a friend" to compete for their time, attention and loyalty.

(pp. 17–26)

This type of "smart marketing" uses data to determine what customers want, and then it offers planning and social media strategy that attempts to account for return on investment (ROI). A solid social marketing plan must account for labor and technology costs related to social media operation, and then determine if the effort produces satisfactory results. A SWOT analysis of strengths, weaknesses, opportunities and threats frequently is followed by the identification of measurable SMART goals.

Specific – clear and specific goals can be broken down into "social channel, social tactic, or social metric."

Measurable – quantify outcomes that can be shared within an organization and beyond.

Attainable – recognize what can be changed compared to outcomes controlled by others.

Relevant – consider importance, values and impact.

Time-bound – identify outcomes that can be observed within a time after a benchmark is set.

(Sprout Social, 2019)

Social media managers may need to create a checklist that begins with an audit of existing and potential future social channels. Once created, account profiles are very important in branding and driving social commerce traffic. Planning through a social media calendar to post and monitor outcomes will help an organization to develop over time its brand voice. This may feature relevant and branded hashtags based upon broader marketing strategies, audience interests, analytics, and optimization of content (Samuels, 2019). Social media strategies and tactics should be based upon ongoing organizational strategic planning processes and long-term media monitoring that lead to benchmarking key performance indicators (KPI) that offer a return on investment (Freberg, 2019; Quesenberry, 2019). A social media audit helps benchmark how to do real-time listening, schedule posts from potentially unlimited "inventory," and track brand "health" across sites (Freberg, 2019, p. 97). Social media managers use their budget to create and maintain a "persona" that brands keywords, tagging, and other thematic "assets" over time (Quesenberry, 2019, p. 266). "Exits," for example, are one potential KPI with Instagram Stories that go beyond typical engagement measures (p. 270). Luttrell and Capizzo (2019) rely upon a set of historic planning models:

- Research, Action, Communication and Evaluation (RACE)

- Research, Objectives, Strategies and Planning, Implementation and Evaluation (ROSIE)

- Research, Objectives, Strategies, Tactics, Implementation and Reporting (ROSTIR) (pp. 10–11).

Social media managers may develop a KPI spreadsheet for benchmarking and tracking paid, earned, shared, and owned (PESO) media (pp. 18–19). The PR use of corporate social responsibility (CSR) within content goals, however, may create ethical transparency issues based upon "any hypocrisy or perception of hypocrisy" (Page & Parnell,

2019, p. 119). Management, then, returns to the broader concerns about community and employee relations programs that require special attention to accuracy, authenticity, and shared values of mutual respect. Prioritization of organizational goals, activities, and outcomes must be consistent.

Some brands also build into their efforts a crisis communication plan. The largest brands may have a concern, for example, that their Instagram use could become the next *Saturday Night Live* parody sketch (Dessem, 2019). Nevertheless, the job of a social media manager frequently is under-valued. Glassdoor in 2020 suggested that average salaries vary by location: San Francisco, $68,772; Washington, DC, $61,829; and Chicago, $49,200. Cost of living impacts pay, but these data tend to be impacted by the scarcity of applicants with available skill sets.

▢ BOX 5.1

4 P's – Product, Price, Place, and Promotion Marketing Mix

E. Jerome McCarthy, a marketing professor at Michigan State and Notre Dame, developed the often-mentioned marketing decisions first known as the 4 P's in his book *Basic Marketing: A Managerial Approach* (1960/1981). Product refers to goods, services, and support. Price is about the cost of something, including money and time. Place refers to either a point-of-sale or other contexts, such as online, geography, demographic target, or sales experience. Promotion is about advertising, publicity, and branding. The model helps companies ask the right marketing questions in development of a plan. For example, marketers want to know how a product satisfies consumer wants and needs, which features are unique to the competition, and who wants it. Pricing is a function of perceived value, profit margins, and price points. Place focuses on where consumers can find the product or service. Promotion is the P that we are interested in most when examining social media. Online conversation may be very important in terms of friends functioning as opinion leaders. Traditional marketing media may diffuse to individual influencers within social media spaces. For example, Pinterest is considered a good platform for sharing product photographs and descriptions. This may trigger sharing, questions, and even website clicks that could be converted to sales.

McCarthy (1960/1981) explored what he called a "marketing mix" within a "dynamic social and political environment" (pp. v–vi). By the seventh edition of the popular book, he viewed "social responsibility" and "consumerism" as "hot" marketing topics (p. vi). Yet, in advance of what later was called the corporate responsibility movement, McCarthy's marketing focus was on individual cognitive steps in the process: motivation, investigation, organization, and utilization (p. viii). The idea that "selling" and "advertising" were "negative" words (p. 3) cultivated an idea that we produce and consume: "Consumers and producers must continually interact" (p. 11, 13). If the four P's happen within "controllable" spaces that are "cultural" and within a "social environment" (p. 52), then marketing would need to be focused on how to "manage channels" (p. 338). The match between "target customers and media" (p. 495) was somewhat uncertain because of challenges in tracking media exposure. Marketing, then, was a promotion challenge of "informing, persuading, reminding" within a "frantically competitive" environment (p. 600). The traditional marketing view in 1981, however, could barely see the coming impact of the personal computer and electronics industry. New products were about to be introduced in very new places.

By 2013, a *Harvard Business Journal* posting urged that it was time to update the marketing mix. The **business-to-business (B2B)** model is less focused on products and more related to "the imperative to deliver solutions" (Ettenson, Conrado, & Knowles, 2013, para. 1). Research suggested that the four P's approach has three shortcomings: it leads to technology and quality, which do not differentiate; it does not emphasize enough the value of solutions; and it "distracts them from leveraging their advantage as a trusted source of diagnostics, advice, and problem solving" (para. 2). Their SAVE model shifts each of the four P's:

- Products → **Solutions**
- Place → **Access**
- Price → **Value**
- Promotion → **Education**

The SAVE marketing approach fits nicely into the social media context of talking to favorite brands for informational purposes.

Sources: Ettenson, R., Conrado, E., & Knowles, J. (January–February 2013). Rethinking the 4 P's. *Harvard Business Review*. http://hbr.org/2013/01/rethinking-the-4-ps/ McCarthy, E. J. (McCarthy, 1960/1981). *Basic Marketing: A Managerial Approach*, seventh edition. Homewood, IL: Richard D. Irwin. Mind Tools (n.d.). The Marketing Mix and 4 Ps, Understanding How to Position Your Market Offering. www.mindtools.com/pages/article/newSTR_94.htm

Beyond the 4 P's, there are other new perspectives on marketing. Kareh (2018), for example, added *people* and *process* because marketing automation emphasizes data and efficiency:

> Focusing on processes means channeling discipline … This is accomplished by utilizing insights to create win-win relationships with suppliers and partners to increase efficiency and drive down cost and by turning data delivered into recommendations that steer production toward consumer-driven goods and services that meet consumers' needs.
>
> (para. 11)

In this increasingly complex environment, marketing efforts must rely upon customer-focused employees. So-called "customer care" happens everywhere, including within social media sites. Business goals that drive consumers to action should identify boundaries of ethical behavior. Critical perspectives see what is happening across screens as feeding unlimited consumption:

> Media marketing narratives engage in materially oriented hegemonic address to consumer citizens, seeking to align and reconcile the interests of all … Our immersing in brandscapes from Coffee Bean culture to Starbucks connoisseurship may be imagined … Consumption across these familiar forms of life does not so much require our engaging in the diversified "work of culture."
>
> (Wilson, 2011, pp. 29–30)

Product branding is seen as immersing individuals in physical and virtual spaces that help define meaning for consumers. "They are not only public but private (e.g., the personal branding of the self as a subject to trust on Facebook)" (p. 117).

CONSUMER PSYCHOLOGY AND ELECTRONIC WORD-OF-MOUTH (eWOM)

The selling process typically has been structured by generating leads for sales people, who qualify a prospect and make a pitch or proposal. This also may involve a selling process that ends with closing or losing a sale. Paige Miller (2013), however, proposes that consumers follow a social media marketing customer-driven path of *finding* sites and content, *learning* through engagement and listening, *validating* information through reviews and community conversation, *using* via demonstrations or a trial, *buying* through a sales process, and *advocacy* after the purchase (p. 95). The last step is perhaps most unique to social media. Companies may announce through social media that they have a new client, or the new customer may endorse the product. A company may reward brand loyalty through a special program that has a linkage to their social media marketing communication plan. Throughout the process, social media conversation plays an important role in strengthening public perceptions of the brand.

Electronic word-of-mouth (eWOM) helps explain how mediated consumer communication "builds upon decades of traditional personal influence communication research" (Lipschultz & Smith, 2016, p. 5). Content or argument quality, source and message credibility, relevance, and other factors help explain the diffusion and adoption of eWOM (Chu & Choi, 2011; Doh & Hwang, 2009; Lu & Keng, 2014; Sandes & Urdan, 2013). Studies have linked eWOM to impressions, social comparison and message sentiment. Lu and Keng (2014) connect eWOM to cognitive dissonance and other traditional psychological concepts and constructs to explore untruthful and negative truthful messages. Social media content sharing, then, involves complex psychological and sociological engagement processes that may be related to branding.

BRANDING

Corporate brand management may be seen as a PR function of "promoting and protecting the reputation of the corporation" (Morley, 2009, p. 4). At the same time, advertising agencies see that their work is to "build a strong, distinctive, memorable brand" (Williams, 2005, p. 3). Branding is closely related to a company's purpose, or "reason for being" (p. 9). This may drive a desire to position the brand as being distinct from all others. "It means not only deciding what you are, but what you are not" (p. 10). Leaders of a "focused, engaged business" (p. 181) must determine how to execute branding through communication. In an age of social media, branding involves both purposeful online communication and also recognition of critical moments when the best choice is silence.

Branding involves a "bond," which has been described as "a powerful emotional connection" (Morley, 2009, p. 7). Social media engagement creates real-time opportunities for brand representatives to connect with the public and establish or reinforce relationships. Advertisers showed a lot of early interest in buying space on Facebook. Edwards (2013) noted that nearly all of Facebook's quarterly revenue **were** generated by advertising (para. 1), and it more than tripled in three years to more than $7 billion in 2016 and $17.6 billion in 2019 – nearly all of it from mobile ads (Constine, 2016; Statista, 2020). Facebook and Google dominate the digital advertising industry (Gjorgievska, 2016), and within social media Facebook has nearly 80% of the US social networking advertising revenue (eMarketer, 2016; Statista, 2019).

The top 200 advertisers now spend more than $100 billion per year, with top spenders shifting over time (Edwards, 2013; O'Reilly, 2015):

TABLE 5.1 *Largest Advertiser Spending*

	Corporation (2019 spending)	*2015 Rank*	*2013 Rank*
1.	**Comcast ($6.12 billion)**	Procter & Gamble	Samsung
2.	**AT&T ($5.36 billion)**	AT&T	Procter & Gamble
3.	**Amazon ($4.47 billion)**	General Motors	Microsoft
4.	**Procter & Gamble ($4.3 billion)**	Comcast	AT&T
5.	**General Motors ($3,14 billion)**	Verizon	Amazon
6.	**Disney ($3,12 billion)**	Ford	Verizon

(Continued)

TABLE 5.1 *(Continued)*

Corporation (2019 spending)	2015 Rank	2013 Rank
7. **Charter Comms. ($3.04 billion)**	American Express	Nestlé
8. **Alphabet Google ($2.96 billion)**	Fiat	Unilever
9. **American Express ($2.8 billion)**	L'Oréal	American Express
10. **Verizon ($2.68 billion)**	Disney	Walmart

Source: De Luce, I. (October 4, 2019). Ten companies that spent more than $1 billion in ads so you'd buy their products. *Business Insider.* https://www.businessinsider.com/10-biggest-advertising-spenders-in-the-us-2015-7.

The majority of the largest advertisers were technology companies. Coca-Cola, the 11th largest 2013 advertiser, also had more than 82 million Facebook fans, which was more than any other brand at the time. By 2016, the brand had more than 100 million Facebook page fans. However, growth stagnated and Samsung became a top Facebook brand with more than 156 million fans. Other leaders included McDonald's, Disney, KFC, Red Bull, and MTV. Top brands build strategies that take advantage of organic and paid social media, as well as paid advertising. These worlds are blending over time within social media.

PROMOTIONS, MARKET RESEARCH, AND SEGMENTATION

Customers use social network sites to create and distribute "brand-centric" content and media (Tuten, 2008, p. 101). Within this broad concept are several types of potential relationships with companies:

- Simple consumer-generated media is created without prior request.

- Consumer-solicited media, or participatory advertising, occurs when brands ask consumers to create, for example, their own advertisement.

- Incentivized consumer-generated media offers prizes for submissions.

- Consumer-fortified media result occurs when a professional advertisement sparks trusted consumer conversation.

- Compensated consumer-generated media is a term used to describe paid bloggers and other arrangements.

(pp. 102–103)

The various arrangements may create a more democratic form of advertising, may encourage crowdsourcing, may develop engagement, and may offer opportunities for long-term relationships. Social media are a "touchpoint" for consumers (Carter, 2019, para. 2). Sprout Social encourages social media managers to listen first, respond quickly, personalize conversations, show a human side, offer rewards, study feedback, "delight customers with something unexpected," and "embrace user-generated content" (UGC) (paras. 35–39).

INTEGRATED MARKETING COMMUNICATION (IMC)

The IMC concept addresses a need to integrate brand-marketing communication across previously separate industries of PR, advertising, and marketing. IMC is designed to take a step back from specific messaging and employ the integration of approaches to achieve strategic goals. Clow and Baack (2011) saw IMC as involving coordination of all marketing – including promotions and social media. An IMC plan, for example, might address shifting funds from traditional advertising to non-traditional media, including social media platforms. This involves more than simply having a presence on a social media site. Vaynerchuk (2013), an early promoter of social marketing, identified his rules of engagement:

> Brands and small businesses want to look relevant, engaged, and authentic, but when their content is banal and unimaginative, it only makes them look lame. Content for the sake of content is pointless. Tone-deaf posts, especially in the form of come-ons and promos, just take up space, and are justifiably ignored by the public. Only outstanding content can cut through the noise.
>
> (p. 16)

Vaynerchuk defined outstanding content as that which: 1) is native to platform; 2) does not interrupt the social media flow; 3) rarely makes demands; 4) leverages pop culture; 5) contains micro-nuggets of "information, humor, commentary, or inspiration"; and 6) stays consistent and self-aware (pp. 16–28). Within this framework, social media storytelling may resonate with viewers and sometimes spread at a viral rate. The "native to platform" idea is an extremely important social media consideration. A photograph posted on Facebook may not fit the context and moment within Instagram, which is stylized. A tweet with a Twitter handle, shortened words, and a hashtag will appear out of place on Pinterest. Likewise, Twitter feeds are a good example of a flow that changes by the moment. VaynerMedia developed a 2020 Super Bowl campaign built around the death of 104-year-old Mr. Peanut (Graham, 2020). It included social media ahead of scheduled TV advertisements before the game. Kraft Heinz Planters had launched with a "cryptic tweet" and a YouTube video that quickly received more than 1 million views of the commercial (para. 3). Mr. Peanut's television funeral was supposed to be based upon Internet reaction to other entertainment characters passing: "What would happen and how would the world react if he passed away?" (para. 8). However, following the death of basketball star Kobe Bryant, his daughter and others in a helicopter crash, Planters halted the campaign. "We are saddened by this weekend's news and Planters has paused all campaign activities, including paid media, and will evaluate next steps through a lens of sensitivity to those impacted by this tragedy" (Tucker, 2020, para. 1).

While it may be useful for a content manager to use Hootsuite or another management tool to organize social media conversations, it is crucial to recognize what is being said within a particular platform at a given time. Online engagement translates to conversation that is aware of what is happening within the culture – from Super Bowl chatter to a storm response. A social media brand manager understands her or his personal brand, company brands, and those of others. Consistent and sensitive messages help build online trust over time, which may be leveraged in the future.

SOCIAL MEDIA STRATEGIC PLANNING, AWARENESS, AND ENGAGEMENT

One important distinction between social networking site activity and social media is the role of social business models. Cha (2013) identified value creation, sources of competency, target market, and revenue as four business considerations. Value is theoretically created through successful brand positioning within the market, but branding also is considered a specific competency (p. 63). Social media engagement is created through positive interaction within a specific social media online space. For example, Twitter's real-time information positioning is different from LinkedIn's professional and job seeker target market, which typically is not as connected to a moment in time (p. 76). It is important within advertising and marketing perspectives for a team to develop social media plans that guide responses during a crisis, but also direct the general purposes and goals of ongoing engagement. Increasingly, teams employ an integrated media approach that weds PR, advertising, marketing, and general business plans. Social media sites are noisy, and it is not easy to reach consumers and make them aware of current branding. A top marketing goal is increasing brand awareness, and social media sites may be seen as "a playground for engaging with one another" and an opportunity "to engage with customers at every stage of their journey" (Mosley, 2019, para. 11).

Awareness begins with online **impressions**. An advertising buyer may bid on a sponsored search keyword that matches a user search and produces a high page ranking. This creates a consumer point of entry (Jansen, 2011, p. 77). A click-through rate (CTR) may be measured as the number of clicks divided by impressions (p. 77). In other words, advertisers are interested in how a sponsored search was observed by consumers and served as a catalyst to drive a percentage of these users to a website for possible conversion. Social media conversation is important as a means to either spark the initial search or generate traffic through the use of a direct link. CTRs appear to be in decline from the height of an era in which people searched for online content. This is being replaced by content that is pushed out across social media sites. Awareness is a cognitive processing of initial information about a product or service. Through engagement with other consumers, paid brand managers, or other representatives may increase motivation to learn more.

Google (2013) studied rapidly growing mobile media usage. In a Nielsen study, Google explored the purchase path when consumers use mobile devices, such as smartphones and tablets. The research team studied 950 people, as well as a panel of mobile users over two weeks, and found the following points to be true:

1. **Consumers spend time researching on mobile.** Consumers spend 15+ hours per week researching on their smartphone and, on average, visit mobile websites six times.

2. **Mobile research starts with a search.** More smartphone users start researching products or services on a search engine vs. a branded mobile site or app.

3. **Location proximity matters to mobile consumers.** 69% of consumers expect businesses to be within 5 miles or less of their location.

4. **Purchase immediacy is key.** Over half of consumers want to make a purchase within an hour of conducting research on their smartphone.

5. **Mobile influences purchases across channels.** 93% of people who use mobiles to research go on to purchase a product or service. Most purchases happen in physical stores.

(p. 3)

More recently, Kaushik (2020) encouraged "step change analytics," such as improving (dramatically reducing) website bounce rates to reduce cost per acquisition (paras. 5–8). Historic desire to optimize through data reflects a motivation to use continuous improvement.

The proliferation of smartphones is leading marketers to focus on the mobile path to purchase in order to strategically develop campaigns that start with a search trigger and end with purchasing at a local store or online destination. A website visit is part of the process, but not all of it. The social media component of the mobile path to purchase is an important role that consumer reviews play in the process. Google talks about consumer research, with 93% of the people in their study using mobile devices to help them decide. This is consistent with Stanford University's research findings: "As you might suspect, the research shows that a wealth of online product information and user reviews is causing a fundamental shift in how consumers make decisions" (Richtel, 2013, para. 2). Traditionally, consumers would pick a mid-priced option between three choices, but reviews now allow consumers to dig deeper in determining value. This finding has important social media implications. Research consistently has found that "not only are reviews extremely valuable in influencing a purchase decision, but a number of circumstances factor into when and how reviews shape customer value" (Spiegel, 2019, slide 4). Displayed reviews may increase conversion by as much as 270%, and variables include price, risk perception, negative reviews, and the number of reviews (slide 5). It means every consumer has the power to be an influencer through his or her reviews on sites such as Amazon and Yelp. Advertisers and marketers that engage with consumers who were likely to be reviewers have an opportunity to create positive experiences, brand loyalty and future purchasing persuasion.

SEARCH ENGINE OPTIMIZATION (SEO)

Online searches remain one of the most important methods for finding information on the Internet. While information pushed out through social media is increasingly a factor, SEO literacy skills help practitioners achieve successful reach with their messages. More people, for example, will see bloggers' content, if headlines and tags are SEO friendly. Likewise, an online press release should be optimized with the SEO words that people associate when thinking about specific ideas. A Google search begins with a person thinking about what they are looking for and then entering a word or phrase. Quickly, Google, the number one search engine, begins to suggest keywords (also identified within computer coding of a site) that are popular, and continuously changing computer algorithms that also drive the other top global sites Bing (Microsoft), Baidu, Yahoo!, and Yandex (Law, 2019). These benefit some pages over others. Website and content operators can control **search engine result placements (SERP)** (Fleischner, 2013, p. 24). "Off-page optimization" is a function of links to a page from other popular and similar pages (p. 61). Social media may positively impact SEO through profile links and rankings:

> If you have a Facebook account it likely includes links of various kinds – links to books you're reading, products and websites you recommend, and hopefully links back to your websites and blogs. By the very nature of Facebook, it carries tremendous authority. If you are linking to your own website, it passes that authority back to you.
>
> (p. 120)

Beyond links, social media activity – likes, favorites, comments, etc. – may be influential. Google property YouTube, for example, is an important social media site for practicing great SEO. Through keywords and links, video offers access to "one of the largest sources of traffic on the planet" (Fleischner, 2013, p. 123).

Kaushik (2010) offered a comprehensive model for understanding SEO. He uses clickstream data, multiple outcomes analysis, and experimentation and testing to focus massive consumer data into usable customer information (p. 7). Customer voice, competitive intelligence, and insights help businesses understand why products are purchased or not:

> The degree of positive or negative engagement lies on a continuum that ranges from low involvement, namely, the psychological state of apathy, to high. An engaged person is someone with an above-average involvement … Customers can be positively or negatively engaged with a company or product.
>
> (p. 57)

Kaushik (2010) viewed this involvement as connected to "emotional states and rational beliefs" (p. 57). One can easily see how social media conversation, with its use of trust, may elevate or lower involvement. For example, a company post might express pride in winning an award, and this may be connected to an increase in trust levels. Likewise, a company representative engaging with a complaining customer might express sympathy and offer to correct the problem.

Google has an approved set of strategies to improve a page rank, and this is referred to as "white hat SEO" (Williams, 2013, p. 7). There also are "black hat" SEO strategies, such as "on-page keyword stuffing to backlinking blasts using software" (p. 7). Google and other search engines seek to point users to trusted sites, whether or not high search rankings are a function of payment. An historically trusted site has a lot of positive

SEO, and search engine algorithms allow for some negative SEO that would label a new site as spam. Social media interaction is an important way to generate positive conversation: "if they ask a question, make sure you answer it as this starts a dialogue with your target audience and builds trust and authority" (p. 87). Google Analytics offers free online courses and certification in the ever-changing world of search algorithms. Of particular interest is how traffic flows across the Web and social media sites. For example, Google Analytics can be used to track organic traffic and paid traffic from a Facebook fan page link to a business website. The Google Analytics dashboard provides a simple overview of site sessions and users, page viewers, and time at specific pages. Typically, active users are tracked over 30-day periods. Demographics, interests, geo-location, the technology used, and other behaviors may be important. Tools allow for benchmarking site data over time.

RETURN ON INVESTMENT (ROI)

Most of what we call advertising and marketing is predicated on the goal of converting consumers into customers of products or services. The consumer process may begin with an online search that leads to social media engagement. The use of a search engine, such as Google, involves entry of a "term" that may be linked to a "keyword," an advertisement or a "sponsored-search result" (Jansen, 2011, p. xviii). For businesses, ROI measurement is related to the use of online platforms for generated leads and conversions to sales:

> The objective of the advertiser is to find the "sweet spot" of terms that will generate significant volumes of convertible traffic. This set of keywords is advertiser-dependent. This selection can generally be done through concentration of a few keywords in the head, a lot of terms in the tail, or a combination of both.
>
> (p. 55)

ROI can be achieved through the alignment of social media terms used with advertising and marketing website keywords. In order to be effective, these keywords must surface in specific screen locations identified through "eye-tracking patterns" research (p. 72). In general, paid searches were most effective when they appear at the top of a page or on the left side of it. These were hot areas of screen viewers for those using languages that read left to right, such as in the United States.

There is an ongoing debate about whether or not ROI can or should be computed for social media activities. Initially, there was an interest in justifying social media to the C-suite managers who did not understand it by making an ROI argument. ROI social media measures, though, tended to be secondary and indirect. Some have focused on clear social media benefits: "the new metrics evaluate social media strategies in terms of audience-building, brand awareness and customer relations" (Heggestuen, 2013, para. 3). Marketers moved away from revenue per customer metrics, at the same time as they increased social media budgets. From this perspective, "audience reach, engagement, and sentiment" are most important (para. 9). A Facebook friend's share, for example, is more likely to be seen in news feeds (29–35%) than brand pages (para. 10). According to *Business Insider*, "Post reach is the most fundamental indicator of reach on Facebook, but it's important to track it relative to the number of page fans and enrich it with complementary indicators" (para. 12). Fans and likes alone are seen as "feel good" or "vanity measures" that do not reflect a meaningful marketing context (para. 16). Social media probably have more in common with traditional personal influence than advertising or marketing impact. Still, advertising media buyers now seek to develop integrated marketing campaigns in which social media components reinforce other messages. Marketers want to be able to pinpoint how a campaign produces the conversion of customer sales. Additionally, new **enterprise** business tools are being developed to provide sales teams with secure environments for updating product information and improving customer relations (Rekdal, 2017). Two areas of interest are an efficient use of "content in engaging with customers" and "advanced permissions, tracking, encryption and forensic watermarks" to keep marketing videos private until release (paras. 6–7). At the same time, social media have the potential to spark negative sentiment within social network conversations. Brand managers must tune in on regular and systematic conversation monitoring and engagement in order to avoid missing important moments of influence.

COST OF IGNORING (COI)

MacLean (2013) identified the cost of ignoring (COI) as a measurement of "social shyness" (para. 2). Companies need to respond to those consumers and customers using social media to communicate. Therefore, social listening and engagement is a very important strategy for customer service, reputation management, crowdsourcing, collaboration, and recruitment (para. 5–9). Engagement may drive customer loyalty and help manage any negative sentiment being expressed by consumers. By being a part of social media communities while not in an advertising or marketing mode, it is possible to build credibility that may be important to use later. This is what industry professional Randa Zalman (@RandaZalman) calls ROR – return on relationship. Social media help personal and corporate brands cultivate meaningful relationships over time.

Before beginning a social media marketing campaign, there are at least 12 considerations:

1. Define campaign goals for specific actions.

2. Use numbers to define and measure success.

3. Focus one platform at a time.

4. Create a social media mission statement, and write all expectations.

5. Use visuals because they drive nearly all Facebook engagement, and help on other sites.

6. Use Google Analytics and other tools to monitor the campaign.

7. Use a social media management tool.

8. Profile an ideal customer.

9. Audit social presence on all sites.

10. Use metrics as success indicators.

11. Test ideas on Twitter.

12. Create and curate highly engaging content (Crawford, 2016).

This overview of social media planning is related to social media marketing trends: live-streaming video, buy and shop now buttons, the establishment of customer data trust, and use of messaging apps (Brychta, 2016). Recognize that professional development is key to keeping up with these ongoing changes in social media marketing strategies and best practices.

ADVERTISING AND MARKETING CASE STUDIES

The University of Chicago, within the south side neighborhood of Hyde Park, was a bit of a food desert with few stores and restaurants until recently. Food truck vendors saw opportunities for driving onto campus and offering students, faculty, and staff a variety of selections from convenient locations. These changed from day to day, so the food trucks used Twitter and other social media to identify daily locations and cuisines.

> @BridgeportPasty1m: UofC, you get to see us again for our scheduled day, you lucky dogs! Try the new Gobbler AND Broccoli and Cheese soup while they last. Yum! (November 13, 2013)

> @taquerofusion54m: #HydePark (58th & Ellis) We'll be in your area by 11 am!! Come and get your #HumpDay Taco on! @UChicago @uchiNOMgo. (January 30, 2013)

REAL-TIME SOCIAL MARKETING

Social media marketing frequently happens in real-time without much of a delay between the time of an initial conversation and commercial response. Mobile smartphones position a consumer at a specific location within a specific amount of time. Applications such as FourSquare encouraged users to check-in at a business for access to specials and coupons, and Facebook later recognized the importance of location. Mobile apps, such as Yelp, offer consumer reviews of nearby restaurants and other local businesses. Customer loyalty programs can take advantage of communication tools by literally reaching out to nearby customers with new offers. Macy and Thompson (2011) connected real-time social marketing to a system of **customer relationship management** that includes customer satisfaction, loyalty, and retention (pp. 40–41). "When marketers approach social media as a viable business intelligence platform, they often get unexpected insights into consumer opinions and shared experiences" (p. 58).

Wendy's turned fast-food marketing on its head with a campaign designed to shift the focus away from issues often associated with consuming unhealthy food. The pretzel

FIGURE 5.1 *Downtown Toronto, Ontario Canada food trucks are popular. @foodtrucksTO launched in 2011 and has about 43,000 followers on Twitter. The site shows food photos #Toronto. Photo by Jeremy Harris Lipschultz, August 2019. In recent years, the number of food trucks grew nationally at about 8% per year. Portland, Oregon, and Austin, Texas, were among the most popular cities in the more than $1 billion industry. The mobile trucks continue to use social media for posting location and menu items. Pop-up shops and stores similarly use social media to promote events (Score, 2019).*

pub chicken sandwich was promoted using overly dramatic soap opera YouTube videos that were produced based on tweets that used the #PretzelLoveStories hashtag, such as:

> @Cborbzz3: You caught my eye, your scent made me float, you make my mouth salivate. I miss you. #PretzelLoveStories.
>
> (July 8, 2013)

The user-generated content featured humor that engaged the audience and potential customers. Wendy's initiated the campaign with two videos – one about a love triangle and the other with a woman behind bars. The result was positive social media across platforms. On Facebook, for example, a video was shared more than 2,000 times and liked more than 12,000 times. The use of crowdsourcing for video content development was a unique way to utilize engagement. At the same time, though, some complained about not knowing that the hashtag was related to a Wendy's sandwich promotion.

The successful social media campaign also opened the door to brand confusion, as some users tweeted about other pretzel brands. Edgy tweets continue to be the norm for most other fast-food brands, such as this post and replies:

@PopeyesChicken: Coming over with Popeyes #SeduceSomeoneInFourWords.

(January 17, 2020)

@jexkax: I want that thigh!!!

(January 17, 2020)

@SweetnessOMG87: My mouth wants You!

(January 17, 2020)

It is less understood that social media marketing campaigns now extend to non-profit strategy. Branding and customer loyalty are no less important in this sector.

⟨⟨ᵗ⟩⟩ BOX 5.2

Thought Leader Robert Moore

Before the advent of social media, institutions had the opportunity to be more considered and/or deliberate in how they addressed their stakeholders or the public-at-large. While there might have been rumors or word-of-mouth concerns about certain actions of the institution, these were circulated relatively "locally" among existing communities, alumni groups, or other interested observers. With Twitter, Snapchat, Instagram, and other immediate-response platforms, that has entirely changed. "News" now breaks on a social media platform – entirely unedited or un-curated or, at times, untrue – and can spread like wildfire. As a result, the institution has to balance

FIGURE 5.2 *@LipmanHearne.*
Courtesy of Lipman Hearne

on a knife-edge of conflicting responsibilities: the need for transparency and engagement with its concerned stakeholders, and the need to actually be sure of what's going on before responding – which isn't always easy. In an era when an immediacy of response is expected, silence can be seen as consent or passive agreement, and a lack of instant response is often interpreted as an admission of guilt. This also brings up the issue of "who speaks for the institution" and whether or not a staff member tweeting on his/her feed is authorized to be the transmitter of official information or if the tweets are strictly personal.

Institutions must stay current and integrate traditional (print, earned media, print, and out-of-home advertising, etc.) and emerging media in strong, effective programs that build upon each other in order to capitalize on the strength and potential of each medium or channel – rather than cannibalizing one to feed the other or having it all run amok. And, as is often the case in higher education, having to manage all of these emerging media without significant additional staff, new training investments, new technology, and other resources remains and will remain a real problem.

"Engagement management" is going to be a big issue moving forward: the training and deployment of communications professionals who can understand, integrate, and utilize the complex opportunities that traditional and emerging media offer in terms of outreach, behavioral tracking, analytics, program design, and refinement for timely and effective response, budget allocation, and the like. Professionals trained or experienced in more traditional media will have to learn the new realities, and digital communicators will have to understand and deploy the "tried and true" methods that still work with many stakeholder audiences. To date, training and professional development tend to go down these two separate paths; in the future, the integration will be absolutely necessary.

Robert Moore, Ph.D. is Senior Consultant and CEO emeritus at Lipman Hearne – a firm that acts as a marketing partner for visionary organizations. He is a nationally recognized authority on non-profit branding and effective marketing practices in higher education. Moore has more than 30 years of experience providing marketing counsel and creative services for non-profit organizations and has written two books on higher education marketing – both published by CASE. Outside of the academe, his clients have included the Ford Foundation, Mayo Clinic and others. His doctorate is in English from the University of Illinois at Chicago.

During the earliest social media communication era, numerous companies struggled to use the new form of branding. Miller (2013) reported on KFC's use of #IatetheBones – a Twitter campaign that continued to produce negative sentiment. In attempting to raise awareness about its new boneless chicken brand, KFC's hashtag led to "sharing memes of people choking on chicken bones, or Hannibal Lecter" (para. 7). Apparently, neither KFC nor its agency predicted that the brand would be associated with the cannibalistic killer featured in the film *The Silence of the Lambs*.

At about the same time, social media erupted over the automaker Hyundai's use of a failed suicide attempt in a video designed to say its emissions are clean (Brockwell, 2013). It sparked an open letter from a woman whose father had died in a similar suicide:

> Surprisingly, when I reached the conclusion of your video, where we see that the man has in fact *not* died thanks to Hyundai's clean emissions, I did not stop crying. I did not suddenly feel that my tears were justified by your amusing message. I just felt empty. And sick. And I wanted my dad.
>
> (para. 7)

The competition for attention within social media in some cases has led advertisers and marketers to ignore the risks associated with edgy content. In a digital world in which everyone has a platform to respond, more than ever creative teams must be able to predict all possible responses. Among social media failures over the years:

- The drink @sunnydelight acted as a depressed person and appeared to make fun of mental illnesses when it tweeted: "I can't do this anymore." (February 3, 2019)

- @DCComics posted a photo it said was translated from Pakistan instead of the Urdu language, and fans responded that, "Here's why @Marvel is winning ..." (January 4, 2016).

- @Gap tweeted, following Hurricane Sandy, "All impacted by #Sandy stay safe! We'll be doing lots of Gap.com shopping today. How about you?" The company removed the tweet following a negative reaction (Fiegerman, 2012).

Clearly, some of the largest brands ran into trouble for a variety of reasons – poor advertising content, unsupervised content managers, weak editing for real-time processes, and even hacked accounts. It appeared that brands were learning through trial and error to be careful within social media.

A case can be made that all digital marketing departs from traditional forms, and social media magnify the differences. Greg Satell (@Digitaltonto, 2013) contrasted the traditional purchase funnel: "Awareness → Opinion → Consideration → Preference → Purchase

... with a triangular visualization of Awareness, Advocacy and Sales" (para. 8). Within it, consideration and loyalty flow. The non-linear continuum should lead marketers to "shift from grabbing attention to holding attention" (para. 10). The idea is to create a valuable exchange between the brand and the consumer. For example, the Nike+ community page tells users which Facebook friends have joined, and shares competitive training data across social networks.

Richards and Yakob (2007) were among the first to recognize that consumers began to see traditional advertising as an interruption:

> Today, in response to an aversion to advertising, some of the world's leading brands have begun to craft an entirely new model for communications to help them earn the right to talk to consumers. They're doing this by making their marketing valuable, developing brand communications that deliver a genuine service value to consumers, free and with no strings attached.
>
> (para. 4)

Social media fit nicely into the marketing shift toward creating valuable consumer services – so valuable that people want to share positive experiences with connections on their social networks. The early skepticism about the effectiveness of social media marketing was replaced with an understanding that "social networks have a 'huge indirect influence' on shopping decisions by building brand and product awareness" (Fiegerman, 2013, para. 3), as well as growing direct impact on sales. Adobe Digital Insights reported that Cyber Monday sales grew more than 12% in 2016, and then nearly tripled in 2019 to $9.4 billion (Gustafson, 2016, para. 2; Klebnikov, 2019). Social marketers improved customer tracking methods to attribute sales traffic to search, social media, email and other sources.

There continue to be calls to reform social media advertising fundamentals. After Twitter banned political candidate advertising, there was pressure on Facebook to do the same. The Twitter policy change did not impact political action committees or others influencing elections. Among the most salient concerns are: "microtargeting," the need for fact-checks, unlimited reach, and disruption of the traditional regulation "in the time leading up to an election" (Gillespie, 2019, para. 4). Britain's Conservative Party, for example, changed its Twitter account name to "factcheckUK" during a television debate: "The renaming made the account look like a neutral fact-checker, raising new concerns about all the creative ways groups and individuals can use social media to deceive voters" (Ortutay, 2019, para. 3). Businessman Mike Bloomberg, former New York mayor and presidential candidate (@Mike2020), even attempted to collaborate with the @ElBloombito parody Twitter account of his weak humorous attempts (Gallucci, 2020). Twitter temporarily suspended El Bloombito without explanation.

It also was not clear how Twitter would define political advertising, or how Facebook's fact-checking would work during future elections. The challenge is balancing access to political information against the threat of voter manipulation. Voters were targeted in traditional TV advertising, but social media precision strikes at undecided voters in swing states makes the practice more effective and potentially dangerous. Facebook sought to push responsibility to be informed back to voters, but some worry it is too easy to mislead some with sophisticated posts that lack transparency and honesty. Given the breadth of global Internet freedom, it may be too late to limit the increasing power of social media communication through government regulation, but US House Speaker Nancy Pelosi has called Facebook "shameful" and "very irresponsible" (Eadicicco, 2020, para. 1). In the face of public criticism, Facebook halted plans to include advertising within WhatsApp (Sapra, 2020).

Kevin Shively (@kevinsaysthings, 2015) at Simply Measured noted that social media marketing budgets continue to dramatically grow, as there is value in direct reach to billions of users. "Social media teams have three distinct goals: Centralized strategy and planning, direction tied to business goals, and dedicated tactical execution" (p. 6). Social businesses growth spike may be related to the launch of Facebook and Twitter advertising and greater awareness of digital value. Survey data indicate that social business is about seeking brand awareness, website traffic growth, share of audience voice, generation of leads, and customer service (p. 15). Shively and co-author Lucy Hitz (@LLHitz) later found that, although social media are *the* marketing channel to more than 2 billion users, "much of that potential is untapped" (Shively & Hitz, 2016, p. 2). The focus on social media is within two-thirds of marketing departments, but less than one in ten say they are able to quantify the ROI from social revenues: "76.5% of marketers say they aren't getting the budget they need to do their best work, and 43% cite analytics software as their biggest need" (p. 5). At a time when marketers routinely used Facebook, Instagram, and Twitter, the title of "social media manager" continued to grow in importance (p. 8) – yet nearly half (46.3%) of all teams had just one person, and more than two-thirds (68%) had two (p. 9). At the same time, Sprout Social data more than one-third of larger organizations have 11 or more social team members (Platt, 2019). Engagement metrics (likes, shares, and comments) are more than twice as common as conversion and revenue metrics (web traffic conversions), and more than three times as likely as brand awareness and amplification measures (p. 11). An overall social media marketing model has emerged: "Awareness → Consideration → Decision → Adoption → Advocacy" (p. 12).

At the heart of the consumer process seems to be a new form of social influence:

> Social media is where consumers are having conversations today, and one of the most impactful byproducts to emerge is that of influencer marketing. Now, influencer marketing is part of the everyday marketing mix. At a high level, it is a form of branded engagement where marketers connect with those who boast prominent social footprints. The goal is to plug into new communities and connect the brand/product to new audiences through the voice and trusted relationships of said influencer.
>
> (p. 3)

Marketers have come to see that friends and family are more influential on some topics, but celebrities with huge social media followings also may exert tremendous influence over behaviors. For example, in the marketing field itself, there are social networks of top influencers and brands (Fields, 2016). Marketers began to use new automated technologies to leverage big data and develop models that predict consumer behavior (Lockhorn, 2016). This was facilitated by and also made more complex because of the diffusion of "Internet of Things" (IoT) devices – from drones to the "connected home" (Heater, 2016, para. 4). Each January, the annual Consumer Electronics Show reveals new ways to keep homes, automobiles, and their owners connected. Virtual and augmented reality devices present new opportunities to reach customers, as they also present marketing data challenges. On Twitter during the 2020 Consumer Electronics Show, the top hashtags included #ai, #iot, #robotics, and #5g (NodeXL, 2020).

The bottom line in social media marketing is developing a program with an eye toward generating new leads and sales, whether or not there is an immediate ROI (Baer, 2013). Social interaction requires patience. "That doesn't mean it will, or should, take you multiple years to start seeing return on your useful marketing, but recognize that you are planting seeds that will bloom in time, not necessarily overnight" (p. 184). Development of blog content as a marketing vehicle, for example, may have some links back to a commercial website, but not too many. "These blogs should add value and be high quality ... and post unique information" (Williams, 2013, p. 64). Authenticity of branding is built upon the role of quality content in developing reputation and relationships (Morley, 2009, p. 204). All industries interact with audiences through content presented within media networks (Ognyanova & Monge, 2013). "In a new media landscape characterized by networked production, networked distribution and networked consumption, relational thinking should be an essential aspect" (p. 85). Contextual social media should yield positive outcomes for advertisers and marketers. Cultural ideologies, "generally associated with the deep-rooted beliefs and values that characterize a culture and endorse a particular worldview," are "those core views" and understandings that bind a society together in support or "without fierce resistance" (Kelso, 2019, p. 120). The Western definition and spread of commercial values, however, is being challenged and redefined around the world (Hanitzsch, Hanusch, Ramaprasad & de Beer, 2019). Social media clearly are central to democratization and related forms of capitalism (Mohammad, 2020). US models of marketing technologies defined the first few digital decades, but this is likely to evolve over time. Creativity remains central to social media storytelling, such as when Panera Bread hired the character "Phyllis" from the popular NBC and Netflix TV show The Office to respond to customer complaints over dropping French onion soup (Wohl, 2020):

> Rather than simply responding to fans' comments on social media (it did that as well), Panera ... released an online video showing Phyllis Smith, the actress who played Phyllis on the U.S. series, reading the mean tweets from a desk at Panera's St. Louis headquarters. The chain took a social media listening exercise and turned it into more of a marketing effort.
>
> (para. 3)

In 2020, social media marketing is rapidly changing. Neil Patel (2019) suggested that planning needs to move beyond Website Google Analytics, and dig deeper into data, including increased use of voice in search. Consumers' path to purchase, or what marketers call conversion, is complex. It may include last-minute decisions to respond to an "upsell," and buy a more expensive product. In a world of increased automation, branding will be more important than ever, as will be marketing that understands buyers at a personal level. Social media data offer marketers a targeted profile of consumers, and this is why online sales at sites such as Amazon have skyrocketed. During the next few years, there will be more competition for attention across paid and organic social media content.

DISCUSSION QUESTIONS: STRATEGIES AND TACTICS

1. How can we better understand relationships consumers have with brands through social media sites? What are the most important benefits and constraints within these interactions?

2. What risks may exist for brands using native advertising and sponsored content to drive media exposure within contexts that appear similar to traditional news stories?

3. How can brands leverage the importance of social media interaction with consumers to grow product sales through indirect effects from ongoing online communication?

4. What is the likelihood that nations will move to regulate advertising? What are the forces for and against regulation?

REFERENCES

Baer, J. (2013). *Youtility, Why Smart Marketing is about Hype Not Help*. New York, NY: Penguin Group.

Brockwell, H. (2013, April 25). An Open Letter to Hyundai. *Slate*. www.slate.com/blogs/browbeat/2013/04/25/hyundai_suicide_ad_an_ad_exec_responds_with_memories_of_her_father.html

Brychta, B. (2016, March 16). 4 Social Media Marketing Trends that Won't Go Away. *PR Daily*. www.prdaily.com/Main/Articles/4_social_media_marketing_trends_that_wont_go_away_20346.aspx

Carr, D. (2013, September 15). The Media Equation: Storytelling Ads May Be Journalism's New Peril. *The New York Times*, B1 (September 16). www.nytimes.com/2013/09/16/business/media/storytelling-ads-may-be-journalisms-new-peril.html

Carter, R. (2019, February 26). 8 Tips to Build Customer Relationships with Social Media. *Sprout Social*. https://sproutsocial.com/insights/build-customer-relationships/

Cha, J. (2013). Business Models of Most-visited U.S. Social Networking Sites. In A. B. Albarran (Ed.), *The Social Media Industries*, pp. 60–85. New York, NY: Routledge.

Chu, S. C., & Choi, S. M. (2011). Electronic Word-of-Mouth in Social Networking Sites: A Cross-Cultural Study of the United States and China. *Journal of Global Marketing* 24(1), 263–281.

Clow, K. E., & Baack, D. (2011). *Integrated Advertising, Promotion and Marketing Communications*, fifth edition. Boston, MA: Prentice Hall.

Constine, J. (2016, November 2). Facebook Scores Big in Q3 Earnings: $7.01B Revenue and 1.79B Users. *TechCrunch*. https://techcrunch.com/2016/11/02/facebook-earnings-q3-2016/

Crawford, C. (2016, August 3). 12 Things to Consider before Starting a Social Media Marketing Campaign. *Social Media Today*. www.socialmediatoday.com/marketing/12-things-consider-starting-social-media-marketing-campaign

Dessem, M. (2019, November 17). Watch the *Saturday Night Live* Sketch that Ruined the Official Sara Lee Instagram Account. *Slate*. https://slate.com/culture/2019/11/harry-styles-snl-sara-lee-instagram-bowen-yang-cecily-strong-julio-torres.html

Doh, S. J., & Hwang, J.-S. (2009). How Consumers Evaluate eWOM (Electronic Word-of-Mouth) Messages. *Cyberpsychology & Behavior 12*(2), 193–197.

Eadicicco, L. (2020, January 18). Nanci Pelosi Slams Facebook, Calling the Tech Giant 'Shameful' and 'Very Irresponsible.' *Business Insider*. www.businessinsider.com/nancy-pelosi-slams-facebook-mark-zuckerberg-video-2020-1

Edelman, D. (2013, October 30). Say Hi to the Social Media Elephant in the Room. *LinkedIn*. www.linkedin.com/today/post/article/20131030130324-1816165-say-hi-to-the-social-media-elephant-in-the-room

Edwards, J. (2013, November 28). These are the 35 Biggest Advertisers on Facebook. *Business Insider*. www.businessinsider.com/top-advertisers-on-facebook-2013-11#ixzz2mKOsoSGf

eMarketer (2016, July 25). Facebook Gets Strong Majority of World's Social Ad Spending. *eMarketer*. www.emarketer.com/Article/Facebook-Gets-Strong-Majority-of-Worlds-Social-Ad-Spending/1014252

Ettenson, R., Conrado, E., & Knowles, J. (2013, January-February). Rethinking the 4 P's. *Harvard Business Review*. http://hbr.org/2013/01/rethinking-the-4-ps/

Fiegerman, S. (2012, November 25). 11 Biggest Social Media Disasters of 2012. *Mashable*. http://mashable.com/2012/11/25/social-media-business-disasters-2012/

Fiegerman, S. (2013, November 30). Social Media Drove Just 1% of Black Friday Online Sales. *Mashable*. http://mashable.com/2013/11/30/black-friday-statistics/

Fields, J. (2016, June 29). Content Marketing 2016: Top 100 Influencers and Brands. *Onalytica*. www.onalytica.com/blog/posts/content-marketing-top-100-influencers-and-brands/

Fleischner, M. H. (2013). *SEO Made Simple, Strategies for Dominating the World's Largest Search Engine*, third edition. Lexington, KY: Michael H. Fleischner.

Fletcher, P. (2016, November 30). Native Advertising Will Provide A Quarter of News Media Revenue by 2018. *Forbes*. www.forbes.com/sites/paulfletcher/2016/11/30/native-advertising-will-provide-a-quarter-of-news-media-revenue-by-2018/

Freberg, K. (2019). *Social Media for Strategic Communication, Creative Strategies and Research-Based Applications*. Los Angeles: SAGE.

FTC. (2019). Disclosure 101 for Social Media Influences. *Federal Trade Commission*. www.ftc.gov/system/files/documents/plain-language/1001a-influencer-guide-508_1.pdf

Gallucci, N. (2020, January 18). Bloomberg's Campaign Tried to Work with the El Bloombito Parody Account but Got Shut Down. *Mashable*. https://mashable.com/article/mike-bloomberg-el-bloombito-parody-twitter-account/

Gillespie, T. (2019, November 15). We Need to Fix Online Advertising. All of It. *Slate*. https://slate.com/technology/2019/11/twitter-political-ad-ban-online-advertising.html

Gjorgievska, A. (2016, April 21). Google and Facebook Lead Digital Ad Industry to Revenue Record. *Bloomberg*. www.bloomberg.com/news/articles/2016-04-22/google-and-facebook-lead-digital-ad-industry-to-revenue-record

Goldmacher, S., & Bui, Q. (2019, October 14). Biden Goes Old. Sanders Goes Young. Warren is in Between. What Facebook Ads Reveal about 2020. *The New York Times*. https://www.nytimes.com/interactive/2019/10/14/us/politics/democrats-political-facebook-ads.html

Google. (2013, November). Mobile Path to Purchase, Five Key Findings. *Google Insights*. www.google.com/think/research-studies/mobile-path-to-purchase-5-key-findings.html

Graham, M. (2020, January 23). Why Planters Killed Off Mr. Peanut. *CNBC*. www.cnbc.com/2020/01/23/planters-ad-agency-vaynermedia-explains-why-they-killed-off-mr-peanut.html

Gustafson, K. (2016, November 29). Online Sales Hit Another Record on Cyber Monday, as Shoppers Continue Gobbling up Deals. *CNBC*. www.cnbc.com/2016/11/29/online-sales-hit-another-record-on-cyber-monday-as-shoppers-continue-gobbling-up-deals.html

Hanitzsch, T., Hanusch, F., Ramaprasad, J., & DeBeer, A. S. (Eds.) (2019). *Worlds of Journalism, Journalistic Cultures around the Globe*. New York: Columbia University Press.

Heater, B. (2016, December 21). What to Expect from CES 2017. *Tech Crunch*. https://techcrunch.com/2016/12/21/ces-2017/

Heggestuen, J. (2013, October 22). The Death of Social ROI – Companies are Starting to Drop the Idea that They Can Track Social Media's Dollar Value. www.businessinsider.com/the-myth-of-social-roi-2013-10

Jansen, J. (2011). *Understanding Sponsored Search, Core Elements of Keyword Advertising*. New York, NY: Cambridge University Press.

Kareh, A. (2018, January 3). Evolution of the Four Ps: Revisiting the Marketing Mix. www.forbes.com/sites/forbesagencycouncil/2018/01/03/evolution-of-the-four-ps-revisiting-the-marketing-mix/#41d8c6a11200

Katz, H. (2007). *The Media Handbook*, third edition. Mahwah, NJ: Lawrence Erlbaum.

Kaushik, A. (2010). *Web Analytics 2.0, The Art of Online Accountability & Science of Customer Centricity*. Indianapolis, IN: Wiley.

Kaushik, A. (2020, January 7). Deliver Step Change Impact: Marketing and Analytics Obsessions. *Occam's Razor*. www.kaushik.net/avinash/top-ten-profitable-marketing-analytics-obsessions/

Kelley, L. D., Jugenheimer, D. W., & Sheehan, K. B. (2012). *Advertising Media Workbook and Sourcebook*, third edition. Armonk, NY: M. E. Sharpe.

Kelso, T. (2019). *The Social Impact of Advertising*. Lanham, MD: Rowman & Littlefield.

Klebnikov, S. (2019, December 3). Cyber Monday 2019 by the Numbers: A Record $9.4 Billion Haul. *Forbes*. www.forbes.com/sites/sergeiklebnikov/2019/12/03/cyber-monday-2019-by-the-numbers-a-record-94-billion-haul/#5d6168982ef0

Law, T. J. (2019, March 12). Meet the Top 10 Search Engines in the World in 2019. *Oberlo*. www.oberlo.com/blog/top-search-engines-world

Lipschultz, J. H., & Smith, M. A. (2016). Social Media Engagement: Advertising Practices, Measurement, Issues, and Constraints. In R. E. Brown, V. K. Jones, and M. Wang (Eds.), *The New Advertising: Branding, Content, and Consumer Relationships in the Data-Driven Social Media Era, Volume Two – New Media, New Uses, New Metrics*, pp. 3–28. Santa Barbara, CA: Praeger.

Lockhorn, J. (2016, March 6). The Next Imperative for Brands: Predicting Consumers' Needs. www.forbes.com/sites/onmarketing/2016/03/06/the-next-imperative-for-brands-predicting-consumers-needs/

Lu, Y. L., & Keng, C.-J. (2014). Cognitive Dissonance, Social Comparison, and Disseminating Untruthful or Negative Truthful eWOM Messages. *Social Behavior and Personality* 42(6), 979–994.

Luttrell, R. M., & Capizzo, L. W. (2019). *Public Relations Campaigns, An Integrated Approach*. Los Angeles: SAGE.

MacLean, H. (2013, May 28). The Cost of Ignoring Social Media. *Salesforce Marketing Cloud Blog*. www.salesforcemarketingcloud.com/blog/2013/05/cost-of-ignoring-social-media/

Macy, B., & Thompson, T. (2011). *The Power of Real-Time Social Media Marketing*. New York, NY: McGraw-Hill.

McCarthy, E. J. (1960/1981). *Basic Marketing: A Managerial Approach*, seventh edition. Homewood, IL: Richard D. Irwin.

Mickey, B. (2013, October 10). Forbes BrandVoice Accounts for 20 Percent of Total Revenue. www.foliomag.com/2013/forbes-brandvoice-accounts-20-percent-total-advertising-revenue#.UmE4cJTwKeu.

Miller, P. (2013). Social Media Marketing. In A. B. Albarran (Ed.), *The Social Media Industries*, pp. 86–104. New York, NY: Routledge.

Mind Tools. (n.d.). The Marketing Mix and 4 Ps, Understanding How to Position Your Market Offering. www.mindtools.com/pages/article/newSTR_94.htm

Mohammad, M. (2020). *Social Media and Democratization in Iraqi Kurdistan.* Lanham, MD: Lexington Books.

Morley, M. (2009). *The Global Corporate Brand Book.* New York, NY: Palgrave Macmillan.

Mosley, M. (2019, February 4). How Social Media Increases Brand Awareness. *Business 2 Community.* www.business2community.com/social-media/how-social-media-increases-brand-awareness-02165638

NodeXL. (2020, January 12). #CES2020. *Social Media Research Foundation.* http://nodexlgraph-gallery.org/Pages/Graph.aspx?graphID=219968

Nunis, V. (2020, January 19). Facebook Blocks the Spinner's 'Brainwashing' Technique. *BBC News.* www.bbc.com/news/technology-51134738

O'Reilly, L. (2015, July 6). These are the 10 Companies that Spend the Most on Advertising. *Business Insider.* www.businessinsider.com/10-biggest-advertising-spenders-in-the-us-2015-7/#4-comcast-corporation-ad-spend-down-17-to-3-billion-for-comcast-2014-was-a-year-marred-with-criticism-of-its-customer-service-nevertheless-the-company-still-spent-big-on-ads-in-2014-including-its-star-trek-themed-super-bowl-spot-7

Ognyanova, K., & Monge, P. (2013). A Multitheoretical, Multilevel, Multidimensional Network Model of the Media System. In E. L. Cohen (Ed.), *Communication Yearbook 37*, pp. 67–93. New York, NY: Routledge.

Ortutay, B. (2019, November 20). Phony 'Fact Check' Account On Twitter Raises New Concerns. *Associated Press.* https://apnews.com/6d007bd571024031a327cec509242037

Page, J. T., & Parnell, L. J. (2019). *Introduction to Strategic Public Relations: Digital, Global, and Socially Responsible Communication.* Los Angeles: SAGE.

Patel, N. (2019, November). Marketing Trends for 2020: Here's What Will Happen that Nobody Is Talking About. *Blog.* https://neilpatel.com/blog/marketing-trends/

Platt, R. (2019, August 9). Social Media Team Size. *Social Media Network.* https://socialmedia.mayoclinic.org/discussion/social-media-team-sizes-vs-org-size/

Quesenberry, K. A. (2019). *Social Media Strategy: Marketing, Advertising and Public Relations in the Consumer Revolution*, second edition. Lanham, MD: Rowman & Littlefield.

Rekdal, A. (2017, January 4). Mediafly Scores $10M for up to 30 New Hires. *Built In Chicago.* www.builtinchicago.org/2017/01/04/mediafly-10m-funding

Richards, B., & Yakob, F. (2007, March 19). The New Quid Pro Quo. *Adweek.* www.adweek.com/news/advertising/new-quid-pro-quo-88322

Richtel, M. (2013, December 7). There's Power in All Those User Reviews. *The New York Times.* www.nytimes.com/2013/12/08/business/theres-power-in-all-those-user-reviews.html

Samuels, R. (2019, January 4). A Complete Calendar of Hashtag Holidays for 2019. *Sprout Social.* https://sproutsocial.com/insights/hashtag-holidays/

Sandes, F. S., & Urdan, A. T. (2013). Electronic Word-of-Mouth Impacts on Consumer Behavior: Exploratory and Experimental Studies. *Journal of International Consumer Marketing 25*(1), 181–197.

Sapra, B. (2020, January 18). Facebook Has Cancelled Efforts to Put Ads in WhatsApp, More than a Year after Its Founders Resigned in Protest of the Effort. *Business Insider.* www.businessinsider.com/facebook-pauses-push-to-sell-ads-on-whatsapp-2020-1

Score. (2019, February 13). Marketing Tips for Your Pop-Up Shop. www.score.org/blog/marketing-tips-your-pop-shop

Sebastian, M. (2013, December 2). Need a Native-Ad Rock Star? Find a Former Forbes Exec. *Ad Age*. http://adage.com/article/media/forbes-breeding-ground-native-ad-experts/245475/

Shively, K. (2015, June 23). The State of Social Marketing, 2015 Report. *Simple Measured*. http://simplymeasured.com/blog/the-2015-state-of-social-marketing-report/

Shively, L., & Hitz, L. (2016, June 20). The State of Social Marketing, 2016 Annual Report. *Simply Measured*. http://simplymeasured.com/blog/introducing-the-2016-state-of-social-marketing-report

Spiegel. (2019). How Online Reviews Influence Sales. *Spiegel Research Center*. https://spiegel.medill.northwestern.edu/online-reviews/

Sprout Social. (2019). What Smart Goals for Social Look Like. *SproutSocial*. https://media.sproutsocial.com/uploads/2019/10/SMART-Goals-Chart.pdf

Statista. (2018). Social Networking Ad Revenue Market Share of Facebook in the United States from 2015 to 2018. www.statista.com/statistics/241805/market-share-of-facebooks-us-social-network-ad-revenue/

Statista. (2019). Facebook's Global Revenue as of 3rd Quarter 2019. www.statista.com/statistics/422035/facebooks-quarterly-global-revenue/

Stelter, B., & Haughney, C. (2013, January 15). Media Decoder: The Atlantic Apologizes for Scientology Ad. *The New York Times*. http://mediadecoder.blogs.nytimes.com/2013/01/15/the-atlantic-apologizes-for-scientology-ad/

Tucker, E. (2020, January 27). Planters' Super Bowl Ad Campaign Featuring Mr. Peanut's Death Halted After Kobe Bryant Crash. *Daily Beast*. www.thedailybeast.com/planters-super-bowl-ad-campaign-featuring-mr-peanuts-death-halted-after-kobe-bryant-crash

Tuten, T. L. (2008). *Advertising 2.0, Social Media Marketing in a Web 2.0 World*. Westport, CT: Praeger.

Vaynerchuk, G. (2013). *Jab, Jab, Jab, Right Hook*. New York, NY: HarperCollins.

Willens, M. (2019, May 14). Forbes Media's Content Solutions Now Account for 40% of Its Direct Revenue. *Digiday*. https://digiday.com/media/forbes-medias-content-studio-now-accounts-40-direct-revenue/

Williams, A. (2013). *SEO 2013 & Beyond, Search Engine Optimization Will Never Be the Same Again!* Lexington, KY: Andy Williams.

Williams, T. (2005). *Take a Stand for Your Brand, Building a Great Agency Brand from the Inside Out*. Chicago, IL: The Copy Workshop.

Wilson, T. (2011). *Global Advertising, Attitudes and Audiences*. New York, NY: Routledge.

Wohl, J. (2020, January 8). Panera Bread Hires Phyllis from 'The Office' to Handle French Onion Soup Fallout. *Ad Age*. https://adage.com/article/cmo-strategy/panera-bread-hires-phyllis-office-handle-french-onion-soup-fallout/2225436

Social Media Metrics and Analytics 6

I would argue that 80% or more of your touches are gonna be two or more. It's not going to be a cold touch, which is your first touch. Therefore, to have high relevance, most of your targeting is going to be driven by what they last did with you, therefore retargeting … IF they just became a fan on Facebook or filled out a lead form, THEN this.
— Dennis Yu, Blitz Marketing (@dennisyu, 2020)

Look beyond surface metrics – align social media metrics with business goals.
— Hootsuite (@Hootsuite, 2018)

Communication researchers have different agendas, methods, and assumptions behind what they do.
— Donald Tredwell (@SAGE_APAC, 2017)

The evolution of social media during its first decade reflects a shift from euphoria over new apps to a need to measure business outcomes. Instagram, for example, rapidly acquired more than 1 million users in 2010, was sold to Facebook two years later for more than $1 billion ($33 per person), and now has more than 1 billion users (Yurieff, 2019). A mere two years after the Instagram deal, Facebook paid "a staggering $22 billion" for WhatsApp (para. 7). In light of these large amounts of money, as well as the business landscape that includes Snapchat and TikTok, there is fierce competition between sites. Older media, such as television, have managed to incorporate social media communication into their business models. Nielsen (2019) noted that their Social Content Ratings measured more than 120 million mentions of television across Facebook and Twitter (para. 3). The most social series in 2019 was the final season of Game of Thrones. "Arya's epic vanquishing of the Night King in this season's third episode became the most talked-about social event across all TV series, sparking over

TABLE 6.1 *Nielsen (2019) Social Television Rankings*

Rank	Program Name [N of Episodes]	Engagements Total [Ave.]	Total Interactions (000)
1	Game of Thrones (HBO, HBO Latino) [6]	31,975,000 [5.3 million]	31,975
2	WWE Monday Night RAW (USA Network) [46]	89,445,000 [1.9 million]	89,445
3	WWE Friday Night SmackDown (FOX, Deportes) [8]	13,249,000 [1.7 million]	13,249
4	America's Got Talent (NBC) [30]	42,263,000 [1.4 million]	42,263
5	American Idol (ABC) [18]	23,538,000 [1.3 million]	23,538
6	WWE SmackDown! (USA Network) [39]	44,633,000 [1.1 million]	44,633
7	The Bachelorette (ABC) [13]	12,180,000 [0.9 million]	12,180
8	The Bachelor (ABC) [12]	9,219,000 [0.8 million]	9,219
9	Grey's Anatomy (ABC) [26]	18,961,000 [0.7 million]	18,961
10	Dancing with the Stars (ABC) [11]	7,868,000 [0.7 million]	7,868

80,000 Twitter interactions in that single moment" (para. 4). WWE wrestling, talent shows, and reality TV topped the list of programs with the most social interaction.

Nielsen (2019) social TV data reflect an increasingly fragmented television audience across broadcast and cable channels in a competitive environment that favors live-action and reality programming. This may be contrasted with Netflix, Hulu, Disney+, Amazon Prime, and other streaming services that release ("drop") seasons and receive social media activity over longer periods of time. From being early viewers to later adopters, watchers may go to social media communication channels and use memes, gifs, and other branded icons. In late 2019, for example, baby Yoda – the child from the Disney+ *Star Wars: The Mandalorian* series – frequently was seen in posts drinking from a cup.

Social media sites offer a unique opportunity to measure human nature and communication behavior. With every online click, we leave a digital trail. There are huge economic realities behind the interest in social media communication. For example, during 2019 Black Friday holiday online sales, $2.9 billion was spent using smartphones, and there was an estimated $7.4 billion total on tablets and computers (Lunden, 2019, para. 1). Mobile phones now include sophisticated cameras designed for Instagram, Snapchat, TikTok, and other social media posts. Companies, such as Adobe and SalesForce track metrics and connect online activity to product sales. Smartphones increasingly are the way people click and buy: "These conversions are growing faster than online shopping overall, so we are now approaching a tipping point where soon smartphones might outweigh web-based purchases through computers" (para. 4).

There are two general categories of data: public and private. In the first decade, nearly all data could be seen, but monetization has meant that increasing amounts of data are seen by companies, but not the public. Instagram, for example, conducted global testing and implementation of hidden likes, and this was believed to reduce the reach of influencers (Constine, 2019). One dataset suggested that a startling 86% of young Americans aspire to be a social media influencer, a $6.6 billion industry (Min, 2019, paras. 1–2). One in five young social media users claim to know an influencer, and this is about twice the estimate of those considering themselves one. Most of this activity is happening on youth-oriented sites.

Snapchat, which from the start limited public access to data, grew from about 150 to 190 million daily users between 2016 and 2019 (Omnicore, 2019; Smith, 2016). The site tended to attract Millennial Internet users in the United States:

- 310 million monthly active users

- 190 million daily active users

- 24% of US social media accounts use Snapchat

- 3 billion Snaps created each day

- 75% of Snapchat users are under age 34.

(Omnicore, 2019, paras. 1–9)

Similarly, newcomer TikTok rapidly grew with 66% of its users under age 30, 500 million monthly US active users, and a whopping 660 million app downloads in 2018 (MediaMix, 2019, para. 6). TikTok Chinese owner ByteDance is monetizing over 1 billion app downloads and potential users through social commerce links. ByteDance also was poised to compete with Spotify and other streaming music services with the launch of Resso in India and Indonesia. It "displays real-time lyrics alongside songs and allows users to leave comments," and "users can also make music accompanied gifs and videos, reminiscent of the lip-syncing feature which made TikTok so popular" (Hamilton, 2019, para. 4). The company continued to attract a youth audience. In rapidly growing Asian markets, apps are challenging traditional e-commerce. Facebook, for example, backed Indian start-up Meesho that "connects buyers and sellers on WhatsApp and … enables them to showcase and sell their goods and works with a range of logistics companies to service their orders" (Singh, 2019, paras. 6–9).

The phenomenal growth of Facebook reached 2.38 billion monthly active users (MAUs), and 1.56 billion daily active users (DAUs), and both data points continued to grow at a rate of about 55 million per quarter (Hutchinson, 2019, paras. 1–2). While growth slowed in North America and Europe, the number of users in India nearly tripled to 313.6 million. Facebook projects 444.2 million users there by 2023 (para. 5). The company estimated that every day 2.1 billion people used Facebook, Instagram, WhatsApp, or Messenger – its "family of services" – "massive" reach that translates into quarterly earnings of more than $15 billion (paras. 9–11). If Facebook continues to increase annual profits by more than 25%, then we may conclude that data privacy concerns will not damage its business model. The tipping point for Facebook appeared to come when it surpassed 1 billion active users in 2016, with most outside of the US and Canada (Fontein, 2016). No wonder that social business people target and engage specific audiences through marketing (63%), communications (16%), public relations (5%), and customer support (1%) departments (Shively & Hitz, 2016, p. 8). It is not easy because Facebook users tend to be different from Instagram or other users: "Facebook interactions are more clearly weighted towards family, friends, and acquaintances, while celebrities get much more precedence on Instagram" (Hutchinson, 2016, para. 9). Globally, soccer athletes rule social media sites, such as Instagram (Clement, 2019).

Ronaldo, from Portugal, and James, from the US, dominate social media by extending their personal and professional brands beyond sports into entertainment, movies, and modeling. A photo of Ronaldo kissing the Euro trophy in 2016 established his dominance in sports and social media communication (Sports Illustrated, 2016, p. 19). Twitter also tends to be very popular in global sports, but Instagram and Snapchat have been the place to make money for Kim Kardashian, Kanye West, and the other Kardashian reality stars (Paul, 2016). Rob Kardashian, for example, "announced to his 8.2 million Instagram followers that his fiancée and mother of their month-old daughter had abruptly left him and taken the baby with her" (Cohen, 2016, para. 1). Imagine the drama for each of his five sisters – who had more than 50 million Instagram followers at the time. The family has mastered the art and science of television and social media cross-platform audience reach, but in order to monetize their efforts, marketers want to see data.

Experts in measurement metrics and analytics discovered how to collect, analyze, and present data. Internet research includes proprietary social media studies, such as the Facebook experiment in 2014 that asked "whether there is a relationship between Facebook content to which you are exposed and your emotional status" (Treadwell, 2017, p. 53). Such A–B testing of two groups relies upon experimental design. Facebook's

TABLE 6.2 *Statista (2019) Athletes Instagram Rankings*

Rank	Name	No of October 2019 Followers
1.	Cristiano Ronaldo (soccer)	184.35 million
2.	Lionel Messi (soccer)	131.37 million
3.	Neymar de Silva Santos Junior (soccer)	126.32 million
4.	David Beckham (soccer)	58.52 million
5.	LeBron James (basketball)	51.61 million
6.	Ronaldinho (soccer)	48.55 million
7.	James Rodriguez (soccer)	43.27 million
8.	Gareth Bale (soccer)	41.64 million
9.	Marcelo Viera Jr. (soccer)	41.38 million
10.	Zlatan Ibrahimović (soccer)	38.33 million

manipulation of positive and negative newsfeed stories raised ethical concerns. Methodologists are also concerned about sampling: "The biggest theoretical problem with Internet sampling is that we cannot develop an Internet sampling frame because we do not know who or what the Internet population consists ..." (p. 150). It is not always the case that human users rather than robots ("bots") are behind a specific social media account, but media industries continue to develop Web analytics:

> Social media monitoring is about listening to what your audience is saying about you on social media. It is about analyzing the data and finally, it is about creating insights that will improve your social media strategy or even your overall marketing strategy.
> (Mytton, Diem, & van Diem, 2016, p. 145)

An application programming interface (API) essentially allows data to be shared across social media sites. Collection of "big data" – large amounts of information – makes new forms of research possible. For example, a single tweet on Twitter has dozens of chunks of meta-data, such as location, date, and time. Location data are particularly important.

The California Consumer Privacy Act of 2018 (AB-375) treated data privacy as an "inalienable" right: "Fundamental to this right of privacy is the ability of individuals to control the use, including the sale, of their personal information" (Section 2). This included disclosure of (a) "specific pieces of personal information the business has collected"; (b) informing consumers, including "the purposes for which the categories of personal information shall be used." As model legislation, California pivoted the US toward European General Data Protection Regulation (GDPR) as a human right. Starting January 1, 2020, an overhaul to the privacy law expanded consumer rights to view personal data and halt sale of it (Chin, 2019).

In *California v. TWC* (2019), the state sued The Weather Channel app (owned by IBM) over continuously tracking and selling user location data without informing consumers of their intention to sell data to third parties. *The New York Times* reported that the app had 45 million active users, and that about 75 companies harvested individual streaming location data (Valentino-DeVries & Singer, 2019). The conflict, in part, arose because complex user agreements may disclose data collection and selling, but users click without reading legal jargon. Some have called for a national privacy law that aligns with the European international law model. Huge social media companies, such as Facebook, are forced to comply with the largest state in the US, as well as international law. Going forward, data battles over Messenger and WhatsApp targeted advertising based upon user data will be important because FTC staff have limited resources to investigate and bring cases (Confessore & Kang, 2018).

The Federal Trade Commission data privacy consent decree agreement with Facebook in 2011 did not stop the apparent violation of rules (Singer, 2019). In 2007, the Facebook Beacon program had shared user purchases with their friends. Facebook had promised users that their data were safe. The Facebook 2012 settlement included the promise to limit data sharing to user privacy settings by "obtaining their express consent before sharing their information beyond" and "by maintaining a comprehensive privacy program to protect consumers' information, and by obtaining biennial privacy audits from an independent third party" (FTC, 2012, para. 2). Cambridge Analytica was among third-party companies that leveraged the data during the 2016 US election. Facebook was among many of the largest digital companies that appeared to use private data. "In the case of Facebook, terabytes of daily user data remain available for descriptive, prescriptive, and predictive analytics" (Lerbinger, 2019, p. 113).

Beyond location data, social media analysts may group content and influencers. Software also allows for categorizing the sentiment of words as positive, neutral, or negative. Social network algorithms may organize groups of tweets around centers of influence. Similarly, text may be analyzed within "word clouds" that identify key text within a social media conversation.

Social media measurement serves basic business goals, which include raising revenue, lowering costs, and increasing satisfaction among customers. In other words, measurement helps make the ROI case for social media tactics to sometimes-skeptical C-suite managers. Traditional communication research methods emphasize rigorous and transparent methodologies. Researchers seek to ground studies in social theory, conceptualize measurement, and operationalize definitions. Scientific research offers **reliability** or consistency of measurement from one time to the next (Wimmer & Dominick, 2013). This is important when using sampling to generalize about larger populations, as is the case in survey research. We hope to be able to reproduce the results of our systematic observation. "Mass media researchers have a great deal to see, and virtually everyone is exposed to this information every day" (p. 5). The research process can be divided into "phases" – the medium, its uses, medium effects, and improvement (p. 6). Academic researchers also have concerns about the **validity** of measures because we cannot assume to know what social phenomena are being measured. Data points may or may not measure what we think is a valid observation. Only through repeated measures and replication of data can we build concepts around predictive theory and analytics. While social science involves statistical tests or rigorous qualitative frameworks, these requirements have not always been applied in the new field of social media measurement. Academic rigor is beginning to come to social media research through **transparency** of methods, but "cool" new online tools, more than scientific method, tended to drive proprietary social media measurement.

Social media communication is still a young field that tends to be grounded in the business of social media marketing. As we become interested in social media, we naturally seek to measure online behavior. Unlike traditional experimental research, survey research, focus groups, or content analyses, measurement of social media involves tracking online behavior and responding to it in real-time. Savage (2011) explained that Twitter, for example, is "a surprising window" into "moods, thoughts, and activities of society" that may not be discovered by traditional research data: "Researchers are finding they can measure public sentiment, follow political activity, even spot earthquakes and flu outbreaks, just by running the chatter through algorithms that search for particular words and pinpoint message origins" (p. 18). We conceptualize social media measurement around awareness, engagement, persuasion, conversion and retention (Sterne, 2010, p. 15). We are interested in those users visiting sites, as well as their behavior while there.

SOCIAL MEDIA MEASURES

Sterne (2010) was one of the first to understand the power of social media data and catalog dozens of possible measures. Some of the earliest important measurements of social media marketing consumers were (pp. xx–xxv):

- Buzz based upon the number of impressions at a given time, on a specific date, time of year, channel, etc.

- Popularity

- Mainstream media mentions

- Number of fans, followers, friends, etc.

- Reach, or second-degree impressions

- Likes or favorites

- Sentiment

- Number of interactions or engagement rate

- Conversions to purchases

Behind these sometimes-crude measures was a desire to demonstrate social media ROI, which may also be measured as a business cost. Just as companies typically do not attach ROI to a receptionist's work, technologist Phil Gomes has asked, so why measure social media ROI? Further, a Cost of Ignoring (COI) was introduced as a way to say that social media offer both opportunities and risks (Radian6, 2013): "The COI of social media comes down to missed opportunities ... you need to question your opportunity costs" (para. 4). These reflect an interest in measuring what could have been done with resources, including time and money. So, social media managers must use strategy, goals and tactics to evaluate what to do, as well as what *not* to do.

Miller (2013) viewed social media marketing as part of the larger marketing task for businesses. This includes "relationship building" with prospects and customers, "earned exposure" through "unrequested endorsement" and customer sharing, "authentic insight" from comments, "search engine visibility" from posts, "cost savings" and tractable "results" (pp. 89–90). The marketing process involves ongoing engagement with customers. Much of what happens within social sites may be seen through the lens of earned media, or content the user spends time creating. In other words, ROI exchanges the cost of staffing brand community managers against measurable results that translate to new clients, potential new business, and increased revenue opportunities. It can be argued that no business can afford to miss any opportunity to engage with potential clients and customers, but targeting business purposes must be front of mind.

THE BARCELONA PRINCIPLES 2.0 AND SMART GOALS

The International Association of Measurement of Communication (AMEC, 2010, 2015) emphasizes data quality and transparency. The original AMEC Barcelona Declaration of Measurement Principles (2010) guided practitioners by emphasizing goal setting, measurement, and business results. AMEC goals and objectives focused on outcomes that offer seven updated PR (public relations) requirements: goal setting and measurement; outcomes over outputs; organizational performance measurement; qualitative and quantitative methods; rejection of advertising equivalencies for value; consistent social media measurement; and transparency that leads to validity. As a fundamental goal, social media campaign effectiveness measurement must avoid historic **advertising value equivalency (AVE)**, which remains popular among some PR clients. In truth, organic and earned social media cannot be valued based upon current pricing for paid content.

A strategic way to approach a campaign is by identification of **SMART Goals** (**Specific, Measurable, Attainable, Relevant**, and **Timely**) as a basis for evaluation of effectiveness over time. Social media managers armed with appropriate planning ahead of a campaign may be able to target specific audiences, measure impression, tone, credibility, and other **key performance indicators (KPIs)**. Through content analysis, SEO, **customer relations management** data, and surveys, it is possible to focus on engagement and conversion measures within a networked community context. AMEC (2015) specifically rejected the value of, for example, "likes," as **vanity metrics** that do not relate to business outcomes.

SEE, SAY, FEEL, DO

Similar to the AMEC principles, another group has conceptualized social media measures as breaking down behavior into four fundamental types linked to ROI:

> The greatest obstacle to determining ROI doesn't happen on the back end once you've collected mounds of user engagement data like RTs, bounce rates, and the number of "Likes." The main obstacle to determining ROI comes from a failure to define the "R" on the front end. What is the return you are trying to create? Without knowing what you are trying to accomplish, it's impossible to measure your success.
>
> (Gordon, 2012, p. 2)

Gordon found that social media are frequently related to "see" measures. Reach, for example, is a function of the number of eyeballs seeing a Facebook post. Impressions are this type of measure. Gordon (p. 5) lists the following "see" metrics:

- Facebook Page Like totals
- Twitter Follower totals
- Website traffic

- Email sign-ups

- RSS subscriptions

- Advertising impressions

- Earned media impressions

As social media content may activate users through engagement, Gordon's "say" measures – content likes, shares, retweets, email forwards, and snaps – all are data that can be measured. Beyond the quantitative measures, we can examine the qualitative comments and sentiment. It is easier to measure online comments than to track those offline statements activated by the original content. Social media users may have emotional responses to what they see or comment about, and the reaction, or the sentiment, may be important. Totaling the number of likes also provides a quantitative measure for "feel." At the end of the social media measurement process, "do" metrics allow us to track behavioral outcomes, such as making a product purchase. Conversion to sales is the most obvious behavioral objective. Organizations, such as non-profits, may be more interested in increasing the number of members, event participants and donations. Public radio stations, for example, need to raise money during annual fund drives, and social media tactics have become an important way to grow the numbers. Likewise, a campaign may be designed to increase attendance at a sponsored event, activate advocacy for a political position or candidate, or identify a new crop of volunteers to replace those leaving. Social media campaigns usually are connected to organization or company websites, which also offer opportunities to measure activity. Even if direct ROI cannot be shown, nearly every personal brand, organization, or company benefits from raising awareness through maintaining a strong and consistent presence within social media.

GOOGLE ANALYTICS

On websites, individuals, organizations, or companies may interest users in owned media, or content residing on sites that are maintained by owners. A strategic campaign may use techniques, such as banner advertising on other sites, email marketing, or social media to attempt to drive traffic back to a homepage. By incorporating Google Analytics tracking code on a page, owners are provided with data on the sources of Web traffic, such as search engines, referrals from other sites, direct traffic, and social media linkages. The importance of searching to find online content means that the keywords need to be carefully selected and tracked. Google Adwords has maintained a tool for analyzing data on keywords and phrases. A Keyword Tool (https://keywordtool.io/) search of "social media" in 2020 found 659 unique keywords that may be related and relevant – marketing, manager, icons, sites, platforms, etc. Keywords allow us to strive for search engine optimization. By identifying popular searches, content creators can focus on some words and avoid others. The top words should generate more clicks at the owned website. Words such as "sale," for example, may generate new traffic and interest. Web coders need to incorporate the tags that align with the words used by customers or brand fans.

Referrals – online traffic that comes from a link on another page – are an important way to generate interest. An analysis of referrals on a site, for example, might reveal that visitors clicked on a link while spending time on Twitter, Facebook, or a blog site. This could be the result of owned or earned media. By checking the source of referrals, users learn more about what works. A check of similar or competitor sites should reveal Web traffic secrets. At some level, referrals could be the result of a social relationship that may be built over time, maintained, or even reinforced through a strategic social media plan and tactics.

Once users land on a website, we are interested in learning more about the type of content and its placement that generates clicks, time spent, or other results. Analytics allow a site manager to examine page bounce rates, which measure how quickly a user exits an individual page. Engaging content keeps users on a page, or it moves them to another page that meets the goals for the site. For example, a news or sports site may

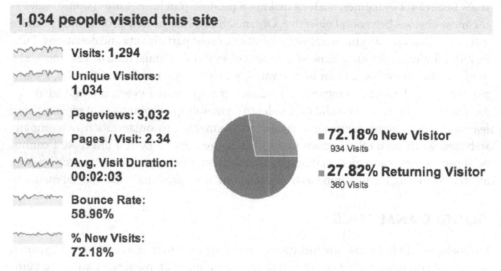

1,034 people visited this site

Visits: 1,294

Unique Visitors: 1,034

Pageviews: 3,032

Pages / Visit: 2.34

Avg. Visit Duration: 00:02:03

Bounce Rate: 58.96%

% New Visits: 72.18%

■ **72.18%** New Visitor
934 Visits

■ **27.82%** Returning Visitor
360 Visits

FIGURE 6.1 *Keywords are very useful in social media searches, and this helps explain why search engine optimization remains important.*

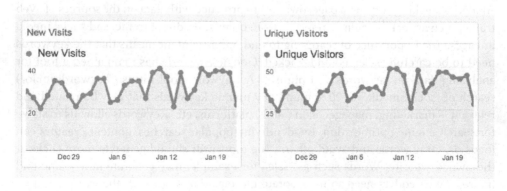

FIGURE 6.2 *Page views include data on the number of visitors returning to a page.*

be selling a cap or t-shirt. The goal would be to display the product on a main page and persuade users to click on a "buy now" link.

Google data **segmentation** helps separate mobile and desktop site visitors, **benchmark** data histories, and content optimization. The Alexa Keyword Difficulty Tool targets keywords used in highly ranked searches. The Google Analytics tool constructs a customer journey from how they found a website to what they viewed and clicked. Kaushik (2010) defined a continuous improvement process of realistic, positive outcome goals. He frequently urges analysts to avoid confusing activities with outcomes, such as shopping versus product sales. The measurement of **clickstream** may include the use of A/B testing that varies content. The Google Analytics Academy offers free training and certificates that demonstrate the ability to leverage data **attribution, last-click attribution**, and other concepts used to measure site visitor conversion to the desired action. Again, planning is critical for social media managers in order to refine tactics. Google data include **dimensions,** such as demographic characteristics, and **metrics** during a site visitor session. A visitor clicking on a Facebook post may find that the link takes her to an owned media website. Google compares this activity to those users visiting a site based upon a search or direct URL address typing. Google Analytics tracks interaction **pageviews** and events, time on page, and **bounce rate** as the "percentage of sessions with only one user interaction." Google search algorithms frequently change, but page effectiveness can be compared to competitors at the Alexa.com site.

For social media sites, such as Facebook pages, we are interested in increasing the number of page views, unique visitors, and likes (which are similar to fans, followers, and members on other social sites). While we want visitors to respond to each post, we also seek higher levels of engagement through liking comments of others and making comments of our own. Within the comments section, we are interested in sentiment analysis of those opinions as positive, neutral, or negative. Frequently, there is a lack of neutral commenting within most social media sites. Long-term analyses tend to find a preponderance of either very negative criticism or glowing praise. Obviously, the goal typically is to maximize positive sentiment and minimize the negative feelings that may exist toward a personal or organizational brand. Some brand managers, however, see negative sentiment as an opportunity to engage and respond in a way that strengthens loyalty among fans. At a minimum, measuring sentiment offers a benchmark starting point for moving the needle away from negativism and toward positive outcomes and relating total engagement to KPIs.

Strong bonds between social media users and media content should produce these benchmark data. By identifying a standard for measuring success, we can set goals for tracking growth in unique visitors and their levels of engagement through time spent, as well as satisfaction. For products, sales create customers – some of whom require additional support. In fact, a lot of brands see the ROI of social media as found within the customer service and care business function. Social media have become important online spaces for responding to complaints, engaging with customer problems, solving issues, converting unhappy customers to loyal fans, and promoting brands. A good customer experience will generate likes, positive comments, and informational shares.

FACEBOOK INSIGHTS

Facebook developed a useful set of free insight data. For each Facebook fan page created, a site manager can download and analyze real-time data compared each week. Ideally, a site sees continuous growth in the number of likes, increases in the **reach** of posts beyond those users liking the page and following it on their feeds. By creating engaging content, a manager can spark comments, shares, and post clicks. Some managers export insight data to an Excel spreadsheet and track long-term data for seasonal shifts or the effectiveness of post attributes. Beyond the quantitative measures of engagement, a page manager should drill down and qualitatively examine the most engaging content.

In the example here, the weekly reach spiked higher because of a newly posted YouTube video. In this example, the post had a small number of likes, but there were clicks through to watch the video. Facebook seeks through its algorithm to promote videos on the site over external links that send a user elsewhere. Facebook has added to its Creator Studio dashboard some Traffic Source Insights, including "video watch time and retention metrics within four separate categories" – followers, shares, recommended and paid (Hutchinson, 2020, para. 1).

Reach can be used to identify promising potential for future content. Although the content generated only two likes, so far, the clicks through to the video and relatively high reach offer promising potential. It also was possible to link a Facebook page to a Twitter account. By posting on the page, an automatic tweet generates a headline and link for Twitter followers. This, in turn, may also increase the reach for content. On a news-sharing page, for example, Twitter can be used to boost the number of clicks for an item of high interest. However, the linkage of Facebook and Twitter profiles is weaker than strengthening overall brand awareness and activity through posts that resonate within unique site norms.

Week of 3rd February, 2014

UNO School of Communication
Build Audience · Promote Page

See Insights

	LAST WEEK	PREVIOUS WEEK	TREND
Total Page Likes	750	750	0.0%
New Likes	1	0	0.0%
Weekly Total Reach	2,295	523	338.8%
People Engaged	206	126	63.5%

FIGURE 6.3 *Analysts examine individual Facebook page posts for clues about fan engagement.*

TWITTER ANALYTICS AND INSTAGRAM INFLUENCE

The open environment of Twitter, as compared to the gated online communities of Facebook and LinkedIn, presents a unique opportunity to access and analyze open and accessible data. On Twitter, there are obvious measures, such as number of followers, number of retweets, and replies. Twitter includes the activity of human users and automated robot "bots," which are computer-generated and scheduled tweets. On Twitter, we can measure following to followers as a ratio, we can study content, and we can explore social networks. One raw measure is the number of tweets per day.

The Twitter Analytics website allows a social media manager to download account data in monthly chunks. Twitter faced stiff competition from Hootsuite, Sprout Social, Union Metrics, and other management tools (Perez, 2017). There is sharp competition to win loyal customers. Sprout Social emerged with its plan to raise more than $150 million by selling public stock in an IPO (Pletz, 2019). However, it is also important to note that the company lost $21 million in 2018 on $78.8 million in social media monitoring software revenue. Social measurement and management tools evolved to become big businesses, but a decade earlier they were merely in-house research projects.

For example, Edelman Digital had generated a TweetLevel.com score based upon four dimensions: influence, popularity, engagement, and trust. The current Berland "Edelman Intelligence" client tools, however, now are not available to the public. Still, these dimensions are important measures from a PR perspective, as they offer opportunities to score and improve the online behavior of influencers. Trust is viewed as an association, such as through a retweet. Engaging content generates new connections and may increase influence. The "permanent beta" model attempted to develop measurement variables important within social media, as seen in Figure 6.4.

🔲 BOX 6.1

Historic Tweetlevel Methodology

Beyond followers (Fo) and follower to following ratio (Fo:Fg), the model focused on updates (UP), retweets (Rt), broadcast to engagement ratio (B:E), the Topsy.com influence score (To), as well as engagement (e) and trust (t). Edelman TweetLevel (2013) was removed in early 2014: "We are currently assessing new methods and technologies to measure influence on Twitter. We appreciate your patience as we explore the realm of possibility. Please reach out to tweetlevel@edelman.com for more information." Trust is a proprietary measure that is not disclosed. TweetLevel also includes in the Edelman formula number of name pointing (@U) and recent replies (@R). It also is important to appear on follower lists and exhibit measures of influence (i). Overall popularity (p) tends to be an obvious measure, although it is vital to filter raw numbers of followers for the presence of bots and spammers using Twitter for direct marketing. While the overall model is transparent, some of the actual data fall under proprietary company information. So, we cannot fully evaluate reliability of measures for trust and influence. Likewise, without clear evidence of data consistency, it is impossible to be sure about the validity of the measurement.

$$TweetLevel = Rg \left| \frac{Fo + Fg + Fo:Fg + Up + Up^{30} + L^Q + Up^v + @U + [RtQ/Ed] + @R^{30} + B:E + Is + To + li + Vi}{Z} \right|$$

$$\times w\,(i \backslash p \backslash e \backslash t)$$

Variables

Fo	= Number of followers	Fg	= Number of users following
Fo:Fg	= Follower to Following ratio	Up	= Number of updates all time
UP^{30}	= Updates over the past 30 days	L^{Q}Fo	= Number of lists following you related to the number of people following that list
Up^v	= Number of updates over specific time period	@U	= Number of name pointing
(Rt Q/Ed)	= Retweets related to quoted and edited proportioned to all	@R^{30}	= Replies sent related to all-time and previous 30 days
B:E	= Broadcast to engagement ratio	Is	= Idea Starter score
To	= Topsy influence score	Li	= Involvement index score
Vi	= Velocity index score	W	= Weight assigned each attribute
Z	= Standardized score	P	= Popularity
e	= Engagement	I	= Influence
t	= Trust	Rg	= Range assigned to score

FIGURE 6.4 *Tweetlevel aggregates many measures in generating a standardized score.*

Source: https://tweetlevel.edelman.com/insights (Accessed January 2014; as of February 2014, the site had been discontinued for updates to the model, as Edelman PR assessed "new methods to measure influence on Twitter.") The firm later settled on Berland tools and branded the proprietary data as "Edelman Intelligence – a global insight and analytics consultancy" before pivoting to their Edelman.com site that hid social media measurement methodology and instead focused on its annual Trust Barometer.

Social media measurement is considered "a discipline" rather than "a tool" under the AMEC (2015) principles. Principle 6 calls for "clearly defined goals and outcomes," multi-method analysis, quantity, and quality evaluation, of "no 'single metric'" for conversation and communities, and precision of data: "Understanding reach and influence is important, but existing sources are not accessible, transparent or consistent enough to be reliable; experimentation and testing are key to success" (Principle 6, bullet 6). Public relations professionals have concluded that transparency is central to credible and trusted social media measurement: "PR measurement should be done in a manner that is transparent and replicable for all steps in the process" (Principle 7). The content source and method of analysis ("whether human or automated, tone scale, reach to target, content analysis parameters") should be transparently reported to clients and the public (Principle 7, bullet 2).

The exploratory efforts to measure social media behavior are important in identifying general strengths and weaknesses, as long as one understands that current data may reflect a fairly large amount of **measurement error**. No social measure is exact and without various sources of error, but we would like to look at individual scores and be able to *estimate error*. Currently, this is not a standard for social media measurement.

Once we can measure a Twitter user type, it is also valuable to be able to examine **word clouds** to see keywords frequently used by and about an influencer. Lady Gaga, with more than 80.7 million global followers, is an interesting example of a brand using social media to reinforce fan relationships. By 2020, however, she was an aging singer and movie star who was replaced among the top social media stars, such as Katy Perry, Justin Bieber, Rihanna, and Taylor Swift. From a PR and branding perspective, the words of the influencer should mirror personal and professional branding of a consistent message to the Twitter audience. The most important branded words should appear in a word cloud as the largest words shown. All of the important brands should at least appear within the cloud. If not, the speaker should adjust the message over time and re-examine the data.

In the example in Table 6.3, we see the top ten Instagram influencers, based upon following fan numbers and engagement. These celebrities include international soccer stars, but mainly reflect entertainment leaders on TV, in movies, and popular music. By using multiple tools to connect a brand with words, we can look for rough patterns in the data. As was noted earlier in this chapter, a few global athletes rise to the level of widely-known entertainers and use social media to transform their brands beyond sports.

It is noteworthy that Kim Kardashian's audience growth slowed after she stopped her real-time posts following a Paris, France, robbery in 2016 in which she was held at gunpoint after wearing expensive jewelry in a photograph. Still, she charges about $500,000 for each sponsored Instagram post (Leskin & Rogers, 2019). While Instagram is home for top influencers, Twitter data remained more public and open:

- TweetReach by Union Metrics (https://tweetreach.com) – Measures reach (accounts reached), exposure (impressions) and activity. It creates a hashtag snapshot of estimated accounts reached, exposure (impressions), weekly activity, top contributors, most retweeted items, and a timeline.

FIGURE 6.5 *Reporters and fans gather outside Lady Gaga's hotel in Bucharest prior to a performance in 2012.*
Courtesy of Shutterstock, Inc

TABLE 6.3 *Top December 2019 Social Media Influencers*

Name	Rank	Engagement
Kylie Jenner	1. @kyliejenner	4.4 million
Cristiano Ronaldo	2. @cristiano	3.9 million
Selena Gomez	3. @selenagomez	3.7 million
Leo Messi	4. @leomessi	3.5 million
Kim Kardashian	5. @kimkardashian	1.6 million
Beyoncé	6. @beyonce	1.7 million
Kendall	7. @kendalljenner	2.2 million
Ariana Grande	8. @arianagrande	1.2 million
neymarjr	9. @neymarjr	1.3 million
Billie Eilish	10. @billieeilish	4.3 million

Sources: Influencer Marketing Hub (2019). Top 25 Instagram Influencers in 2019, Most Followed Instagrammers. https://influencermarketinghub.com/top-instagram-influencers-in-2019/. Three years earlier, Twitter was more important than Instagram. In 2016, the WeFollow Wizoid.com list was dominated by technology and marketing sector influencers: @GuyKawasaki, @garyvee, @ThisIsSethsBlog, @kimgarst, @MariSmith, @chrisbrogan, @MarketingProfs, @MichaelHyatt, @mashable, @kevinrose, and @aplusk.

- NodeXL (https://nodexlgraphgallery.org/Pages/Default.aspx) – The open-source, open data and open science tool of the Social Media Research Foundation visualizes Twitter neighborhoods searched by topics, accounts, hashtags or other content.

- Tweetdeck (https://tweetdeck.twitter.com/) – Twitter provides a free, real-time tool for watching tweets by specific searches. This provides users with a sense of the volume of tweets at a given moment, while also archiving content by user columns.

The trend over the past six years has been for numerous startups to fail, as Facebook, Instagram, Twitter, and Snapchat limit third-party data and incorporate this function within in-house functions and their business models. The potential to measure Twitter influence is an exciting development, even if it cannot capture offline influence. Still, popularity on Twitter also cannot be directly associated with the measurement of other social media activity. The centrality of engagement is important across all social media. Hootsuite, Sprout Social, Nuvi, and other paid platforms have attempted to integrate and aggregate social media data across sites with varying degrees of access and success. Twitter, for example, controls the technology for limiting access to data retrieval. Likewise, news sites now behind paywalls require paid licensing to access their social media data. The Hootsuite Platform Certification is training courseware for educational and enterprise settings that helps users learn effective use of the product. In general, free software is very limited. Data collection on Nuvi is a function of the cost of downloading chunks of data.

Many companies now offer to clients what is called a **social media dashboard**. Adobe Marketing Cloud, for example, integrates social content management and analytics. The idea is to synthesize key insights on a screen to offer the user key data without needing to jump from screen to screen. Universal Information Services (@Universal_Info) is an international media tracking and news monitoring company that sells a measurement dashboard. CEO Todd Murphy (@Todder4News) says the company responded to AI by developing an Alpha Clips mobile app that follows AMEC measurement principles. Other companies, such as Cision (@cision) and Burell Communications (@BurrellPR) also combine computer tools with human coding. Dashboards track top hashtags, total word counts, top tweeters, top mentions, influence via social **network visualization**, top websites, impressions, top journalists, key topics, impressions by state, and other measures. The goal is to measure impact and publicity value for influencers.

A dashboard provides the client with the aggregate amount of social media conversation, but it goes further in breaking down types of content across key platforms. Facebook and Twitter in this example are stronger social media spaces for an organic packaging of the message, but Facebook is much more active in a debate over mustard versus ketchup. At the same time, charity engagement appears stronger on blogs and YouTube. A user would need to drill down deeper into the data to examine specific content and posts to better understand how the results align or fail to measure up to strategic goals.

BOX 6.2

Thought Leader Timothy Akimoff

Social media are constantly evolving to become more immersive. Where we once linked readers back to our website through social media, publishers are creating the content within Facebook, Snapchat and Instagram. With live streaming, immersive 360-degree videos, and virtual reality, social media have taken much of the gusto from even specialized Web storytelling templates and allowed audiences to experience news in real-time as if they were there. Social media are the common template of our digital lives.

FIGURE 6.6 *@timakimoff.*
Photograph by Jeff Rivet, courtesy of Tim Akimoff, WBEZ

Social media grow exponentially because of rapid advances in the core technology and ever-increasing accessibility. The more iPhones and Androids sold, the more people use Twitter, Facebook, Instagram, and other social media services to document their lives. The biggest challenge will be to keep ahead of the fast-paced changes taking place on the social media landscape due to technology improvements and user proficiency as well as advanced storytelling techniques. Mobile-only applications, such as Snapchat and Instagram, are true disruptions, redefining the very nature of content. Younger users value privacy and are cognizant of data costs enough to want limited-duration content. Business are putting press releases out on social media and holding live-streamed press conferences.

Looking ahead, immersive experiences will become increasingly desirable to news consumers. They will seek to be where the story is whether by virtual reality or another immersive storytelling technique. Transferring storytelling skills from well-known techniques like video, audio and print to emerging styles like virtual reality, Facebook Live/Periscope and 360-degree video as well as virtual gaming as we saw with Pokémon GO, will create more demand for this kind of content by people who are spending more time using social media in all aspects of their lives from getting news to crowd-sourcing dinner.

Timothy Akimoff is Social Media Coordinator for the Oregon Department of Fish and Wildlife. He previously held positions at Chicago Public Radio, which includes public radio stalwart WBEZ, KTUUTV in Anchorage, Alaska, and at Lee Enterprise and the Missoulian/Ravalli Republic in Missoula, Montana. He studied journalism at the University of Oregon and has reported in Oregon and in Kiev, Ukraine.

SOCIAL NETWORK ANALYSIS (SNA)

Academic researchers explore online behavior and measurement through the application of social network theory. The systematic study of how individuals interact in social settings has been the focus of research for more than 50 years. Tubbs and Moss (1983), for example, traced investigations in the nature of "popular" or "over-chosen" and "unpopular" or isolated people (pp. 108–109). In describing social interaction between popular and unpopular people, they diagrammed through the "sociogram" how positive traits, such as enthusiasm and maturity, may be related to judgments about "sincerity" of another's conversation (p. 110). In the current era of social networks and social media, these connections are important to journalism and public relations. Social networking generates measures of branding, influence, trust and dispersion of ideas through Twitter and Facebook, and offers an opportunity to be seen as an opinion leader.

Information theory and models emphasize the flow of messages through channels. The perception of communication depends upon situations and context (Severin & Tankard, 2001). Much of this work was grounded in Heider's balance theory and Festinger's cognitive dissonance theory from the 1950s, which may be related to social judgment (Milburn, 1991). Burnett and Marshall (2003) link communication models to Internet discussion:

> At the very core of the meaning of the Web is linkage and connection: it is fundamentally about modes of communication and presenting possibilities about how those modes might intersect. Thus, the Web is simultaneously a mass-mediated *and* one-to-one form of communication. It is a site of incredible cultural consumption *and* cultural production and makes it harder to establish the boundary between these two activities.
>
> (p. 59)

Twitter users (sometimes called "tweeps") may be analyzed to identify "visual patterns found within linked entities" (Hansen, Shneiderman, & Smith, 2011, p. 32). Researchers have proposed and developed methods for the analysis of structure and grouping of categories and clusters in a social network. One model is called Group-In-A-Box (GIB):

> One particularly important aspect of social network analysis is the detection of *communities*, i.e., sub-groups of individuals or entities that exhibit tight

> interconnectivity among the other wider population. For example, Twitter users who regularly retweet each other's messages *may form cohesive groups* within the Twitter social network. In a network visualization they would appear as clusters or sub-graphs, often colored distinctly or represented by a different vertex shape in order to convey their group identity.
>
> (Rodrigues et al., 2011, para. 2, emphasis added)

Some researchers call the network graph that is produced by analysis software a "sociogram," which has "vertices (also called nodes or agents) and edges (also called ties or connections)" (Hansen, Shneiderman, & Smith, 2011, p. 33). In social network analyses, Twitter users are connected by a series of lines in social space. The maps represent a center of people at the core of a network, as well as "isolates" at the periphery.

Network analyses are grounded in nearly 300 years of study in graph theory. In modern terms, "It is often useful to consider social networks from an individual member's point of view" (Hansen, Shneiderman, & Smith, 2011, p. 36). Information from journalists and PR practitioners, either to one another or spreading to the general public, may be visually displayed through computer-generated mapping. As early as the 1930s, researchers were developing hand-drawn "pictures of patterns of people and their partners" (p. 38). This theoretical perspective has influenced the modern study of relationships. For example, Heaney and McClurg (2009) applied social networks to the study of American politics. They found social networks useful in understanding information flow, as well as collaboration within political organizations. Garton, Haythornthwaite, and Wellman (1997) describe social network analysts as examining relations:

> They treat the description of relational patterns as interesting in its own right – e.g., is there a core and periphery? – and examine how involvement in such *social networks* helps to explain the behavior and attitudes of *network members* … They use a variety of techniques to discover a network's densely-knit clusters and to look for similar role relations.
>
> (para. 3)

Communication theory also has been concerned with how networks relate to personal influence. Cooley (1909/1966) identified four factors: expressiveness, permanence, swiftness and diffusion of communication – he viewed the extension of messages as "enlargement" and "animation" (pp. 149–159).

> Social contacts are extended in space and quickened in time, and in the same degree the mental unity they imply becomes wider and more alert. The individual is broadened by coming into relation with a larger and more various life, and he is kept stirred up, sometimes to express, by the multitude of changing suggestions which this life brings to him.
>
> (p. 150)

Baran and Davis (2006) suggested that the influence of opinion leaders may be understood through similar interests and social stratification of leaders and their followers. At one time, the shift from interpersonal to mediated communication reduced feedback (Westley & MacLean, 1957), but the lines between interpersonal and media communication have now blurred. Even so, Gumpert and Cathcart (1986) concluded that, "Every type of communication, from face-to-face to mass communication, is still basically an interpersonal communicative act" (p. 19). Influence may disperse from the center of a social network. This influence often accelerates when a leader is "stimulating" what has been called "virtual communities" (Koh et al., 2007, p. 70). In order to be sustainable, the researchers contend that four principles must exist: clear purpose/vision, clear member role definition, moderator leadership, and *online/offline events* (pp. 70–71; emphasis added). Events, in fact, play a key role in strengthening member identification within a social network. It is for this reason that the present research focuses on a specific international event that receives widespread media coverage.

Data analyses can be performed using NodeXL software. A white-listed company on Twitter may collect about 18,000 queries per hour, but a regular user is limited to 150 queries per hour. Researchers use NodeXL, which is a social network analysis tool built into Microsoft Excel in current versions and is specifically designed for non-programmers, to collect, analyze and visualize network data from social media sites, such as Twitter. In a Twitter network, there are times when researchers are less concerned about the importance of a specific account and more concerned about position in the network. A position in the network may have something to do with having access to information or the flow of information. For example, a PR practitioner may appear near the center, if she or he is disseminating new information to be used by electronic news media. Thus, it is important to examine the betweenness centrality measurement. Utilizing the NodeXL filter, tweeps with a low betweenness measurement can be removed. NodeXL has the capability to identify clusters or cliques of tweeps based upon the network structure. The software uses an algorithm that looks for groups of densely clustered tweeps that are only loosely connected to other tweeps in another cluster.

Russo and Koesten (2005) addressed the concepts of centrality and prestige. Within a network, an individual can be placed within a social space occupied by others:

> An actor's *centrality* (out-degree) represents his or her ability to touch others in the network. In particular, centrality is a measure of potential influence and popularity based on who an actor seeks to interact with within the social network … An actor's *prestige* (in-degree) represents the degree to which others seek out a particular actor in a social network.
>
> (p. 256)

It is possible to examine the centrality of network positioning, as contrasted with being on the periphery, to determine importance in the flow of information. A person at the center of a network has a lot of information flowing through them. Prestige is another way to say that influence happens when others seek out an individual in the network. For example, a financial journalist may be sought out by a PR person with a goal of gaining media attention for her or his event. Centrality and prestige may place an individual in the role of being "the object of communication," (p. 256) without necessarily being the original source. Social network influence, in part, is a function of content creator abilities to spark engagement with followers.

📱 **BOX 6.3**

TikTok Influence Grid

InfluenceGrid.com in early 2020 ranked top TikTok users by their huge numbers of followers. As had happened with Instagram and other earlier start-ups, those first to the new social media party gained a critical advantage over later adopters.

Account Followers Country Average Views Engagement
@lorengray 35.8 million USA 6.4 million 17.5%
Total videos: 2,300; Comments per video: 4,000
@babyariel (duet) 30.0 million USA 1.7 million 22.9%
Total videos: 1,900; Comments per video: 1,000
@zachking (magic) 28.6 million USA 334.4 million 0.7%
Total videos: 161; Comments per video: 6,800
@riyaz.14 24.9 million India 959,200 16.1%
Total videos: 1,100; Comments per video: 2,000
@kristenhancher 23.1 million. USA. 856,300 17.0%
Total videos: 1,800; Comments per video: 846

By analyzing the visual appearance of social networks over time, we may see that most users fall into recognizable patterns with opinion leaders at the center of sub-groups. Users may pay attention to each other, and there can be a symmetric exchange of attention and information in this social network (Hansen, Shneiderman, & Smith, 2011). The top ten influencers clustered around media accounts with strong social ties (Hansen, Shneiderman, & Smith, 2011). The users with the highest between-ness centrality revealed the bridging users. These users are vitally important to the structure of the network and are important for three reasons: 1) these users are in a better position than others in terms of having access to information; 2) these users are a bridge to *different people in other networks*, which have the potential to carry the message further and thus increase the reach; and 3) these users are connected to *different people*, and they have greater chances of having access to *different information*.

The measurement of social networks opens the possibility to develop greater sophistication in social media analyses. By understanding communication patterns of influence, as well as the content of the communication, we should be able to observe the impact of Twitter and other social tools. This is important for social networks and media, as well as social marketing efforts.

At the same time, social networks offer an opportunity to understand political communication. Himelboim, McCreery, and Smith (2013) integrated network and content analyses to study political views on Twitter. By mapping conversation on ten controversial subjects, the team discovered subgroups of "highly connected users – clusters – that were loosely connected to users outside their clusters" (p. 167). Conservative and liberal clusters were common, as younger users tended to move away from neutral news sites. Twitter data tend to fall into one of six visual patterns of crowds identified in mapping by Smith et al. (2014):

- **Polarized Crowd** – two large and dense groups with little overlap

- **Tight Crowd** – highly interconnected accounts with few isolated

- **Brand Clusters** – well-known products and services

- **Community Clusters** – conversation about popular topics

- **Broadcast Network** – commentary and breaking news

- **Support Network** – customer service hub and spoke structure.

(paras. 8–13)

There continues to be a need to study the reliability and validity of data visualization. The mapping of social crowds is strongly impacted by search terms used to sample population data found in current social media communication. Academic research will continue to develop and help us better understand the nature of communication on Twitter and other social media sites.

OTHER SOCIAL NETWORK MEASUREMENT ISSUES

As Miller (2013) observed, social media marketing involves a lot of variables and media channels and opportunities:

> Social media are exciting new marketing channels deserving serious experimentation and analysis for integration into marketing programs. They provide hundreds of channels for networking and building relationships ... The conversation must be unfettered ... The company must respond honestly to complaints or criticism and trust its customers to distinguish unfair comments from fact.
>
> (p. 102)

Social media can be a powerful force to reach large audiences with important messages. Audience size and "connectedness" matter in "online word of mouth" campaigns, as well as general conversation (Sterne, 2010, pp. 51, 57).

Social media measurement returns us to the central issues of computer-mediated communication (CMC). These spaces allow us to develop online relations, explore interaction with new people, create identities, and grow communities of interest. Tools such as Klout.com attempted to measure influence across social media platforms. Conversation monitoring of relevant quantitative and qualitative data offers opportunities to learn from social networking and social media. Sentiment analysis techniques continue to be developed that will take us beyond broad measures of influence and trust toward understanding the quality of engagement and the nature of the impact.

The measurement industry offers "deliverables" to clients, and social media metrics and analytics have become big business. The ongoing development of best practices for measuring communication tone, for example, should yield greater precision in the future. Whether or not social media engagement increases or decreases on specific sites over time, scientifically reliable and valid data will be needed.

In the United States, there are few government regulations of the Internet. Smartphone and tablet access now include high-quality video, which is extending the average amount of time users spend online. Video sites are integrating social chats and other functions, and new tools are likely to emerge to measure user behavior. Social media platforms are viewed as branding opportunities for media industries (Greer & Ferguson, 2011). This will push marketers to develop more complex social media measurement tools and techniques.

DISCUSSION QUESTIONS: STRATEGIES AND TACTICS

1. If you were advising a CEO who had never been on Twitter to create a profile, which key concepts would you discuss with her or him?

2. How would you decide whether or not to create a new social media account for your personal or company brand? What are the potential risks of following the crowd to TikTok?

3. Is there ever a case for disengagement from social media? Which circumstances would provide reasons to lower levels of engagement?

4. How could you integrate the findings from data on Facebook, Instagram and Twitter to use best practices at newer social media sites? Which other data points are of interest to you?

5. Explore your social network. What do the data tell you about your use of Twitter? What is missing from the data? How could you improve measurement and your use of Twitter?

REFERENCES

AMEC. (2010, July 19). *Barcelona Declaration of Measurement Principles*. http://amecorg.com/2012/06/barcelona-declaration-of-measurement-principles

AMEC. (2015). Barcelona Principles 2.0. https://amecorg.com/wp-content/uploads/2015/09/Barcelona-Principles-2.pdf

Baran, S. J., & Davis, D. (2006). *Mass Communication Theory*, fourth edition. Belmont, CA: Thomson Wadsworth.

Burnett, R., & Marshall, P. D. (2003). *Web Theory*. London, UK: Routledge.

California Consumer Privacy Act of 2018, AB-375. https://leginfo.legislature.ca.gov/faces/bill-TextClient.xhtml?bill_id=201720180AB375

California v. TWC. (2019). https://int.nyt.com/data/documenthelper/554-1-a-weather-app-location/8980fd9af72915412e31/optimized/full.pdf

Chin, C. (2019, December 19). Highlights: The GDPR and CCPA as Benchmarks for Federal Privacy Legislation. *Brookings*. https://www.brookings.edu/blog/techtank/2019/12/19/highlights-the-gdpr-and-ccpa-as-benchmarks-for-federal-privacy-legislation/

Clement, J. (2019, October 8). Most-followed Athletes on Instagram Worldwide as of October 2019. *Statista*. www.statista.com/statistics/647392/most-followers-instagram-athletes/

Cohen, S. (2016, December 23). Kardashian-Chyna Reality Show Continues on Social Media. *NBC Chicago*. www.nbcchicago.com/entertainment/entertainment-news/Kardashian-Chyna-Reality-Show-Continues-on-Social-Media–408104915.html

Confessore, N., & Kang, C. (2018, December 30). Facebook Data Scandals Stoke Criticism that a Privacy Watchdog Too Rarely Bites. *The New York Times*. www.nytimes.com/2018/12/30/technology/facebook-data-privacy-ftc.html

Constine, J. (2019, November 8). Instagram to Test Hiding like Counts in US, Which Could Hurt Influencers. *TechCrunch*. https://techcrunch.com/2019/11/08/instagram-hide-likes-us/

Cooley, C. H. (1909/1966). The Significance of Communication. In B. Berelson and M. Janowitz (Eds.), *Reader in Public Opinion and Communication*, second edition, pp. 147–155. New York: Free Press.

Fontein, D. (2016, July 27). Top Demographics that Matter to Social Media Marketers. *Hootsuite*. https://blog.hootsuite.com/facebook-demographics/

FTC. (2012, August 10). FTC Approves Final Settlement with Facebook. www.ftc.gov/news-events/press-releases/2012/08/ftc-approves-final-settlement-facebook

Garton, L., Haythornthwaite, C., & Wellman, B. (1997, June). Studying Online Social Networks. *Journal of Computer-Mediated Communication 3*(1). http://jcmc.indiana.edu/vol3/issue1/garton.html

Gordon, J. (2012). See, Say, Feel, Do: Social Media Metrics That Matter. *Fenton*. http://online.fliphtml5.com/ivff/yguy/#p=1 (Accessed March 25, 2020).

Greer, C. F., & Ferguson, D. A. (2011). Using Twitter for Promotion and Branding: A Content Analysis of Local Television Twitter Sites. *Journal of Broadcasting & Electronic Media 55*(2), 198–214.

Gumpert, G., & Cathcart, R. (Eds.) (1986). *INTER/MEDIA. Interpersonal Communication in a Media World*, third edition. New York: Oxford University Press.

Hamilton, I. A. (2019, December 14). TikTok's Owner Has Been Quietly Testing a Spotify Competitor. *Business Insider*. www.businessinsider.com/tiktok-owner-bytedance-testing-music-app-resso-2019-12

Hansen, D. L., Shneiderman, B., & Smith, M. A. (2011). *Analyzing Social Media Networks with NodeXL*. Burlington, MA: Elsevier.

Heaney, M. T., & McClurg, S. D. (2009, September). Social Networks and American Politics. *American Politics Research 37*(5), 727–741.

Himelboim, I., McCreery, S., & Smith, M. (2013). Birds of a Feather Tweet Together: Integrating Network and Content Analyses to Examine Cross-Ideology Exposure on Twitter. *Journal of Computer-Mediated Communication 18*, 154–174.

Hutchinson, A. (2016, July 14). Facebook Releases New Data on What Users are Looking for on Facebook and Instagram. *Social Media Today*. www.socialmediatoday.com/social-business/facebook-releases-new-data-what-users-are-looking-facebook-and-instagram

Hutchinson, A. (2019, April 24). Facebook Reaches 2.38 Billion Users, Beats Revenue Estimates in Latest Update. *Social Media Today*. www.socialmediatoday.com/news/facebook-reaches-238-billion-users-beats-revenue-estimates-in-latest-upda/553403/

Hutchinson, A. (2020, January 9). Facebook Outlines New 'Video Traffic Source Insights' and Provides Video Tips. *Social Media Today*. www.socialmediatoday.com/news/facebook-outlines-new-video-traffic-source-insights-and-provides-video-ti/570067/

Kaushik, A. (2010). *Web Analytics 2.0*. Indianapolis, IN: Wiley Publishing.

Koh, J., Kim, Y.-G., Butler, B., & Bock, G.-W. (2007, February). Encouraging Participation in Virtual Communities. *Communications of the ACM 50*(2), 69–73.

Lerbinger, O. (2019). *Corporate Communication, an International and Management Perspective*. Hoboken, NJ: Wiley Blackwell.

Leskin, P., & Rogers, T. N. (2019, November 7). Kim Kardashian Says She No Longer Posts to Instagram and Social Media in Real-time after Being Robbed at Gunpoint in Paris. *Business Insider*. www.businessinsider.com/kim-kardashian-instagram-social-media-paris-robbery-likes-mental-health-2019-11

Lunden, I. (2019, November 30). Black Friday Sees Record $7.4B In Online Sales, $2.4B Using Smartphones. *TechCrunch*. https://techcrunch.com/2019/11/30/black-friday-sees-record-7-4b-in-online-sales-2-9b-spent-using-smartphones/

MediaMix. (2019). 13 TikTok Statistics Marketers Need to Know: TikTok Demographics & Key Data. https://mediakix.com/blog/top-tik-tok-statistics-demographics/

Milburn, M. A. (1991). *Persuasion and Politics*. Belmont, CA: Wadsworth.

Miller, P. (2013). Social Media Marketing. In A. B. Albarran (Ed.), *The Social Media Industries*, pp. 86–101. New York, NY: Routledge.

Min, S. (2019, November 8). 86% of Young Americans Want to Be a Social Media Influencer. *CBS News*. www.cbsnews.com/news/social-media-influencers-86-of-young-americans-want-to-become-one/

Mytton, G., Diem, P., & van Diem, P. H. (2016). *Media Audience Research, A Guide for Professionals 3e*. Los Angeles, CA: SAGE.

Nielsen. (2019, December 10). Tops of 2019: Social TV. *Nielsen Media*. www.nielsen.com/us/en/insights/article/2019/tops-of-2019:-social-tv/

Omnicore. (2019). Snapchat Statistics. www.omnicoreagency.com/snapchat-statistics/

Paul, K. (2016, December 20). Kim Kardashian Made a Cameo on Snapchat – Here's How Much Money She Has Lost by Staying off Social Media. *MarketWatch*. www.marketwatch.com/story/kim-kardashian-is-losing-300000-a-week-by-staying-off-social-media-2016-11-07

Perez, S. (2017, January 11). Twitter Is Shutting Down Its Business App, Twitter Dashboard. *TechCrunch*. https://techcrunch.com/2017/01/11/twitter-is-shutting-down-its-business-app-twitter-dashboard/

Pletz, J. (2019, December 2). Sprout Social Expects To Raise $156 Million In IPO. *Crain's Chicago Business*. www.chicagobusiness.com/john-pletz-technology/sprout-social-expects-raise-156-million-ipo

Radian6. (2013). The Cost of Ignoring Social Media. *Sales Force Marketing Cloud*. www.salesforcemarketingcloud.com/blog/2013/05/cost-of-ignoring-social-media/

Rodrigues, E. M., Milic-Frayling, N., Smith, M., Shneiderman, B., & Hansen, D. (2011). *Groupin-a-Box Layout for Multi-faceted Analysis of Communities*. http://hcil.cs.umd.edu/trs/2011–24/2011–24.pdf

Russo, T. C., & Koesten, J. (2005, July). Prestige, Centrality, and Learning: A Social Network Analysis of an Online Class. *Communication Education 54*(3), 254–261.

Savage, N. (2011, March). Twitter as Medium and Message. *Communicators of the ACM 54*(3), 18–20.

Severin, W. J., & Tankard, J. W., Jr. (2001). *Communication Theories*, fifth edition. New York, NY: Longman.

Shively, K., & Hitz, L. (2016). *The State of Social Marketing: 2016 Annual Report.* Simply Measured. Available at: http://simplymeasured.com/blog/introducing-the-2016-state-of-social-marketing-report/

Singer, N. (2019, January 18). The Week in Tech: How Google and Facebook Spawned Surveillance Capitalism. *The New York Times.* https://www.nytimes.com/2019/01/18/technology/google-facebook-surveillance-capitalism.html

Singh, M. (2019, November 15). TikTok Tests Social Commerce. *TechCrunch.* https://techcrunch.com/2019/11/15/tiktok-link-bio-social-commerce/

Smith, C. (2016, November 17). 88 Amazing Snapchat Statistics (October 2016). *Expanded Ramblings.* http://expandedramblings.com/index.php/snapchat-statistics/

Smith, M., Rainie, L., Shneiderman, B., & Himelboim, I. (2014, February 20). Mapping Twitter Topic Networks: From Polarized Crowds to Community Clusters. *Pew Research Center, Internet & Technology.* www.pewresearch.org/internet/2014/02/20/mapping-twitter-topic-networks-from-polarized-crowds-to-community-clusters/

Sports Illustrated. (2016, December 12). Scorecard: Social Climbers, p. 19.

Sterne, J. (2010). *Social Media Metrics.* Hoboken, NJ: Wiley.

Treadwell, D. (2017). *Introducing Communication Research*, third edition. Los Angeles, CA: SAGE.

Tubbs, S. T., & Moss, S. (1983). *Human Communication*, fourth edition. New York, NY: Random House.

Valentino-DeVries, J., & Singer, N. (2019, January 3). Los Angeles Accuses Weather Channel App of Covertly Mining User Data. *The New York Times.* www.nytimes.com/2019/01/03/technology/weather-channel-app-lawsuit.html

Westley, B. H., & MacLean, J. M. (1957). A Conceptual Model for Communications Research. *Journalism Quarterly 34*(1), 31–38.

Wimmer, R. D., & Dominick, J. R. (2013). *Mass Media Research: An Introduction*, tenth edition. Boston, MA: Wadsworth.

Yurieff, L. (2019, December 19). From Instagram to TikTok: How Social Media Evolved This Decade. *CNN Business.* www.cnn.com/2019/12/19/tech/social-media-end-of-decade/index.html

New and Mobile Media Technologies, Innovation, and Investment

I think that digital detox will become more prevalent this year, with many people trying to limit the amount of time they spend on social media. I also think that there will continue to be a big push towards making social media more private and secure for its users – this has been a big problem recently, and many people are just realizing how truly dangerous a lack of online privacy can be.

– Lilach Bullock, @lilachbullock (2020)

The real magic of #PokemonGo is the way you look like you're creepily filming strangers, when you're really trying to capture a damn Zubat.

– Nic Healey, @dr_nic (2016)

The last tweet was sent personally by The Queen from her official Twitter account @BritishMonarchy #TheQueenTweets

– Queen Elizabeth, @RoyalFamily (2014)

Innovation drives social media thought leaders and celebrities. Lilach Bullock, for example, is a "lead conversion expert" who has tweeted nearly 400,000 times since 2008. Her content marketing focus in Israel and the UK has attracted more than 101,700 Twitter followers. Social media communication momentum is wide and deep – even members of the Royal Family are active. When Queen Elizabeth II announced the hiring of a digital engagement expert in 2020, it was clear that the Royal Family was ready to expand efforts begun when she first tweeted in 2014 (Aguilera, 2019). From TikTok dance challenges to the use of new technologies, social media communication continued to evolve through the use of innovative professionally created content. There was a surge of early interest in augmented reality (AR) during the summer of 2016, as users swarmed to the Pokémon Go app. BuzzFeed attracted more than 145,000-page views by curating funny Pokémon tweets (Whitehead, 2016). Nearly all of the initial product launch mentions of the app were on Twitter, suggesting the importance of real-time social monitoring, key moments, and trends (Underdown, 2016). However, the app failed to incorporate social functionality within it, and this omission may have limited its durability within an age of social media communication. A 2017 *Trends Report*, though, suggested a more serious business impact – we were seeing "a turning point for immersive content" (Edelman Digital, 2016, p. 4). From live streaming to 360-degree advertisements, it appears that mobile innovation will lead the next wave of social media technologies. Global social media interest continues to grow: more than two-thirds of the world are mobile users, but about one-third of adults in the UK reduced social media use (Carter, 2020, para. 8). "More people are now choosing to 'detox' from social media, deleting apps and profiles in order to step away from it" (para. 7). One estimate concluded that people were spending nearly two days per week on their smartphones: "This whole scale move to social by your prospects, customers, employees, new recruits and investors is a transformation where you need to get onboard otherwise you will never catch up" (Hughes, 2020, para. 5). For students of social media, balancing the need to keep up and the health concerns from living online are real.

There also are critical economic and social perspectives that connect technological innovation to broad trends of a global workforce, use of social media to stay connected, and young professionalism: "Social entrepreneurs have responded to the need to provide lonely foreigners with a means to gather face-to-face with others who are in a similar situation – even if on a superficial level of a new relationship – by using digital platforms" (such as Facebook groups) "to create mobile expat clubs" (Polson, 2016, p. 4). This has implications because of a rise "to embrace a places-less lifestyle" that suggests "a broader set of discourses and practices through which a new global, mobile class is emerging" (p. 5). In development of "a set of cultural practices," critical theorists "re-examine concepts of place, identity, class, and community in a changing context of digital media, mobility, and globalization" (p. 23). Such approaches, though, tend to be overshadowed by business implications. Albarran (2013) examined the structures of the social media industry that emphasize research and innovation:

> Companies are understandably secretive about their internal research and development efforts. Most companies will not detail new products under consideration, nor offer any specifics as to how much funding and support is spent each year on research and innovation efforts.
>
> (p. 9)

Social media industries have developed business models focused on marketing, content, news, and uses in a way that places less value on personal data privacy. For example, millions of SMS text messages were not secure following a huge data breach (Whittaker, 2019). At the same time, the Amazon Ring doorbell camera was considered a privacy problem when it was disclosed that local police agencies have wide access to the data, which also was hacked (Guariglia, 2019). In one case, a hacker was watching a home camera and speaking to children. Increasingly, home cameras, such as the Pet Cube, also offer social media sharing of images. The value of social media are based upon CMC self-image presentation, "spontaneity," appearance, and status:

"In Facebook reality, friendship, resembling rather superficial friendliness ... 'friends' may attest to the person's high social status, others to his/her power, relational skills, or attractiveness" (Bogdanowska & Bogdanowska-Jakubowska, 2016, pp. 26–27). The monetization of psychological use motivation may be at the core of understanding rapid mobile and social media adoption. In this context, there is fertile ground to cultivate entrepreneurship.

Digital media have ushered in an era of continuous innovation. Beginning with multimedia software programs and the early Web in the 1990s, the United States became a global hotbed for an innovation culture that spread to many parts of the world. The investment in new technologies increasingly has a connection to social media communication. Some large corporations created the title of Chief Digital Officer (CDO) to incorporate the need for internal thought leaders who attempt to keep pace with the changing landscape of social and mobile media, as well as to focus the previous work of Chief Information Officer (CIO).

Social networking sites that employ social media must transform innovation into a business model. Social business is complex, involving key sources of value creation (Cha, 2013). A successful social media platform must provide a needed product or service, it must function within user expectations, it must serve a particular market, and it must ultimately generate revenue in order to survive and prosper: "The inherent nature of social networking sites keeps users coming back on a regular basis, which also likely increases the exposure of these returnees to the goods and services marketed on these sites" (p. 78). Amazon.com, for example, offered Today's Deals as a way to motivate customers to return and engage. Each product is rated by a five-star average, and consumers may also read customer reviews. The social media communication of customer engagement provides important texture and context for site visitors. Social media observers have connected customer engagement to sharing, altruism, value creation, influence and other important marketing concepts.

📱 BOX 7.1

Viewpoints Power Reviews: Curated Product and Service Review System

More than 70 million PowerReviews through an "ecosystem of consumers, advocates, and influencers" is designed to promote the creation and curation of "authentic content to accelerate sales." The PowerReviews website lists successes in the areas of health and beauty; apparel and footwear; food and beverage; and home and garden marketing.

The tool has been used by thousands of brands and retailers to collect customer reviews and answer questions (www.powerreviews.com/). It allows in-market shoppers to directly engage with brands through verified reviews. Amazon and other sites have shown that shoppers consider product reviews an accurate way to gauge consumer experiences, and a site known for independent and trusted reviews reached out to marketers. In an age of social media, brands cannot ignore the voice of the people. The challenge, however, is building consumer engagement that does not game the system. Viewpoints.com, a consumer reviews platform, launched Pulse for brands to listen to and engage more directly with consumers.

"For the first time we're giving the brands, the owners of the products, the ability to now claim those products and collect reviews ... manage those reviews and promote them," founder and CEO Matt Moog said. The site attempts to verify reviewers, and uses an editorial process before publishing reviews.

Viewpoints reviewers complete a proactive disclosure form, including required Federal Trade Commission (FTC) disclosure of any payments or products received. Beyond this, every review is screened "at multiple points," Moog said. "We also have a number of fraud detection signals ... that are automated ... We then human moderate every review that comes on the site." Each review is scored, and about 25% are rejected – 20% for poor quality and 5% spam, Moog said.

Viewpoints seeks to know its reviewers and build "a rich social profile of them" by collecting reviews "as an independent third party," Moog said, and organizing and curating them to "validate their authenticity" as a "trusted intermediary." Unlike typical retailer sites designed to sell products, Moog says Viewpoints tells consumers products *not* to buy, highlights those with low ratings, and offers access to negative reviews. By identifying reviewers and their review history and offering reviewer badges (trusted, verified trusted, and VIP), Viewpoints is different from retailers.

By having a large number of reviews and an active community of millions of users, Moog says Viewpoints limits the impact of an illegitimate review that might initially sneak through. Viewpoints questioned reviewers, and Moog says, "if we're not satisfied that it's a legitimate review, we'll remove it."

"I would never tell you or anyone else that it's a perfect system," Moog said, "but you can certainly over time be able to trust more people who contribute regularly, whose opinions are spread across many different products and categories, who have many interlocking relationships."

Online shoppers are not the only ones checking reviews. A growing number of in-store shoppers also read product reviews; survey data suggest. Nearly half of all shoppers check for reviews prior to making a buying decision.

While Viewpoints will allow brands to engage with consumers, marketers will pay to add information – not delete or re-order existing reviews. By creating a corporate account, Pulse offers review collection tools, product description publishing and reply management, analytics, and promotion tools through a partnership with Google Shopping and Google Search, Moog said.

The collection, management, and promotion of reviews also features social media tools that connect with Facebook and Twitter.

Moog sees the model as having an "opportunity to bring greater transparency and accountability to the market" by shining a light on good *and* bad products. "When you think about the environment and sustainability and peoples' need to spend money in places where it matters," Moog says, "I'd rather get something that lasted for a long time, that didn't fill a landfill and go spend my money on health care or education rather than disposable consumer goods."

Source: See Lipschultz, J. H. (January 23, 2014). Consumer Review Credibility, Brand Marketing and Social Media. *The Huffington Post*, Media. www. huffingtonpost.com/jeremy-harris-lipschultz/consumer-review-credibili_ b_4634447.html; Viewpoints (January 14, 2017). Advertisers. http://www. viewpoints.com/

Innovators and entrepreneurs across the county continue to develop ideas and products. When Foursquare co-founder Dennis Crowley launched the location-based app, he saw it as social media communication. The concept of "checking-in" somewhere quickly became connected to the Facebook **social graph**, which Crowley described as "anyone you've ever shaken hands with" (Crowley, 2010, at 0:21). Twitter, Crowley concluded, was more about entertaining people. Foursquare, in its initial concept, was "people you actually overlap with in real life." Crowley began his work in graduate school with "a lot of creative freedom" to follow what he was passionate about (at 2:12): "Creativity is people trying interesting things without the fear of failure or ridicule" (at 2:28). The focus is on "rapid iteration" – building something that probably will not work, and then fixing it and improving the product each week (at 2:46). This is the nature of start-up culture and thinking. It begins with learning what has been done in the social media space and then trying to improve it. In a few short years, social media moved from innovation to important function within small and large established companies.

t📡 BOX 7.2

Thought Leader Zena Weist

My career took a complete shift in 2006 because of social media. I was Group Manager of Online Branding for a telecom and was responsible for all corporate digital marketing and our online voice. It became very apparent that our customers were talking about us on discussion boards and blogs – Facebook was still gated for universities, and Twitter hadn't been launched yet. We began working with our customer service team to create an online response team that listened and responded to customer inquiries. We launched a YouTube "How

FIGURE 7.1 *@zenaweist.*
Courtesy of Zena Weist

To" video channel, and by 2007 we were active on Facebook and Twitter as well. Our mantra was listen, respond, resolve, and engage. I was recruited to become the first Social Media Director at H&R Block in 2010, and I have been focused on integrated marketing, including social media, ever since.

Social media had been "siloed" into marketing or communications. It really flows across all business functions and needs to be part of change management and operations. The shift in thinking that needs to occur to move social media programs from tactical to more strategic and company-wide will be the biggest challenge for organizations. I bumped into this narrow line of thinking while brand-side and agency-side and see it as the largest pain point for current clients.

The opportunity is largest with social media in customer experience and product innovation. We will have our customer service, marketing and communication foundation solid within social media, and organizations will continue to focus more attention on utilizing social media to enhance customer experience and product innovation through predictive analytics from social media listening.

Zena (Monsour) Weist is a Board Member for the Catholic Charities of Northeast Kansas, Digital Storytelling Center of Kansas City, and the Catholic Education Foundation in Kansas. Previously, she was Strategy Director at Level Five Solutions in Kansas City. She has more than 20 years of experience, including at Edelman Digital and H&R Block, leading online marketing and interactive agency branding. In 2011, TopRank named Weist "One of the 25 Women Who Rock Social Media." She is a founding member of the Kansas City Chapter of The Social Media Club.

ENTREPRENEURS

Social media innovation captured the imagination of those energized by an entrepreneurial spirit. The same open approach to development that was seen during the personal computer and Internet revolution seems present with social and mobile media. The development of smartphone apps almost immediately helped define social media as mobile. Rapid diffusion of smartphones and dropping prices for tablets created a ready market for developing social media platforms, such as Snapchat. Initially, entrepreneurs may start projects with little or no money, but eventually it requires investment to launch, grow, and sustain a company as a profitable business.

Digital media entrepreneurship, as is the case with social media, must utilize strategies when it comes to market value (Abernathy & Sciarrino, 2019). "External factors – such as the economic environment and industry sector in which a company operates – have historically exerted an outsized impact, determining as much as 90% of a company's market valuation" (p. 66). Entrepreneurs create "a unique value proposition" (p. 107), and try to turn "value into profit" (p. 117). "Customer journey mapping" within social media may show how the experience "affects loyalty and brand attachment" (p. 144, 147).

In terms of user time spent, apps and mobile browsing rapidly dominated digital media (comScore, 2015). Apps drove most of the early mobile media growth. "Millennials spend an exorbitant amount of time on their smartphone apps, and usage declines with age" (p. 9). Instagram's rapid growth beyond 600 million users, adding 100 million alone in 2016 (Swant, 2016), helps explain why innovative brands such as Airbnb extensively used it for branding (York, 2016). Instagram Stories offered brands creative ways to show inner-workings of their businesses, repurpose blog content, promote upcoming live events, offer product demos, celebrate highlights, and display company creativity (Galek, 2017). Likewise, on Snapchat, marketers fiercely compete to be top influencers (Steimle, 2016). This also happens among apps, as witnessed when Meerkat had an early 2015 successful launch of mobile social video, only to be eclipsed by Twitter Periscope and later Facebook Live as personal streaming social phenomena (Brogan, 2015). While Internet live video streams had been available for years, the "new apps help to incorporate live streaming into the existing social media landscape, potentially bringing it to a much larger audience" (para. 2). Nowhere in the US was this more important than the #BlackLivesMatter protests in #Ferguson Missouri, #Baltimore, and other cities. Streaming accounts attracted large audiences, including mainstream news reporters and organizations attempting to cover real-time developments. The success of each new app motivates developers and investors to search for the next viral sensation.

ANGEL INVESTORS AND START-UPS

Most social media start-ups, once beyond initial development and testing, would be expected to make a "pitch" to an investor or investment group. These are people who have large amounts of money. They are willing to participate in a risky investment because of the potential to earn huge gains. An angel investor brings capital to the business and buys into the start-up. Some investors have organized into groups that share debt and evaluate new ideas within a competitive environment. An investor must weigh **opportunity costs** of what else could be done with the money, if not invested in the concept. It is common for start-ups to be developed with a goal of either selling to a large corporation or issuing public stock.

Many start-ups attempt to take advantage of the fact that we rarely go anywhere without our smartphones. HearHere Radio, a Chicago-based start-up, for example, launched the Rivet News Radio app (Glenn, 2013). The concept was for users to "hear news on their own schedules – starting, stopping, skipping and selecting stories as they wish" (para. 2). Founder John MacLeod found a crowded market for smartphone apps, as developers compete for our limited attention. The start-up pivoted into a telemarketing "news on hold" service, podcasting consultant, and more focused audio feature app. Start-ups must generate revenue and eventually be profitable to survive. Although Pew Internet data suggested that about 60% in the US listened to online radio, music, and podcasts, it is not clear that many companies will be profitable – especially those that fail to take advantage of social media trends.

More often than not, start-ups fail. For example, in 2018, Unicorn Scooters raised $150,000 – a relatively small amount during a time when other companies raised millions over longer periods of time for new ideas. Electric scooters were a hot idea in a competitive space.

> As the story goes, the business spent way too much money on Facebook and Google ads; the startup quickly shut down with no money left over to issue refunds for more than 300 of its $699 scooters that had been ordered.
>
> (Heater, Clark, & Ha, 2019, paras. 27–28)

Social media advertising costs for paid and promoted posts, the seasonal nature of the scooter business, and successful competitors meant that Unicorn Scooters lost customers and revenue needed to keep the business model afloat. For many start-up products targeted at young consumers, a business plan must include purchasing Instagram advertisements. No wonder corporate owner Facebook continues to see huge growth in quarterly earnings.

BIG IDEAS AND BUSINESS

Social media reach billions of people, so it should not be a surprise that this is now about big business. Facebook was one of the earliest social media sites to generate large amounts of revenue by selling advertising. Once Facebook sold stock, it offered small and large investors the opportunity to participate in its growth in exchange for risking money on it. Estimates of active social media users are rough but offer some idea of the size of these businesses, as shown in Table 7.1.

Cha (2013) theorized that business models of social network sites are derived from four components: value creation, target marketing, competencies, and revenue (pp. 62–63). As products or services, they have a scope, distribution and positioning:

> It addresses the value that the firm provides customers and how the firm creates value … The value creation is also directly related to how the firm positions itself in the market … The value that a firm creates, and how the firm creates value, cannot be separated from how the firm positions itself in the marketplace.

(p. 62)

Value, then, is complex and important: "Firms wanting to enter the social networking market should differentiate their value, positioning, and target [a] consumer base from existing social networks" (p. 75).

TABLE 7.1 *Estimates of "Active Users" on Top Social Network Sites (2019)*

SNS Rank 2019 (2016)	Launch Year	Estimated Total Active Users 2019 2016 2013
1. (1) Facebook	2004	2.27 billion 1.59 1.59
2. (2) YouTube	2005	1.90 billion 1.50 1.00
3. (3) WhatsApp	2010	1.50 billion 1.00 600 million
4. (4) Facebook Mess.	2011	1.30 billion 1.00 500 million
5. (6) WeChat	2011	1.08 billion 697 million 438 million
6. (9) Instagram	2010	1.00 billion. 400 million. 150 million
7. (5) QQ (China)	1999	803 million 853 million 438 million
8. (7) QZone (China)	2005	531 million 640 million. 645 million
9. (–) TikTok (Douyin, China)	2016*	500 million. – –
10. (13) Sina Weibo	1999	486 million 222 million 167 million
11. (18) Reddit	2005	330 million 95 million 70 million
12. (10) Twitter	2006	326 million 320 million 232 million

Note: TikTok launched outside of China and in the US in 2017. It soared to 500 million active users after its ByteDance launch and Musical.ly absorption in 2018.

Sources: As many as 3.5 billion daily Snaps – Snapchat photographs and videos – were shared, and that number increased from 760 million in 2016. See Zephoria (October 2019). The Top 10 Valuable Snapchat Statistics – Updated in October 2019. https://zephoria.com/top-10-valuable-snapchat-statistics/. By 2015, 2 billion photos were shared daily on Snapchat, WhatsApp, Facebook, Instagram, and Flickr. https://whatsthebigdata.com/2015/12/14/2-billion-photos-are-shared-daily-on-snapchat-whatsappfacebook-instagram-and-flickr/; Dustin.tv (December 9, 2013). Global Social Media Research Summary 2016. *Smart Insights.* www.smartinsights.com/social-media-marketing/social-media-strategy/new-global-social-media-research/, via Statistica, www.statista.com/statistics/272014/global-social-networks-ranked-by-number-of-users/.

"CRUSH IT" AND THE THANK YOU ECONOMY

Vaynerchuk (2009) was an early adopter of social media platforms as a way to build brand identity. His book *Crush It, Cash in on Your Passion* reflected the entrepreneurial spirit embodied in the social media shift. The Internet "lowered the entry barriers to monetizing," (p. 5) and he argued that personal branding was the key to success through storytelling – writing, podcasts, or videos. Vaynerchuk linked social media content, such as blogs, to marketing principles of making "the extra effort" to "show genuine appreciation" (p. 28). Social media communication ushered in an era in which entrepreneurs comfortable in social media spaces may be able to skyrocket in popularity and become a rock star within the innovation culture. This, in turn, generates interest and potential funding of new ideas.

CROWDFUNDING

A way to fund a start-up is by going to the public and using Internet interest rather than via angel investment. A social media start-up can capture the interest of thousands of small investors through viral media rather than risking the idea on an investment group that may want to control it. Kickstarter.com pioneered the idea, and GoFundMe.com grew it by raising over $3 billion for personal causes. In 2020, the top crowdfunding sites were considered to be Kickstarter, Indiegogo, Causes, Patreon, GoFundMe, CircleUp, and Lending Club (Nguyen, 2019).

☐ BOX 7.3

Kickstarter

Kickstarter described itself as "a new way to fund creative projects" using "direct support of people" (para. 1). It was launched in 2009, and the numbers are impressive: 10 million creative project supporters. In 2015 Kickstarter became a Benefit Corporation for non-profits that are obligated to consider the impact on society with "legally defined goals." More than 34,000 projects have been backed, including one that won an Oscar.

The Kickstarter mission is "to help bring creative projects to life." Kickstarter offers tools within a socially responsible context. It donates 5% of its after-tax profits toward arts and music education, as well as organization fighting inequality.

Source: Kickstarter (January 14, 2013). Kickstarter is a Benefit Corporation. www.kickstarter.com/charter

---

EMERGENCE OF NEW AND MOBILE MEDIA

Much of what we call in this book *social media communication* is happening as users of mobile devices connect with their social networks worldwide. Researchers in South Korea found that it is possible to predict mobile divides by measuring demographic and skill variables (Jung, Chan-Olmsted, & Kim, 2013). While South Korea has "one of the highest smartphone penetration rates," the "younger, more innovative" users downloaded more apps:

> Specifically, male respondents used news/information applications more frequently, whereas female respondents used communication, utility, and commerce applications more frequently ... the observed gender differences in technology might be attributed more to differences in functional preferences ... women prefer online person-to-person communication more than men, and women use social media for relational purposes more frequently than their male counterparts.
>
> (pp. 728–729)

The research team suggested that a gender difference in news and information application use may magnify social and human capital differences. Early on social media also were found to drive mobile video viewing (Harris Interactive, 2012), and mobile phone viewing grew video viewing 233% between 2013 and 2016: "More than half of all video viewing is now happening on mobile, and most of those views come from phones, not tablets" (Roettgers, 2016, para. 1). Video drives more Instagram engagement than any other content; for LinkedIn posts and tweets with video, they spark ten to twenty times more engagement (Ahmad, 2019, para. 3).

🔲 BOX 7.4

The Death of Brickflow

Part of the story of innovation and investment is a willingness to fail. Brickflow, while innovative, ended operations when funding ran out for its project to compete with other social media content aggregators. The model to generate "cinematic slideshows" by tracking social media conversation was eventually converted to an open-source project. The Brickflow team started a new project, Lab.Coop, which was a tech venture incubator to help other start-up teams. It included a product lab, school, and Internet of Things hardware accelerator.

Sources: Lab.Coop (January 14, 2017). Building Ventures. www.lab.coop/; Brickflow (December 31, 2016). Unfortunately, Brickflow's Story Has Ended. http://brickflow.strikingly.com/; Grasty, T. (October 25, 2013). Brickflow Founder Tells His Tale Behind "Social Media Storytelling." *The Huffington Post*. www.huffingtonpost.com/tom-grasty/brickflow-founder-tells-his-tale_b_4138962.html

---

IMPLICATIONS OF REVOLUTIONARY MOBILE AND SOCIAL MEDIA

Social media behavior tends to favor a crowdsourcing desire because mobile technologies create flexibility to briefly bring people together physically or virtually and "plug in valuable information" (Greengard, 2011, p. 20). At the heart of social and mobile media are relationships, social ties, social capital, and motivation (Brown, 2011). Social capital theory has been applied to research on Facebook fan pages. Social interaction, shared values, and trust have been important predictors of future use (Lin & Lu, 2011). The researchers suggested that there is a complex process involving structure, cognition, and relational aspects. As expected, "shared values are an important factor influencing trust" of social media content (p. 568).

Barack Obama was one of the first politicians to harness the power of the social and mobile with an innovative campaign app in 2008 (Kenski, Hardy, & Jamieson, 2010). For example, young voters allowed the presidential campaign app to access their mobile phone contact lists, and then sorted these with a focus on key swing states. The app tracked calls in which users were urged to encourage their friends in these key states to remember to vote on election day. The app also was a mobile portal for campaign information, upcoming events, Obama videos, and positions on key issues. The technology opened the door to mobile and social media campaigning. By 2012 in the key swing state of Ohio, PBS reported that President Obama's campaign utilized an extensive ground network of volunteers, an iPad app for door-to-door campaigning, and a big data approach to filtering and targeting messages at different types of voters.

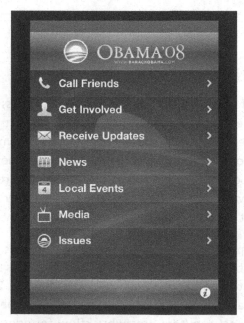

FIGURE 7.2 *Candidate Barack Obama's 2008 presidential election iPhone app changed modern political campaign strategy by incorporating social media communication.*

Facebook also became a battleground for social media sharing in the 2012 presidential election. Facebook's Randi Zuckerberg identified social networking as a social space for activism and change:

> Through social media, people not only donate money, but even more importantly, their reputation and identity. Each time someone clicks "like" or joins a cause on Facebook, they are broadcasting that message to hundreds of their friends, and aligning themselves with a particular issue ... the awareness generated from that simple action has a ripple effect and has the potential to recruit some extremely engaged volunteers and donors in the future.
>
> (Vericat, 2010, p. 177)

Zuckerberg suggested that Facebook may fill a void in face-to-face conversation lost for social or political reasons: "I believe that Facebook's ability to occupy the space of a free and unmoderated media and civil space will bring many more opportunities for meaningful democratic change" (p. 178). Online social networks may allow us to visualize "clear patterns" of affiliation and communication (Langlois et al., 2009, p. 425) – even among weak "acquaintances and other people with shallower connections" (Brown, 2011, p. 31). Early in the 2016 presidential election cycle, Pinterest deleted Rand Paul's board that mocked Hillary Clinton (Killough, 2015). Bernie Sanders, Clinton, and eventual winner Donald Trump all effectively used social media to activate their polarized groups of followers. They relied heavily on email lists for fundraising, events, and regular social media posts. Trump became known for his constant flow of controversial tweets that were reported by news media, and shared on social media and continued throughout his first term, an impeachment process and the 2020 election season.

Facebook responded after the 2016 election to concerns that it had allowed "fake news" to be shared throughout the campaign by rolling out new user tools to flag content. It hired a former TV news reporter and host, Campbell Brown, "to lead its news partnerships team" with news organizations (Rutenberg & Isaac, 2017, para. 2).

At the same time, Twitter suspended some accounts for violation of their terms of service. Edelman President Richard Edelman noted that trust continues to be an issue: "We have witnessed a stunning reversal of power between mainstream and social media: The ability to go direct to end users of information through social channels radically disrupted the mainstream news agenda" (Edelman, 2016, para. 1). Edelman predicted that,

1. "The technology industry will be in the crosshairs" because of privacy and security issues.

2. "Companies will be tempted to imitate Trump," but should not.

3. "The populist genie is out of the bottle."

4. "Local will prevail over global," as brands seek local purposes.

5. "Native advertising will have to change to survive" – "supplanted by video and graphic experiences."

6. "The fake news epidemic will continue, for now."

7. "New voices will fill the void in governance."

8. "Every company must be a media company."

9. "Companies will reach a new level of transparency," with an emphasis on truth and ethics.

10. "Sustainability will be led by business," as household practices become a conversation.

(para. 2)

Mathison (2009) was one of the first who identified the idea that every company is now a media company: Mobile and social media developed direct media channels created and maintained by new players (Mathison, 2009). The Twitter space, for example, lent itself to mobile use at large events (Pogue, 2009). In a stadium crowd, the 140 and then 280-character text format functions with low bandwidth availability when other platforms, such as Facebook, may bog down.

Many residents of large cities commute on trains and buses, and this leaves a lot of time to access mobile devices. In the same way that commuters once read newspapers, magazines, and books while riding, mobile apps offer access to information and entertainment. The difference is that smartphones offer more options and extremely current content. Bloggers have capitalized on the desire for more diverse content (Rettberg, 2008). Access to new points of view may influence social change and acceptance of new political positions and the adoption of ever-newer technologies (Genachowski, 2010; Rogers, 2003). In countries where democracy is struggling to flourish, there have been numerous attempts to use social and mobile media as tools of mobilization, revolution, and international awareness (Motadel, 2011).

While political discussion may account for relatively small proportions of social media on Facebook – especially outside of a presidential election – it was more common among those using Twitter (Pew, 2009). One can envision a social network as a place where opinions are activated by the distribution of news, information, data, and opinion. At the same time, salience of a particular social issue reflects the rise and fall of news cycles and various social contexts.

TWITTER IMPACT

Twitter has been a social media space for #fails – including the many failed attempts by brand managers to take advantage of events in real-time (Time, 2013). For example, baked goods brand Entenmann's tweeted immediately following the Casey Anthony case verdict (and then quickly apologized):

@Entenmanns: Who's #notguilty about eating all the tasty treats they want?!

(July 5, 2011)

Naturally, the failed attempt to hijack a popular hashtag – **hashjacking** – backfired, as Twitter users responded with criticism. Keenan (2013) explains that brands need to research whether or not a hashtag is promoted by another brand or linked to a tragic event. In either case, it is a good idea to avoid using the tag. The key is relevance: "With #RoyalBaby, brands like Pampers and Johnson & Johnson had a perfect opportunity to throw some fun, branded images into the mix" (para. 5). Twitter is a mobile platform that favors smart social media communication. In real-time, mistakes happen, but apologies can work. An American Red Cross social media manager, for example, accidentally tweeted from the official account about getting "slizzered," and a well-timed correction diffused the crisis:

> @RedCross: We've deleted the rogue tweet but rest assured the Red Cross is sober and we've confiscated the keys.
>
> (February 15, 2011)

By responding with a designated driver reference, the Red Cross appropriately used the context of Twitter to apologize and move on. Brands continue to fail. Chase, for example, opened itself to criticism on Twitter:

> @Chase
>
> You: why is my balance so low
>
> Bank account: make coffee at home
>
> Bank account: eat the food that's already in the fridge
>
> Bank account: you don't need a cab, it's only three blocks
>
> You: I guess we'll never know
>
> Bank account: seriously?
>
> #MondayMotivation (April 29, 2019)

Presidential candidate Elizabeth Warren (@SenWarren) parodied the style in a response. "Workers: employers don't pay living wages." Twitter is one of many popular mobile social media apps that take advantage of real-time communication, as well as other characteristics of mobile devices.

BOX 7.5

Thought Leader Brian Zuercher

The company called Seen, a Columbus, Ohio, start-up that uses visual marketing to drive customer engagement, encouraged Indy 500 fan sharing on race day. Twitter and Instagram photographs were tagged by fans with #Indy500orBust. The photos were incorporated into race marketing through an interactive map and geotagging. The Indy 500 gained new followers

FIGURE 7.3 *@bzuerche.*
Courtesy of Brian Zuercber

to their social media accounts, and greater reach across the social media landscape. CEO and co-founder Brian Zuercher identified a continuous environment:

The most significant change for marketing professionals was the concept of "always on." Additionally, it was managing industry information flow, personal identity (i.e., public persona and perception), and channel awareness.

- Industry information flow: We now have access to a fire hose of data and understanding how to manage and synthesize the massive amount of incoming information can be a challenge. At the same time, with the right tools, the data can be turned into actionable insights.
- Personal identity: It's essential to keep your brand's personal voice authentic and in line with your company's positioning. Because of social media, marketing professionals need to be aware of the various networks, apps and services available and then decide on the places to focus their time and effort. For example, instead of road tours and speaking engagements, it's possible to develop an expert view by creating and sharing valuable content to social networks.
- Channel awareness: Marketing professionals must have a true understanding of this and it should not be delegated.

The largest challenge will be having a healthy balance between your time spent participating online and offline. You still need to be aware of the conversation surrounding your industry, but at the same time, as information spreads faster and new platforms pop up, it's easy to get lost in all the information available online. The best way to strike a balance between the two is to understand media and be strategic about which platform makes the most sense for your business's audience.

Our business is focused on consumer visual media. The confluence of data will enable major opportunities to provide marketers critical insights to make smart, quick decisions. As transactional, social, and customer data evolve, it also becomes a major opportunity for marketers to drive growth.

Brian Zuercher is CEO at Hopewell in the Columbus, Ohio area. It is "the first human-focused work experience company using tech to help us build a new way to work." Previously, he was CEO of SEEN, as well as an account manager, product manager, consultant, advisor, reviewer, and company founder. Zuercher has a graduate degree in management and technology from Rensselaer Polytechnic Institute, and an undergraduate degree from Butler University. He has worked for GE, Honeywell, ABM, Clearwish, The Ohio State University Technology Commercialization and others. He was an advisor for UQ Marketing.

MOBILE GEOTAGGING

Location-based services (LBS) leverage mobile and social media by linking "people, places and things to enhance interactions" (Humphreys & Liao, 2011, p. 407). Armed with smartphones, users interact with two-way data interaction that may facilitate real-time social media behaviors. Conceptually, a sense of place may be meaningful to people: "Space is considered a more abstract term. Whereas place is considered more concrete" (p. 408). Researchers did not fully understand how users' mobile geotagging – placing digital tags on people, places, or objects – develops within a social context, but there appears to be "place-based storytelling and self-presentation through place" (p. 415). At the heart of these social networking and social media activities, "people make meaning" (p. 418).

Geospatial information, such as population, climate, and business data, have value and may be connected to social media data streams (Kruse, Crompvoets, & Pearlman, 2018). "The estimation of the value of information (VOI) must be able to describe how the decision-maker's information changes as a result of ... geospatial data" (p. 11). Social media generate "huge amounts of data" that require real-time storage, filtering, and "qualitative approaches" (pp. 214–15). Facebook Insights data, for example, offer precise geographic targeting, along with demographic and psychographic filtering. Consumers using branded mobile apps leave a digital data trail, and this changed advertising and social experiences. The targeting of consumers became a big business with companies growing through "billions of actionable insights" (Lipschultz, 2016, paras. 2–3). Large brands had an interest in the Internet of things, and geo-location data offered a way to hyper-target consumers. The lack of personal data privacy was a problem for employees fired from jobs over social media posts, as well as for high school students turned down for college admission because of an immature moment on social media. As we will see later, all social media users need to develop media literacy skills that help them understand that they are being watched on social media.

GOOGLE GLASS, SNAPCHAT SPECTACLES, AND AR

There was a lot of interest in the Google Glass technology, and more generally virtual and augmented reality. Wearable mobile technologies appear to be the next wave by allowing users to have hands free for activities instead of holding a smartphone. Google released the technology, and developers built some apps for it. Among the ideas: hands-free information for bike riding, cooking, golf, and travel (Google, 2013). It appeared that Glass initially was more suited to specialized business applications. Wearable technologies may either enhance social interaction or inhibit it as a distraction. Snapchat Spectacles was the first to test the link between wearables and social media. The augmented reality (AR) space is full of start-ups that push the technology. Thyng in Chicago, for example, developed AR experiences that can be placed on any surface. A group of iOS and Android developers built mobile apps that allow users to place 3-dimensional objects, personal photographs and video within a digital space. The concept is to allow people to walk around within the digital spaces. Thyng CEO Ed LaHood said, "We really see two market segments, both B2B and B2C as being symbolic in the sense that the more ... that the behavior becomes mainstream, the more it becomes interesting" (LaHood, 2018, 03:46). It will continue to take some time for social media platforms to incorporate data from wearable, AR and VR technologies, but it is easy to see how they may improve the quality of crowdsourcing.

It is difficult to make an accurate prediction about social media use, management, and marketing. This remains a rapidly changing field based upon fragmented attention across many sites. Among a list of predictions made about 2020, these appear to be important long-term concerns:

- The cost of advertising on Facebook and LinkedIn will increase and lead to a re-evaluation of ROI of a paid post. Cost per click (CPC) must be compared to other strategies.

- Platform-specific organic posts may re-emerge in response to rising advertising costs, and Facebook and Instagram Stories will continue to become more popular.

- Brands will focus on personalized customer experiences and micro-engagement, wherever they may happen.

- Noisy social media saturation will require managers to emphasize authentic and creative posts that entertain while not looking like advertising.

- As AI develops, brands will strive to emphasize conversation and human-centered content (Jenkins, 2019).

Technology innovators are risk-takers. Increasingly, start-ups such as YikYak developed social media apps outside of Silicon Valley (Deamicis, 2015). At the same time, YikYak, Burnbook, and other apps allowed for quasi-anonymous harassment and faced legal and ethical challenges – just because a technology works, it does not mean the human behavior is right (Prime, 2015). Tech start-ups also continue to struggle with diversity issues. *Inc.* Reporter Salvador Rodriguez (@sal19) showed how a Dropbox.com tweet attempted to reflect diversity, but a photograph was criticized because it had no African Americans or Latinos: "Though the photo includes CEO Drew Houston surrounded by both men and women, there is not a single person in the image with obviously darker-colored skin" (Rodriguez, 2016, para. 4).

The earliest successful Silicon Valley technology companies have been around for more than 40 years, so those businesses have matured (Ciaccia, 2016). Some have argued that we are witnessing "the end of the age of websites" (Mirkinson, 2016, para. 1). Regardless of how content is found and shared, in a social media age employees and others in personal and professional social networks have become the bread and butter of amplification. Lenovo, for example, urged its 60,000 employees ("Social Champions") to share company information: "Users post relevant content for their coworkers to see, and everyone has the ability to share those stories on external social networks" (Wegert, 2015, para. 5). The stream of technological innovation – from 5G mobile to VR and AR headsets – continues at a rapid pace, and the **Internet of Things** will require bandwidth and infrastructure, such as needed towers, to power connected devices (Adler, 2016; Hendel, 2019). Mobile technologies allow for new relationships between people and technologically mediated social communication, and they raise issues about personal privacy, law, ethics, and media literacy.

DISCUSSION QUESTIONS: STRATEGIES AND TACTICS

1. How is the push toward technological innovation changing your life? How do you think it may impact work during your career?

2. What are the challenges of connecting mobile technologies to social media communication? What are the new opportunities to benefit from this connection? What are the realistic limits of the new technologies?

3. What are the privacy concerns about geo-location and tagging mobile social media services? How do you think these services and concerns will evolve in the future?

REFERENCES

Abernathy, P. M., & Sciarrino, J. (2019). *The Strategic Digital Entrepreneur*. Medford, MA: Wiley Blackwell.

Adler, R. (2016, July 13). Here Comes 5G. *Recode*. www.recode.net/2016/7/13/12108888/here-comes-5g-fcc-spectrum-frontiers-order-broadband-wireless

Aguilera, J. (2019, December 13). Queen Elizabeth Hiring 'Digital Engagement' Expert to Run Her Social Media Channels. *Time*. https://time.com/5750078/royal-family-social-media-job/

Ahmad, I. (2019, October 30). Video Marketing Statistics for 2020. *Social Media Today*. www.socialmediatoday.com/news/video-marketing-statistics-for-2020-infographic/566099/

Albarran, A. B. (2013). Introduction. In A. B. Albarran (Ed.), *The Social Media Industries*, pp. 1–15. New York: Routledge.

Bogdanowska, N., & Bogdanowska-Jakubowska, E. (2016). Face and the Ethics of Social Networks. In K. Zilles and J. Cenca (Eds.), *Media Business Models: Breaking the Traditional Value Chain*, pp. 13–31. New York: Peter Lang.

Brogan, J. (2015, March 27). Meerkat and Periscope Aren't Changing the News. *Slate*. www.slate.com/articles/technology/technology/2015/03/meerkat_and_periscope_the_live_streaming_apps_aren_t_changing_the_news.html

Brown, A. (2011, March–April). Relationships, Community, and Identity in the New Virtual Society. *The Futurist 29–31*, 34.

Carter, J. (2020,January 8). Social Media Marketing Trends 2020. *Smart Insights*. https://www.smartinsights.com/social-media-marketing/social-media-strategy/social-media-marketing-trends–2020/

Cha, J. (2013). Business Models of Most-Visited U.S. Social Networking Sites. In A. B. Albarran (Ed.), *The Social Media Industries*, pp. 60–85. New York, NY: Routledge.

Ciaccia, C. (2016, April 1). Apple Turns 40 – Here's the 7 Best Apple Products Ever. *The Street*. www.thestreet.com/story/13488276/1/7-best-apple-products-ever-including-the-apple-watch.html

comScore. (2015, September 22). The 2015 U.S. Mobile App Report. *comScore*. www.comscore.com/Insights/Presentations-and-Whitepapers/2015/The-2015-US-Mobile-App-Report

Crowley, D. (2010, May 16). Foursquare Co-Founder Dennis Crowley. *YouTube*. www.youtube.com/watch?v=UjEc85wosw4

Deamicis, C. (2015, March 30). Yik Yak's Secret Advantage: It's outside the Silicon Valley Bubble. *Readwrite*. https://readwrite.com/2015/03/30/yik-yak-secret-weapon-outside-silicon-valley-bubble/ (Aceessed March 27, 2020).

Edelman. (2016, December 15). 6 A.m.: The Way Ahead. *Edelman*. www.edelman.com/

Edelman Digital. (2016, December 15). *2017 Trends Report*. http://edelmandigital.com/trends/

Galek, C. (2017, January 6). 6 Ways to Use Instagram Stories to Boost Audience Engagement. *Social Media Today*. www.socialmediatoday.com/

Genachowski, J. (2010, October 15). U.S. Senate Committee on Small Business and Entrepreneurship, FCC Chair's Response. http://fjallfoss.fcc.gov/edocs_public/attachmatch/DOC-302374A1.pdf

Glenn, L. R. (2013, December 5). Press Release. *Chicago-based Startup Launches App to Reinvent Radio News for Smartphone Era*. https://www.rivetsmartaudio.com/ourstory (Acessed March 27, 2020).

Google. (2013). Glass. www.google.com/glass/start/

Grasty, T. (2013, October 25). Brickflow Founder Tells His Tale Behind "Social Media Storytelling." *The Huffington Post*. www.huffingtonpost.com/tom-grasty/brickflow-founder-tells-histale_b_4138962.html

Greengard, S. (2011). Following the Crowd. *Communications of the ACM 54*(2), 20–22.

Guariglia, M. (2019, November 20). Five Senators Join the Fight to Learn Just How Bad Ring Really Is. *Electronic Frontier Foundation.* www.eff.org/deeplinks/2019/11/five-senators-join-fight-learn-just-how-bad-ring-really

Harris Interactive. (2012, March 15). *One in Five Adults With Mobile Devices Will Use Social Media to Follow March Madness in 2012.*

Heater, B., Clark, K., & Ha, A. (2019, December 26). Remembering the Start-ups We Lost in 2019. *TechCrunch.* https://techcrunch.com/2019/12/26/startups-lost-in-2019/

Hendel, J. (2019, December 29). The Big Barrier to Trump's 5G America. *Politico.* www.politico.com/news/2019/12/29/big-barrier-trump-5g-america-089883

Hughes, T. (2020, January 9). People are Spending Nearly 2 Days a Week on Their Smartphones. *Abacus News.* www.abacusnews.com/culture/people-china-spend-nearly-2-days-week-their-smartphones/article/3044471

Humphreys, L., & Liao, T. (2011). Mobile Geotagging: Reexamining Our Interactions with Urban Space. *Journal of Computer-Mediated Communication 16*(3), 407–423.

Jenkins, L. D. (2019, December 2). 12 Social Media Marketing Predictions From The Pros. *Social Media Examiner.* www.socialmediaexaminer.com/2020-social-media-marketing-predictions-from-the-pros/

Jung, J., Chan-Olmsted, S., & Kim, Y. (2013). From Access to Utilization: Factors Affecting Smartphone Application Use and its Impacts on Social and Human Capital Acquisition in South Korea. *Journalism & Mass Communication Quarterly 90*(4), 715–735.

Keenan, C. (2013, July 25). *Hashjacking: Hot or Not? Social Solutions Collective.* http://socialsolutionscollective.com/hashjacking-hashtag-hot-or-not/

Kenski, K., Hardy, B. W., & Jamieson, K. H. (2010). *The Obama Victory: How Media, Money, and Message Shaped the 2008 Election.* New York, NY: Oxford University Press.

Kickstarter. (2013). Seven Things to Know about Kickstarter. www.kickstarter.com/hello

Killough, A. (2015, February 17). Pinterest Deletes Rand Paul's Mock Hillary Clinton Page. *CNN.* www.cnn.com/2015/02/17/politics/rand-paul-hillary-clinton-pinterest/

Kruse, J., Crompvoets, J., & Pearlman, F. (Eds.) (2018). *GeoValue: The Socioeconomic Value of Geospatial Information.* Boca Raton: CRC Press.

LaHood, E. (2018, Feb. 5). Ed LaHood, CEO at Thyng. *YouTube.* https://youtu.be/nCqzvC4dx0Y

Langlois, G., Elmer, G., McKelvey, F., & Devereaux, Z. (2009). Networked Publics: The Double Articulation of Code and Politics on Facebook. *Canadian Journal of Communication 34*(3), 415–434.

Lin, K. Y., & Lu, H. P. (2011). Intention to Continue Using Facebook Fan Pages from the Perspective of Social Capital Theory. *Cyberpsychology, Behavior, and Social Networking 14*(10), 565–570.

Lipschultz, J. H. (2014, January 23). Consumer Review Credibility, Brand Marketing and Social Media. *The Huffington Post, Media.* www.huffingtonpost.com/jeremy-harris-lipschultz/consumer-review-credibili_b_4634447.html

Lipschultz, J. H. (2016, October 6). Digital Data Trails, Brand Insights and Mobile Users. *The Huffington Post, Contributors.* www.huffingtonpost.com/entry/digital-data-trails-brand-insights-and-mobile-users_us_57f27bbbe4b095bd896a14c9

Mathison, D. (2009). *Be the Media.* New Hyde Park, NY: Natural E Creative Group.

Mirkinson, J. (2016, May 1). Google's New Media Apocalypse: How the Search Giant Wants to Accelerate the End of the Age of Websites. *Salon.* www.salon.com/2016/05/01/googles_new_media_apocalypse_how_the_search_giant_wants_to_accelerate_the_end_of_the_age_of_websites/

Motadel, D. (2011). Waves of Revolution. *History Today* 61(4), 3–4.

Nguyen, S. (2019, November 20). The 7 Best Crowdfunding Sites of 2020. *The Balance Small Business*. www.thebalancesmb.com/best-crowdfunding-sites-4580494

Pew Research Center. (2009, June 24). Strong Public Interest in Iranian Election Protests: Many Know Iranians Using Internet to Get Message Out. *Pew Research Center*. http://peoplepress.org/report/525/strong-public-interest-in-iranian-election-protests

Pogue, D. (2009). *The World According to Twitter*. New York, NY: Blackdog & Levanthal.

Polson, E. (2016). *Privileged Mobilities: Professional Migration, Geo-Social Media, and a New Global Middle Class*. New York: Peter Lang.

Prime, J. A. (2015, March 23). Bossier Sheriff Warns About Burnbook App. *Shreveport Times*. www.shreveporttimes.com/story/news/local/2015/03/23/bossier-sheriff-warns-burnbook/70351250/

Rettberg, J. W. (2008). *Blogging*. Cambridge, UK: Polity.

Rodriguez, S. (2016, December 14). Dropbox Photo Fail Shows How Not to Celebrate Diversity. *Inc*. www.inc.com/salvador-rodriguez/dropbox-diversity-picture.html

Roettgers, J. (2016, December 6). More than Half of All Video Viewing Now on Mobile, Tablet Viewing Flat (Report). *Variety*. http://variety.com/2016/digital/news/mobile-video-viewing-stats-1201934907/

Rogers, E. (2003). *Diffusion of Innovations*, fifth edition. New York, NY: Free Press.

Rutenberg, J., & Isaac, M. (2017, January 6). Facebook Hires Campbell Brown To Lead News Partnership Team. *The New York Times*. www.nytimes.com/2017/01/06/business/media/facebook-campbell-brown-media-fake-news.html

Steimle, J. (2016, September 15). The Top 50 Marketing Influencers on Snapchat (That Aren't DJ Khaled). *Mashable*. http://mashable.com/2016/09/15/top-50-snapchat-marketing-influencers/

Swant, M. (2016, December 15). This Instagram Timeline Shows the App's Rapid Growth to 600 Million. *AdWeek*. www.adweek.com/news/technology/instagram-gained-100-million-users-6-months-now-has-600-million-accounts-175126.

Time. (2013, November 4). Twitter: The 140 Moments That Made Twitter Matter. Tech. *Time*. http://techland.time.com/2013/11/04/the-140-moments-that-made-twitter-matter/slide/all/

Underdown, M. (2016, July 12). Gotta Catch 'Em All: Learnings from the Launch of Pokémon Go. *Sysomos Blog*. https://blog.sysomos.com/2016/07/12/gotta-catch-em-all-the-social-media-business-impact-from-pokemon-go/

Vaynerchuk, G. (2009). *Crush It, Cash in on Your Passion*. New York, NY: Gary Vaynerchuk.

Vericat, J. (2010). Accidental Activists: Using Facebook to Drive Change. *Journal of International Affairs* 64(1), 177–180.

Wegert, T. (2015, September 11). How Lenovo Gets 60,000 Employees to Share Company Content. *Contently*. https://contently.com/strategist/2015/09/11/how-lenovo-gets-60000-employees-to-share-company-content/

Whitehead, M. (2016, July 7). Literally Just 25 Hilarious Tweets About People Playing Pokémon Go. www.buzzfeed.com/matwhitehead/gotta-tweet-em-all

Whittaker, Z. (2019, December 1). Millions of SMS Messages Exposed in Database Security Lapse. *TechCrunch*. https://techcrunch.com/2019/12/01/millions-sms-messages-exposed/

York, A. (2016, December 6). 21 Instagram Accounts to Follow for Brand Inspiration. *Sprout Social*. http://sproutsocial.com/insights/instagram-accounts-to-follow/

Yu, D. (2020). Video IS Your Funnel. *Blitz Metrics*. https://blitzmetrics.com/blog/

Big Data and Privacy

This is some real-life Black Mirror stuff that we're seeing here.
— US House Representative Alexandria Ocasio-Cortez (@AOC, 2020)

Governments are increasingly purchasing sophisticated technology to monitor their citizens' behavior on social media.
— Adrian Shahbaz & Allie Funk (@freedomhouse, 2019, para. 1)

Mapping … boozy tweets can show where people are drinking – or, more specifically, drinking too much – and could help cities point out important trends when it comes to alcohol policy and public health.
— Alissa Walker (@awalkerinLA, 2014)

From WikiLeaks to other attacks on online security, the computer science of privacy may depend upon behavioral cybersecurity and the application of personality psychology (Patterson & Winston-Proctor, 2019). Users need to understand the science of "intrusion detection" (p. 51), as well as individual factors behind "hackers" and "fake news" creator motivation (pp. 253–254). In one view, "surveillance capitalism" reduces our social media communication posts to "free raw material for translation into behavioral data" (Zuboff, 2019, p. 8). Computers may facilitate gaming a system through hacking, or understanding it by collecting and analyzing free and open data. In California, an overhaul of the California Consumer Privacy Act took effect on January 1, 2020. It strengthened consumer rights to review personal data, bulk delete it, and stop the sale to data brokers (Lerman, 2019). There were expected legal challenges to the nation's strongest state law. Privacy must be understood within an evolving context of data analysis (Electronic Communications Privacy Act, 1986).

Former Gizmodo writer (now @Curbed) Alissa Walker reported that a six-month computer science study found more than 11,000 New York geotagged drunk tweets:

"The team developed a machine-learning algorithm to automatically find tweets that are composed while drunk" (Walker, 2016, para. 3). The research is an example of big data collection available from social media sites. *Journalism & Mass Communication Quarterly* devoted its Summer 2016 issue to "Information Access and Control in an Age of Big Data" – "in the context of mass communication to explore the problems and possible solutions surrounding the issue of who controls Big Data and how to access the information" (Carter & Lee, 2016, p. 269). In the special issue, Youm and Park (2016) examined the European Union's "**Right to Be Forgotten**" law, which allows individuals "to demand that Google and other search engines erase links" considered "prejudicial" to them (p. 273). The EU Charter grants a set of access and privacy rights: "Everyone has the right of access to data which has been collected concerning him or her, and the right to have it rectified" (p. 275, quoting EU Charter, Art 8(2)). Meanwhile, US National Security Agency (NSA) surveillance included social media monitoring of Facebook: "While proponents of such programs argue surveillance is essential for maintaining national security, more vetting and transparency is needed ..." (Stoycheff, 2016, p. 308). One global study found that,

> Advances in artificial intelligence (AI) have opened up new possibilities for automated mass surveillance. Sophisticated monitoring systems can quickly map users' relationships through link analysis; assign a meaning or attitude to their social media posts using natural-language processing and sentiment analysis; and infer their past, present, or future locations. Machine learning enables these systems to find patterns that may be invisible to humans, while deep neural networks can identify and suggest whole new categories of patterns for further investigation. Whether accurate or inaccurate, the conclusions made about an individual can have serious repercussions, particularly in countries where one's political views, social interactions, sexual orientation, or religious faith can lead to closer scrutiny and outright punishment.
>
> (Shahbaz & Funk, 2019, para. 4)

Social media and the ability to track and collect behavioral data have created "issues at the center of a polarized debate" (Lee, 2013, p. 146). By providing personal information in exchange for the use of social media sites, there are risks:

> Information on social media sites may not only be searched without permission or knowledge but may be permanently stored, meaning some material intended to be private may never enjoy a cloak of privacy. Photos, rants, relationship statuses, and people's whereabouts, for example, may always be "out there" for future employers, dates, neighbors, police investigators, and commercial businesses to mine, share, and utilize.
>
> (p. 147)

Mills (2015) concluded that there is an inherent conflict between all forms of media and a desire for personal privacy: "Pervasive intrusion works to choke the exact human characteristics that free press itself is intended to foster – free thought and open expression of ideas" (p. 148). He proposed a "human dignity" model in the US that would be similar to Europe:

> In the new world, an Internet intrusion by new media could be to falsely friend a person on Facebook and then use that person's profile information to publish an embarrassing blog post, detailing that individual's private life. In many U.S. courts today, there would be a finding of no expectation of privacy and therefore no remedy for this harm.
>
> (p. 173)

Under the Mills (2015) framework, there would be six principles:

1. Sanction disclosure of certain intimate private facts.
2. Utilize and adapt existing torts.
3. Utilize law punishing intrusions upon space, property, and personal information.
4. Avoid the initial disclosure of sensitive information.
5. Punish defamation including outrageous falsity.
6. Promote and support media creating self-defining ethical standards that include new media.

(p. 182)

Privacy protection depends upon a patchwork of state and national laws, and these provide little in the way of consistency across the large global social network. The collection, organization, analysis, distribution, and use of big data – huge online datasets tracking user action and interaction – is very relevant for those concerned about social media communication privacy.

PRIVACY DEVELOPMENT

The concept of privacy was conceived by Cooley (1888), theorized by Warren and Brandeis (1890), and later developed in law by Brandeis as a right "to be let alone" (*Olmstead v. United States*, 1928, p. 478). Cooley viewed privacy as an absolute protection, while Warren and Brandeis sought to challenge the right of newspapers to invade domestic life through words and flash photography. Many years later, Prosser (1960) and Bloustein (1964) debated a framework, but Prosser's categories were widely accepted: "intrusion upon seclusion or solitude; public disclosure of private facts; false light; and appropriation of persona for commercial exploitation" (Lipschultz, 1988, p. 509). Growing from British common law, the tort of invasion of privacy captured the idea that even the King was not allowed to enter into a private home without invitation. In the 20th century, concern focused on news media disclosure of embarrassing facts, a newsworthiness defense, and notions of community decency (*Sidis v. F. R. Publishing Corp.*, 1940). New technologies of their times – aerial photography and satellite imagery – sparked concerns beyond the traditional on-the-ground photography. At the same time, governmental intrusion by law enforcement raised constitutional Fourth Amendment questions about search and seizure privacy law. Whether or not an intrusion is connected to governmental activities, continuous surveillance may be seen as an intrusion upon one's expectation of privacy. Invasion of privacy has the potential to disclose embarrassing information, defame reputation, or commercialize persona. Under current law, privacy protection is judged as "a matter of community mores" (*Virgil v. Time, Inc.*, 1975, p. 1129).

In an era of surveillance and data, the US Supreme Court has held that landline telephone booth wiretaps violated what courts have defined as a close zone of privacy around a person (*Katz v. United States*, 1967). The Electronic Communications Privacy Act of 1986 criminalized the interception of computer data. Additionally, special classes of records, such as health and educational information, are protected under federal statutes (HIPAA, 1996). After the September 11, 2001 terrorist attacks, the PATRIOT Act gave law enforcement agencies new rights to monitor previously private personal data and share it with other police that might be seeking to avert future attacks:

> It relaxed restrictions on the sharing of information between domestic law enforcement agencies and intelligence agencies, enhanced the government's subpoena power to obtain and inspect e-mail records of suspected terrorists, expanded bank record-keeping requirements to track transactions of money laundering, and permitted roving wiretaps of suspected terrorists.
>
> (Terilli & Splichal, 2014, p. 315)

The NSA, as was disclosed by former government contractor employee Edward Snowden, has engaged in broad surveillance of online communication, including social media activities. Publication of details by WikiLeaks, *The Guardian*, *The Washington Post*, *The New York Times*, and others forced the Obama Administration to defend its practices and review processes. A secret FISA court under the Foreign Intelligence Surveillance Act of 1978 is assigned the job of reviewing surveillance, but critics have claimed that few safeguards remain to protect personal privacy in an age of big data. Humbach (2012) contended that any right of privacy must defer to constitutional First Amendment freedom of expression rights, and should be treated as an exception.

The right of users to protect private data on social media sites is not clear because only lower courts, so far, have taken these cases (*Moreno v. Hanford Sentinel, Inc.*, 2009). Facebook was forced to settle with users whose online data was gathered and distributed without consent (*Lane v. Facebook, Inc.*, 2012). The Appeals Court affirmed a $9.5 million settlement approved by a lower court, and a rehearing was later denied (*Lane v. Facebook*, 2013). In the *Lane* case, it was disclosed that Facebook had launched a program in 2007 called Beacon, which involved member sharing of information about website visits outside of Facebook. Beacon updated profiles with personal information useful to Facebook's business partners: For example, Blockbuster would give Facebook data about video rentals, and then Facebook would share this with a user's friend network:

> Although Facebook initially designed the Beacon program to give members opportunities to prevent the broadcast of any private information, it never required members' affirmative consent. As a result, many members complained that Beacon was causing publication of otherwise private information about their outside web activities to their personal profile without their knowledge or approval. Facebook responded to these complaints (and accompanying negative media coverage) first by releasing a privacy control intended to allow its members to opt out of the Beacon program fully, and then ultimately by discontinuing operation of the program altogether.
>
> (*Lane v. Facebook*, 2012, p. 816)

Unsatisfied with these responses, a group of 19 plaintiffs filed a putative class action in federal district court against Facebook and a number of other entities that operated websites participating in the Beacon program. The class-action complaint alleged that the defendants had violated various state and federal privacy statutes. Each of the plaintiffs' claims centered on the general allegation that Beacon participants had violated Facebook members' privacy rights by gathering and publicly disseminating information about their online activities without permission. The plaintiffs sought damages and a variety of equitable remedies for the alleged privacy violations (*Lane v. Facebook*, 2012, pp. 816–817).

The *Lane* court upheld the settlement as fair, although it may have been too small and directed away from the users who lost their privacy. In a dissenting opinion, a judge pointed out that some go online to shop in order to keep purchases private, but Facebook marketed Beacon to retailers, such as Blockbuster, Zappos, and Overstock, to enable brands "to gain access to viral distribution" and "act as word-of-mouth promotion" that "may be seen by friends who are also likely to be interested" in purchasing the products (p. 827). Beacon was implemented over the objections of Facebook users:

> Worse, Facebook made it very hard for users to avoid these broadcasts. The user had to actively opt out. And opting out required video game skills. The user would get a pop-up on his screen asking whether he wanted to opt out, but the pop-up would disappear in about ten seconds. Too slow reading the pop-up or clicking the mouse, and all a user's "friends" would know exactly what he had bought. Since the pop-up disappeared so quickly, someone looking at another window, or answering the phone, or just not paying attention, would likely not even be aware of the opt-out option before it disappeared.
>
> (p. 827)

The dissenting opinion made it clear that the settlement money went to lawyers and an educational program rather than those wronged by the privacy invasion. Class members received "no compensation," and they did "not get even an injunction against Facebook doing exactly the same thing to them again" (p. 835).

Feldman (2012) has asked what seems to be a persistent question: "Is privacy dead?" in an analysis published in *The Huffington Post*. "Even in this new exhibitionist environment, anyone doing business utilizing user or customer information should make sure to implement fair and transparent privacy policies" (para. 7). "Is privacy dead? No. But we are changing how we feel about it" (para. 11). Not so, say technology promoters from Palo Alto to New York.

Data aggregators are in the business of selling consumer data. The nearly complete adoption of mobile smartphones presents perhaps the most troubling aspect of the privacy question. Whether or not you check in or broadcast your location, telecommunication firms may collect continuous data on your whereabouts. They do not have to tell what they are doing with the data.

BOX 8.1
Lack of Privacy and Social Networks

The Social Media Research Foundation's Marc A. Smith (@marc_smith) suggested in 2012 that the United States does little to protect privacy. Germany, for example, has a law protecting employee privacy. US employers may analyze employee email for valuable patterns. The NodeXL software allows for analysis of social networks of Outlook email users.

Computers read 130 million tweets per day. Smith has tracked daily snapshots of topics, such as Occupy Wall Street and the Tea Party. "Anytime two people interact in email or otherwise," Smith said, "it leaves a graph."

"Nothing is private," Smith claims. He sees it as similar to an iceberg with about 10% "above the water line" and public. Smith views this as an issue because, for example, an employer may decide to fire an employee for being at the periphery rather than the center of a company email social network.

Source: Lipschultz, J. H. (August 28, 2012), Privacy Is Dead? – Really? *The Huffington Post*. www.huffingtonpost.com/jeremy-harris-lipschultz/online-privacy_b_1831956.html

The technologies continue to morph with the adoption of facial recognition. The US Supreme Court has yet to take on the definition of privacy within a social media context. There are some European safeguards, such as those from the Council of Europe Privacy Convention, that go beyond US law in terms of data protection. Popular live streaming and recording video on Facebook, Twitter, and other sites, for example, appears to be protected First Amendment speech, as "intrusion and public disclosure torts are unequipped to provide remedies for potential privacy harms" (Stewart & Littau, 2016,

p. 312). Further, social media companies used contract law of terms of service agreements with users to protect business growth interests. Increasingly, non-disclosure agreements, which were popular within corporate America employee relationships, have spread beyond HR and PR offices to even include public events (Elle, 2019). Comedian Pete Davidson was among the first to do this, as he ran counter to ubiquitous social media communication apps.

TIKTOK, INSTAGRAM, AND TWITTER POLICIES

The TikTok app responded to criticism that it was being used as a surveillance tool by releasing a January to June "transparency report" in December 2019. TikTok (2019), which soared as a popular new app that year, encouraged safe expression: "We believe that when people feel safe, their creativity can flourish" (Para. 1). One privacy challenge is when law enforcement agencies use social media communication apps to seek data during an investigation: "TikTok is committed to assisting law enforcement in appropriate circumstances while respecting the privacy and rights of our users" (para. 4). TikTok developed Law Enforcement Data Request Guidelines (para. 5). At times, there are requests to remove content: "We review such requests closely and evaluate the specified content in accordance with our Community Guidelines and local laws" (para. 8). TikTok (2019) community guidelines appeared to be strict about protecting copyrights: "Upon receiving an effective notice from a rights holder of potential intellectual property infringement, TikTok will remove the infringing content in a timely manner" (paras. 9–10). The company also has a separate intellectual property policy. As with other large social media sites, TikTok has a contract with users in its Safety Center: account privacy settings, content rules, and instruction on blocking other accounts. Anti-bullying policies include a user's ability to deny followers and delete fans. TikTok included information for parents, as well as a Wellness section with external links, such as to suicide prevention and crisis lifelines.

Instagram (2020) also has a Terms of Use page with community guidelines, instructions about privacy and blocking, safety and parental information, law enforcement rules, and specifics about eating disorders. Terms of Use frame user experience in a positive way:

- **Offering personalized opportunities to create, connect, communicate, discover, and share.**
  People are different. We want to strengthen your relationships through shared experiences you actually care about. So we build systems that try to understand who and what you and others care about, and use that information to help you create, find, join, and share in experiences that matter to you. Part of that is highlighting content, features, offers, and accounts you might be interested in, and offering ways for you to experience Instagram, based on things you and others do on and off Instagram.

- **Fostering a positive, inclusive, and safe environment.**
  We develop and use tools and offer resources to our community members that help to make their experiences positive and inclusive, including when we think they might need help. We also have teams and systems that work to combat abuse and violations of our Terms and policies, as well as harmful and deceptive behavior. We use all the information we have – including your information – to try to keep our platform secure. We also may share information about misuse or harmful content with other Facebook Companies or law enforcement. Learn more in the Data Policy.

- **Developing and using technologies that help us consistently serve our growing community.**
  Organizing and analyzing information for our growing community is central to our Service. A big part of our Service is creating and using cutting-edge technologies that help us personalize, protect, and improve our Service on an incredibly large scale for a broad global community. Technologies like artificial intelligence and machine learning give us the power to apply complex processes across our Service. Automated technologies also help us ensure the functionality and integrity of our Service.

- **Providing consistent and seamless experiences across other Facebook Company Products.**
  Instagram is part of the Facebook Companies, which share technology, systems, insights, and information – including the information we have about you (learn more in the Data Policy) in order to provide services that are better, safer, and more secure. We also provide ways to interact across the Facebook Company Products that you use, and designed systems to achieve a seamless and consistent experience across the Facebook Company Products.

- **Ensuring a stable global infrastructure for our service.**
  To provide our global Service, we must store and transfer data across our systems around the world, including outside of your country of residence. This infrastructure may be owned or operated by Facebook Inc., Facebook Ireland Limited, or their affiliates.

- **Connecting you with brands, products, and services in ways you care about.**
  We use data from Instagram and other Facebook Company Products, as well as from third-party partners, to show you ads, offers, and other sponsored content that we believe will be meaningful to you. And we try to make that content as relevant as all your other experiences on Instagram.

- **Research and innovation**
  We use the information we have to study our Service and collaborate with others on research to make our Service better and contribute to the well-being of our community.

(Instagram, 2020, paras. 5–9)

The Instagram Data Policy makes clear the vast amount of user data collected from content, networks, devices, and purchases. The policies reflect Facebook ownership of Instagram.

Twitter (2020) structures its Terms of Service as Who May Use the Services; Privacy; and Content on the Services. Twitter reserves the right to remove content that violates its use contract. It also protects its right to have third-parties advertise on the site. Users have a license:

> Twitter gives you a personal, worldwide, royalty-free, non-assignable and non-exclusive license to use the software provided to you as part of the Services. This license has the sole purpose of enabling you to use and enjoy the benefit of the Services as provided by Twitter, in the manner permitted by these Terms.
>
> The Services are protected by copyright, trademark, and other laws of both the United States and other countries. Nothing in the Terms gives you a right to use the Twitter name or any of the Twitter trademarks, logos, domain names, other distinctive brand features, and other proprietary rights. All right, title, and interest in and to the Services (excluding Content provided by users) are and will remain the exclusive property of Twitter and its licensors. Any feedback, comments, or suggestions you may provide regarding Twitter, or the Services is entirely voluntary and we will be free to use such feedback, comments or suggestions as we see fit and without any obligation to you.
>
> (paras. 23–24)

Twitter limits its legal liabilities by treating the services in an "as-is" context (paras. 27–28). It is worth reading all contracts that, as a user, have been accepted when first creating an account. The end-user agreements frequently are updated, and users need to know potential issues. Other social media site Terms of Service contracts have similar language.

BIG DATA AND PRIVACY

There appears to be no standard big data definition, but it is related to predictive analytics, data mining, and trends (Nelson & Simek, 2013):

> Facebook has a huge amount of our data. In fact, it has more than some people think because they never read the Terms of Service, which allow Facebook to monitor your online activities while you are logged in. That very valuable data is sold to advertisers so that they can have ads related to your online activities pop up or show on visited web pages. Not so bad if you're searching for a new car, but what if you hang out (while married) in dating sites? Or you frequent pornography sites? What are you doing online that you'd prefer to be kept private? How about searching for help in treating a substance abuse problem? Or how to file a bankruptcy? Perfectly innocent activities certainly deserve to be private but privacy is eroding fast in the big data world.

> We just don't think about our digital privacy. We use our car's GPS, we post on Facebook, we buy on Amazon, and we use location service apps on our smartphones. We create our own "big data" cloud about who we are, where we are, what we do, what we like and what we don't.
>
> (pp. 34–35)

Allen (2013) considered whether or not individuals have an ethical responsibility to protect privacy within the big data information pool. One challenge is that, "People are giving away more and more personal data to intimates and strangers for a variety of self-interested, altruistic, or civic-minded reasons" (p. 847). Further, there are practical limits to managing data privacy given technological complexities: "I am suggesting a new, richer way to think about the moral relationship of consumers to business and government – as partnerships in ethical goodness" (p. 865). Allen believed that assertive consumers do not give social media businesses and government a pass on privacy and ethics, but rather create the potential for a stronger system of safeguards.

BOX 8.2

Germany and Privacy

Germany has been a leader in online data privacy protection since the 1970s. At that time, West Germany passed laws to avoid abuse of personal data, which citizens had experienced under Hitler and saw in East Germany before the fall of the Berlin Wall (Somaskanda, 2013). The scale of the US NSA PRISM spy program, as disclosed by Edward Snowden, fell outside of what is legal under German law:

> Under German data protection law, the BND is not allowed [to] register and store communications data on a wide scale, or randomly tap phone conversations. Instead, they have to use sensors and look for keywords within phone and email conversations – but even there, they are only allowed to scan 10 percent of international communication.
>
> (para. 21)

The German government, however, has been unable to use its courts to fully protect social media privacy. Facebook and other sites locate their European operations in Ireland, which has weaker data privacy laws. The German government has expressed the view that Google and other large companies use their size and power to ignore concerns (Overdorf, 2013). More recently, German regulators sought to stop Facebook from collecting and using some of its user data. Anti-trust regulator Bundeskartellamt targeted its concerns toward WhatsApp and Instagram.

Sources: Ghosh, S. (January 14, 2019). Facebook's Entire Business Model Is Being Dissected in Germany, Where Regulators Are Getting Tough On Tech. *Business Insider*. https://www.businessinsider.com/facebook-is-under-increasing-threat-from-german-regulators-2019-1

Somaskanda, S. (July 26, 2013). NSA Spying Rankles Privacy-Loving Germans. *The Atlantic*. www.theatlantic.com/international/archive/2013/07/nsa-spying-rankles-privacy-loving-germans/278,090/; Overdorf, J. (November 5, 2013,). Germany: Privacy Protections Must Go Beyond "No-Spying Act." *MINNPOST*. www.minnpost.com/global-post/2013/11/germany-privacy-protections-must-go-beyond-no-spying-act

FTC REGULATION

In the United States, the strongest privacy protections for social media consumers derive from Federal Trade Commission regulation. Nearly a decade ago, the FTC called upon Congress to enact laws that would address data security, breaches of security, and brokering of data (FTC, 2012). The FTC identified three critical areas for businesses to address (paras. 4–6):

Privacy by Design – companies should build in consumers' privacy protections at every stage in developing their products. These include reasonable security for consumer data, limited collection and retention of such data, and reasonable procedures to promote data accuracy;

Simplified Choice for Businesses and Consumers – companies should give consumers the option to decide what information is shared about them, and with whom. This should include a Do-Not-Track mechanism that would provide a simple, easy way for consumers to control the tracking of their online activities.

Greater Transparency – companies should disclose details about their collection and use of consumers' information, and provide consumers access to the data collected about them.

The FTC raised specific concerns about large platforms and mobile use, which would impact social media sites such as Facebook. In its full report, the FTC noted enforcement action in 2010 against Facebook:

> Brought enforcement actions against Google and Facebook. The orders obtained in these cases require the companies to obtain consumers' affirmative express consent before materially changing certain of their data practices and to adopt strong, company-wide privacy programs that outside auditors will assess for 20 years. These orders will protect the more than one billion Google and Facebook users worldwide.
>
> (p. ii)

The FTC took action with orders against Google, Facebook, and online advertising networks, and used fair credit reporting and child online privacy protection laws to force changes. "To the extent that large platforms, such as Internet Service Providers ('ISPs'), operating systems, browsers, and social media, seek to comprehensively track consumers' online activities, it raises heightened privacy concerns" (p. 14). The FTC held workshops to better understand tracking issues and consider the need for tougher regulation. At the same time, "the Commission generally supports the exploration of efforts to develop additional mechanisms, such as the 'eraser button' for social media ... to allow consumers to manage and, where appropriate, require companies to delete the information consumers have submitted" (p. 29). That idea, however, may conflict with free commercial speech constitutional rights. "While consumers should be able to delete much of the information, they place on a particular social media site, there may be First Amendment constraints to requiring third parties to delete the same information" (p. 71, fn. 358).

In recent years, the FTC has focused on guidelines that warn Instagram influencers against deceptive posts, including content that fails to disclose paid advertising:

> If you endorse a product through social media, your endorsement message should make it obvious when you have a relationship ("material connection") with the brand. A "material connection" to the brand includes a personal, family, or employment relationship or a financial relationship – such as the brand paying you or giving you free or discounted products or services.
>
> (FTC, 2019)

Telling your followers about these kinds of relationships is important because it helps keep your recommendations honest and truthful, and it allows people to weigh the value of your endorsements.

As an influencer, it's **your responsibility** to make these disclosures, to be familiar with the Endorsement Guides, and to comply with laws against deceptive ads. Don't rely on others to do it for you (FTC, 2019, paras. 3–4).

In some cases, the FTC has fined companies for violating commercial speech regulation (*Central Hudson v. Public Service Commission*, 1980; Lord & Taylor, 2016).

PRIVACY AND LEGAL IMPLICATIONS

Social media communication privacy is likely to spawn industry guidelines and standards for self-regulation, future regulation and legislation, and court cases challenging the status quo in the United States. At the international level, there will be continued political and legal pressure on large social media platforms to be transparent and offer users more opportunities to protect their data. Still, the very nature of social media sharing is that social networks negotiate privacy through friend, follower, and fan interaction. The commercialization of social media, sophistication of data collection and tracking, and desire of advertisers to target consumers ready to act present numerous ongoing privacy challenges. Judges and juries will be faced with interpreting legal conflicts over the protection of privacy.

While privacy may be seen as a matter of user literacy, site terms of service, or government regulatory protection, it is also connected to the norms of information flow. Traditional journalists seek to access as much information as possible, but there may be a cultural shift. Social media spaces encourage the sharing of private stories to an audience. Bloggers, for example, use sometimes-personal narrative storytelling to attract readers. Blogger Tracy Solomon wrote about her daughter's battle with leukemia to increase public understanding, and in doing so she and her family voluntarily gave up some of their privacy.

The social norms of privacy will continue to evolve, just as lawmakers and social network sites adjust to new uses of technology. Data protection is a social, political, and legal issue. Social media communication by mobile smartphone or other Internet device identifies the speaker, and there is no complete online anonymity. Therefore, users must rely upon businesses and government to be more careful with data. At the same time, social media users must act with an understanding of the public nature of most online communication.

BOX 8.3

Thought Leader Tracy Solomon

Before I started blogging in 2002, information seemed to pass through some sort of "viable" source that it could be traced back to, a line of responsibility. The reason I started blogging was to update a large amount of people on my youngest daughter's quickly changing health issues foregoing the timely process of phone calls and emails. However, the source would still be me, directly.

Fast forward 18 years to 280-character tweets changing events around the world, alerting readers and news outlets immediately of unfolding tragedies and/or current conditions on the ground, anywhere at any time and from unknown people before sourcing can often take place.

Facebook has become more than just an acceptable place to act as a family chain or circle but also a very needed place of comfort at those most horrific moments following tragedies waiting to hear from family members or friends to see if they are okay and can "check-in."

Social Media are often the first places many people check in the morning, during the day, and shortly before going to sleep. As users, journalists, curators, parents, and leaders knowing our words can so quickly move and so broadly spread, social media have become so much more than a social outlet and require more understanding, patience, respect and responsibility.

Imagine how it can continue to grow and influence lives and our world over the next ten years and coming generations.

Before I started Katia's blog in November 2002, there had already been identity issues with pictures of others being used to start fake fundraising cancer sites. I made it a point to tell many cancer organizations about Katia's blog. Also, the media was covering her story, and I posted links to those articles. There were continuous marrow drives done nationwide trying to find a match for her over a six-month period in 2002–2003, so her story was widely covered.

Internet security is very important to me, and keeping my own name and Katia's name clear is important. We are always willing to share and take part in something when asked. We just prefer to be asked: Social media create ease of access to a variety of forms of available information; it challenges journalism to not focus on being first to report something or running a story that is sensationalized – something to grab more followers/viewers. Readers run the risk of having too much information quickly at their fingertips, some sourced and some not. This can cause a great deal of confusion and put people at risk, causing avoidable harm.

In the future, I would like to see a more collaborative effort in bringing social media to the forefront of schools, news organizations, emergency services, and more. This requires a better understanding of fact-checking and the need to provide source information along with what is posted to avoid the misunderstanding of what is opinion versus what is fact. If social media are used correctly, they can save lives. So many can benefit from a tool that ties our world together if it is used in a positive way. We can reach out to people we were never able to before to sell our product, brand or service and/or have a message heard.

Tracy Solomon is author of *Shadows to Light Your Way* (2019). Follow her on Twitter (@tracysolomon), Facebook (tracysolomon) and Instagram (tracysolomonpics). She has written the Change Happens blog at TracyLSolomon.com and for the Tampa, Florida *Examiner*'s Political Buzz. She blogged about her daughter's battle with leukemia.

FIGURE 8.1 *@tracysolomon.*
Courtesy Tracy Solomon

Data privacy continues to be a complex area of law. Some states, following the protection of workers, have considered student social media privacy legislation (Viera, 2015). Surveys show that among about four in ten young adults, there is confusion about how businesses protect personal data privacy (Schwarz, 2015). Further, among social movements that use Twitter and other tools to grow, "the technology also opens them up to an unprecedented degree of scrutiny" (The Economist, 2016, para. 3). Data scientists have the ability to collect big data and answer a variety of questions. Marketers, too, seek "the business value as 'contextual intelligence' which we're able to extract through big data dives" (Neely, 2016, para. 1). Unlike academics working under ethical review systems, marketers may not protect individual data privacy. Recent developments include the study of automated "bots" and "chatbots" on Twitter and elsewhere (Kollanyi, Howard, & Woolley, 2016). Beyond academic researchers and marketers, mobile telephone providers have profited from offering government access to big data (Lipp, 2016). In Europe, the momentum is in the direction of increased data protection for users of WhatsApp, Facebook, Google, and other sites (Gibbs, 2017). Still, worries persist over facial recognition, ubiquitous cameras, and analyses of massive databases using machine learning (Feathers, 2020; Hill, 2020; Holmes, 2020). In the next chapter, we will address a broader set of legal and regulatory social media issues and cases.

DISCUSSION QUESTIONS: STRATEGIES AND TACTICS

1. What do the Terms of Service say for your favorite social media app? What rights are granted to the company? What rights are given to users? What, if you could, would you change about the policies?

2. How have your expectations for personal privacy changed, if at all, in the age of social media? What are your most important concerns?

3. What do you think can be done to align United States privacy policies with those in the European Union? What are the advantages and disadvantages of global policies?

4. What are the significant implications for privacy based on the use of mobile smartphones and tablets to access social media sites? Which areas might lead to litigation or changes in the law?

REFERENCES

Allen, A. L. (2013). An Ethical Duty to Protect One's Own Information Privacy? *Alabama Law Review 64*, 845.

Bloustein, E. J. (1964). Privacy as an Aspect of Human Dignity: An Answer to Dean Prosser. *New York Law Review 39*, 962.

Carter, E. L., & Lee, L. T. (2016). Information Access and Control in an Age of Big Data. *Journalism & Mass Communication Quarterly 93*(2), 269–272.

Central Hudson Gas & Electric Corp. v. Public Service Commission, 447 U.S. 557 (1980).

Cooley, T. M. (1888). *Cooley on Torts 2d*, 29.

The Economist (2016, March 26). Tracking Protest Movements, A New Kind of Weather. www. economist.com/news/special-report/21695192-social-media-now-play-key-role-collective-action-new-kind-weather

Electronic Communications Privacy Act. (1986). 18 U.S.C. Sec. 2510.

Elle, J. (2019, November 27). Pete Davidson Holds SF Comedy Show – But Makes Attendees Sign $1M Agreement for Entry. *NBC Bay Area*. www.nbcbayarea.com/news/local/Pete-Davidson-Holds-SF-Comedy-Show–But-Makes-Attendees-Sign-1M-Agreement-for-Entry-565572142. html

Feathers, T. (2020, January 17). Ubiquitous Surveillance Cameras are Changing Our Understanding of Human Behavior. *Motherboard*. www-vice-com.cdn.ampproject.org/c/s/www. vice.com/amp/en_us/article/qjdbxm/ubiquitous-surveillance-cameras-are-changing-our-understanding-of-human-behavior

Feldman, M. J. (2012, February 28). Is Privacy Dead? *The Huffington Post*. www.huffingtonpost. com/miles-j-feldman/internet-privacy_b_1306701.html

FTC. (2012, March 26). *FTC Issues Final Commission Report on Protecting Consumer Privacy. Federal Trade Commission*. www.ftc.gov/news-events/press-releases/2012/03/ftc-issues-final-commission-report-protecting-consumer-privacy [Full report downloaded at: FTC Report: *Protecting Consumer Privacy in an Era of Rapid Change*. www.ftc.gov/sites/default/files/documents/reports/federal-trade-commission-report-protecting-consumer-privacy-era-rapid-change-recommendations/120326privacyreport.pdf]

FTC. (2019, November). Disclosures 101 for Social Media Influencers. *Federal Trade Commission*. www.ftc.gov/tips-advice/business-center/guidance/disclosures-101-social-media-influencers

Gibbs, S. (2017, January 10). WhatsApp, Facebook and Google Face Tough New Privacy Rules under EC Proposal. *The Guardian*. www.theguardian.com/technology/2017/jan/10/whatsapp-facebook-google-privacy-rules-ec-european-directive

Hill, K. (2020, January 18). The Secretive Company that Might End Privacy as We Know It. *The New York Times*. www.nytimes.com/2020/01/18/technology/clearview-privacy-facial-recognition.html

HIPAA. (1996). Health Insurance Portability and Accountability Act of 1996. 42 U.S.C.A. Sec. 1320d, 4.

Holmes, A. (2020, January 2020). AOC Is Sounding the Alarm about the Rise of Facial Recognition: 'This Is Some Real-Life "Black Mirror" Stuff.' *Business Insider*. www.businessinsider.com/aoc-facial-recognition-similar-to-black-mirror-stuff-2020-1

Humbach, J. A. (2012). Privacy and the Right of Free Expression. *First Amendment Law Review 11*, 16.

Instagram (2020). Terms of Use. https://help.instagram.com/581066165581870/

Katz v. United States (1967). 389 U.S. 347.

Kollanyi, B., Howard, P. N., & Woolley, S. C. (2016, November 17). Bots and Automation over Twitter during the U.S. Elections. *COMMPROP Data Memo*. http://politicalbots.org/

Lane v. Facebook. (2013). 709 F.3d 791.

Lane v. Facebook, Inc. (2012). 696 F.3d 811 (9th Cir.).

Lee, L. T. (2013). Privacy and Social Media. In A. B. Albarran (Ed.), *The Social Media Industries*, pp. 146–165. New York, NY: Routledge.

Lerman, R. (2019, December 29). Calif. Vastly Expands Digital Privacy. Will People Use It? *Associated Press*. https://apnews.com/62ee3095c0c04cebb89cedbf771a929f

Lipp, K. (2016, October 25). AT&T Is Spying on Americans for Profit, New Documents Reveal. *The Daily Beast*. www.thedailybeast.com/articles/2016/10/25/at-t-is-spying-on-americans-for-profit.html

Lipschultz, J. H. (1988). Mediasat and the Tort of Invasion of Privacy. *Journalism Quarterly* 65(2), 507–511.

Lipschultz, J. H. (2012, August 28), Privacy Is Dead? – Really? *The Huffington Post.* www.huffingtonpost.com/jeremy-harris-lipschultz/online-privacy_b_1831956.html

Lord & Taylor, LLC, In the Matter of. (2016). Federal Trade Commission Settlement. www.ftc.gov/enforcement/cases-proceedings/152-3181/lord-taylor-llc-matter

Mills, J. L. (2015). *Privacy in the New Media Age.* Gainsville, FL: University Press of Florida.

Moreno v. Hanford Sentinel, Inc. (2009). 172 Cal. App. 4th 1125.

Neely, J. (2016, March 2). Do You Have the Context You Need? Unlocking the Value of Big Data Marketing. *Social Media Today.* www.socialmediatoday.com/marketing/do-you-have-context-you-need-unlocking-value-big-data-marketing

Nelson, S. D., & Simek, J. W. (2013). Big Data: Big Pain or Big Gain for Lawyers? *The Vermont Bar Journal & Law Digest 39*, 33.

Olmstead v. United States. (1928). 227. U.S. 438, p. 478.

Overdorf, J. (2013, November 5). Germany: Privacy Protections Must Go Beyond 'No-Spying Act'. *MINNPOST.* www.minnpost.com/global-post/2013/11/germany-privacy-protections-must-go-beyond-no-spying-act

Patterson, W., & Winston-Proctor, C. E. (2019). *Behavioral Cybersecurity, Applications of Personality Psychology and Computer Science.* Boca Raton, FL: CRC Press.

Prosser, D. (1960). Privacy. *California Law Review 48*, 383.

Schwarz, H. (2015, May 13). Millennials are a Little Confused When It Comes to Privacy. *The Washington Post.* www.washingtonpost.com/news/the-fix/wp/2015/05/13/millenials-dont-trust-government-to-respect-their-privacy-but-they-do-trust-businesses-what/

Shahbaz, A., & Funk, A. (2019). Freedom on the Net 2019 Key Finding: Governments Harness Big Data for Social Media Surveillance. *Freedom House.* www.freedomonthenet.org/report/freedom-on-the-net/2019/the-crisis-of-social-media/social-media-surveillance

Sidis v. F. R. Publishing Corp. (1940) 113 F.2d 806.

Somaskanda, S. (2013, July 26). NSA Spying Rankles Privacy-Loving Germans. *The Atlantic.*

Stewart, D. R., & Littau, J. (2016). Up, Periscope: Mobile Streaming Video Technologies, Privacy in Public, and the Right to Record. *Journalism & Mass Communication Quarterly* 93(2), 312–331.

Stoycheff, E. (2016). Under Surveillance: Examining Facebook's Spiral of Silence Effects in the Wake of NSA Internet Monitoring. *Journalism & Mass Communication Quarterly* 93(2), 296–311.

Terilli, S. A., Jr., & Splichal, S. (2014). Privacy Rights in an Open and Changing Society. In W. W. Hopkins (Ed.), *Communication and the Law*, 2014 edition, pp. 291–316. Northport, AL: Vision Press.

TikTok (2019). TikTok Transparency Report. www.tiktok.com/safety/resources/transparency-report

Twitter (2020). Twitter Terms of Service. https://twitter.com/en/tos

Viera, M. (2015, April 10). Maryland Governor to Consider Student Social Media Privacy Bill. *Student Press Law Center.* www.huffingtonpost.com/student-press-law-center/maryland-governor-to-consider-student-social-media-privacy-bill_b_7042374.html

Virgil v. Time Inc. (1975). 527 F.2d 1122 (9th Cir.).

Walker, A. (2016, March 16). An Algorithm Can Tell If You're Drunk Tweeting. *Gizmodo.* www.gizmodo.in/software/An-Algorithm-Can-Tell-If-Youre-Drunk-Tweeting/articleshow/51432774.cms

Warren, S., & Brandeis, L. (1890). The Right to Privacy. *Harvard Law Review 4*, 193.

Youm, K. H., & Park, A. (2016). The "Right to Be Forgotten" in European Union Law: Data Protection Balanced with Free Speech? *Journalism & Mass Communication Quarterly* 93(2), 273–295.

Zuboff, S. (2019). *The Age of Surveillance Capitalism, The Fight for A Human Future at theNew Frontier of Power*. New York: Hachette Book Group.

Law and Regulation

9

We need to update electoral laws so they can handle 21st-century issues including social media, dodgy data use and digital foreign interference. The future of our democracy depends on it.
– David Lammy, British Labour Party Member of Parliament @DavidLammy (2020)

Given the news industry's significant and ongoing financial troubles, the need to address a nearly century-old debate about piracy of news and information has attracted the attention of government officials, who have acknowledged the consequences of a weak press to democratic governance.
– Victoria Smith Ekstrand, @vekstra (2015, p. 188)

Our audience, our clients, and our colleagues expect that we, as professional communicators, become expert in using all available communication tools to do our respective jobs – and to do so in a way that dodges potential legal and ethical pitfalls.
– Daxton R. "Chip" Stewart, @MediaLawProf (2013)

What a lot of people don't realize is that when they decide to start a blog or post comments... they are potentially making themselves open to being liable to the laws of that country.
– Anthony Fargo, @AnthonyFargo1 (2012)

Tweets, whether from celebrities or those less prominent, frequently present public relations, if not legal issues. Technology innovator Elon Musk won a case filed against him for a misguided post on Twitter that raised defamation issues.

In another case, WSAV-TV television reporter Alex Bozarjian used the medium to publicly respond to inappropriate contact: A Georgia man was charged with a misdemeanor sexual battery count for slapping the female reporter's rear during live TV coverage of a bridge run slapping the woman's rear. The incidents reflect elements of social media law (Bynum, 2019).

Another has to do with huge companies that control user data and marketing.

Facebook has aggressively moved to combine its flagship brand with its Instagram and WhatsApp app acquisitions, but the Federal Trade Commission in late 2019 reviewed these business plans (Wolverton, 2019). Facebook Blueprint already connects the three apps in strategies it teaches to businesses and students. The regulatory review in the US followed the action in the European Union against Google based upon anti-competitive advertising practices.

Lawmakers, regulators, and the courts are slow to keep pace with technological change, including the evolving social media landscape, but previous law remains important. "Centuries of jurisprudence about media law provide a foundation for understanding particular challenges we face when using social media" (Stewart, 2013, p. vii). For example, Facebook claimed user Christopher Peter Tarquini posted deceptive messages that promised to show others a video of celebrities Justin Bieber and Selena Gomez having sex. At the time, Bieber had more than 49 million Twitter followers (more than 107.5 million in 2020), as shown in Table 9.1 – second only in 2016 to Katy Perry – and Gomez more than 17 million Twitter followers at the time (46 million in 2016). When people clicked on the link, they were reportedly led to spam that automatically posted the link on their Facebook walls (Crook, 2013). *TechCrunch* learned that Facebook spent $5,000 investigating Tarquini's social media commission scam, which violated its Terms of Service (paras. 3–5). Facebook went to court to recover its costs and have Tarquini banned for life from the social networking site. Spamming as commercial speech is one form of behavior that may spawn case law. Facebook filters organic content, but the company has also removed some advertising. A controversial HIV-prevention drug created a public controversy, and then Facebook responded by removing personal injury lawyer advertising about potentially harmful side effects (Sapra, 2019).

Federal Trade Commission (FTC) warnings to Instagram bloggers, vloggers, and other social media influencers about clear and transparent labels for commercial sponsors to obvious cases of online deception and misrepresentation indicate that we have

TABLE 9.1 *Top Twitter 2020 and 2016 Followers and Instagram 2020 Rank*

Twitter Account (Facebook Rank)	Followers 2020	Followers 2016	Instagram 2020
@BarackObama	1. 110.7 million	68.2 million	– 26.4 million
@katyperry	2. 108.3 million	94.7 million	20.86 million
@justinbieber	3. 107.4 million	90.5 million	13.125 million
@rihanna	4. 94.9 million	53.3 million	– 9.1 million
@taylorswift13	5. 85.4 million	69.5 million	12.122 million

Sources: Brandwatch (December 27, 2019). www.brandwatch.com/blog/most-twitter-followers/and www.brandwatch.com/blog/top-most-instagram-followers/; Track Analytics (December 27, 2019). www.trackalytics.com/twitter/profile/barackobama/; Fan Page List (December 27, 2019). https://fanpagelist.com/category/top_users/

been moving toward regulated social media (FTC, 2016). In a Lord and Taylor consent order, the FTC targeted a fake news article and Instagram post for a clothing line, and alleged that "the company paid 50 online fashion 'influencers' to post Instagram pictures of themselves wearing a paisley dress from the new collection, but failed to disclose they had given each influencer the dress, as well as thousands of dollars ..." (para. 3). Nevertheless, other companies continued to flood the influencer market with products and payments, leaving influencers with a responsibility to disclose business relationships. "In any advertising medium (and they consider social media advertising), you must disclose your relationship with a #client, #sponsored or similar identifier" (Dietrich, 2015, para. 11). Lord and Taylor (2016) stands for the principle that "each endorser" must be provided "with a clear statement of his or her responsibility to disclose, clearly and conspicuously" the connection (p. 4).

Concern over illegal online behavior in cyberspace is nothing new (Branscomb, 1996), but the openness of social media publishing generates many more cases and concerns. The complexity of social networking also impacts groups of people with every networked communication. For example, a District of Columbia Court of Appeals panel had backed the Federal Communications Commission (FCC) plan to reclassify wired and mobile Internet Service Providers (ISPs) as common-carrier utilities that exercise no content controls (*US Telecomm v. FCC*, 2016). While the decision was hailed as a Net Neutrality victory, the Trump Administration FCC in 2017 quickly repealed the rules in its Restoring Internet Freedom order.

At the start of 2020, the top ten Instagram accounts were:

1. Instagram (316 million)

2. Cristiano Ronaldo (189 million)

3. Ariana Grande (167 million)

4. Dwayne ("The Rock") Johnson (161 million)

5. Selena Gomez (161 million)

6. Kim Kardashian (151 million)

7. Kylie Jenner (151 million)

8. Lionel Messi (136 million)

9. Beyoncé (134 million)

10. Neymar (128 million)

The top Facebook individual celebrity accounts in early 2020 were:

5. Cristiano Ronaldo (122.4 million)

8. Shakira (103.5 million)

10. Vin Diesel (100.4 million)

11. Lionel Messi (89.5 million)

12. Eminem (89.3 million)

13. Rihanna (81 million)

14. Justin Bieber (78.3 million)

16. Will Smith (76.9 million)

18. Taylor Swift (74.4 million)

In 2016, Facebook held the top three spots. The top celebrities on Facebook were: 4. Cristiano Ronaldo (118.4 million); 5. Shakira (104.5 million); 6. Vin Diesel (100.8 million); 9. Eminem (91.2 million); and 10. Lionel Messi (87.6 million). Soccer held four of the top ten spots in 2016, but only two of the top eleven in 2020.

In the United States, social media users are governed by the British common law tradition, constitutional development of free expression rights through case law, and federal statutes and regulation. The FCC has addressed texting while driving, disability, and access issues that impact social media law. The FTC's concerns about online privacy, email hacking, crowdfunding deception, deceptive advertising, marketing disclosure, and mobile identity theft are also important.

FREE EXPRESSION AND THE FIRST AMENDMENT

The First Amendment of the US Constitution, while not interpreted as providing an absolute right of free expression, remains a strong statement in favor of it:

> Congress shall make no law respecting an establishment of religion, or prohibiting the free exercise thereof; or abridging the freedom of speech, or of the press; or the right of the people peaceably to assemble, and to petition the Government for a redress of grievances.
>
> (First Amendment. Constitution of United States of America 1789)

The *Alien and Sedition Acts of 1798* were not considered before the US Supreme Court, but the constitutionality of government action was reviewed beginning with the *Espionage Act of 1917*. Although the Court upheld convictions for publishing and distributing anti-war fliers, a clear and present danger test began to emerge, as well as support for what later became known as the marketplace of ideas. Milton (1644) offered the earliest marketplace of ideas articulation that remains a free speech justification:

> Though all the winds of doctrine were let loose to play upon the earth, so Truth be in the field, we do injuriously by licensing and prohibiting to misdoubt her strength. Let her and Falsehood grapple; who ever knew Truth put to the worse in a free and open encounter?
>
> (Milton 1644)

As the US Supreme Court struggled with 20th-century free speech cases, dissenters offered defenses for speech. Justice William O. Douglas (1951) expressed what became known as the near-absolutist position:

> Unless and until extreme and necessitous circumstances are shown, our aim should be to keep speech unfettered and to allow the processes of law to be invoked only when the provocateurs among us move from speech to action.
>
> – *Dennis v. US* (1951, p. 590)

Fifty years ago, *New York Times v. Sullivan* (1964) convinced a majority of US Supreme Court justices to support constitutional protection for political speech, which includes a debate on public issues that is "robust" and "wide open" (p. 271). So it is with Twitter and other platforms. Social media pages empower users to be global publishers through blogs, podcasts, and social sites. Although anonymity is more "a complicating factor" on Twitter, even for Facebook, LinkedIn, and other sites, it challenges attempts to regulate social media:

> Like traditional media, the Internet allows speakers to communicate their messages to a large consuming public. However, because the content providers include independent speakers – whose information may be subject to minimal editing – as well as traditional media speakers – whose information is often verified and edited – defamatory speech has greater potential to reach a widespread audience ...
>
> Given the speed with which such content can be disseminated and reputations injured as a result, the level of First Amendment protection available for defamatory Internet speech must be critically evaluated ... Thus, defamatory statements published online have serious potential to cause both reputational injury and economic harm ...
>
> (Sanders & Olsen, 2012, pp. 365–366)

Sanders and Olsen (2012) suggested the need for a psychological sense of community rather than one based upon traditional legal geography. Social media are global (Ali, 2011), and online freedom brings a unique set of legal responsibilities. Social media transform every user through their interactions with others. The international distribution of unfiltered media across a mosaic of legal systems and structures means technological freedom as a trend is colliding with governmental, corporate, organizational, and individual desires to control messages. For example, in Pakistan, an English literature professor was sentenced to death in 2019 after making anonymous secular Facebook posts in 2013 that the court determined to be blasphemy (Shah & Gillani, 2019). The professor had a Fulbright award to study at Jackson State University in Mississippi before returning to Pakistan, posting, and then being jailed for more than six years. The massive and ubiquitous Internet may be too large to completely control (Fang, 2008), but legal systems and structures attempt to incorporate new cases within traditional rules. Social media have triggered a new set of expectations in journalism (Briggs, 2020), and present new legal challenges (Nockleby et al., 2013).

INTERNET LIBEL

Internet Service Providers have protection from liability for libel. America Online, for example, could not be sued for potentially libelous content distributed using its network (*Blumenthal v. Drudge and America Online*, 1998). AOL was protected, a lower court ruled, because of the limited exercise of editorial control and a mostly passive role. In a social media context, it is interesting to think about the use of the RT on Twitter, which may or may not be passive depending upon the context of tweets. In any case, social media make it more difficult to measure economic impact because of the absence of a definable mass media audience. Social media crowds instead are dependent upon individual social networks for distribution. Further emergence of a sharing culture, promoted by sites that encourage users to share content with online friends or fans, introduces a new media model. Current concerns include legal protection of outrageous speech (Calvert, 2014), and the statutory protection for revenge porn posts after a relationship breakup (Goldnick, 2015).

Content owners who benefit from advertising revenue generated by increased numbers of site visitors must also try to protect property rights. A group of advertisers, for example, was allowed by the US Supreme Court to go forward with a lawsuit against Google claiming its AdWords program displayed their advertising on "low quality" websites (Revesz, 2016, para. 2). In a separate case, the US Supreme Court declined a challenge in the Google Books case, which allows Google to maintain millions of digital library books without paying "authors who said the project amounted to copyright infringement on a mass scale" (Liptak & Alter, 2016, para. 1). Google has scanned more than 20 million books since 2004, and keyword searches may offer users content found within social media sites.

At the same time, some brands use social media to promote valuable content or services that generate revenue (Mathison, 2009). In this model, each user has the power to be her or his personal media outlet. It is a world in which sites such as Twitter generate unique content (Pogue, 2009), leverage digital assets (Keller, Levine, & Goodale, 2008; Pavlik, 2008), and internationalize thinking (Groggin & McLelland, 2009). "Yet the evolution of the Internet has brought with it the reality that the custody or ownership of content is questionable, or problematic at best, in cyberspace" (Lisby, 2020, p. 226).

FACEBOOK, TWITTER, AND THE LAW

While journalists are, of course, not the only social media users, they have a particular need to verify accuracy of online information (Chow, 2013). In the early years, social media sites went from being unheard of in the courts to the subject of hundreds of cases each year (Stewart, 2013). Media law scholar Derigan Silver noted that social media law may be eroding First Amendment protections for free speech:

> One of the biggest issues facing non-media users of social media is the distinctions some courts have created between the constitutional protections afforded the media and those afforded to average individuals … in effect, lower courts are removing a wide range of speech from constitutional protections at the very time new communication

technologies such as email, Facebook, Twitter, and blogs are giving non-media individuals the power to reach wider and wider audiences.

(Silver, in Stewart, 2013, pp. 39–40)

For example, in *Tatro v. University of Minnesota* (2012), a state Supreme Court upheld university discipline against a mortuary science student posting what she said were "satirical" comments on her Facebook wall. Amanda Tatro, who later died in 2012, had violated student conduct code and program rules designed to professionally respect privileged access to human cadavers. According to court records, the University of Minnesota focused on four Facebook posts:

- **Amanda Beth Tatro:** Gets to play, I mean dissect, Bernie today. Let's see if I can have a lab void of reprimanding and having my scalpel taken away. Perhaps if I just hide it in my sleeve … (November 12, 2009)

- **Amanda Beth Tatro:** Is looking forward to Monday's embalming therapy as well as a rumored opportunity to aspirate. Give me room, lots of aggression to be taken out with a trocar (December 6, 2009)

- **Amanda Beth Tatro:** Who knew embalming lab was so cathartic! I still want to stab a certain someone in the throat with a trocar though. Hmm … perhaps I will spend the evening updating my "Death List #5" and making friends with the crematory guy. I do know the code … (December 7, 2009)

- **Amanda Beth Tatro:** Realized with great sadness that my best friend, Bernie, will no longer be with me as of Friday next week. I wish to accompany him to the retort. Now where will I go or who will I hang with when I need to gather my sanity? Bye, bye. Bernie. Lock of hair in my pocket

(Undated, p. 513)

While the postings broke no laws, Tatro was barred from the lab during an investigation of her comments. Meanwhile, two local television newsrooms interviewed her, and this generated public pressure on the university. As the investigation continued, Tatro was allowed to return and take final examinations. Tatro testified at a hearing that she did not understand that Facebook posts fell under a rule that prohibited blogging. Anatomy Laboratory Rule #7 specified that, "Blogging about the anatomy lab or the cadaver dissection is not allowable." Tatro's punishment included a grade of "F" in the course, as well as these requirements: that she completes an ethics course, writes a letter to faculty, and completes a psychiatric evaluation. Additionally, she was placed on probation for the remainder of her undergraduate work. Relying primarily on elementary and high school cases, the Minnesota Supreme Court rejected Tatro's First Amendment argument, noting that she had signed a contract to follow lab rules:

We acknowledge the concerns expressed by Tatro and supporting amici that adoption of a broad rule would allow a public university to regulate a student's personal expression at any time, at any place, for any claimed curriculum-based reason. Nonetheless, the parties agree that university may regulate student speech on Facebook that violates established professional conduct standards. This is the legal standard we adopt here, with the qualification that any restrictions on a student's Facebook posts must be *narrowly tailored* [emphasis added] and directly related to established professional conduct standards. Tying the legal rule to established professional conduct standards limits a university's restrictions on Facebook use to students in professional programs and other disciplines where student conduct is governed by established professional conduct standards ... we limit the potential for a university to create overbroad restrictions that would impermissibly reach into a university student's personal life outside of and unrelated to the program. Accordingly, we hold that a university does not violate the free speech rights of a student enrolled in a professional program when the university imposes sanctions for Facebook posts that violate academic program rules that are narrowly tailored and directly related to established professional conduct standards.

(p. 521)

Meanwhile, the National Labor Relations Board (NLRB) pushed back against company social media policies that limited what employees may say about their employers. An NLRB judge ruled that Chipotle Mexican Grill's social media policy violated labor laws (Sass, 2016). An employee in Pennsylvania had been fired after responding to a customer on Twitter: "@ChipotleTweets, nothing is free, only cheap #labor. Crew members only make $8.50hr how much is that steak bowl really?" (para. 2). The tweet was later deleted after a supervisor referenced social media policy against "disparaging" statements (para. 3). Only labor conditions and employee redress appear to be covered under restrictions, but company social media policies cannot violate general First Amendment principles. The National Labor Relations Act of 1935 also was applied when a grocery chain in 2014 social media policy was found to be too broad, violated speech rights, and inappropriately required employee disclaimers on all social media posts (*Kroger Co. of Mich. v. Granger*, NLRB, 2014). More recently, the NLRB (2018) clarified employer business rights and employee First Amendment rights. In a case involving CVS Health, the NLRB emphasized its precedent to "differentiate" among "different industries and work settings" in the application of the National Labor Relations Act (NLRA) covering employee unions (p. 2). The CVS Health Code of Conduct covered all traditional media relations: "Colleagues who speak on social media about the company in any way must make it clear that they are a CVS Health employee, but not speaking on behalf of the Company or as an official Company Representative" (p. 3). The use of the branded company logo was also limited under the code, and the NLRB found this to be lawful. The social media policy also required that employees distinguish professional and personal posts, but the NLRB recognized limits: "The Board has recognized that requiring employees to self-identify in order to participate in collective action would impose a significant burden ..." (p. 5). Nevertheless, companies are allowed to protect privacy and security within employee social media posts that must not violate laws. The CVS Health Social Media Policy Colleague Handbook contained important First Amendment language:

> Nothing in this policy is meant to limit your legal right to use social media to speak about your political or religious views, lifestyle and personal issues, working conditions, wages, or union-related topics or activities with others inside or outside the Company, or to restrict any other legal rights.
>
> This policy is not intended to interfere with any rights provided by the National Labor Relations Act.
>
> (p. 7)

The NLRB urged companies to elaborate on employee labor rights when they communicate with each other through social media. The balancing approach to social media policy included concern over any requirement that an employee must identify themselves: "Although the savings clause is in some ways comprehensive, it does not mitigate the chilling effect of the self-identification requirement" (p. 11). The NLRB left to companies and employee bargaining units to settle specifics about disclosure of employee information and self-identification requirements. While this law covers only employees covered under collective bargaining agreements, it offers language guidance to non-union employees about fair employer social media policies that offer some First Amendment protection. In 2019, there was an informal settlement reached in the case.

As a general rule, social media and other Internet communication are not immune to traditional media law – libel, privacy, copyright, and commercial speech. When a user signs on to a site, such as Facebook, she or he agrees to a Terms of Service (TOS) agreement that is essentially a contract. Each Facebook user should explore terms and policies, as these are a legal contract between the social media site and the SNS participant. Too frequently, users click to gain access without reading and understanding terms, which specify rules covering vague areas of the law. Facebook divides its terms into three categories: Rights and Responsibilities, Data Use, and Community Standards.

Facebook has explained how it collects user data to monetize its commercial products. "This can include information in or about the content you provide (like metadata), such as the location of a photo or the date a file was created" (Facebook Data Policy, 2020, para. 3, www.facebook.com/privacy/explanation). The company tracks users over time:

> We collect information about how you use our Products, such as the types of content you view or engage with; the features you use; the actions you take; the people or accounts you interact with; and the time, frequency and duration of your activities.
>
> (para. 5)

Users and their social networks also are studied. "This can include information about you, such as when others share or comment on a photo of you, send a message to you, or upload, sync or import your contact information" (para. 7)

Facebook has previously noted that deleted content "may persist in backup copies for a reasonable period of time (but will not be available to others)." Some computer program applications seek user permission and then use the content that is posted. Additionally, content shared as "public," such as a profile picture, can be seen by "everyone, including people off of Facebook."

Facebook "cannot guarantee" safety, and its TOS has user "commitments" to "not post unauthorized commercial communications (such as spam)," not "collect users' content or information" without prior permission, "not engage in unlawful multi-level marketing," "not upload viruses," and not "access an account belonging to someone else." The Facebook TOS contract also requires that users "will not bully, intimidate, or harass any user," "will not post content that: is hate speech, threatening, or pornographic; incites violence; or contains nudity or graphic or gratuitous violence." So-called "mature" content requires "appropriate age-based restrictions." In general, Facebook is not to be used "to do anything unlawful, misleading, malicious, or discriminatory."

Under the heading "Registration and Account Security," Facebook requires the use of "real names and information." As with other TOS provisions, the site relies upon complaints, if a user registers a fake name. Social networking sites rarely require identity verification beyond an email address, and this makes it easy to dodge the rules.

Under the rules, users are to create only one personal account for themselves. Under the TOS, "You will not use your personal timeline primarily for your own commercial gain, and will not use a Facebook Page for such purposes." Convicted sex offenders are not allowed to use Facebook, under the rules. It is recommended that readers frequently should read Facebook data privacy policies, as they continue to be revised.

Twitter also presents a number of legal issues.

☐ BOX 9.1

Emerging Twitter Law

Tweets, messages of no more than 140 (now 280) characters on Twitter, received increasing attention from lawyers. *The National Law Journal* reported in 2008 that micro-blogging was a quick way to get an employee or an employer in trouble (Baldes, 2008). Social media interaction can be subpoenaed during a case, and tweets create a legal record of communication and behavior. The tech website Mashable.com (@Mashable; Cashmore, 2008) identified four potential lawsuit areas: company secrets, invasion of privacy/defamation, trademark violations, and wrongful employee termination claims.

In 2009, for example, Horizon Group Management, which manages rental property in Chicago, sued tenant Amanda Bonnen for $50,000 after she tweeted as @JessB123: "You should just come anyway. Who said sleeping in a moldy apartment was bad for you? Horizon realty thinks it's okay." Bonnen had just 20 followers on Twitter, but the libel lawsuit claimed the tweet damaged Horizon's reputation. A Cook County judge dismissed the case in finding the tweet was too vague. Other examples of Twitter law include:

- In *US v. Fumo*, 655 F.3d 288 (2011), a Pennsylvania state senator's criminal convictions were upheld, but the appeals court ordered re-sentencing. During deliberations, a TV station reported that a juror had posted on Twitter, as well as on Facebook. After watching the report the night before the verdict, the juror panicked and deleted the postings, which included this tweet: "This is it ... no looking back now!" On the same March 2009 evening the juror also deleted this Facebook wall post: "Stay tuned for the big announcement on Monday everyone!" A District Court judge found that the juror violated instructions to avoid discussing the case outside the jury room, but there was no evidence of outside influence. The posts were called "nothing more than harmless ramblings with no prejudicial effect" and that, "They were so vague as to be virtually meaningless" (p. 301).
- The Kentucky Supreme Court cited New York rules that allow a lawyer to search social media sites to research prospective jurors, as long as there is no contact or attempt to "friend" the person. It is also considered ethical for a lawyer to visit public sites during trial evidence and deliberations to monitor but not engage in discussion (*Sluss v. Commonwealth*, 381 S.W.3d 215, 2012).
- The Florida Bar Association, which regulates attorney advertising, found that, "If access to a lawyer's Twitter postings is restricted to the followers of the particular lawyer, the information posted there is information at the request of a prospective client and is not subject to the lawyer advertising rules under Rule 4–7. I(h)" (Faehner, 2012, p. 36).

In the area of public relations, Hall (2013) suggests that every strategic social media policy must address legal concerns that are now central to social media communication on sites, such as Twitter – transparency, privacy, employee control, intellectual property, and tone (pp. 223–224). In particular, social media audiences should know who is speaking to them and have some sense of content producer motivation. Social media communication happens within contexts that include employee roles and obligations, content property rights, and normative expectations for personal and company branding.

Sources: Baldes, T. (December 22, 2008). Beware: Your "Tweet" on Twitter Could Be Trouble, *National Law Journal*. www.law.com/jsp/nlj/PubArticleNLJ.jsp?id=1202426916023&slreturn=20131026150648 Cashmore, P. (December 20, 2008). Twitter Lawsuits: 4 Reasons Your Tweets Might be Trouble, *Mashable*, http://mashable.com/2008/12/20/twitter-lawsuits/ Chicagoist (January 21, 2010). Twitter Lawsuit Dismissed http://chicagoist.com/2010/01/21/twitter_lawsuit_dismissed.php Faehner, M. J. (June 2012). Advertising. *Florida Bar Journal 86* (6), 36–37. Hall, H. K. (2013). Social Media Policies for Advertising and Public Relations. In D. R. Stewart (Ed.), *Social Media Law, A Guidebook for Communication Students and Professionals*, pp. 212–226. New York, NY: Routledge. Wang, M. (2009). UPDATED: Rounding up the Buzz. ChicagoNow. http://culture wav.es/public_thought/72,990

For Facebook and other sites around the world, the rapid global shift to mobile media through smartphones and tablets has presented new legal challenges. From Asia to the Middle East, high-speed mobile networks opened social media communication and challenged traditional legal restrictions.

INTERNATIONAL SOCIAL MEDIA

Internet access broadened with mobile and real-time applications ("apps"), and social media law and regulation have been evolving with rapid global adoption. Out of 7.8 billion people in 2020, more than 5 billion were mobile users, and about one-half were active social media users (Lipschultz, 2020, p. 197; Silver, 2019). The leading countries for Internet use were China (829 million), India (560 million), the United States (312 million), Brazil (149 million), Indonesia (143 million), Japan (118 million), Nigeria (111 million), Russia (109 million), Bangladesh (92 million), and Mexico (85 million) among 4.4 billion worldwide (p. 197).

The US had a diffusion advantage in the 1990s, but rapid global growth is happening almost everywhere across cultures and cybercultures (Bell & Kennedy, 2007). Mergers, such as Facebook's purchase of the popular WhatsApp messaging application, continue to face scrutiny. The European Commission in early 2017 reviewed whether or not Facebook misled regulators during the 2014 merger (Associated Press, 2016). At issue is whether Facebook deliberately changed course in its August 2016 terms of service and privacy policies update in a way that could now link WhatsApp telephone numbers to Facebook accounts. The FTC reached a $5 billion settlement with Facebook in 2019 (Fair, 2019).

The 2010 re-licensing of Google in China was also contingent upon regulatory limitations. So-called "law-based management" required Google to accept government filtering. In the application letter, Guxiang (Google) pledged to "abide by Chinese law," and "ensure the company provides no law-breaking content as stipulated in the 57th statement in China's regulations concerning telecommunications" (Xinhua, 2010). The statement says that any organization or individual is prohibited from using the Internet to spread any content that attempts to subvert state power, undermine national security, infringe on national reputation and interests, or that incites ethnic hatred or secession, or transmits pornography or violence. Guxiang also accepted that all content it provides is subject to the supervision of government regulators, said the official.

Broad issues of global cybercrime fall under the relatively new area of "Internet governance," which address a variety of activities, including online pharmacies' marketing of nationally regulated medicines:

> Conceptually, it is defined as the establishment of shared principles, norms, rules, decision-making procedures and programs developed by governments, the private sector, and civil society on the use and evolution of the Internet. Reflecting a heretofore decentralized, multi-stakeholder, multi-country, interconnected, self-governed and autonomous group of actors, the UN has made Internet governance a global priority despite its highly challenging nature.
>
> (Mackey & Liang, 2013, para. 36)

A UN-initiated World Summit on the Information Society (WSIS) established the Internet Governance Forum (IGF), and it has begun to address global Internet governance issues, such as the marketing of counterfeit medicines. This involves both technical and

FIGURE 9.1 *In China, hundreds of millions have access to Weibo, but they are officially blocked from Facebook, Twitter and other international sites.*

behavioral concerns, as stakeholders seek "solutions to issues arising from the misuse of the Internet" (para. 37). Similar to early Internet studies, social media communication presents both challenges and opportunities (Ali, 2011). Former Egyptian President Mubarak, for example, sought to stifle Internet communication at the height of protests in Cairo's Tahrir Square because of "the incredible power of social media" (p. 185). "The story of social media in developing nations so far is one of individual empowerment" (p. 209). In the Arab world, free speech has been challenged because of the need for "state security," which can be weakened as people discuss and debate social change on social media sites:

> The Internet and social media are important because of their intrinsic value and the possibility they create of starting a campaign, spreading news about what is going on, or even starting a movement that demands change. But what is important to remember is that these are only tools used by people who desire change – and want it because of the current situation in which they live.
>
> (AbuZayyad, 2013, p. 40)

While social networking sites may be used to mobilize protests, more often legal issues arise based upon the power to distribute messages to a wide audience.

PRIOR RESTRAINT AND TERRORISM

The post-9/11 world is sensitive to the dangers posed online by terrorists who may use social media to plan violent acts. The law, however, provides centuries of cases highlighting the protection of free expression. Blackstone's *Commentaries on the Laws of England* (1765–1769) defines prior restraint doctrine:

> In this, and the other instances which we have lately considered, where blasphemous, immoral, treasonable, schismatical, seditious, or scandalous libels are punished by the English law, some with a greater, others with a less degree of severity; the *liberty of the press*, properly understood, is by no means infringed or violated. The liberty of the press is indeed essential to the nature of a free state: but this consists in laying no *previous* restraints upon publications, and not in freedom from censure for criminal matter when published. Every freeman has an undoubted right to lay what sentiments he pleases before the public: to forbid this, is to destroy the freedom of the press: but if he publishes what is improper, mischievous, or illegal, he must take the consequence of his own temerity.
>
> (Blackstone, 1979)

In Blackstone's widely accepted view,

> Every freeman has an undoubted right to lay what sentiments he pleases before the public; to forbid this is to destroy the freedom of the press, but if he publishes what is improper, mischievous or illegal, he must take the consequences for his own temerity.

Therefore, the larger social good was achieved by placing responsibility in the hands of individuals. It would be somewhat more likely that individuals would challenge the order with new ideas than that a censor would allow such controversial ideas out. Once available to the public, these could be judged. However, it is not clear that Blackstone's legal theory afforded any protection beyond the point of publication, even under the framers' view. Four types of expression that could be punished under common law were:

- *Seditious libel* – words "designed to bring the government into dispute," meant that truthful criticism was subject to greater punishment.

- *Obscenity* – words that tended to corrupt people through "immoral influences," meant that sexuality was taboo.

- *Blasphemy* – words against the church were seen as "offenses to God," meaning that the state could inflict punishment.

- *Libel* – words against other individuals were thought to threaten peace, meaning that government would punish the offender rather than allow for retribution.

In *Near v. Minnesota* (1931), the Supreme Court established an American prior restraint doctrine. The Court left open the possibility for a narrow class of prior restraints: where national security in a time of war was threatened, in times when publication might incite the violent overthrow of the government, publishing fighting words or obscenities.

For social media communication, prior restraint law places a burden on government to limit a speaker before online publication, but it does not protect her or him from subsequent punishment through civil lawsuit or the criminal justice system. The Web, over time, was less revolutionary than first predicted and more an extension of traditional media in terms of American communication law. A difficult challenge is how to define offensive material. For example, Senator Joseph Lieberman in 2008 complained to Google about the existence of YouTube videos posted by terrorist organizations, such as al-Qaeda. Google operates YouTube, and it protects free speech for legal, nonviolent, and non-hate speech videos.

☐ BOX 9.2

Social Media Terrorism

Professor Gabriel Weimann (2010) recounts the exchange between two Palestinians – one with homemade explosives asking for instructions, and the other explaining how to make a bomb on the public site, *Izz al din al Kassam*:

> The internet has enabled terrorist organizations to research and coordinate attacks; to expand the reach of their propaganda to a global audience; to recruit adherents; to communicate with international supporters and ethnic diasporas; to solicit donations; and to foster public awareness and sympathy for their causes.
>
> (p. 46)

Beginning with the chat room and electronic forum, and developing within social media communication, there is a "cyber-jihad" movement (p. 46). The US has warned that Twitter could be "an effective communication tool for terrorists trying to launch military attacks" (p. 48). Wary that Facebook and similar sites do not guarantee anonymity, terror groups look for apps that are not focused on individual identity. On the other hand, there have been examples of recruiting on Facebook.

YouTube is one of the oldest social media sites, and it is the most popular global video space. Since its launch in 2005, terrorist groups "realized the potential of this easily accessed platform for the dissemination of their propaganda and radicalization videos" (p. 51). One user posted more than 100 such videos in 2009 alone (p. 52). YouTube videos considered "jihadist content" have been spread "far beyond traditional jihadist websites" (p. 52). Social networking is an effective tool for those wishing to fuel political sympathies and even convert individuals to a cause by luring them to extremist messages.

Source: Weimann, G. (2010). Terror on Facebook, Twitter, and YouTube. *Brown Journal of World Affairs 16* (2), 45–54.

The US First Amendment perspective tends to promote freedom of expression by limiting government action against media – including social media. In most countries, though, there are few protections for freedom of speech and publication. Consider the 2013 conviction of Jeremy Forrest in the United Kingdom. Authorities investigated tweets that named his victim, which were against the law. Sussex police said the Crown Prosecution Service monitors social media sites for violation of law designed to protect the identity of sexual assault victims. The British law provides for lifetime anonymity. *The Guardian*'s David Banks (@DBanksy) observed that the identity of the victim had been made public at the time of her abduction, and this may have confused some, but not all, Twitter users:

> Others clearly knew the legal position, but were intent on defying it because it did not make sense to them, or somewhat disturbingly, they did not think the victim had deserved anonymity in this case. One taunted the authorities to sue him for it if they dared (apparently unaware that this is not a civil matter, it is a criminal one; naming a victim of a sexual offence is itself a sexual offence).
>
> (Banks, 2013, para. 8)

In the UK, there are guidelines of the Crown Prosecution Service (CPS) for prosecution of social media communication. These attempts to strike a public interest balance between protecting individuals and allowing for balanced freedom of speech. British common law made through cases is a foundation for US law, which also provides constitutional First Amendment protection. Nevertheless, British social media guidelines offer instructive principles to consider.

📱 **BOX 9.3**

CPS Guidelines On Prosecuting Cases Involving Social Media

The British guidelines offer prosecutors "clear advice" on making consistent decisions in social media cases. UK law applies to all social media, including "to the resending (or retweeting) of communications."

General principles test two stages of a case: "The first is the requirement of evidential sufficiency and the second involves consideration of the public interest." Cases require "sufficient evidence to provide a realistic prospect of conviction," and this "means that an objective, impartial and reasonable jury (or bench of magistrates or judge sitting alone), properly directed and acting in accordance with the law, is more likely than not to convict."

* * * *

An initial assessment is made of "the content of the communication and the conduct in question so as to distinguish between,"

1. Communications which may constitute *credible threats* of violence to the person or damage to property.
2. Communications which *specifically target an individual or individuals* and which may constitute harassment or stalking within the meaning of the Protection from Harassment Act 1997.
3. Communications which may amount to a *breach of a court order*. This can include offenses under the Contempt of Court Act 1981, section 5 of the Sexual Offences (Amendment) Act 1992, breaches of a restraining order or breaches of bail. Cases where there has been an offense alleged to have been committed under the Contempt of Court Act 1981 or section 5 of the Sexual Offences (Amendment) Act 1992 should be referred to the Attorney General and via the Principal Legal Advisor's team where necessary.
4. Communications which do not fall into any of the categories above and fail to be considered separately (see below): i.e., those which may be considered *grossly offensive, indecent, obscene or false*.

* * * *

The guidelines distinguish "credible threats of violence," referencing Lord Chief Justice in *Chambers v DPP* [2012]: *"a message which does not create fear or apprehension in those to whom it is communicated, or may reasonably be expected to see it, falls outside [section 127(i)(a)], for the simple reason that the message lacks menace"* (para. 30).

Threats should not be prosecuted if they are not credible. The guidelines urge prosecutors to look for "evidence of hostility or prejudice," and criminal law encourages an "increase in sentences for racial and religious aggravation," as well as "increase in sentences for aggravation related to disability, sexual orientation or transgender identity."

* * * *

The British are concerned about "targeting specific individuals through harassment or stalking," which are defined as "repeated attempts to impose unwanted communications or contact upon an individual in a manner that could be expected to cause distress or fear in any reasonable person" and "contacting, or attempting to contact, a person by any means." Courts in the UK, as is the case in the US, may issue a restraining order against an individual engaged in online stalking. British law also restricts "grossly offensive, indecent, obscene or false" communication. At the evidence stage of an investigation, the guidelines call for a "high threshold" because of the millions of daily social media messages, which create "the potential that a very large number of cases could be prosecuted before the courts" and "the potential for a chilling effect on free speech." Prosecutors are urged to "exercise considerable caution before bringing charges."

> The British also reference Article 10 of the European Convention on Human Rights: Everyone has the right to freedom of expression. This right shall include the freedom to hold opinions and to receive and impart information and ideas without interference by public authority and regardless of frontiers …
>
> Article 10 "protects not only speech which is well-received and popular, but also speech which is offensive, shocking or disturbing."
>
> (citing *Sunday Times v UK (No 2)*, 1992)

The UK standard is "communication that is *grossly* offensive" for there to be criminal charges. "Just because the content expressed in the communication is in bad taste, controversial or unpopular, and may cause offense to individuals or a specific community, this is not in itself sufficient reason to engage the criminal law." The context of a social media communication is considered, as in the case of an Internet bulletin board:

Instead, prosecutors should focus on cases "where a specific victim is targeted and there is clear evidence of an intention to cause distress or anxiety, prosecutors should carefully weigh the effect on the victim, particularly where there is a hate crime element." Interestingly, age is also considered because children and young people "may not appreciate the potential harm and seriousness of their communications and a prosecution is rarely likely to be in the public interest."

Source: The Crown Prosecution Service (2012). Guidelines on prosecuting cases involving communications sent via social media. www.cps.gov.uk/legal/a_to_c/communications_sent_via_social_media/

The emphasis on a public interest standard is similar to what is found under US broadcast regulation, and may be applied to social media disinformation regulation (Napoli, 2019). While the Federal Communication Commission reconsiders its regulation of electronic media, the US Supreme Court has rejected public interest regulation for Internet communication, which now includes social media.

US INTERNET INDECENCY

A portion of the *Telecommunications Act of 1996*, called the *Communications Decency Act (CDA)*, set the stage for several attempts to regulate the Internet and social media communication by making it explicitly illegal to knowingly send or make available to minors any indecent or obscene material. The US Supreme Court, however, found part of the CDA's indecency provisions unconstitutional. The case of *Reno v. ACLU* (1997) acknowledged Congress' concern with preventing children from being the targets of, or having access to, sexually explicit communications, but it said the CDA's ban on indecency was vague and overbroad.

The Internet uses nearly unlimited digital space, which makes it very different from the limited broadcast public spectrum. Further, people are not as likely to be exposed inadvertently to sexually explicit material on the Internet as they might be on broadcast stations. Still, obscene material may be banned from the Internet because the First Amendment does not protect any obscene messages, regardless of medium. Website operators act as publishers: "Publishers may either make their material available to the entire pool of Internet users, or confine access to a selected group, such as those willing to pay for the privilege" (p. 853). The Court has consistently called for narrowly tailored restrictions on Internet speech and application of traditional obscenity law. From a legal perspective, the Internet has been viewed as similar to print media.

Social media communicators have First Amendment rights, but they also are subject to its narrow restrictions. In the *Reno* case, former Justice Sandra Day O'Connor was ahead of her colleagues on the bench in calling for zoning the Internet by using .xxx domain names – it was a technological solution that took more than a decade to begin to materialize.

Courts use *Miller v. California* (1973) to define obscenity across all media – including social media. An early computer bulletin board operator in California, for example, was charged in Memphis under federal law with transmitting obscene content, and the conviction of two people was upheld (*United States v. Thomas*, 1996). When judging obscenity, a jury must examine three parts of the *Miller* legal test for media content:

1. *Prurient Interest.* An average person, applying contemporary local community standards, must find that the work, taken as a whole, appeals to prurient interests.

2. *Patently Offensive.* The work must depict in a patently offensive way sexual content specifically defined by applicable state law.

3. *Value of Work.* The work lacks serious literary, artistic, political or scientific value.

The *Miller v. California* approach to obscenity requires all three items to be satisfied for a jury to find that the media content is obscene. Justice John Paul Stevens observed in one case, though, that prurient appeal is a problem by potentially forcing the most puritanical village standards on everyone. For social media, it may be quite difficult to identify "the work" in the context of "a whole," as mobile social platforms such as Snapchat are brief and temporary. Likewise, it is unclear how state law can be applied within the international context of social media. Finally, the value test is a matter of generational and cultural definition that is very challenging for judges and juries. Online pornography remains profitable, and commercial interests often clash with restrictive local community standards (*Nitke v. Gonzalez*, 2005). Pornography spammers continue to be a problem, and Facebook is among those social media sites filing lawsuits to stop it (Crook, 2013).

REGULATED MEDIA TECHNOLOGIES

The growth of media technologies and a free market economic system helped generate a 20th-century information economy that included commercial newspaper "metropolitan distribution networks" (Pool, 1983, p. 20). It is easy to see how potentially powerful social networks are now replacing the importance of newspaper networks.

Likewise, United States global media "imperialism" through traditional channels (Innis, 1972, p. 169) is also being weakened in the 21st century by social media. Printing presses gave way to the Internet, and social media sites that offered anyone access destroyed professional journalism norms of gatekeeping.

Despite the weakening of controls over media communication, the US government maintains a regulatory interest in information accuracy and consumer perception of claims.

⚡ BOX 9.4

Thought Leader Misty Montano

The relationship between the journalist and the news consumer has had the greatest impact from social media. The basic rules of journalism will always be the backbone of good, solid reporting. However, journalism has been greatly impacted by social media when applied to each person who engages with the story. Journalists have found themselves being the "who" because readers expect them to actively talk with people about their stories on social media. The witness on the scene of a breaking news situation who tweets it or posts it anywhere on social media is now the one who "breaks" the news and is often thrown into a citizen journalist role. Social media requires journalists to have a transparent relationship with news consumers, and this includes attribution of information and editorial process.

FIGURE 9.2   @Misty – Montano.
Courtesy of Misty Montano

News travels to family and friends through their social networks even though many of these people wouldn't normally seek out news items. News organizations now have an integrated social media marketing plan to engage regular and new audiences to move them to the end product: TV, online, and mobile news.

Many people do not understand why they see what they see in their news feed on Facebook. Many do not understand that Facebook is constantly changing based on user behavior. Many who have Twitter accounts don't know how to make Twitter useful in their lives other than being forced into using it to participate in favorite TV shows or to find out emergency information from local law enforcement or news agencies.

News organizations expect employees to use social media but may provide little to no training or guidelines, and could end up in a situation where either the social communities aren't developed or one action of an employee on social media could harm the organization.

Weaving one's personal life with his work and public life on social media is truly an art form. Anything posted on social media can have an impact on one's employment.

Disclaimers in "about me" and "bio" sections with phrases like "views are my own" and "RTs are not an endorsement" provide no protection to someone whose actions on social media are seen as damaging to the company for which that person works.

The law protects an individual's right to free speech and protects an individual from being forced to give their social network passwords to their employers; however, nothing is truly private on social media and the right to have a job is not protected by law. One's use of social media becomes one's personal brand. Employers have the right to protect their company profile and brand. Employers have the right to search the digital footprint of its employees.

The main rule I preach wherever I go is this, "Don't BE the news." This simply means to think first and be smart in all you do. Behave on social media the way you would behave in front of the important people in your life – managers, colleagues, parents, teachers, grandparents, etc. If you wouldn't say or do it in front of these people, then don't do it on social media.

Misty Montano is Digital Director at KUSA-TV in Denver, Colorado. She is an Emmy award-winning journalist. She previously was Assignment Editor at KCNC-TV and received her B.A. in Media Communication from Hastings College.

Commercial broadcasters, such as Misty Montano, rely upon advertising revenues to pay the bills and turn a profit. Media businesses and their advertising are governed in the US by commercial speech law and regulation.

FTC REGULATION: ADVERTISING, PR, AND SOCIAL MEDIA

The Federal Trade Commission regulates advertising in the United States utilizing a "clear and conspicuous" legal standard. Commercial speech, defined by Supreme Court Justice John Paul Stevens as "expression related solely to the economic interests of the speaker and its audience" (Hayes, 2013, p. 264) is a special class of communication under the law. The FTC has as its mission: "To prevent business practices that are anti-competitive or deceptive or unfair to consumers; to enhance informed consumer choice and public understanding of the competitive process; and to accomplish this without unduly burdening legitimate business activity" (FTC, 2014a, para. 1). The FTC seeks "vigorous competition among producers and consumer access to accurate information, yielding high-quality products at low prices and encouraging efficiency, innovation, and consumer choice" (para. 2). Their top strategic goal is consumer protection: "Prevent fraud, deception, and unfair business practices in the marketplace" (para. 3). The FTC has jurisdiction over a variety of privacy and identity concerns in the digital age: limiting unwanted calls and emails; computer security; online safety of children; protection of identity from theft; and repairing identity after theft (FTC, 2014b). After Typhoon Haiyan, for example, the FTC urged consumers "to do some research to ensure that your donation will go to a reputable organization" rather than "fraudsters" (Tressler, 2013, paras. 2–3).

The FTC has used a *reasonable consumer* standard as the legal test for deception since 1983, when a policy statement defined this:

> The Commission believes that to be deceptive the representation, omission or practice must be likely to mislead reasonable consumers under the circumstances. The test is whether the consumer's interpretation or reaction is reasonable. When representations or sales practices are targeted to a specific audience, the Commission determines the effect of the practice on a reasonable member of that group. In evaluating a particular practice, the Commission considers the totality of the practice in determining how reasonable consumers are likely to respond.
>
> (FTC, 1983)

Advertising is considered deceptive, if it lacks a reasonable basis (*Firestone*, 1973). The FTC determines deception based upon false advertiser claims that would give a consumer a false impression (Ibid., fn. 5). In particular, disclosure needs to be written, clear, and conspicuous.

The FTC also has investigated complaints about the Yelp review site (Forbes, 2013). Questions persist about whether or not Yelp offered search benefits to those restaurants advertising on the site – an allegation that Yelp firmly denies. Still, at sites such as Yelp and Amazon, the influence of reviews opens the possibility that some may try to "game" the system in their favor by encouraging positive reviews or promoting the placement of negative reviews against competitors. This is a very difficult social media environment to control or regulate because it is fluid and dispersed.

The FTC clear and conspicuous standard is reflected through the guidance to be prominently placed using easily understood words. Disclosures need to be located in places where they will be seen, as well as near a review or claim that is being made. A social media site that buries important details in fine print would not be following FTC standards. Font size is an issue because of the use of small, mobile devices and various operating systems or device settings.

In 2004, the FTC investigated Amazon.com's online Toy Store because of concerns over the protection of child privacy. The FTC responded to complaints by finding that the purpose of the site was to sell toys to adults, Amazon used adult language and there were no activities targeted at kids: "Thus, the FTC staff does not believe the overall character of those websites indicates that they are targeted at children" (FTC, 2004, p. 2). Children under 13 are protected under the COPPA online privacy law, but the FTC found that a "Kid's Review Form" was not promoted to attract children. The FTC also has been concerned with the issue of paid blogging. The FTC (2010) issued guidelines reflecting truth-in-advertising principles:

- Endorsements must be truthful and not misleading;

- If the advertiser doesn't have proof that the endorser's experience represents what consumers will achieve by using the product, the ad must clearly and conspicuously disclose the generally expected results in the depicted circumstances; and

- If there's a connection between the endorser and the marketer of the product that would affect how people evaluate the endorsement, it should be disclosed.

(p. 1)

Although the principles and guidelines are not new, the FTC revised these to emphasize that they apply to social networking sites and social media marketing:

The FTC revised the Guides because truth in advertising is important in all media – including blogs and social networking sites. The FTC regularly reviews its guides and rules to see if they need to be updated. Because the Endorsement Guides were written in 1980, they didn't address social media. The legal principles haven't changed. The FTC revised the examples to show how these standards apply in today's marketing world.

(p. 2)

The FTC said financial arrangements between paid bloggers and advertisers may not be apparent to readers, and the law defines deceptive practices as those misleading "'a significant minority' of consumers" (p. 2). FTC enforcement focuses on advertisers rather than endorsers. The FTC has the authority to regulate deceptive advertising as commercial speech, which does not have full First Amendment rights. "If you have a relationship with a marketer who's sending you freebies in the hope you'll write a positive review, it's best if your readers know you got the product for free" (p. 3). The guidelines emphasize transparency in communication.

On a personal Facebook page, for example, FTC urges identifying an employer, if products are mentioned: "People reading that discussion on your Facebook page might not know who you work for ... readers might not realize the products you're talking about are sold by your company" (p. 4). The onus is on advertisers and marketers to train people, monitor content, and review "questionable practices" (p. 6).

In one case, the Bureau of Consumer Protection notified Hyundai Motor America that gift certificates given to bloggers encouraging links to Hyundai videos or comments on Super Bowl advertisements may have run afoul by failing to disclose the relationship. The law "requires the disclosure of a material connection between an advertiser and an endorser when the relationship isn't otherwise apparent to consumers" (Fair, 2011a, p. 1). A staff letter read: "An advertiser's provision of a gift to a blogger for posting specific content promoting the advertiser's products or services is likely to constitute a material connection that would not be reasonably expected by readers of the blog" (p. 1).

Still, the FTC closed its investigation without further action. The FTC found that Hyundai may not have known in advance about the arrangement, "a relatively small number of bloggers received the gift certificates," and some bloggers did disclose the payments (p. 1). Hyundai had hired a media firm, which developed the blogging campaign, as noted by FTC staff:

> Although advertisers are legally responsible for the actions of those working directly or indirectly for them, the actions at issue were contrary both to Hyundai's established social media policy, which calls for bloggers to disclose their receipt of compensation, and to the policies of the media firm in question. Moreover, upon learning of the misconduct, the media firm promptly took action to address it.
>
> (p. 2)

It is important to recognize the responsibilities of all parties. The advertiser has ultimate responsibility for its social media campaigns, and the correct path is compensation disclosure. While the company received some initial cover for having hired a firm to run the campaign, its social media policies were also relevant. The FTC draws three rules from its Endorsement Guides: 1. Mandate a disclosure policy that complies with the law; 2. Make sure people who work for you or with you know what the rules are; and 3. Monitor what they're doing on your behalf (p. 2). FTC also has become interested in the so-called "blurred lines" – "the blending of ads with news, entertainment, and other content in digital media – sometimes called 'native advertising' or 'sponsored content'" (Fair, 2013a, p. 1). As public relations firms venture into advertising work, previous divisions between traditional PR earned media and sponsored or paid media become difficult to separate. In all areas, the FTC calls for disclosure and transparency.

Privacy also continues to be a regulatory issue. The FTC issued a complaint against Facebook for "deceptive or unfair" privacy practices (Fair, 2011b, p. 1). The FTC-proposed order stated that information "from or about" individual consumers, such as names, addresses, email addresses and telephone numbers, are covered by privacy rules. FTC staff (pp. 1–2) said that:

- Facebook can't misrepresent what covered information it collects or discloses.

- When Facebook offers privacy settings on its site, it has to honor them. For example, it can't offer settings that restrict information to "Only Friends" and then share it with others.

- Facebook can't mislead people about the extent to which it shares covered information with third parties, like apps or advertisers.

- Facebook can't mislead people about the steps it takes to verify the privacy or security that third parties provide – for example, apps used on its site.

- Facebook can't mislead people about the extent to which their covered information is accessible after they've deactivated or deleted their accounts.

- Facebook can't mislead people about the extent to which the company complies with the government or third-party privacy programs – like the US-EU Safe Harbor Framework.

The FTC says Facebook needs to "clearly and prominently" disclose data sharing and receive consent from its users. The guidance called for severing control of user data within 30 days of account terminations, as well as an independent assessment, monitoring and compliance reporting.

One other developing FTC concern is the use of Internet "spycam" technologies (Fair, 2013b, p. 1). Some software has offered "detective mode" settings that triggered webcams without awareness and consent. The FTC concludes, "Technologies that track or monitor consumers can raise privacy and security eyebrows" (p. 2). In business settings, the FTC urges "appropriate notice and consent safeguards" (p. 2). Some employers, for example, monitor employee social media usage or prohibit it. If spyware is used for monitoring, then employees should know this within a set of clear rules. The FTC may attempt to impose broad liability through its lawsuits, including software developers, corporate officers and companies using monitoring. Beyond the FTC, courts also rule on commercial property rights within social media communication.

COPYRIGHT INFRINGEMENT, FILE SHARING, AND FAIR USE

Social media communication extended intellectual property rights issues beyond the early Internet cases. Copyright protects original material upon its creation, and the creator has exclusive rights to reproduce and distribute it, as well as the right to create other works derived from the original. Therefore, uploading a document or media file such as a photograph, copying a posting, and re-transmitting it without permission all could violate copyright and digital theft statute law (*Digital Theft Deterrance Act*, 1999). Content owners may exercise rights for specific periods of time, which have been extended under US law to sometimes more than a century. At some point content falls into the public domain and can be copied and shared without restriction.

Social media which emphasize creative content sharing on sites, such as YouTube, raise numerous important legal issues. When a user sees a posting, the computer temporarily loads the file, which might be considered illegal copying. Of course, downloading the file by taking a screenshot or saving it more clearly reflects copyright infringement under US law.

The *Digital Millennium Copyright Act of 1998* eliminated loopholes by addressing streaming media and licensing fees for music and videos (*Eldred v. Ashcroft*, 2003). There is a long history of copyright cases against illegal use of media content. From music bootleggers to video thieves, the US government has attempted to protect the property rights of copyright owners. Social media, however, generate holes in these enforcement efforts by dispersing illegal activity across user networks and sites. Given these enforcement challenges, corporate owners seek to manage and control use and payments through social media sites, such as iTunes and YouTube. The **Digital Rights Management (DRM)** approach seeks to collect user payments for media, and control downloading/uploading and sharing. To some extent, social media sites make it easier to track, charge, and restrict illegal copying than the earlier websites. However, DRM has proven difficult to enforce. Some critics believe that a better system may emerge over time, based upon user behavior.

In the US, the so-called "hot news" doctrine affords property rights to a breaking news story for a very short period of time (Ekstrand, 2015, p. 2). "Theoretically speaking, this means that I own the fact that a plane has crashed – if I have gathered that information myself – for a very (indeed VERY) short time" (pp. 2–3). News pirates may be held liable under misappropriation law, although "only the most egregious violators – those who persistently pirate fresh news, often from the same source – are the ones who are pursued in court" (p. 3).

Copyright law has become particularly important on photo-sharing sites, such as Instagram and Snapchat. It turns out that a photographer rather than the camera owner has an intellectual property right over photos based upon the protection of the creative process. If a user hands a smartphone to a friend to take a picture, technically the friend owns rights to the photo – even though it resides on the original user's phone. An exception may be professional photographers using equipment owned by their employer under a work-for-hire agreement.

A different spin on copyright law happened when a crested black macaque monkey in 2014 grabbed a nature photographer's camera and took a "selfie" that went viral on social media. Ninth circuit courts twice ruled that the photo fell into the public domain (*Naruto v. Slater*, 2018). "Monkeys are not persons and cannot own copyrights" (Lisby, 2020, p. 228). "Works from non-human sources aren't copyrightable, unless a person makes substantial changes and edits to the photograph" (p. 228).

SOCIAL PERSPECTIVES ON LAW

Social media communication, as with earlier computer and Internet law, has raised new concerns about free expression. From hopes to fears, the marketplace of ideas brings with it norms expressed in the law. Freedom of expression is at odds with, for example, a general right of privacy or right to be forgotten:

> The concept of a privacy interest arising out of the obscurity of information, as a socio-normative principle, and the right to be forgotten, as a legal mechanism concerned with the European idea of dignity-based privacy, are both fundamentally at odds with the established theories that undergird the American First Amendment right of freedom of speech ... It appears that the differences between the long tradition of vigorously protecting free speech and the concepts of obscurity and the right to be forgotten are irreconcilable.
>
> (Larson III, 2013, pp. 119–120)

Privacy came to the forefront in the United States in 2016. Celebrity gossip website *Gawker* halted publication after losing an appeal of an initial $140 million judgment in a case brought by professional wrestler Hulk Hogan, legally known as Terry Bollea

(Carmody, 2016). The lawsuit stemmed from a 2012 story, "Even for a Minute, Watching Hulk Hogan have Sex in a Canopy Bed is Not Safe for Work but Watch Anyway" (p. 1). About 90 seconds of a 2007 30-minute video was shared, and a jury initially awarded Hogan $55 million in actual economic damages and $60 million for emotional distress (later increased to a total $140 million, including punitive damages). *Gawker* was sold to Univision, which closed the main site, but continued to operate *Gizmodo*, *Jezebel*, and other valuable assets (p. 4). As part of a bankruptcy filing, Gawker settled the 5-year-old case with Bollea for $31 million plus cash from the sale of Gawker (Kennedy, 2016). "Bollea's case against Gawker was bankrolled by Silicon Valley billionaire Peter Thiel, whom Gawker outed as gay back in 2007 ..." (para. 7).

The US Supreme Court ruled in *Carpenter v. United States* (2018) on a Fourth Amendment data privacy in a criminal law case. Timothy Ivory Carpenter's mobile phone data located him possibly nearby a series of 2011 robberies. At his trial, Carpenter's lawyers attempted to suppress digital evidence collected without a warrant or evidence of probable cause. Data histories may show the movement of an individual, and Chief Justice John Roberts, a conservative, was joined by four liberal justices in a narrow split five to four decision. The Court ruled that the search of mobile data was illegal. The majority found an "expectation of privacy in the record of his physical movement." Four dissenting justices, however, ruled that mobile data are no different from business records.

In other invasion of privacy cases, an individual may violate the privacy of another. Playboy model Dani Mathers took a Snapchat and body-shamed a naked 70-year-old woman at a LA Fitness gym changing room. Mathers was sentenced to one month removing graffiti in Los Angeles, and the California legislature passed a tougher privacy law (NPR, 2017).

Normative theory within a social context has been defined as how media *ought* to operate based upon values (Lipschultz, 2008). Normative legal theories, including classical liberalism, are tested through cases and case law. As a function of technology, social media communication challenges traditional industrial assumptions about control. Normative laws restrict prior restraint on publication, including the types happening in social media communication, but also enable subsequent punishment for harmful speech through libel suits. Economic forces influence which cases are brought, as well as outcomes. In its simplest form, libel involves damage to reputation.

In a libel case, a plaintiff must prove publication, identification, falsity, fault and damages. Proving publication on the Internet, in some cases, could be more difficult than earlier mass media forms. Unless the offending pages were downloaded and saved or printed, it is possible that the defamation could vanish in cyberspace. Assuming the social media communication content was saved, identification of the plaintiff should be fairly straightforward and not unlike other media forms. The plaintiff's evidence that the material in question is false is always one of the most difficult aspects of a libel suit, regardless of media form. The Internet might pose some special problems because of the ability to "cut and paste" images and words digitally. The standards of fault depend upon whether the plaintiff in a libel suit is a public figure or not. For most people alleging libel, they merely must show that the social media publisher was negligent with the facts. Because most content providers are not trained journalists, it would seem that standards for negligence might be lower and more difficult to prove in court. For public figures and officials, the standard is "actual malice" – defined legally as reckless disregard for the truth and entertaining serious doubts about the information. If all of these elements can be shown, a plaintiff in a libel suit must still make a case for economic damages. For example, a tweet would have to be proven to cost an individual or organization a specific amount of money. Or, if a Facebook post led to someone being fired, a court could examine actual damages of lost wages, as well as additional costs.

Libel cases can be won or lost. For example, innovator Elon Musk successfully defended himself after a cave explorer sued over a tweet in 2018. Musk had called a British rescuer "pedo guy" during a Thailand search for 12 trapped soccer players. The CEO of Tesla and SpaceX, Musk apologized and then deleted the defamatory post (Logan & Matousek, 2019, para. 3). While the plaintiff's attorneys claimed Musk was calling him a pedophile, Musk's defense was that this was a common expression in his native country of South Africa. After winning the case, Musk (@elonmusk) tweeted, "My faith in humanity is restored."

Once a plaintiff has made his or her case, the defendant in a libel suit has several defenses to follow. Had someone published a libel on a social media site, the simplest defense would be that the information was the truth. That judgment depends upon the Internet communication of millions of people. Baym (1995) was an early observer of the nature of online culture and communities:

> If language use is an important locus of cultural meaning making in traditional cultures, it is only more so for Usenet cultures, which are so heavily linguistic in nature ... There are few if any shared spaces, face-to-face encounters, or physical artifacts to provide cultural foundations. Thus, the discourse, shaped by the forces of the system and object of interest as well as the idiosyncrasies of the participants, carries inordinate weight in creating a group's distinct environment.
>
> (p. 33)

But the once-isolated online communities began to take on traditional qualities within social networking sites. Facebook, for example, offered the possibility for political opponents to confront each other amid the heat of a contested political campaign. Top social media communication sites at any given time represent "self-sustaining" forms of interaction (Rogers, 1995, p. 313). Legal rules may encourage a marketplace of ideas, but they exist within a much broader set of social, political, and economic constraints. Stevenson (1995) viewed modern media as a form of radical democratization with "a plurality of voices" in a "fragmented culture" (pp. 68–69). Early computer-mediated communication norms were harbingers for social media communication. Although global in nature, users in the United States tend to adopt a First Amendment perspective. On the one hand, social media provide a platform for free speech and access to potentially large audiences. On the other, use leads to loss of personal privacy.

SOCIAL MEDIA PRIVACY ISSUES

Social media users continue to express concerns about the protection of their privacy on sites such as Facebook. At the same time, Facebook is among those sites that attempt to protect users from spammers. YouTube owner Google continues to make technological changes in an attempt to limit, if not eliminate, spam email and comments. The site also has banned some videos, targeting those intended to promote illegal activities or incite violence.

Employees at work also have very limited privacy rights while online. They are subject to company social media policies, which vary greatly in the level of restrictiveness. A very real legal question remains about whether or not First Amendment rights extend into the workplace, as other constitutional rights do.

New technologies also threatened to erode traditional common law views about the sanctity of privacy in one's own home. Privacy becomes a question when law enforcement authorities tap into computer transmissions. While a court order is required, it may be possible for computer users to encrypt transmissions. In 1993, the National Security Agency (NSA) proposed a clipper chip to allow decoding. The government's homeland security efforts since September 11, 2001, to fight terrorist threats also have caused new privacy concerns. The US Court of Appeals, District of Columbia Circuit, for example, upheld the Federal Communications Commission decision that law enforcement agencies require wiretap compatibilities to listen in on mobile telephone and network use (*Am. Council of Educ. v. FCC*, 2006). The NSA has come under scrutiny in recent years for accessing large stores of social media and other data through orders of a secret court. The global nature of emerging spy centers in various countries make it likely that virtually every email and other social media communication may be tracked by governments. In the US, the Fourth Amendment protections against illegal search and seizure have been seriously weakened by the emerging security state. Documents released in 2013 by ex-NSA contractor Edward Snowden and published in *The Washington Post* and *The Guardian* raised concerns about the widespread government surveillance of communication networks, including social network sites. The media coverage was shared across social media and generated a public backlash. The ongoing WikiLeaks release of classified government information offers a new model of networked news (Beckett, with Ball, 2012).

The changing social and political conditions created by the September 11, 2001 terrorist attacks presented a new level of complexity. New communication technologies may be used for good or evil, and regulators struggle to allow for advancements without making it easier to harm people. Within sites such as Facebook, the company warns users about data it collects on postings and even user locations. As Facebook (2014) has told users: "Remember, when you post to another person's timeline, that person controls what audience can view the post. Additionally, anyone who gets tagged in a post may see it, along with their friends." User settings may limit public viewing, but data are saved for use by the company for advertising purposes and for the government, if subpoenaed.

The US Supreme Court reversed and remanded convictions on four of five counts against Anthony Elonis for making Facebook threats against his estranged wife and a former employer – in violation of federal statute law (*Elonis v. United States*, 2015). The Court rejected a reasonable person standard and concluded that a federal jury must evaluate a defendant's state of mind. Elonis has used a "Tone Dougie" pseudonym in Facebook posts and claimed the content was rap lyrics that should be given First Amendment protection. A third circuit federal appeals court, however, reinstated an earlier "true threats" conviction (Kendall, 2016; *US v. Elonis*, 2016). In criminal cases, future juries and judges will need to assess the state of someone using a social media site to make alleged threats.

☎ BOX 9.5

Thought Leader Jeana Goosmann

Social media exploded over the last decade. Facebook. Twitter. Snapchat. Instagram. LinkedIn. It's a great tool for connecting with customers or clients, and other organizations. But how have social media impacted the law?

Here are three ways social media have impacted the law over the past decade:

1. Social Media Policies

Business owners now need social media policies. How many employees are members of one or more of these sites? How many employees are active on one or more of these sites? If so, does the employer know what they post or tweet or snap on those sites? Does the employer know if customers, investors, or competitors can see what employees are saying?

FIGURE 9.3   *@GoosmannLawFirm.*
Courtesy of Goosmann Law Firm and Fels Photo

Employees' presence on these sites could be affecting a business in positive and negative ways. Businesses are still catching up to the consequences that social media hold (and to the numerous social media accounts one employee can hold). Some of those consequences are within business control, while others are not. One area a business can control is the influence on employee use of social media. Although employees can use social media on their own time, every business needs to be aware of how an employee's statements on social media might be construed as the employer's statements.

Businesses need to protect their brands, and one way of doing this is by putting a social media policy in place within their employee handbook.

2. Discovery

What is discovery? It is a series of questions and requests that one party in a lawsuit sends to another party. The purpose of discovery is to allow both sides to gather the information that they may need to prove their arguments, if the case were to go to trial. Social media evidence can be obtained either within or outside of the formal discovery process.

There are more devices connected to the Internet than there are people on Earth. It may come as no surprise that a Plaintiff or Defendant's online activities often fall squarely within the scope of discoverable information during civil litigation. Additionally, electronically stored information ("ESI") isn't just email anymore, with extensive and almost instantaneous mobile access to the Internet, uploads and downloads, status updates, texts, and "tweets," social media must be considered part of almost every legal investigation into discoverable evidence. Over 100,000 tweets are sent and over 684,478 pieces of content shared on Facebook every minute of every day.

Before formal discovery commences, a simple Internet search (Google and Bing) or search of other social media sites can be conducted to determine if the party or witness in question has a social media presence. It is a relatively common practice for opposing counsel and/or their staff to search for a party or a witness's Facebook or other social media pages, as well as their kids, spouse, siblings, and friends. This is an especially popular practice in the worlds of family law, medical malpractice and personal injury/tort defense.

3. Ethics

The increase of social media use has raised several questions regarding what attorneys ethically can or cannot do on social media. For example, is it ethical for attorneys to connect with clients of former clients on social media? Clearly, it is *not* ethical to communicate with a client regarding matters relating to their representation over social media networking sites.

Law can get complicated when it comes to unrepresented individuals. An attorney may contact an unrepresented (someone without a lawyer) person on social media, as long as they are clear about their identity and purpose. However, the moment a conversation turns to matters that could be privileged, the conversation must be moved off social media.

What about researching a juror's social media? An attorney may review a juror's social media presence but may not communicate directly with the juror. This includes messaging them or sending them a friend or follow request.

As social media continue to grow, so will the impact on the law. If you're not sure if something is appropriate to post or ethical to use in discovery, it's best to err on the side of caution and contact your lawyer as social media maintains its popularity.

Jeana Goosmann is the founder, CEO, and Managing Partner of the Goosmann Law Firm in Sioux City, Iowa. As the CEO's Attorney, she is general counsel to company presidents, CEOs, corporate executives, business owners, and business leaders. Jeana teaches, counsels, and inspires business leaders to level up their business to launch them toward success. She successfully leads one of the nation's fastest-growing law firms. Jeana has represented clients on the Forbes billionaire's list, senators in trial, and companies involved in an anti-trust class action, toxic tort, business fraud, piercing the corporate veil, adversary proceedings, mass product recall, breach of contract, explosion litigation and business torts. In addition to practicing law, Jeana is the author of the business leadership book, *Worth It*, which teaches her RED Philosophy – Ready, Execute, Deliver.

The boundaries and limitations of communication and business in cyberspace remain unsettled. Twitter, for example, has blocked US intelligence agencies from having access to a Dataminr tool used to track breaking news, apparently "worried about the 'optics' of seeming too close to American intelligence services" (Gilmer, 2016, para. 3). Social media freedom seemed to be at odds with an interest in national security concerns. As one scholar of computer-mediated communication has noted, digital and Internet technologies present a paradox: "Utopian and dystopian views about the future of the Internet describe two very different future scenarios" (Barnes, 2003, p. 331). Increasingly, events such as the 2014 Olympics in Sochi offered contexts controlled by a hosting government and economic entity focused on profits rather than free speech (Dickey, 2013). For athletes and even audience members, there may be social media restrictions when entering controlled venues, such as concerts, private clubs, or other property.

As Pool (1983) noted:

> The onus is on us to determine whether free societies in the twenty-first century will conduct electronic communication under the conditions of freedom established for the

domain of print through centuries of struggle, or whether the great achievement will become lost in a confusion about new technologies.

(p. 10)

It remains to be seen what happens now that the powerful must deal with potentially billions of social media "publishers" communicating through complex and unpredictable computer networks. The spreading of, for example, distorted images and superimposed text to create false information during a 2017 crisis in Cameroon ended with a 93-day government shutdown of the Internet, use of a 2014 terrorism law, and jail sentences (Ngange & Mokondo, 2019). Unfortunately, governments around the world are quick to censor and disconnect online access during political tension.

These can be seen as part of a larger technological system driving social change and resistance to it (Ellul, 1980). These new media force examination of social and legal assumptions (Lievrouw & Livingstone, 2006). The emerging social media communication environment is mobile and wireless (Raychaudhuri & Mario, 2011), and it is ahead of the legal rules designed to protect individuals, social systems, and political actors.

The challenge for us is to see concepts such as "marketplace of ideas," "social responsibility," and "public interest" in light of social, political, and economic factors. If we do this, it will follow that new technologies such as the Internet may not fundamentally change the tilt of power. Nowhere can this be seen more than among bloggers who speak their minds and sometimes exert influence (Rettberg, 2008). Social media communication technology can encourage open international communication (Thussu, 2009). It also may activate meaningful exchanges, collaboration, and social change. Social media communication law mirrors older media law in that it remains fluid as policies and regulations adapt to change (Wiley, Abernathy, & Wadlow, 2007). The ambiguity of law in this environment leaves space for behavior evaluated in terms of values and ethical norms. These may be viewed as politically liberal or conservative, depending on the control of power at any given moment (Luthi, 2019).

The global nature of social media communication presents many opportunities and challenges going forward. Young Saudis, for example, lack freedoms in their country, but they had found freedom to "debate" on Twitter and "flirt at the mall" using WhatsApp and Snapchat (Hubbard, 2015, para. 1). As is the case in much of the world, social media in Saudi Arabia was a liberating force amid strict laws and norms: "Confronted with an austere version of Islam and strict social codes that place sharp restrictions on public life, young Saudis are increasingly relying on social media to express and entertain themselves, earn money and meet friends and potential mates" (para. 3). It remains unclear the extent to which new practices there and elsewhere will be met with government responses that include new restrictions. The general tendency is to see social media as potential tools for political instability – especially amid protests or other political strife.

Even in the more liberal European nations, there are new social media regulations. The online publication *The Daily Beast* noted that tweeting from the UK "racist or otherwise libelous bile can land you in jail" (Moynihan, 2014, para. 1). A 44-year-old Staffordshire shopkeeper, for example, "was arrested, fingerprinted, and had his computer seized by police when he made a pair of tasteless jokes about Nelson Mandela" (para. 12). Although newspapers reprinted the tweets, only the Twitter user was targeted by authorities. Likewise, in the area of US libel law, users can be sued for defamation, but Facebook and other social network sites are immune from liability (*Finkel v. Facebook*, 2009) under provisions of the *Communications Decency Act* of 1996 (47 USC 230). Nevertheless, journalists using social network sites to source their reporting that turns out to be inaccurate may be sued for libel (Chow, 2013).

When BuzzFeed in early 2017 shared a 35-page private intelligence document known as "The Trump Dossier," journalists debated the ethics of publishing at a time when other news organizations withheld it (FiveThirtyEight, 2017). In the wake of the devastating Gawker case, BuzzFeed took a legal chance in exposing on the Internet private, yet unsubstantiated allegations. US privacy law is unsettled, and this created publication concerns for journalists and others using social media. Social media law and ethics appear to be an evolving landscape that requires a deep understanding by users. In the end, as legal scholar Kimberly Chow warns, social media communication should be handled with care.

DISCUSSION QUESTIONS: STRATEGIES AND TACTICS

1. How are social media a significant change for US and global rules of law? In this redefinition, what are important limitations on free expression?

2. How are social media rules applied within workplaces? What differences exist between government restrictions on use and those limits imposed by others?

3. What can we conclude about the existence of social media privacy? How does interest in having access to content and wanting to share it conflict with privacy?

4. What alternatives to draconian censorship exist when a government deals with false social media information during a political uprising?

REFERENCES

AbuZayyad, Z. K. (2013). Human Rights, The Internet and Social Media: Has Technology Changed the Way See Things? *Journal of Politics, Economics & Culture 18*(4), 38–40.

Ali, A. H. (2011, Summer). The Power of Social Media in Developing Nations: New Tools for Closing the Global Digital Divide and Beyond. *Harvard Human Rights Journal 24*(1), 185–219.

Am. Council of Educ. v. FCC, U.S. App. LEXIS 14174 (2006).

Associated Press (2016, December 20). EU Watchdog Probes Facebook over WhatsApp Merger. http://abcnews.go.com/Technology/wireStory/eu-watchdog-probes-facebook-whatsapp-merger-44303762

Baldes, T. (2008, December 22). Beware: Your "Tweet" on Twitter Could Be Trouble. *National Law Journal*, www.law.com/jsp/nlj/PubArticleNLJ.jsp?id=1202426916023&slreturn=20131026150648

Banks, D. (2013, June 26). Jeremy Forrest Case: Twitter Users Could Have Broken the Law. *The Guardian*. www.theguardian.com/media/2013/jun/26/jeremy-forrest-twitter-users

Barnes, S. (2003). *Computer-Mediated Communication, Human-to-Human Communication across the Internet*. Boston, MA: Allyn and Bacon.

Baym, N. (1995). The Emergence of Community in Computer Mediated Communication. In S. G. Jones (Ed.), *CyberSociety: Computer-Mediated Community and Communication*, Chapter 7, pp. 138–163. Thousand Oaks; CA: Sage.

Beckett, C., with Ball, J. (2012). *WikiLeaks, News in the Networked Era.* Cambridge, UK: Polity Press.

Bell, D., & Kennedy, B. M. (Eds.) (2007). *The Cybercultures Reader*, second edition. London: Routledge.

Blackstone, W. (1769). *Commentaries on the Laws of England: A Facsimile of the First Edition of 1765–1769*, pp. 150–153 (Commentaries 4). The University of Chicago. http://press-pubs. uchicago.edu/founders/documents/amendI_speechs4.html

Blumenthal v. Drudge and America Online, 992 F. Supp. 44 (D.D.C. 1998).

Branscomb, A. W. (1996, June). Cyberspaces: Familiar Territory or Lawless Frontiers. *Journal of Computer-Mediated Communication 2*(1). http://onlinelibrary.wiley.com/doi/10.1111/ j.1083-6101.1996.tb00178.x/full

Briggs, M. (2020). *Journalism Next, A Practical Guide to Digital Reporting and Publishing*, fourth edition. Los Angeles: SAGE.

Bynum, R. (2019, December 13). Man Videotaped Slapping Reporter's Rear On Live TV Charged. *NBC News.* www.nbcchicago.com/news/national-international/man-videotaped-slapping-reporters-rear-charged/2189166/

Calvert, C. (2014, November). Public Concern and Outrageous Speech: Testing the Inconstant Boundaries of IIED and the First Amendment Three Years after *Snyder V. Phelps. University of Pennsylvania Journal of Constitutional Law 17*, 437–477.

Carmody, C. (2016, Summer). *Gawker* Shuts down after Losing Its Initial Appeal of $140 Million Judgment in Privacy Case. *The Silha Bulletin*, pp. 1–5.

Carpenter v. U.S. 585 U.S. ___, 138 S.Ct. 2206 (2018).

Cashmore, P. (2008, December 20). Twitter Lawsuits: 4 Reasons Your Tweets Might Be Trouble. *Mashable.* http://mashable.com/2008/12/20/twitter-lawsuits/

Chicagoist (2010, January 21). Twitter Lawsuit Dismissed. http://chicagoist.com/2010/01/21/ twitter_lawsuit_dismissed.php

Chow, K. (2013, Fall). Handle with Care: The Evolving Actual Malice Standard and Why Journalists Should Think Twice before Relying on Internet Sources. *N.Y.U. Journal of Intellectual Property & Entertainment Law 3*, 53–75.

Crook, J. (2013, November 21). Don't Spam Facebook with Fake Bieber Porn unless You Want to Get Sued. *TechCrunch.* http://techcrunch.com/2013/11/21/dont-spam-facebook-with-fake-bieber-porn-unless-you-want-to-get-sued/

The Crown Prosecution Service (2012). Guidelines on Prosecuting Cases Involving Communications Sent via Social Media. www.cps.gov.uk/legal/a_to_c/communications_sent_via_social_media

Dennis v. U.S., 341 U.S. 494, 590 (1951).

Dickey, J. (2013, August 12). Express Yourself. Or Not. *Sports Illustrated*, p. 20.

Dietrich, G. (2015, January 6). The FTC and Social Media: You Have to Disclose. *Spin Sucks.* http://spinsucks.com/communication/ftc-social-media-rules/

Digital Theft Deterrence Act, 17 U.S.C. § 504(a), (c)(1) (1999).

Ekstrand, V. S. (2015). *Hot News in the Age of Big Data: A Legal History of the Hot News Doctrine and Implications for the Digital Age.* El Paso, TX: LFB Scholarly Publishing.

Eldred v. Ashcroft, 537 U.S. 186, *reh'g denied*, 538 U.S. 916 (2003).

Ellul, J. (1980). *The Technological System, Translated from the French by Joachim Neugroschel.* New York: Continuum.

Elonis v. United States, 35 S.Ct. 2001 (2015).

Facebook (2014). *Choose Who You Share With.* m.facebook.com/help/www/459934584025324

Facebook, Rights and Responsibilities. 2. Sharing Your Content and Information. www.facebook.com/legal/terms

Faehner, M. J. (2012, June). Advertising. *Florida Bar Journal 86*(6), 36–37.

Fair, L. (2011a, December 22). *Using Social Media in Your Marketing? Staff Closing Letter Is Worth a Read*. Washington, DC: Federal Trade Commission.

Fair, L. (2011b, December 1). *Facebook's Future: What the FTC Order Means for Consumer Privacy*. Washington, DC: Federal Trade Commission. https://www.ftc.gov/news-events/blogs/business-blog/2011/12/facebooks-future-what-ftc-order-means-consumer-privacy

Fair, L. (2013a, November 18). *Blurred Lines*. Washington, DC: Federal Trade Commission.

Fair, L. (2013b, October 22). *How Aaron's Erred: What Your Business Should Take from the Latest Spycam Case*. Washington, DC: Federal Trade Commission.

Fair, L. (2019, July 24). FTC's $5 Billion Facebook Settlement: Record-Breaking and History-Making. *Federal Trade Commission*. www.ftc.gov/news-events/blogs/business-blog/2019/07/ftcs-5-billion-facebook-settlement-record-breaking-history

Fang, I. (2008). *Alphabet to Internet, Mediated Communication in Our Lives*. St. Paul, MN: Rada Press.

Federal Trade Commission (FTC), (1983, October 14). Policy Statement on Deception: Appended to Cliffdale Associates, Inc., 103 F.T.C. 110, 174 (1984). www.ftc.gov/ftc-policy-statement-on-deception

Federal Trade Commission (FTC) (2004, November 24). *Letter to Marc Rotenberg, Electronic Privacy Information Center*. Washington, DC: Federal Trade Commission.

Federal Trade Commission (FTC), (2010, June). *The FTC's Revised Endorsement Guides: What People are Asking*. Washington, DC: Federal Trade Commission.

Federal Trade Commission (FTC). (2014a). *About the FTC*. www.ftc.gov/about-ftc

Federal Trade Commission (FTC). (2014b). *Consumer Information. Privacy & Identity*. www.consumer.ftc.gov/topics/privacy-identity

Federal Trade Commission (FTC). (2016, May 23). FTC Approves Final Lord & Taylor Order Prohibiting Deceptive Advertising Techniques. www.ftc.gov/news-events/press-releases/2016/05/ftc-approves-final-lord-taylor-order-prohibiting-deceptive

Finkel v. Facebook (2009). N.Y. Misc. LEXIS 3021, NY Slip Op 32248(U).

Firestone, 81 F.T.C. 398, 1972, *aff'd*, 481 F.2d 246, 6th Cir., *cert. denied*, 414 U.S. 1112 (1973).

FiveThirtyEight. (2017, January 12). Should Rumors like the Trump Dossier Be News? *FiveThirtyEight*. https://fivethirtyeight.com/features/should-rumors-like-the-trump-dossier-be-news/

Forbes, P. (2013, January 23). FTC Complaints About Yelp Allege Extortion, Libel, More. http://eater.com/archives/2013/01/23/ftc-complaints-about-yelp-allege-extortion-libel-more.php

Gilmer, M. (2016, May 8). Twitter Blocks U.S. Intelligence Agency Access to Social Media Tool, Report Says. *Mashable*. http://mashable.com/2016/05/08/twitter-blocks-dataminr-access/

Goldnick, L. (2015). Coddling the Internet: How the CDA Exacerbates the Proliferation of Revenge Porn and Prevents a Meaningful Remedy for Its Victims. *Cardoza Journal of Law & Gender 21*, 583–629.

Groggin, G., & McLelland, M. (Eds.) (2009). *Internationalizing Internet Studies, Beyond Anglophone Paradigms*. New York, NY: Routledge.

Hall, H. K. (2013). Social Media Policies for Advertising and Public Relations. In D. R. Stewart (Ed.), *Social Media Law, A Guidebook for Communication Students and Professionals*, pp. 212–226. New York, NY: Routledge.

Hayes, A. S. (2013). *Mass Media Law, The Printing Press to the Internet*. New York, NY: Peter Lang.

Hubbard, B. (2015, May 22). Young Saudis Bound by Conservative Strictures, Find Freedom on Their Phones. *The New York Times*. www.nytimes.com/2015/05/23/world/middleeast/saudi-arabia-youths-cellphone-apps-freedom.html

In the Matter of Lord & Taylor, LLC. Federal Trade Commission C-4576 (May 20, 2016).

Innis, H. A. (1972). *Empire and Communications*. Toronto: University of Toronto Press.

Keller, B. P., Levine, L., & Goodale, J. C. (2008). *Communications Law in the Digital Age 2008*, Three volumes. New York: Practicing Law Institute.

Kendall, B. (2016, October 28). Conviction Reinstated in Facebook Threats Case. *The Wall Street Journal*. www.wsj.com/articles/conviction-reinstated-in-facebook-threats-case-1477666807

Kennedy, M. (2016, November 2). Hulk Hogan Reaches Settlement With Gawker Worth Over $31 Million. *NPR*. www.npr.org/sections/thetwo-way/2016/11/02/500389355/hulk-hogan-reaches-settlement-with-gawker-worth-over-31-million

Kroger Co. of Mich. v. Granger, NLRB. No. 07-CA-098566 (April 22, 2014).

Larson III, R. G. (2013, Winter). Forgetting the First Amendment: How Obscurity-based Privacy and a Right to Be Forgotten are Incompatible with Free Speech. *Communication Law & Policy 18*(1), 91–120.

Lievrouw, L. A., & Livingstone, S. (Eds.) (2006). *The Handbook of New Media, Updated Student Edition*. London: Sage.

Lipschultz, J. H. (2008). *Broadcast and Internet Indecency, Defining Free Speech*. New York, NY: Routledge.

Lipschultz, J. H. (2020). New Communication Technologies. In W. W. Hopkins (Ed.), *Communication and the Law 2020 Edition*, pp. 195–222. Northport, AL: Vision Press.

Liptak, A., & Alter, A. (2016, April 18). Challenge to Google Books Is Declined by Supreme Court. *The New York Times*. www.nytimes.com/2016/04/19/technology/google-books-case.html

Lisby, G. (2020). Intellectual Property. In W. W. Hopkins (Ed.), *Communication and the Law 2020 Edition*, pp. 223–248. Northport, AL: Vision Press.

Logan, B., & Matousek, M. (2019, December 6). Elon Musk Wins In Defamation Trial Over His 'Pedo Guy' Tweet. *Business Insider*. www.businessinsider.com/elon-musk-wins-defamation-trial-over-pedo-guy-tweet-2019-12

Luthi, S. (2019, December 22). How Trump Is Filling the Liberal 9th Circuit with Conservatives. *Politico*. www.politico.com/news/2019/12/22/trump-judges-9th-circuit-appeals-court-088833

Mackey, T. K., & Liang, B. A. (2013). *Globalization and Health 2013 9*(45). www.globalization-andhealth.com/content/9/1/45.

Mathison, D. (2009). *Be the Media*. New Hyde Park, NY: Natural E Creative Group.

Miller v. California, 413 U.S. 15 (1973).

Milton, J. (1644). *Areopagitica: A Speech for the Liberty of Unlicensed Printing to the Parliament of England*. Project Gutenberg. http://gutenberg.readingroo.ms/6/0/608/608-h/608-h.htm

Moynihan, M. (2014, January 23). Can a Tweet Put You in Prison? It Certainly Will in the UK. *The Daily Beast*. www.thedailybeast.com/articles/2014/01/23/can-a-tweet-land-you-in-prison-it-certainly-will-in-the-uk.html

Napoli, P. M. (2019). *Social Media and the Public Interest, Media Regulation in the Disinformation Age*. New York: Columbia University Press.

Naruto v. Slater, 888 F.3d 418 (9th Cir.) (2018).

Near v. Minnesota, 283 U.S. 697 (1931).

New York Times v. Sullivan, 376 U.S. 254, 271 (1964).

Ngange, K. L., & Mokondo, M. S. (2019, December). Understanding Social Media's Role in Propagating Falsehood in Conflict Situations: Case of the Cameroon Anglophone Crisis. *Studies in Media and Communication 7*(2), 55–67.

Nitke v. Gonzalez, 413 F. Supp. 2d 262 (S.D.N.Y.) (2005), *affd.*, 547 U.S. 1015 (2006).

NLRB (2018, September 5). CVS Health, Case 31-CA-210099, National Labor Relations Board, Office of the General Counsel, Advice Memorandum. www.nlrb.gov/case/31-CA-210099

NPR (2017, May 25). 'Playboy' Model Sentenced Over Body-Shaming Woman At Gym. https://www.npr.org/sections/thetwo-way/2017/05/25/529999618/playboy-model-sentenced-over-body-shaming-woman-at-gym

Nockleby, J. T., Levinson, L. L., Manheim, K. M., Dougherty, F. J., Gold, V. J., Ides, A. P., & Martin, D. W. (2013). *The Journalist's Guide to American Law*. New York, NY: Routledge.

Pavlik, J. V. (2008). *Media in the Digital Age*. New York, NY: Columbia University Press.

Pogue, D. (2009). *The World According to Twitter*. New York, NY: Black Dog & Leventhal.

Pool, I. D. S. (1983). *Technologies of Freedom*. Boston, MA: Harvard University Press.

Raychaudhuri, D., & Mario, G. (Eds.) (2011). *Emerging Wireless Technologies and the Future Mobile Internet*. New York, NY: Cambridge University Press.

Reno v. ACLU, 521 U.S. 844 (1997).

Rettberg, J. W. (2008). *Blogging*. Cambridge, UK: Polity Press.

Revesz, R. (2016, June 6). US Supreme Court Rejects Google Appeal in Lawsuit Brought by Advertisers. *Independent*. www.independent.co.uk/news/world/americas/us-supreme-court-rejects-google-appeal-in-lawsuit-brought-by-advertisers-a7067566.html

Rogers, E. M. (1995). *Diffusion of Innovations*, fourth edition. New York, NY: Free Press.

Sanders, A. K., & Olsen, N. C. (2012, Autumn). Re-defining Defamation: Psychological Sense of Community in the Age of the Internet. *Communication Law & Policy 17*(4), 355–384.

Sapra, B. (2019, December 30). Facebook Reverses Course after Backlash, Deciding to Remove Ads about HIV-prevention Drug that Were Called 'Factually Inaccurate' and a Risk to Public Health. *Business Insider*. www.businessinsider.com/facebook-removes-inaccurate-hiv-prevention-prep-ads-after-lgbtq-backlash-2019-12

Sass, E. (2016, August 23). Chipotle's Social Media Policy Violated Law, Says NLRB. *MediaPost: Social Media Daily*. www.mediapost.com/publications/article/283060/chipotles-social-media-policy-violated-law-says.html

Shah, S., & Gillani, W. (2019, December 21). Pakistani Professor Sentenced to Death for Blasphemy on Social Media. *The Wall Street Journal*. www.wsj.com/articles/pakistani-professor-sentenced-to-death-for-blasphemy-on-social-media-11576936022

Silver, L. (2019, February 5). Smartphone Ownership Is Growing Rapidly around the World, but Not Always Equally. *Pew Research Center, Global Attitudes & Trends*. www.pewresearch.org/global/2019/02/05/smartphone-ownership-is-growing-rapidly-around-the-world-but-not-always-equally/

Stevenson, N. (1995). *Understanding Media Cultures*. London, UK: SAGE.

Stewart, D. R. (Ed.) (2017). Preface. In *Social Media and the Law, A Guidebook for Communication Students and Professionals*, second edition, pp. vii–xiv. New York, NY: Routledge.

Tatro v. University of Minnesota, 816 N.W.2d 509 (2012), Minn. LEXIS 246.

Thussu, D. K. (Ed.) (2009). *Internationalizing Media Studies*. London, UK: Routledge.

Tressler, C. (2013, Nov. 12). *How to Help Victims of Typhoon Haiyan in the Philippines*. www.consumer.ftc.gov/blog/how-help-victims-typhoon-haiyan-philippines

U.S. Telecomm v. FCC. (2016, June 14). D.C. Cir., No, 15-1063, slip opinion 1619173.

U.S. v. Elonis. 841 F.3rd 589 (3rd Cir., 2016).

United States v. Fumo. 655 F.3rd 298, 301 (2011).

United States v. Thomas. 74 F.3rd 701 (6th Cir.) (1996).

Wang, M. (2009). UPDATED: Rounding up the Buzz. *ChicagoNow*. http://culturewav.es/public_thought/72990

Weimann, G. (2010). Terror on Facebook, Twitter, and YouTube. *Brown Journal of World Affairs 16*(2), 45–54.

Wiley, R. E., Abernathy, K. Q., & Wadlow, R. C. (Eds.) (2007). *25th Annual Institute on Telecommunications Policy & Regulation*. New York, NY: Practicing Law Institute.

Wolverton, T. (2019, December 12). Federal are considering Blocking Facebook from Combining WhatsApp, Instagram and Its Other Apps. *Business Insider*. www.businessinsider.com/facebook-could-face-an-injunction-from-the-ftc-2019-12

Xinhua (2010, June 30). *Google Says to "Abide by the Chinese Law" in Order to Renew License.* http://news.xinhuanet.com/english2010/china/2010-07/01/c_13377786.htm

Social Media Ethics

Public life in the twenty-first century is undergoing a historic alteration through ubiquitous multimedia technologies, and ethics is essential for coming to grips with them.

– Clifford G. Christians (2019, p. 31)

Editorial discretion forms the critical core of any media company. However, in their emerging role as news providers, social media platforms should exercise ethical transparency in their policies and practices for curating and disseminating the news.
– Lori Bergen, AEJMC (@AEJMC, 2016)

Hyping transparency distorts media ethics in several ways: It misunderstands the basis of media ethics, while blurring crucial differences among concepts; it wrongly implies that transparency can replace other principles and can resolve ethical issues created by new media.
– Stephen J. A. Ward (@MediaMorals, 2013)

Social media ethics are complicated and rapidly changing (Elliott & Spence, 2020). From how and when to correct errors to distinguishing news from opinion, social media content creators, editors, and managers face constant questions about truth, accuracy, and trust. Journalists and others "grapple with both situational decision-making and professional philosophy" (Mellinger, 2020, p. xxiii). Likewise, journalism educators have been drawn into controversies over factual information.

In mid-2016, the Association for Education in Journalism and Mass Communication (AEJMC), the largest group of journalism educators, issued a statement targeting Facebook and other social media site transparency (AEJMC, 2016). Then-President Lori Bergen, dean at the University of Colorado at Boulder, said she spoke for educators in responding to media coverage about Facebook manipulation of trending news during the presidential election. "This accusation is predicated on Facebook's professed desire to be a trusted platform for users and media partners" (para. 2). The AEJMC statement offered a normative statement that, "Facebook is powerful and undoubtedly influential, and it should exercise ethical transparency in curating and disseminating news" (para. 6). The statement sought to separate Facebook from "legacy" media:

> If Facebook is biased or is purposely inaccurate in what news and information it says is "trending," it should be judged as a social media platform, not as a news media company that embraces the news values that are essential to a free and democratic society.
>
> (para. 7)

Media ethicists, however, look beyond transparency and platform nature to editorial independence in the foundational nature of ethics.

Social media communication raises important ethical issues because it can be perceived as anonymous – crossing borders and cultures worldwide. From its computer-mediated communication origins to state-of-the-art PR and advertising campaigns, a lack of transparency and communication independence may trigger a social media response. Caldiero (2016), for example, has applied postmodernism to PR in finding "multiple truths" to present a basic challenge: "it may be more effective and useful to, at least in part, acknowledge uncertainty, understanding of alternate perceptions, and awareness of publics' increasing wariness of "organizational truth," as promoted in managed PR messaging" (p. 28).

Transparency, then, is an oversimplified value, but it is not "a magical idea – a norm with seemingly magical powers to restore democracy" (Ward, 2013a, para. 6). Ward suggests that "responsible publication for democracy," not transparency, is the ethical foundation in journalism, and "editorial independence" also is a basic idea (para. 11) – especially in an era of nonprofessional journalists:

> Without a stress on independence, and without a constant critical eye for conflicts of interest, I fear that questionable, non-independent journalism will fly under the flag of transparent journalism. One can be a transparent journalist, yet still be inaccurate or care little for minimizing harm. But more than this, even if a journalist is transparent, accurate, and minimizes harm, we still are left with a crucial question for her: How free are you to tell the stories that the public needs to hear? Telling people "where you come from" as a journalist is to be commended. But it is not enough for journalism ethics.
>
> (para. 32)

Editorial independence may be compromised when special interests override larger public interests. Facebook, for example, temporarily offered news media payments for Facebook Live broadcasts, so there was a clear lack of independence in the broader sense. Ward suggests that lack of independence leads to "propaganda" or "narrow advocacy," if "non-professional journalists" do not "make a strong ethical argument for ignoring considerations of independence" (paras. 29–30). In the online world, the speed of information distribution, for example, leads to incorrect information distributed on

Twitter about nearly every breaking news national story – from the Boston Marathon bombings to the shootings in 2013 at the Los Angeles airport. In Ward's view, "irresponsible reporting" happens when we ignore some values, "such as verification and minimizing harm," and instead emphasize being first with the story.

The professional context of journalism ethics frequently may create "conscience" moments within a real-time social media and 24-hour news cycle context: "Some of these considerations merely call for good journalism: seek the truth, verify, be fair" (Mathewson, 2014, p. 198). Yet, the search for a singular definition of truth clashes in social media spaces with Caldiero's (2016) Neo-PR understanding of "meaning creation" as not so much "fluid" or "inconsistent," but open to new voices on Twitter and other sites: "technology such as social media and the increasing diversity of an organization's constituents reinforces the postmodern idea that plurality of meaning is the standard ..." (p. 34). This seems to move us beyond the traditional tension between journalists and publicists, as the degree of transparency and independence play out in the public sphere of social media sites. The "fake news" debate in 2017 made this clear, as some media commentators sought to return to facts:

> Instead, call a lie a lie. Call a hoax a hoax. Call a conspiracy theory by its rightful name. After all, "fake news" is an imprecise expression to begin with ... What's more, the term is being used to discredit – or at least muddy the waters for – legitimate fact-checking efforts.
>
> (Sullivan, 2017, paras. 10, 12)

It seemed clear that partisans were using social media to spread interpretations, and portray them as facts.

Even within the legacy and credible new media sector, The Trump Dossier case discussed in the last chapter offers ethical issues about whether or not the public was served by the release of unsubstantiated information. Poynter Vice President Kelly McBride told *Vox* that there was no ethical basis to publish:

> Not by the standards of professional journalism. The professional journalists that I work with take their responsibility to verify information, add context to it, and present it to the audience in a way that the audience can make sense of it – they take that responsibility quite seriously. And there didn't seem to be any attempt to do any of that on Buzzfeed's part.
>
> (Illing, 2017, para. 12)

McBride suggested that media can be transparent and responsible by telling readers what they possess (even if it is leaked and stolen) that is unverified. She distinguished the case from the historic Pentagon Papers – verified documents.

The longer-term interest is in the difference between *The New York Times'* and a publication such as Buzzfeed's social media ethics. A document dump seems to narrow the gap between Buzzfeed and Wikileaks in terms of its function within journalism as mere release to the public of private and potentially damaging information.

Social media communication tools and practices are beginning to mature, so it makes sense to discuss and debate values that underlie behavior. Journalists, PR, and advertising managers and marketers must confront changing norms. Ward has made a case for "radical" change in the view of journalism ethics and global practices. Beyond the implications of an interconnected world, Ward is concerned with the proliferation of activist journalism:

> But when are activist journalists not propagandists? When are journalists partisan political voices and when are they journalists with a valid cause? Rather than simply dismiss activist journalism on the traditional ground of objectivity, how can we develop a more nuanced understanding of this area of journalism?
>
> (Ward, 2013b, para. 21)

This relates to the problem of real-time public sourcing on Twitter of the separation of rumors from story facts – particularly when journalists work across cultural norms.

It comes down to credibility and trust. In Ward's view, "independence, not transparency, distinguishes journalism from propaganda, journalism from narrow advocacy." He challenges a key point in *The New Ethics of Journalism* (2014), a volume edited by

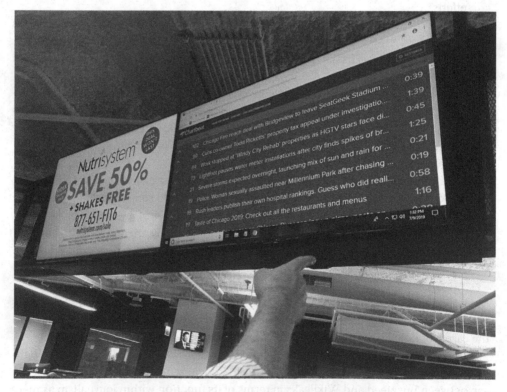

FIGURE 10.1 *A large screen at the Chicago Tribune in 2019 used Chartbeat software to track second-by-second website views.*

Kelly McBride and Tom Rosenstiel (@tbr1) – Ward wants to reform independence rather than replace it. To be fair, McBride and Rosenstiel discuss transparency within the context of 20th-century mass media scale and neutral voice:

> These two precepts, which grew out of both an economic and a democratic imperative, led to an ethical principle of *independence:* the notion that the organization and the individuals who create the news should not advocate for outcomes or slant the news in favor of a particular point of view.
>
> (pp. 89–90)

Reading further, their perspective values "independent observers" and not lowering standards because "true transparency is more than disclosure" requiring "producing the news in ways that can be explained and even defended." The book explains this in Adam Hochberg's (@adamhochberg) chapter discussing the Wisconsin Center for Investigative Journalism's concerns related to non-profit news organizations: donor transparency, editorial independence, the firewall between journalism and fundraising, and conflicts of interest (Hochberg, 2014, p. 132).

Ward (2019) revisited normative ethics that may be guided by professional codes, profits, consumer marketing and economic realities. "Impartiality" of journalists, for example, may not include a neutral stance, but it should strive for "holistic ethics" that favor traditional concepts of human dignity and justice (Ward, 2019, pp. 25, 89). The use of reason and logic can be challenging within competitive social media, but the key is to lean toward restraint.

We should also recognize that independence has always been an ideal, and local news organizations regularly struggle with the need to keep advertisers happy. This has not changed in the digital era. If a newspaper uses its official news brand on Facebook and Twitter to promote a grand opening, it sacrifices a degree of editorial independence. There is a conflict of interest if it fails to report a problem, such as a traffic jam, that affects the public interest.

But do not limit thinking to journalism. Failure to disclose interests is a huge social media communication problem with public relations, advertising and marketing. From sponsored content to native advertising, the lines between content and vested interests are crossed in ways that promote neither transparency nor independence. On LinkedIn, for example, Felix Salmon (@felixsalmon; Salmon, 2013) noted that, "there is very little distinction between editorial and advertising" because it "is all just posts" (para. 13):

> LinkedIn is about people more than it is about companies, but that really only helps – it makes everything feel more personal and less corporate, and that in turn makes the message more likely to be well received. No one cares about the editorial/advertising divide: the very concept seems silly. Indeed, if any disclosure is needed, readers would much rather know whether a certain CEO wrote a given post himself, or whether he had it written for him. (Good luck finding that out.)
>
> (para. 13)

Therein lies the deeper issue of social media communication ethics. Real-time interaction and engagement happen within the context of individual social networks and marketing strategies. CEOs are now being called upon to be social media "thought leaders" and participants, according to one study, in order to show innovation, build media relationships, provide a human face for the company, and other aspects of reputation management. Joe Mathewson (@joemathewson) and his challenge of truth-seeking through a need to "verify, and be fair" seems to imply a safeness in simply finding enough sources, regardless of *their* independence (Mathewson, 2014, p. 198) – social media fairness, instead, seems in the eye of the beholder. Corporate executives, meanwhile, worry about their participation in social media communication – even within the professionally oriented LinkedIn platform, where their specific concerns include (Toomey, 2013, p. 8):

1. Can I keep my contacts private? "Contacts can be visible only to you, or to all of your connections."

2. Do I have to connect with everyone who asks me to? "Your connections should be people you know personally and/or have done business with, and who you might be able to refer to others."

3. What types of content should I share on LinkedIn? "Share your company's news, thought leadership and blog posts."

4. What are the differences between Endorsements and Recommendations? "an Endorsement is a one-click way for your connections to validate your Skills & Expertise ... A Recommendation is a detailed, written statement ..."

5. When should I connect with new contacts? "Growing your network is an ongoing process"

Information verification goes a long way toward finding an ethical path. Fairness is more challenging because we make subjective judgments. In a political context, the deep divide in social media realities may be a function of divergent cultural values. It owes a lot to traditional ethical concerns about morality, justice, virtue and safety of others. In journalism, for example, media ethics regarding traditional roles are stressed by the lack of social media control and traditional gatekeeping:

> The public is swamped with information through more traditional sources as well as via the Internet, and its social media "children," the bloggers, Facebook updaters and tweeters ... It is our contention that this new "role" of the mass media is to sift through all that information... The gate-keeping role of journalists has not ended, but the number of non-journalistic gates is increasing and editors are competing against more sources, more outlets and more voices.
>
> (Patching & Hirst, 2014, p. 218)

Social media communication should not alter fundamental values and ethical principles, but we must be open to differing values, principles, and practices that we encounter within global social networks. Pompper (2015) addresses how the idea of corporate social responsibility (CSR) within PR is negotiated in areas such as environmental sustainability:

> Public relations practitioners and scholars use the sustainability narrative to enhance corporate image/reputation, which ultimately supports bottom-line profits. Less plentiful are critical scholars urging for public relations practitioners to act normatively from inside organizations; as a means for inspiring organizations' authentic, ethical commitment to a wide number of stakeholders (people), while also being respectful of natural environments (planet) and earnings (profit).
>
> (p. 2)

There sometimes appears to be an ethical struggle between reputation management (that now happens within social media) and a greater social good "to confront instances of injustice and immorality – negative impacts on the public sphere – in order to inspire positive social change" (p. 19). The normative nature of social media ethics depends upon social agreement on scientific facts, as well as consensus on ethical responses.

The early debate about social media ethics is not a threat. It is healthy and serves our desire to promote democracy, community and freedom. At the same time, however, social media sites may be platforms for political extremism on the left and right. To the extent that such social media communication threatens democratic freedom, there must be engagement in search of shared values. Brian Solis (2014) expressed concern about "the grey zone" of social media perception:

> The ethical practice of social media starts with an ethical foundation. Without it, you risk falling victim to social media's relentless and unforgiving nature of real-time relevance or irrelevance. You are competing for the moment and for the future in all you do. Without a strong ethical foundation, you unintentionally make perilous decisions driven by what's right ... right now, rather than what's truly right.
>
> (p. xvi)

Social media "impressions and opinions" may be treated as "truth" and "reality" in ethics that are "open to interpretation" (p. xvi). Still, transparency and authenticity fall short of a theoretic and philosophical understanding of ethics.

THEORIES AND PHILOSOPHIES

Media ethics developed as a field within the context of issues surrounding 20th-century mass media. Christians, Rotzoll, and Fackler (1991) used the Potter Box as a way to think about morality within "a systematic process" (p. 2). Potter's moral reasoning box moves a person through a process of definition, values, principles and loyalties (p. 4). For example, media may decide to publish – "even if some people get hurt or are misunderstood" (p. 4) – if they value the information as representing truth. The first definition stage of the process begins with a "situation" (p. 8). There are a variety of ethical principles, such as:

- Aristotle's Golden Mean is that which lies "between two extremes" (pp. 11–12).

- Kant's Categorical Imperative is that "moral law is unconditionally binding" (p. 14).

- Mill's Principle of Utility is that "happiness was the sole end of human action" (p. 15).

- Rawl's Veil of Ignorance seeks to have the "most vulnerable party" receiving "priority" (p. 18).

- Judeo-Christian Persons as Ends is the ethics of loving "your neighbor" (p. 19).

Media ethicists have advanced thinking to bring it into a global and digital media context, which may create an "open media ethics" (Ward & Wasserman, 2010, p. 276). Opening media ethics is a matter of "meaningful participation" and "significant influence on the course of discussion" (p. 277), "content determination and revision" (p. 278), and transformation related to "citizen-based new media" with a "potential to create a global ethics discourse" (p. 281). Social media communication may be media critiques or activism that can be understood within the framework of "mobilization efforts" (p. 282). Consider what Ward and Wasserman (2010) describe as "peer-to-peer ethics" on a global scale:

> This peer-to-peer accountability can take the form of comments or blog posts, responses to Twitter feeds, or exchanges that take place parallel to citizen journalism posts … citizen journalists are held accountable for misrepresentations or inaccuracies by fellow commentators or visitors to the site.
>
> (p. 286)

Drawing upon the work of Habermas, Ward and Wasserman (2010) suggest that ethical processes and "reasoning should aim at an ideal mode of inclusive and equal discourse" (p. 288), which aligns with the veil of ignorance. A global context within journalism ethics addresses, for example, cultural sensitivities in "times of grief and trauma" (Motlagh et al., 2013, p. 1). There is initial evidence that media credibility is related to "role conceptions of professional journalists while social trust was positively associated with both professional and citizen journalists' role conceptions" (Chung & Nah, 2013, p. 274). Transformative credibility standards and role perceptions may represent the beginning of more open ethical processes.

IDEALISM AND RELATIVISM

Ethical idealism of truth, independence, and minimization of harm have been altered by digital media realities. While truth remains an ideal principle, emerging values include transparency and community engagement: "Clearly articulate your journalistic approach, whether you strive for independence or approach information from a political or philosophical point of view" (McBride & Rosenstiel, 2014, p. 3). Shirky (2014) wrestles with the Internet dilemma of beliefs, facts, and "post-fact" assertions:

> The Internet allows us to see what other people actually think. This has turned out to be a huge disappointment. When anyone can say anything, we can't even pretend most of us agree on the truth of most assertions any more.
>
> (p. 15)

The fundamental shift is from a world in which media function within a structure that offered a degree of scarcity and exclusivity.

> What does change, enormously, is the individual and organizational adaptations required to tell the truth without relying on scarcity and while hewing of ethical norms without reliance on a small group of similar institutions that can all coordinate around those norms.
>
> (p. 20)

As a new expectation of transparency is offered by open ethics, the very fact that storytellers are confronted in real-time with their audience members suggests a philosophical level of social media communication ethics ambiguity:

> What's harder to gauge is the power – and tension – that social media interaction will bring to this kind of storytelling. As journalists tell their stories via Twitter, they will certainly also receive questions and comments from their followers. Some of that interaction will no doubt interrupt and change the course of the storytelling.
>
> (Huang, 2014, p. 50)

Social media storytelling, journalism, and other forms, are likely to align with practices of collaboration in which communities contribute to their development. The shift from professional ethical norms to small group behavioral rules could replace the need for normative ethical rules with the engaged community desires to crowdsource and correct story narratives. Christians (2019) focuses on a "human-centered" approach:

> Global media technology is not just a world of technological artifacts. The problem is the dominance of the technological modes of thought over the human orders of politics, ethics, and culture. Philosophers of technology worry about a debilitating loss of morality through instrumentalism. Rather than be content with the critique only, and live with traditional dualism of means and ends, the instrumentalist worldview needs to be challenged at its roots.
>
> (p. 51)

Social media communication best practices, then, are not simply a matter of what works best from a marketing perspective. Instead, practitioners should reflect upon concerns for data privacy, truth and other moral challenges.

MORAL DEVELOPMENT

While traditional ethics seeks to cultivate individual moral development through its principles, rules, codes and processes, the emergence of fluid community narratives might be a function of interpersonal and small group communication and agreement. Typically, codes of ethics serve to guide media professionals, including those engaged in social media communication (Roberts, 2012). Tension exists, as codes may blur "distinctions between minimal expectations and ideal standards" (p. 115). It is debatable that media ethics codes are effective in training new employees, or even that they serve a valuable public relations function for media industries. Yet, research has found that codes reflect values: "Decision makers need to identify their values to understand the reasons behind their actions" (p. 116). Based on Rohan's (2000) dimension contrasting individual and social context outcomes, Roberts (2012) identifies key concerns. While an individual may seek "achievement" or "power," society may be driven by "universalism" (i.e., "tolerating"), and "benevolence" (i.e., "enhancing the welfare") (pp. 117–18). Likewise, an organization may be concerned with "tradition" (i.e., "commitment"), "security," and even "conformity," at the same time that opportunity is stimulating (pp. 117–118). After examining 15 ethics codes, Roberts (2012) confirmed that they tend to emphasize social context rather than individual values:

> These values make fundamental claims about the interdependent relationships among media, society, and the environment. The reliance upon benevolence and universalism themes is not surprising, given that nearly all of these codes were created by organizations that espouse some level of social responsibility … and desires by the code-writing organizations to reflect values that society would respect.
>
> (p. 122)

The values, while important ideals, may present difficult challenges for social media communicators. The search for truth, for example, is highly valued across media fields. Yet, social media communication may blur truth by valuing subjectivity and opinion. Further, personal branding places pressures on individuals to differentiate themselves from the social media crowd, while ethical guidelines urge caution. Within such an environment, it is not clear how the process of moral development advances individual and organizational thinking.

TRUST AND TRANSPARENCY

Social media communication practitioners may assume that by being as transparent as possible, they will build trust. The examination of conflict between individual and social values, however, suggests that transparency alone will not be effective. Bowen (2013) listed 14 other values – fairness, avoiding deception, dignity and respect, eschewing secrecy, reversibility, viewpoint identification, rationality, clarity, disclosure, verification, responsibility, intention, community good, and consistency: "Consistency allows publics to know and understand you, and you can meet their expectations" (p. 126). If we build trust through consistency rather than transparency alone, then social media ethics needs to be understood within a very broad context.

The importance of trust and transparency helps explain why it is neither ethical nor effective to buy followers on, for example, YouTube. Instead, Cooper (2019) offers a list of Hootsuite constructive alternatives:

1. Ask viewers to subscribe.

2. End videos with a mention about the next one.

3. Interact with audience members, and make new friends.

4. Update channel art.

5. Brand thumbnail images.

6. Embed videos on blogs and websites.

7. Use tools, such as video watermarks.

8. Develop playlists.

9. Run contests.

10. Celebrate subscriber milestones.

11. Schedule consistent release of videos.

12. Cross-promote through posts on other social media channels.

13. Effectively use keyword research in video titles.

14. Use creative new video content.

15. Frequently, new video should be topical, and not "evergreen."

16. Develop partnerships with other channels.

17. Collaborate with celebrities.

(paras. 19–75)

Each tactic should be filtered through ethical decision-making, regardless of whether the purpose of the content is to entertain or inform. Social media may replace traditional media communication in areas such as political discussion, as distrust of institutions leads to new forms of "interaction and information consumption" (Himelboim et al., 2012, p. 106):

> Whereas trust of one's *outer circle* was a good predictor for a variety of online behaviors and attitudes, political openness was found to be more sensitive to differences between types of spaces preferred for gaining political information. Trust in the *outer circle* predicted the use of all types of online media (consumption and interaction), where political openness successfully predicted only the use of social media.
>
> (p. 107)

In other words, social media behavior is more aligned with expressing political opinions or support for a candidate than it is trust in information coming from others. Social media communication spaces may be useful to people with a need to express opinions, even when they may be controversial or even potentially harmful in an ethical sense.

At a fundamental level, CMC anonymity may cultivate a different form of communication, which breaks down social taboos or reaffirms narrow social norms (Leonard & Toller, 2012). In a study of MyDeathSpace.com communication, several themes emerged: sympathy for deceased and loved ones, suicide method, judging the deceased and others, explanations for suicide, regret for death, and loved ones' response to posters (pp. 392–399):

> we found that the Web site MyDeathSpace provided a setting for individuals to write in and discuss the death of an individual due to suicide rather than a site for the bereaved to commiserate and make sense of the death of their loved one.
>
> (p. 400)

Such CMC may serve individual more than social needs. This site did not "serve as a venue where survivors of suicide can reach out to others for social support and encouragement" (pp. 400–401). "Online spaces that allow for primarily absolute and pseudo-anonymity appear to encourage extremely disinhibited communication that demonstrates no regard for others involved in the communication" (p. 402). As an ethical issue, individuals had the freedom to discuss the frequently avoided issue of suicide, but the anonymous communicators did so without regard for potential harm inflicted on family and friends. Clearly, social media communication raises ethical issues of human dignity.

ᯤ BOX 10.1

Thought Leader Craig Newmark

Something big is happening: the public is effectively using the Internet to build global societal movements. Online, people are connecting at almost instantaneous speeds to share information, relate to one another, and serve the public interest.

Some years ago, as people were still figuring out this art form, I started reading about the history of large-scale change. It dawned on me, and many others, that the leaders of societal movements, even those from hundreds of years ago, are effective in what we now call "blogging." Tom Paine and Ben Franklin used new communication tools, like the printing press and movable type, to blog compellingly that the Colonies should declare their independence. John Locke used the same methods to blog about individual rights in the context of British representative democracy.

These bloggers used the best technologies of their time. Networked distribution involved what we now call "store and forward" methods, which means using places where groups of people come together, such as churches and cafés, to spread information. A number of folks have made these observations, best documented by *Economist* Deputy Editor Tom Standage in *Writing on the Wall*.

Massive societal change seems to involve tipping points that are inspired by the compelling voices of their time. French poet and novelist Victor Hugo said in *The History*

FIGURE 10.2 *@craignewmark*.
Photograph by Stephanie Canciello, Unali Artists via Craig Newmark

of a Crime something that approximately translates to, "There is nothing as powerful as an idea whose time has come." Compelling bloggers both manifest and articulate ideas, creating those tipping points. Tom Standage eloquently points out, "History retweets itself."

Nowadays, the Internet provides people on a large scale with their own kind of printing press and the means to distribute their work, with the potential to influence the public and seriously serve the common good.

However, there are consequences that come with the conveniences of this technology. Bad actors use social media and other Internet platforms to spread disinformation at rapid speeds. The stakes in this information war are a free press, an informed public, and a strong democracy. Making sure that trustworthy news and information prevails is an all-hands-on-deck task. It will take everyone, including my fellow engineers, tech companies, third parties, and the government, to ensure that the Internet keeps the public informed so that we can all be thoughtful voters, citizens, and neighbors.

After all, a nerd's gotta do what a nerd's gotta do.

Craig Newmark is a Web pioneer, philanthropist, and leading advocate. Most commonly known for founding the online classified ads service Craigslist, Newmark works to support and connect people and drive broad civic engagement. In 2016, he founded Craig Newmark Philanthropies to advance people and grassroots organizations that are "getting stuff done" in the areas of trustworthy journalism and information security, voter protection, women in technology, and veterans and military families. At its core, all of Newmark's philanthropic work helps to strengthen American democracy by supporting the values the country aspires to – fairness, opportunity, and respect.

HUMAN DIGNITY FRAMEWORKS

In the early days of using social media for public relations purposes, there were many examples of lack of transparency and disclosure. Bowen (2013) utilized the 2006 case of a fake blog – a "flog" created by Edelman PR for Wal-Mart – which posed a personal and positive RV couple interacting "with happy Wal-Mart employees" (p. 126). By concealing the identities of paid bloggers and its source, "the website does not respect the dignity of the public, nor does it respect their intellectual need for open and honest information to form independent judgments" (p. 127). Deception is an ethical violation of human dignity. "Deliberately concealing sponsorship, astroturfing, and flogging are practices that violate the moral duty communicators have to society to be universally honest, to communicate with dignity and respect, and act with good will" (p. 127).

Waters (2014) has examined social media openness and disclosure – identifying new efforts and challenges within the PR context. Practitioners have "healthy skepticism" about the value of online relationships (p. 11). The PRSA code of ethics and the Arthur W. Page society are examples of promoting PR disclosure in the interest of building industry trust: "Despite these suggestions from industry leaders, many organizations fail to disclose who maintains the brands' accounts" (p. 15). From "ghost blogging and ghost commenting" (Gallicano, Bivens, & Cho, 2014, p. 21) to Facebook page "impression management" (DiStaso, 2014, p. 44), transparency alone falls short of explaining social media ethical struggles for both PR and journalism practitioners. "While truth is generally thought to be the norm of communication as a whole, truth also has priority in media theory and practice" because among journalists, "truth telling is … generally understood around the world" (Christians, 2019, p. 134).

PRACTICAL SOCIAL MEDIA ETHICS

As social media have developed in recent years, traditional media organizations adapted to the new interaction with audience members. National Public Radio, in response to ethical concerns, has offered its journalists specific rules of engagement.

▢ BOX 10.2

NPR Social Media Guidelines

NPR Ethics Handbook (2017)

NPR emphasized that real-time breaking news coverage of events "present new and unfamiliar challenges" and has urged reporters to "tread carefully." The guidelines urged that online behavior – "just as you would in any other public circumstances" – means treating people with "fairness, honesty and respect." NPR has emphasized verification of information: "Verify information before passing it along." In NPR's current document, "social media communities" are explicitly mentioned:

> The Internet and the social media communities it encompasses can be incredible resources. They offer both a remarkably robust amount of historical material and an incredible amount of "real-time" reporting from people at the scenes of breaking news events. But they also present new and unfamiliar challenges, and they tend to amplify the effects of any ethical misjudgments you might make. So tread carefully. Conduct yourself online just as you would in any other public circumstances as an NPR journalist. Treat those you encounter online with fairness, honesty and respect, just as you would offline. Verify information before passing it along. Be honest about your intent when reporting. Avoid actions that might discredit your professional impartiality. And always remember, you represent NPR.
>
> (para. 1)

Under an accuracy heading, NPR told reporters to be "careful and skeptical" of social media information:

> When determining whether to pass along information being reported on social media sites by other news outlets or individuals, be thoughtful. When we point to what others are saying, in the eyes of many we are effectively reporting that information ourselves. This is true whether the platform is an official NPR social media webpage, a personal blog or a Twitter page that is written by an NPR journalist.

The guidelines expressed concern about false online identities. Under an offline follow-up heading, NPR again urged caution. "So, when appropriate, clarify and confirm information collected online through phone and in-person interviews."

Likewise, NPR has expressed concern about manipulated photographs and old videos that are distributed online: "bring a healthy skepticism to images you encounter, starting with the assumption that all such images or video are not authentic."

The guidelines also address honesty, including avoiding political partisanship, a lack of Web privacy and independence:

> It's important to keep in mind that the terms of service of a social media site apply to what we post there and to the information we gather from it. Also: The terms might allow for our material to be used in a different way than intended. Additionally, law enforcement officials may be able to obtain our reporting on these sites by subpoena without our consent – or perhaps even our knowledge. Social media is a vital reporting resource for us, but we must be vigilant about keeping work that may be sensitive in our own hands.

NPR reminds reporters that their "standards of impartiality also apply to social media." The traditional rules apply to personal pages and joining groups – whether or not the employee identity is "readily apparent."

"In reality, anything you post online reflects both on you and on NPR." The guidelines also address the important issue of media accountability. Social media happen in "public spaces." NPR adds, "don't behave any differently online than you would in any other public setting." The standard is a conservative one in recommending that reporters avoid online norms that sometimes may be looser than the face-to-face world.

As such, reporters are asked to consider legal implications, "regardless of medium." In respecting community norms, there is a need for awareness: "Our ethics don't change in different circumstances, but our decision might." Finally, the NPR guidelines conclude: "Social media are excellent tools when handled correctly."

Source: NPR (May 2, 2012, accessed January 15, 2017). *NPR Ethics Handbook*. Social media. http://ethics.npr.org/tag/social-media/

An emphasis on "practical ethics" addresses online anonymity and the obvious limitation of written rules:

> Rules alone don't work because often they seem imposed externally. They come across as punitive and can be easily broken if there's nothing more fundamental to support them other than the fear of being caught.
>
> (Elliott & Spence, 2018, p. 186)

In digital journalism, for example, media ethicists explore "the public good," "truthful, reliable, and trustworthy information," and "the public interest" (p. 187). Even the most well-meaning journalism may suffer from the fact that "storytellers have their own cultural blinders" (p. 192). Difficult ethical issues frequently are decided based upon "moral courage," or "doing the right thing even at the risk of inconvenience, ridicule, punishment, or loss of job, security, or social status" (Mintz, 2019, p. 63).

EQUALITY AND FAIRNESS

Lack of disclosure to the public raises issues of fairness. Paid tweets by celebrities, for example, earn some thousands of dollars. Bowen (2013) concluded that failure to be transparent about sponsorship violates fundamental ethical principles:

> Be transparent; paid speech should be identified as such. Identify communication
> as personal, individual speech and opinion versus speech as a representative of
> the organization, so that publics have the information to evaluate it appropriately.
> Check relevant facts. A rational analysis should examine messages from all sides and
> viewpoints.
>
> (p. 129)

While deception through failure to disclose sponsorship may not lead to harmful outcomes, it runs the risk of creating public misperception that could be influential. For example, if a healthy-looking movie star is paid to promote an unhealthy product on Twitter, the social media communication may lead some to buy and consume it. Federal Trade Commission guidelines emphasized the responsibility of social media influencers to disclose "financial, employment, personal, or family relationship with a brand" (FTC, 2019, p. 3). Even tags, likes, and other responses have been considered as endorsements.

Twitter also has been the social media site for numerous crises in public relations. Caldiero (2016) examined the Susan G. Komen Foundation's decision to "defund" Planned Parenthood (p. 30). Following a January 31, 2012, AP news report, "social media sites erupted," as "over 100,000 tweets were sent or retweeted that night" (p. 36). Hashtags, such as #stopthinkingpin, #shameonkoman and #Raceforthecrazy helped frame a plurality of narratives (p. 36):

> If Komen had been prepared to acknowledge the multiple truths at play in this delicate
> scenario, understand the co-creation of meaning inherent in today's organization/
> publics relationships. And reject the dominant metanarratives of modernistic PR, the
> organization may have fared much better than it did.
>
> (p. 41)

Still, Komen and Planned Parenthood emerged from the PR crisis, and some would argue that organizations are caught between the demands of traditional news media framing and the realities of pluralistic social media spaces. In this sense ethics for journalists and PR practitioners are being redefined by new technological and social circumstances.

When a Yelp employee published a critical open letter to the CEO about low pay and struggling employees, clearly it was newsworthy (Winchel, 2016). A variety of personal and professional ethics may be applied to employee use of social media sites, but the Yelp post sparked a public debate. The ethical considerations are easier to judge when tweets devolve into social media attacks and bullying (Gettys, 2015). This happened when news reporter Alyssa Marino (@alyssa_marino) reported on the Memories Pizza Indiana shop refusal to sell pizzas for a gay wedding.

The problem of cyberbullies spawned a #MoreThanMean campaign that included a YouTube video confronting online harassment faced by women in sports media (Lipschultz, 2016). Chicago Sportswriter Julie DiCaro blocked Twitter accounts that represented a "constant ... stream of sexism and misogyny and threats" (para. 2). Two of about twenty women asked agreed to participate in the #MoreThanMean project. DiCaro also suggests that during the 2016 election, "there was a noticeable lack of kindness, civility and compassion" (para. 6). Clearly, a lack of mutual respect within Twitter and other social media sites reflects a failure of ethical behavior in treating others with human dignity.

NATURAL LAW AND HARM

Beyond the legal implications of potentially harmful social media communication, it is ethically fundamental to follow the principle to do no harm. "Communication professionals who implement social media initiatives would be well advised to consider the harm to their reputations that can be caused by ignoring ethics in the technological space" (Bowen, 2013, p. 132). Particularly when young people are present in social media spaces, which may be difficult to know, safety is a concern: "In response to concerns about online predators, illegal downloading, and imprudent posting of content online, a number of cyber safety initiatives have emerged online and in schools around the country" (James et al., 2010, pp. 218–219). Core and salient issues include: "identity, privacy, ownership and authorship, credibility, and participation" (p. 219), and one research group calls for the use of "good play" rules to address ethical online behavior from a positive perspective to encourage "meaningful and engaging" participation within a community:

> Definitions of responsible or ethical conduct in online spaces may differ markedly from offline definitions. Here we consider the new digital media as a playground in which the following factors contribute to the likelihood of good play – (1) technical literacy and technology availability; (2) cognitive and moral person-centered factors (including developmental capacities, beliefs, and values); (3) online and offline peer cultures; and (4) presence or absence of ethical supports (including adult or peer mentors, educational curricula, and explicit or implicit codes of conduct in digital spaces). Our approach to ethics does not focus solely on transgressions but strives to understand why, how, and where good play happens.
>
> (p. 226)

The approach emphasizes media literacy rather than rules to cultivate and "develop ethical reflection and conduct as a key foundation for youth empowerment" (p. 277).

While the application of moral development through online play may be appropriate in an educational learning context, social media communication practitioners are expected to adhere to organizational standards and industry guidelines. Privacy, such as that when a user is on Facebook or adjusts settings, is a fundamental expectation: "Crucially, these rights and obligations hold regardless of the perceptions that users have of their online interactions" (D'Arcy & Young, 2012, pp. 535–536). In a twist, a California teenager filed a class action lawsuit against TikTok. Lawyers claim that the app surreptitiously collects user data and stores files in Chinese servers (Hamilton, 2019). TikTok allowed users to draft videos before they created an account. The American teen claimed that a "user" account associated with "her phone number" was created and stored with "other private user data" (paras. 5–6). It would seem difficult to protect personal data privacy when downloading and using mobile apps.

RECONSIDERING COMMUNITY

Ethical issues are all around us in social media communication, which offer competing values to the traditional world of journalism and media. As the NPR social media guidelines mentioned earlier, "Realize that different communities – online and offline – have their own culture, etiquette, and norms, and be respectful of them." Data suggest that during the 2016 election cycle, people un-friended, blocked, and battled each other in social media spaces (Dann, 2016). It was unclear in early 2017 that the polarized mood had changed much in the United States (Thompson, 2016). Respect for others is an important community value. Too often, organizations run into online and offline difficulties because of a breakdown of respect for others.

Social media tools, such as Storify, created spaces that were not as limited by space as Twitter. However, Storify closed in May of 2018. Facebook and Instagram Stories, Twitter Moments, and Snapchat Snaps came to define storytelling spaces by learning from start-up innovation. At the same time, organizations across the social media communication landscape are developing understanding about the need to provide employee guidance, support and ongoing feedback. However, there also are continuing concerns over the movement within public relations to promote employee advocacy programs that clearly lack ethical independence (Stein, 2016).

The global nature of social media has challenged ethicists "to account for a diversity of ethical perspectives globally, while avoiding cultural relativism" (Wasserman, 2011, p. 791). Post-colonial criticism of traditional media ethics is that "constructs such as freedom and responsibility, which are often presented as having universal validity, are themselves 'local' in that they have originated from particular epistemological traditions rooted in Western thought and experience" (p. 792). In Africa, for example, there is "a contested terrain" of "development journalism," "indigenization," and "professionalization and social responsibility" (p. 800). While media practitioners in the US push for First Amendment freedoms, a global perspective must take into account stages of development and cultural assumptions within the language used to describe normative ethics.

In the wake of the apparent Russian cyber-attack on American politics (Lipton, Sanger, & Shane, 2016), journalism opinion leaders find hope in professional practices. *Washington Post* Executive Editor Martin Baron told CUNY journalism graduates:

> We can be better and smarter and wiser – and the public can be more informed – By what you've witnessed over a lifetime and what you now see and hear. You will have the opportunity and the power to transport people into a world they otherwise would never have known. Journalism can do that.
>
> (Baron, 2016, paras. 4–5)

Baron suggested that journalists need to listen more and quit making assumptions. From an ethical frame of reference, journalists, their sources, and the public should seek truth through a more careful process.

LIMITATIONS OF ETHICS

Social media ethics are typically applied as a set of professional guidelines. Formal law rarely governs them. Organizations have attempted to incorporate traditional ethical guidelines based upon a set of values, even though social media norms may differ among online communities. There will continue to be tension between the practice of social media communication and the constraints desired by media organizations.

Facebook (2016) Trending Review Guidelines had imperfectly sought to guide an "editorial team," "topic detection team," and "content ranking team." Its largest failure may have been to: "ASSUME EVERY TOPIC IN PENDING (category) IS A REAL-WORLD EVENT, UNTIL PROVEN OTHERWISE," which operated opposite to traditional journalistic standards of not publishing until the information is verified. Clearly, publishing news and filtering a Facebook news feed were in conflict. Former Facebook workers had claimed they "routinely suppressed news stories of interest to conservative readers" (Nunez, 2016, para. 1). Yet, data suggested that there was wide sharing of conservative news in 2016 (Beres, 2016). Facebook responded that there was no evidence of manipulation (Owen, 2016), CEO Mark Zuckerberg defended company "principles" (King, 2016, para. 2), and the US Senate investigated (Dinan, 2016; Pegoraro, 2016). Gillmor (2016) called upon news organizations to both "fully participate in the Facebook ecosystem," but also "persuade Facebook to take seriously its growing responsibility to help get quality journalism in front of as many people as possible" (para. 3). The concentration of Facebook power, whether through ever-changing filtering algorithms, company principles, or human management, suggests the need for both greater transparency *and* independence. Gillmor called on news to explain to the public Facebook's problems with data privacy, content filtering, Internet monopolization and ethics: "Facebook constantly pushes the boundaries of acceptable behavior, especially in the way it collects and handles data on its users. It changes its terms of service and privacy policy, often in ways that should alarm people" (para. 11).

We are in an age in which government censorship may be indirect and happen through social media or other online companies and their end-user agreement contract language. For example, in China, its search engine Baidu censored political images (Chricton, 2019). Image filtering led to public criticism, and some employees have left the company. "Unfortunately, far too many companies – and far too many tech companies – blindly chase the dollars and yuans, without considering the erosion in the values at the heart of their own business" (para. 14). At the same time, however, Reddit was among social media companies in a difficult position over banning accounts that were suspected of UK election interference (Kirka, 2019). Some company regulation, though, is less severe. Facebook's Instagram has added new user age disclosure, but the company had no plans to verify the self-reporting (Dave, 2019).

Concern also persists about advertising and marketing ethics in an age of organic and paid posts. As early as 2010, Facebook's research showed that "political mobilization messages" could have an effect on "self-expression, information-seeking and real-world voting behavior" (Raicu, 2019, para. 2). Algorithm design can have an impact on election outcomes: "Some Facebook policies give people voice (while controlling the volume button); some take it away" (para. 18). In this sense, Raicu (2019) argues that the process of moderating public voice requires a complete ethical evaluation. However, Facebook continued to rely on its community-based approach.

The emerging field of social media communication tends to follow traditional media in testing our ideals about freedom and social responsibility within a democratic context (Christians, Rotzoll, & Fackler, 1991). Beyond a desire to avoid harm to others, ethics assumes accountability to others within a social context. Each decision made has implications within society. The best hope is to align individual notions of morality and ethics with industry and organizational values and practices. By communicating with others, including online communities, it is hoped that greater understanding emerges over time. Ward's (2013b) focus on independence strikes a chord when it comes to social media conflicts of interest. The 2016 debate about "fake news" spreading across social media sites, such as Facebook, fell short of understanding that journalistic accuracy and a desire to minimize harm form a core of ethics. Harms must be articulated and processed prior to publication, sharing, and social media engagement. A higher public interest standard would form a social media ethics plateau that resides somewhere above individual personal interests to be noticed, business and brand interests to be economically successful, and political interests for power. These and other issues will be expected to be important, as individual empowerment must be cultivated through social media literacy.

DISCUSSION QUESTIONS: STRATEGIES AND TACTICS

1. Is there a proper role for activist journalists within social media? How should traditional or mainstream journalists differentiate their work?

2. Which values are most important for ethical behavior within social media? In what ways may it be difficult to be governed by traditional ethical guidelines?

3. How are global norms of ethics a challenge to US rules? In what ways will global social media communication influence future directions in ethics?

REFERENCES

AEJMC (2016, June 3). Journalism Educators Urge Social Media Platforms to Ensure Ethical Transparency in Curating and Disseminating News. www.aejmc.org/home/2016/06/pac-060316/

Baron, M. (2016, December 16). Washington Post Executive Editor Martin Baron Delivers Commencement Address at the CUNY Graduate School of Journalism. *The Washington Post.* www.washingtonpost.com/pr/wp/2016/12/16/washington-post-executive-editor-martin-baron-delivers-commencement-address-at-the-cuny-graduate-school-of-journalism/

Beres, D. (2016, May 10). Conservative News is Widely Shared on Facebook, Data Show. *The Huffington Post.* www.huffingtonpost.com/entry/conservative-news-facebook_us_57321975e4b096e9f092d63b

Bowen, S. A. (2013). Using Classic Social Media Cases to Distill Ethical Guidelines for Digital Engagement. *Journal of Mass Media Ethics* 28(1), 119–133.

Caldiero, C. (2016). *Neo-PR, Public Relations in a Postmodern World.* New York: Peter Lang.

Crichton, D. (2019, December 8). In Wake of Shutterstock's Chinese Censorship, American Companies Need to Relearn American Values. *TechCrunch.* https://techcrunch.com/2019/12/08/in-wake-of-shutterstocks-chinese-censorship-american-companies-need-to-relearn-american-values/

Christians, C. G. (2019). *Media Ethics and Global Justice in the Digital Age.* Cambridge, UK: Cambridge University Press.

Christians, C. G., Rotzoll, K. B., & Fackler, M. (1991). *Media Ethics, Case & Moral Reasoning, Third Edition.* New York, NY: Longman.

Chung, D. S., & Nah, S. (2013). Media Credibility and Journalistic Role Conceptions: Views on Citizen and Professional Journalists among Citizen Contributors. *Journal of Mass Media Ethics* 28(4), 271–288.

Cooper, P. (2019, December 5). How to Get Free YouTube Subscribers (The Real Way). *Hootsuite.* https://blog.hootsuite.com/how-to-get-free-youtube-subscribers/

D'Arcy, A., & Young, T. M. (2012). Ethics and Social Media: Implications for Sociolinguistics in the Networked Public. *Journal of Sociolinguistics* 16(4), 532–546.

Dann, C. (2016, December 19). Unfriended: How the 2016 Election Made Us Battle, Avoid and Block Each Other. *NBC News.* www.nbcnews.com/politics/first-read/unfriended-how-2016-election-made-us-battle-avoid-block-each-n698001

Dave, P. (2019, December 4). Instagram will now Require New Users to give their Ages, but won't be able to Verify Birthdays. *Reuters via Business Insider.* www.businessinsider.com/instagram-to-collect-ages-in-push-for-youth-safety-alcohol-ad-dollars-2019-12

Dinan, S. (2016, May 10). Senate begins Probe into Facebook over Conservative Censorship Allegations. *Washington Times.* www.washingtontimes.com/news/2016/may/10/senate-begins-probe-facebook-censorship-allegation/

DiStaso, M. W. (2014). Bank of America's Facebook Engagement Challenges Its Claims of "High Ethical Standards". In M. W. DiStaso and D. S. Bortree (Eds.), *Ethical Practice of Social Media in Public Relations*, pp. 21–32. New York: Routledge.

Elliott, D., & Spence, E. H. (2018). *Ethics for a Digital Era.* Oxford, UK: John Wiley & Sons.

Elliott, D., & Spence, E. E. (2020). *Ethics for A Digital Era.* Hoboken, NJ: John Wiley & Sons.

Facebook (2016). Trending Review Guidelines. https://fbnewsroomus.files.wordpress.com/2016/05/full-trending-review-guidelines.pdf

FTC (2019, November 5). Disclosures 101 for Social Media Influencers. https://www.ftc.gov/system/files/documents/plain-language/1001a-influencer-guide-508_1.pdf

Gallicano, T. D., Bivens, T. H., & Cho, Y. Y. (2014). Considerations Regarding Ghost Blogging and Ghost Commenting. In M. W. DiStaso and D. S. Bortree, *Ethical Practice of Social Media in Public Relations*, pp. 21–32. New York: Routledge.

Gettys, T. (2015, April 2). 'Proud of Yourself Sweeties?': Trolls Attack Reporter Who Quoted Anti-LGBT Pizza Shop Owner. *Raw Story*. www.rawstory.com/2015/04/proud-of-yourself-sweetie-trolls-attack-reporter-who-quoted-anti-lgbt-pizza-shop-owner/

Gillmor, D. (2016, April 9). Journalists: Stop Complaining about Facebook, and do Something about it. *Blog*. https://dangillmor.com/2016/04/09/journalists-stop-complaining-about-facebook-and-do-something-about-it/

Hamilton, I. A. (2019, December 3). A California Student is Suing TikTok, Alleging that It Surreptitiously Hoovered up Her Data and Sent It to China. *Business Insider*. www.businessinsider.com/tiktok-class-action-lawsuit-sending-data-china-2019-12

Himelboim, I., Lariscy, R. W., Tinkham, S. F., & Sweetser, K. D. (2012). Social Media and Online Political Communication: The Role of Interpersonal Informational Trust and Openness. *Journal of Broadcasting & Electronic Media 56*(1), 92–115.

Hochberg, A. (2014). Centers of Investigative Reporting. In K. McBride and T. Rosenstiel (Eds.), *The New Ethics of Journalism*, pp. 123–135. Los Angeles, CA: Sage.

Huang, T. (2014). Centers of Investigative Reporting. In K. McBride and T. Rosenstiel (Eds.), *The New Ethics of Journalism*, pp. 39–59. Los Angeles, CA: Sage.

Illing, S. (2017, January 12). Was BuzzFeed Wrong to Publish the Trump Dossier? This Media Ethicist says Yes. *Vox*. www.vox.com/conversations/2017/1/12/14238688/trump-russia-buzzfeed-putin-poynter-media-ethics

James, C., Davis, K., Flores, A., Francis, J., Pettingill, L., Rundle, M., & Gardner, H. (2010). Young People, Ethics, and the New Digital Media. *Contemporary Readings in Law and Social Justice 2*(2), 215–284.

King, H. (2016, May 12). Zuckerberg Wants to Meet with Conservatives Amid Facebook Bias Allegations. *CNN Money*. http://money.cnn.com/2016/05/12/technology/facebook-trending-guidelines/

Kirka, D. (2019, December 7). Reddit Bans Accounts, Suspects Possible UK Vote Interference. *Associated Press*. https://apnews.com/d09434c0932cde4bbb59ba116670078d

Leonard, L. G., & Toller, P. (2012). Speaking Ill of the Dead: Anonymity and Communication about Suicide on MyDeathSpace.com. *Communication Studies 63*(4), 387–404.

Lipschultz, J. H. (2016, November 11). Dealing with Social Media Bullies. *The Huffington Post*. www.huffingtonpost.com/entry/dealing-with-social-media-bullies_us_582615b3e4b02b1f5257a113

Lipton, E., Sanger, D. E., & Shane, S. (2016, December 13). The Perfect Weapon: How Russian Cyberpower Invaded the U.S. *The New York Times*. www.nytimes.com/2016/12/13/us/politics/russia-hack-election-dnc.html

Mathewson, J. (2014). *Law and Ethics for Today's Journalist: A Concise Guide*. Armonk, NY: M. E. Sharpe.

McBride, K., & Rosenstiel, T. (Eds.) (2014). *The New Ethics of Journalism*. Los Angeles, CA: Sage.

Mellinger, G. (2020). Introduction: Journalism's Ethical Progression. In G. Mellinger and J. P. Ferré (Eds.), *Journalism's Ethical Progression, A Twentieth Century Journey*, pp. ix–xxvi. Lanham, MD: Lexington Books.

Mintz, S. (2019). *Beyond Happiness and Meaning, Transforming Your Life through Ethical Behavior*. Columbus, OH: Gatekeeper Press.

Motlagh, N. E., Hassan, M. S. B. H., Bolong, J. B., & Osman, M. N. (2013). Role of Journalists' Gender, Work Experience and Education in Ethical Decision Making. *Asian Social Science 9*(9), 1–10.

NPR (2017). *NPR Ethics Handbook. Social Media.* http://ethics.npr.org/tag/social-media/

Nunez, M. (2016, May 9). Former Facebook Workers: We Routinely Suppressed Conservative News. *Gizmodo.* http://gizmodo.com/former-facebook-workers-we-routinely-suppressed-conser-1775461006

Owen, L. H. (2016, May 10). Facebook: "No Evidence" that Contractors "Manipulated Trending Topics" or Suppressed Conservative Viewpoints. *Nieman Lab.* www.niemanlab.org/2016/05/facebook-no-evidence-that-contractors-manipulated-trending-topics-or-suppressed-conservative-viewpoints/

Patching, R., & Hirst, M. (2014). *Journalism Ethics, Arguments and Cases for the Twenty-first Century.* London, UK: Routledge.

Pegoraro, R. (2016, May 11). There are Worse Things than Manipulated 'Trending' Story Lists. *Yahoo! Finance.* http://finance.yahoo.com/news/the-only-thing-worse-than-a-manipulated-%E2%80%9Ctrending%E2%80%9D-list--an-unfiltered-on-162716282.html

Pompper (2015). *Corporate Social Responsibility, Sustainability and Public Relations: Negotiating Multiple Complex Challenges.* London, UK: Routledge.

Raicu, I. (2019, December 5). The Ethics of "Giving People Voice" and Political Advertising on Facebook. *The Markkula Center for Applied Ethics.* www.scu.edu/ethics-spotlight/social-media-and-democracy/the-ethics-of-giving-people-a-voice-and-political-advertising-on-facebook/

Roberts, C. (2012). Identifying and Defining Values in Media Codes of Ethics. *Journal of Media Ethics 27*(2), 115–129.

Rohan, M. J. (2000). A Rose by Any Name? the Values Construct. *Personality and Social Psychology Review 4*(3), 255–277.

Salmon, F. (2013, March 15). Too Many Flavors of Native Content. *Reuters Opinion.* http://blogs.reuters.com/felix-salmon/2013/03/15/the-many-flavors-of-native-content/

Shirky, C. (2014). Truth Without Scarcity, Ethics Without Force. In K. McBride and T. Rosenstiel (Eds.), *The New Ethics of Journalism*, pp. 9–24. Los Angeles, CA: Sage.

Solis, B. (2014). Forward: Social Media Is Lost without a Social Compass. In M. W. DiStaso and D. S. Bortree *Ethical Practice of Social Media in Public Relations*, pp. xv–xxiv. New York: Routledge.

Stein, L. (2016, February 26). Edelman Invests in Employee Advocacy Platform Dynamic Signal. *Advertising Age.* http://adage.com/article/agency-news/edelman-invests-employee-advocacy-platform-dynamic-signal/302852/

Sullivan, M. (2017, January 8). It's Time to Retire the Tainted Term 'Fake News'. *The Washington Post.* www.washingtonpost.com/lifestyle/style/its-time-to-retire-the-tainted-term-fake-news/2017/01/06/a5a7516c-d375-11e6-945a-76f69a399dd5_story.html

Thompson, A. (2016, December 8). Parallel Narratives: Clinton and Trump Supporters Really Don't Listen to Each Other on Twitter. *Vice News.* https://news.vice.com/story/journalists-and-trump-voters-live-in-separate-online-bubbles-mit-analysis-shows

Toomey, K. (2013, September). 5 Questions Executives Ask about LinkedIn. *Public Relations Tactics 20*(9), 8.

Ward, S. J. A. (2013a, November 4). Why Hyping Transparency Distorts Journalism Ethics. *PBS Media Shift.* www.pbs.org/mediashift/2013/11/why-hyping-transparency-distorts-journalism-ethics/

Ward, S. J. A. (2013b, August 19). Why We Need Radical Change for Media Ethics, Not a Return to Basics. *PBS Media Shift.* www.pbs.org/mediashift/2013/08/why-we-need-radical-change-for-media-ethics-not-a-return-to-basics/

Ward, S. J. A. (2019). *Disrupting Journalism Ethics, Radical Change on the Frontier of Digital Media*. London and New York: Routledge.

Ward, S. J. A., & Wasserman, H. (2010). Towards an Open Ethics: Implications of New Media Platforms for Global Ethics Discourse. *Journal of Mass Media Ethics 25* 275–292.

Wasserman, H. (2011). Towards a Global Journalism Ethics via Local Narratives, Southern African Perspectives. *Journalism Studies 12*(6), 791–803.

Waters, R. D. (2014). Openness and Disclosure in Social Media Efforts, A Frank Discussion with Fortune 500 and Philanthropy 400 Communication Leaders. In M. W. DiStaso and D. S. Bortree *Ethical Practice of Social Media in Public Relations*, pp. 3–20. New York: Routledge.

Winchel, B. (2016, February 23). Yelp Employee's Angry Open Letter to CEO Starts Online Firestorm. *PR Daily*. www.prdaily.com/Main/Articles/Yelp_employees_angry_open_letter_to_CEO_starts_onl_20213.aspx

Best Practices
in Social Media

When it comes to social media have you figured out the right cadence for posting? Are you repurposing your content?

– Dave Kerpen (@DaveKerpen, 2020)

Every time we do one of those shows, we get all this feedback from the audience. And so they're in constant engagement with the audience, and they get better and better at making stuff. And so their creative process is informed by all of this user data that's coming back, and allows them to make better content.

– Jonah Peretti, Buzzfeed CEO (@peretti, 2016)

I love Twitter. Sure it is noisy. Yes, it has quite a few spammers and bots and "push" marketers… but just about everything good that has happened in my business has had its origin in Twitter. It is surreal quite frankly.

– Kim Garst (@kimgarst, 2013)

Kim Garst is CEO of KG Enterprises (formerly Boom Social) in Tampa, Florida. Her blog (http://kimgarst.com) was among the *Social Media Examiner*'s top sites, and Forbes has called her a social media power influencer. On Twitter, Garst has about 608,000 followers, and she follows more than 241,000, yet she attempts to respond and thank all engaging with her content. She has posted more than 300,000 tweets. Social media have "invaded the very core of the way we communicate," Garst said at the 2012 IBM Global Summit in Orlando. "It affords you the opportunity to connect with people you would never in the ordinary course of life connect to." Facebook, YouTube and LinkedIn are increasingly visual, so photographs, graphics and videos are very important to be an effective social media marketer. Test engagement with various approaches to see which content is "sticky" on specific sites. Garst integrates her social media with a steady stream of free and paid content shared with a growing email list. Increasingly, Facebook Live and other sites offer the lure of video connected to real-time chat and engagement. This is a powerful combination as a way to promote ideas, products and services. The mobile new media environment presents distinct challenges and opportunities for each communicator and medium.

MOBILE MEDIA AND CMC

It is clear that users of smartphones, tablets, watches, and other devices are having a major impact on social media, and this trend will continue. The "new forms of sociability" may reinforce or work against traditional communication, as "mobile communication, along with other network technologies, is associated with increased face-to-face engagements with network ties, bringing people together physically as well as psychologically" (Campbell & Ling, 2011, p. 325). Digital media are very fragmented, as everyone has become an online storyteller. Only the best stories at the precise moment within a strategic space spread beyond small and personal social networks.

However, the "flip side" of networked communication is that it may emphasize "social divisions" through member boundaries "when mobile media are used for network configuration" (Campbell & Ling, 2011, p. 325).

The organization of mobile apps reflects "a fingerprint of sorts" in that these show "the combination of interests, habits, and social connections that identify that person" (Gardner & Davis, 2013, p. 60). Social networking and social media sharing through apps "becomes an integral part of the way" people in general – and particularly youths – "choose to express themselves online" (p. 61). Hunsinger (2014) contended that computer connections, along with social media immediacy, create communal perceptions:

> It is the interactivity that generates the sense of presence and thus community that enables most people to engage with social media. However, it is also this interactivity that encourages people to use it with friends and communities... the interfaces are mediations of data... Social media interfaces engage us through interactivity and the appearance of co-presence, community, and in the end, the appearance of social connection.
>
> (p. 9)

Social presence, interaction, media richness, communities, and networks return us to fundamental CMC concerns (Sherblom, 2020). "Electronic propinquity," or a psychological "feeling of relational closeness, is related to the traditional media concept of para-social interaction" (p. 82). Appearance or reality, these online connections are useful for all forms of media communication. Those seeking to engage with a dispersed media audience can find many of its members now using mobile media devices to access social media platforms. Patel (2016) suggested five social marketing tools that reflected mobile focus and survived in 2020:

1. Buffer – is a scheduling tool that competes with Hootsuite, as a way to post across sites.

2. Social Clout – tracks engagement metrics.

3. Feedly – creates daily aggregated content from RSS content feeds.

4. Canva – is an image creation tool.

5. Socedo – is a social business tool to generate sales leads.

The size and scope of social media require that users manage time and optimize efforts. This helps explain why news professionals have embraced tools that help them navigate social media.

NEWSPAPERS, MAGAZINES, AND JOURNALISM REVISITED

Social media interest is high among journalists. In terms of best practices, the following are popular:

- Live tweet from a news event and create a Twitter Moment summary of a curated list of the best engagement and information.

- Send out links to stories across social media sites to drive traffic to websites.

- Use great photography to spark audience interest in coverage and promote the brand.

- Engage online with people in the community to identify news sources and seek verifiable information.

- Search social media platforms for story ideas and possible new trends.

- Monitor government operations and behavior of politicians.

- Cultivate personal brands of star journalists.

- Respond to criticism of coverage.

- Promote advertisers' events with sponsored posts.

- Curate content from credible news sources to clarify and correct bad information circulating as social media rumors.

- Post photographs from publication archives and offer to sell popular prints.

- Take advantage of convergence opportunities by publishing audio, video, and streaming events in real-time.

- Thank fans for engaging and sharing content.

- Answer questions from readers.

Before his death, Steve Buttry posted dozens of ideas for journalists on Slideshare.net. He suggests that news organization community engagement equates to making a "top priority to listen, to join, lead & enable conversation to elevate journalism" (Buttry, 2013). This happens across many evolving social media platforms, including mobile videos on Facebook, Instagram, and Twitter. Journalists can use social media as a reporting tool by looking for blogs and content in their local communities. Social media offer the opportunity to connect with comments and commentators. Journalists also use crowdsourcing in the search for *verified* news content. From live-tweeting to tracking hashtags, journalists using social media may have an advantage over those ignoring sources and content. Across all forms of journalism, mobile apps and social media create new opportunities and possibilities.

RADIO, AUDIO, AND PODCAST MOBILE APPS

Internet podcasts created competition for local radio stations, as did the movement toward individual purchasing of online song libraries from iTunes. In the social media era, online services such as Spotify and Pandora allowed music listeners to share playlists with friends. One trend was the creation of news and information apps that cater to an increasingly mobile audience. All-news radio, for example, has survived and prospered for decades in large media markets. In an age of mobile smartphones and social media, radio is again changing to meet new habits.

Rivet, a Chicago start-up, launched in late 2013 with an iPhone app, and its developers initially targeted people wanting to personalize story selection. "It shows the power of being free from the tyranny of the clock," President and COO Cindy Paulauskas said. "We can make our traffic reports as long or as short as they need to be, and we can create updated reports whenever the situation changes." The company, however, struggled to attract a growing audience for radio news.

FIGURE 11.1 *Rivet News Radio sought to engage mobile smartphone users with an app that distributed hyperlocal traffic reports and customized news.*
Courtesy of Rivet News Radio

WBBM Newsradio 780 in Chicago countered with its award-winning CBS Radio. com app. It quickly added basic Twitter and Facebook sharing. Director of News and Programming Ron Gleason believed that live radio audiences come and go, and he was not convinced they would make the effort to select and navigate recorded content:

> The good: more and more people are getting valuable information faster and faster. The bad: you can't always trust what you see – because the information is only as good as the source. As a credible source on which Chicagoans rely, we are actively involved in the use of social media to let people know about the stories we're reporting. We reach people with our AM and FM signals, through our stream, at CBSChicago.com, through the CBS local YourDay app, via Twitter, Facebook, etc. The more ways we can reach out, the more people we'll reach. The good news for WBBM: there's still no medium more immediate than Newsradio, and the ability for broadcast outlets to reach the masses during breaking news stories and emergencies is second to none.
>
> (Gleason, 2013)

Rivet, unable to win over live radio news audiences, by 2020 had become "a smart media production and distribution company" that featured: AP national news, branded podcasts, and video, place-based **Digital Out Of Home** advertising, smart speaker alerts, callers on-hold entertainment, and studio production facilities. The larger social media shift demands a visual presence and interaction with fans through engaging audio, video, photographs and text. These may be delivered through social media channels and traditional websites or email newsletters.

⊼ BOX 11.1

Thought Leader Charlie Meyerson

The leveling of the playing field between journalist and, as New York University journalism professor Jay Rosen has dubbed them, "the people formerly known as the audience," has had an astonishing impact. Reporters are subject now more than ever to analysis, criticism and correction by those who once had to content themselves with letters to an editor – who may or may not have chosen to publish them. And a reporter's success (as gauged by audience reach) depends as never before on readers', listeners' and viewers' decision to share ... or *not* to share.

As never before, the news business now needs journalists whose ability to engage an audience matches their ability to gather and report facts.

What I've been saying for more than two decades has become a cliché: Despite the radical and painful transformation the Internet has inflicted on media companies, this is the best time in history to become a journalist.

FIGURE 11.2 *@Meyerson.*
Photograph by Steve Ewert Photography, courtesy of
Charlie Meyerson

The Internet has brought society closer now than ever to the ideal advanced by Justice Oliver Wendell Holmes, who said, "the best test of truth is the power of the thought to get itself accepted in the competition of the market."

The digital revolution means that if you have something true to say – and I mean "true" here broadly: not just "truthful" or "factual," but also "truly funny," or "truly moving," or "truly beautiful" – this new digital world empowers you to communicate it to anyone, anywhere, regardless of medium. You don't need a printing press. You don't need an antenna. All you need is a way with words or sound or pictures and a library card to use a computer.

Beginning in January 2017, I put much of this theory to the test as the creator of a website, *Chicago Public Square* – a daily email news briefing much like those I helped launch in my almost 13 years at the *Chicago Tribune*. Beginning as a simple blog (on Google's venerable Blogger platform) – scraped once a day by MailChimp to be mailed out to a list of subscribers comprising (to begin) just friends and fans notified via Facebook, Twitter, and LinkedIn – *Square* grew into a medium that won critical acclaim (media watchdog Robert Feder dubbed it "excellent") and reaches hundreds of people daily.

Square's distinguishing characteristic has been its independence from any one news organization – its freedom to link to any source with information relevant to a Chicago-centric audience. That – and a fierce devotion to watching which subject lines, links and phrases drive audience engagement – helped build a loyal audience that opened *Square* daily at rates consistently about two-and-a-half times MailChimp's media and publishing industry average.

The *Square* blog and email also became the launchpad for content across several platforms – for instance, a video tour of a restored landmark and a series of podcasts, many recorded before hundreds of people.

That one guy – a veteran journalist, sure, but still just one older guy – could do all that hints at the exciting opportunities awaiting generations of journalists even more technologically sophisticated than I am.

Charlie Meyerson is founder and publisher of *Chicago Public Square*, founding head of news at start-up Rivet Radio and the principal at his consulting practice, Meyerson Strategy. He has devoted a career in Chicago connecting great journalism with growing audiences – online, on air, in print. Meyerson won a national 2016 Edward R. Murrow Award for online audio investigative reporting at Rivet and, at *Chicago Public Square*, a 2018 Chicago Headline Club award for Best Radio Newscast – the latest of dozens of awards for his work at Rivet, FM News Chicago, the *Chicago Tribune*, WNUA, and WXRT-FM. He has held managerial roles at the *Tribune*, WGN-AM, and WNUA. He's contributed to Chicago Public Media WBEZ-FM 91.5 and *Crain's Chicago Business*. And he's served as Adjunct Professor of Journalism at Roosevelt and Northwestern Universities and Columbia College Chicago. With his Rivet colleagues, he shares a US patent for delivering a "contextually relevant media content stream based on listener preference."

Sources:
A Square Video Tour. youtube.com/watch?v=sGG4j1SZzls
Chicago Public Square podcasts.
chicagopublicsquare.com/search/label/Podcasts
The Secret Origin of Chicago Public Square.: medium.com/@meyerson/the-secret-origin-of-chicago-public-square-181d293b12d3

TELEVISION, BRANDING, AND LIVE FROM THE SCENE

For decades, live and local television news produced predictable content. What is new and exciting is the blending of backpack journalism, mobile media technologies, and social media strategies. Livestream viewers go behind the scenes. Much as popular sociologist Erving Goffman might have described "front stage" and "backstage" life, the video stream and chat room offered a backstage glimpse into the workings of TV news. There is a para-social interaction – a sociological term coined to describe how media personalities seem like our friends – when seeing TV people interact with viewers ahead or after a broadcast.

Few reporters and stations are sharing this much about what happens away from the bright lights of TV cameras. Television has an opportunity to be experimenting with this innovative social media approach. It offers the opportunity to drive audience traffic online, on the air, and back online. While this may not be *the* future of local news, it is an attractive real-time model that follows the rules of computer-mediated communication: identity (branding), interaction (two-way), and community building (online).

At the national level, television programming from *The Voice* (#TheVoice) to a live performance of *The Sound of Music* (#SoundOfMusicLive) leveraged online engagement. While musical theatre is challenging on network television, NBC decided that by engaging social media fans, program interest could be magnified. In fact, despite negative comments, NBC's audience of 21.3 million viewers in 2013 was the largest for a non-sporting event in four years (Lane, 2013; RTT News, 2013). The early development of social TV created cultural models for annual live television events – #GoldenGlobes, #Grammys, #Oscars, #SuperBowl, and others. Especially during the winter months when viewing is highest, live events create significant real-time experiences.

TOP MEDIA SITES ON SOCIAL MEDIA

Most readers would be able to identify Facebook and Twitter among the top social media sites, but there are many media sites that benefit from Facebook likes, Twitter re-tweets, and overall social media exposure. Table 11.1 is a list of the top publishers on Facebook.

TABLE 11.1 *Top Facebook Publishers and Website Rank (2018–2019)*

	News Site	Total Monthly Engagements	Web Top 50 Rank (unique visitors)
1.	CNN.com	46.5 million	4 (95 million)
2.	FoxNews.com	40.4 million	6 (65 million)
3.	DailyMail.co.uk	36.6 million	–
4.	NYTimes.com	33.5 million	5 (70 million)
5.	BBC.co.uk	26.7 million	13 (35 million)
6.	DailyWire.com	26.4 million	–
7.	TheGuardian.com	26.3 million	10 (42 million)
8.	WashingtonPost.com	26.2 million	9 (47 million)
9.	CBSNews.com	25.2 million	–
10.	NBCNews.com	23.6 million	7 (63 million)

Sources: NewsWhip (June 2019). The Top Publishers On Facebook In June 2019. https://www.news-whip.com/2019/07/top-publishers-facebook-june-2019/; Sharma, A. (December 25, 2018). 15 Most Popular News Websites In the World – 2019 Edition. *TechWorm.* https://www.techworm.net/2018/12/best-most-popular-news-websites-world.html; Alexa.com (January 26, 2020). The Top 500 Sites on the Web (Top 50 Free). https://www.alexa.com/topsites

Increasingly, partnerships with Facebook and other social media sites made it more difficult to track audience trends through publicly available data.

BLOGGING

Activities identified as blogging may take many forms. An individual may operate a WordPress, Blogger, or other site with complete editorial control and decision-making. At the same time, sites such as *The Huffington Post* originally maintained a blog team to exercise an editorial review process. That changed in 2016 when *HuffPost* developed a Contributor site and shifted editorial control and responsibility to writers. Blogs published there still conform to style and other publishing rules.

The *Chicago Tribune* hosts *ChicagoNow*, a local blog site that promotes wide-open community discussion from many bloggers who often do not sign opinions with their names. Editors at this site promote a local blogger community by hosting regular social hours called "blatherings" and other events. One is called "Blogapalooz-Hour" in which bloggers are given a topic in the evening and have one hour to publish. Following the event, *ChicagoNow* community managers created a summary of the monthly topical posts. The topics are very general, such as, "Write about a great challenge faced by you or someone else" (*ChicagoNow*, 2013). The site in 2020 continued to emphasize sports, movie reviews, entertainment, and life in the city. Beyond full-length blog posts, which may run 500 to 1,000 words or more, microblogging on Twitter, Tumblr, and other social media sites is seen as a way to regularly communicate ideas without the effort and time required by more traditional blogging.

BLOGS FOR PUBLIC RELATIONS AND SOCIAL MEDIA MARKETING

Blogging and microblogging developed from early Internet discussion boards. The principle is the same in that online publishing gives authors exposure to a global audience. In some cases, the combination of blogging and PR alter careers and generate large amounts of interest. Creating, developing, and maintaining a blog are important best practice steps for anyone launching a career or seeking to further develop awareness. Blogging has its roots in the early days of the World Wide Web (WWW) and its fundamentals continue within a social media context.

⟨⟨⟩⟩ BOX 11.2

Thought Leader Robert P. Miles

In the mid-1990s, tech life was hard. "Networking" meant the office computers were linked through a mainframe that filled an entire hermetically sealed room. World Wide Web sites? No graphics! No video! Just *words*.

FIGURE 11.3 *@valueinvestorNE.*
Courtesy of Robert Miles

The words "social" and "media" were never linked – if they were, it meant a group of people watching a *television* show together (suffering through commercials, no less!). No Facebook, no LinkedIn, no Twitter, no blogs! Ah, but we did have "bulletin boards."

Not like Pinterest. Bulletin boards allowed people to post messages that could be read by others who intentionally sought them. As sites such as AOL (get this: known then as America Online) and Yahoo! emerged, it was on just such a bulletin board that I, unwittingly, became an early adopter of what became social media marketing.

In 1993, AOL hosted *The Motley Fool*, a new investment newsletter founded by brothers David and Tom Gardner. Owning a 25-employee business events company meant investing my employee's retirement funds. Believing it as important to know how to invest as what to invest in, I studied strategies. *The Motley Fool* and its bulletin board caught my eye.

One thing I wanted to know was, who was the most successful investor and would he manage my investments? It may have been *The Motley Fool* that led me to Roger Lowenstein's 1995 book, *Buffett: The Making of an American Capitalist*. Already considered "the Oracle of Omaha," Buffett was then a 65-year-old business magnate. I was then a 38-year-old with a 12-year-old company, who'd been raised and lived near Detroit, Michigan. Though Buffett most certainly was not available to manage my investments, his Midwestern perspective and humor resonated with me, another Midwesterner.

But, I realized, a third alternative was available: investing in Buffett himself. After purchasing Berkshire Hathaway stock, I attended my first "Woodstock for Capitalists" the first Saturday in May of 1996, one of 8,000 shareholders and guests (today that number exceeds 30,000) to absorb his sage advice.

The more I learned about and from Buffett, the more enamored I was of his principles. Becoming something of a Buffett geek, I waxed enthusiastic to anyone who would listen. And then I decided to share my enthusiasm more widely, by committing to post "101 Reasons to Own Berkshire Hathaway" on *The Motley Fool* bulletin board dedicated to Buffett's company.

Using the screen name SimpleInvestor, the first post, on December 9, 1998, read:

> INVEST WITH THE BEST – There is simply no better investment than Berkshire Hathaway, and no better investment manager than Warren Buffett. I have been investing in the stock market for 30 years and I have done just about everything imaginable … I have searched high and low throughout this country and abroad. And my search has led me to the single greatest investment that I have ever made … I invite you to sit back and read my 101 REASONS TO OWN BERKSHIRE HATHAWAY. Please feel free to debate, agree or even add your own reasons why you own Berkshire. Fortunately there are more than 101 days until the next annual meeting …

The post drew a whopping 11 recommendations.

Although not posted daily, all 101 reasons were finished before the May 1999 shareholders meeting. "Recommendations" increased and messages rolled in from readers around the world, including a European economist who urged me to publish the posts.

Not being naive about social courtesies, I wrote Mr. Buffett to inform him of this project. Surprisingly, he wrote me back. Even more surprising, he informed me that as a *Motley Fool* reader, he'd read all 101 of the reasons. Topping things off, he included a check for ten copies to give his board of directors.

Reality quickly set in as libraries and bookstores refused to carry the "book." It was self-published, had no LOC number, no ISBN, no bar code. The best option for promotion seemed to be where it started, on *The Motley Fool*. Sales were brisk and soon more books were printed. Then I posted a different message: I'd buy shareholders an ice cream cone at the Dairy Queen the evening before the May 2000 annual meeting, even if they didn't buy the book.

People showed up in droves. The local and worldwide news media appeared. So did Warren Buffett. When he put an arm around my shoulder, flashbulbs (yes flashbulbs) lit up. The book-signing event caught the eye of a John Wiley & Sons publishing company representative attending the reception.

Before I knew it, I was in New York City, receiving an offer for this book and for my next one. To which I said, "I didn't know I was going to write another book." Of course you are, I was told. A check was pushed toward me. A tape-bound copy of "The World's Greatest Investment: 101 Reasons to Own Berkshire Hathaway" was pushed back in return.

Little did I know this simple investor's decision to share my enthusiasm on a bulletin board would forever alter my career path. Three books later, I travel the world speaking about Buffett's investment strategies, appear regularly on cable news, host the annual "Value Investor Conference," and teach an Executive MBA course. If it hadn't been for the "newfangled" online communication that ultimately grew into social media, my enthusiasm for Warren Buffett would never have enthused millions, but only bored my friends to tears.

Robert P. Miles is an author, founder and host of the Value Investor Conference (www.valueinvestorconference.com/) and teaches a unique course at the University of Nebraska at Omaha Executive MBA program, titled *The Genius of Warren Buffett*.

The lessons learned by Bob Miles during the early Internet offer hints as to how social networking and social media may create new opportunities with new people and businesses. By jumping into what some would consider risky social media spaces with ideas and passion, an individual connects with others seeking similar information and interests.

HELPFUL TOOLS

Social media users typically spend a lot of time in an array of spaces, so there is a great need for planning, strategies, and development of best practices that cultivate efficient use of new tools. PostControlMarketing.com offers auditing templates and updated lists of free or low-cost tools (Quesenberry, 2019). Social media dashboards offer content managers an opportunity to synthesize the most relevant and important data in real-time.

For example, it may be important to track the top influencers on Twitter, which can be viewed from different perspectives. As we have explored, a social network can be visualized in terms of who is near the center of it, and who is at the periphery. Likewise, we may want to track hashtags, audience size, mentions, or linked websites. The sheer size of global social media present information and data management challenges – content duplication, content access, timeliness of content, relevance of content to a particular platform and discussion, and efficiency within large networks.

Beyond these issues, businesses worry about the bottom line of social media activities. Evidence has begun to emerge, suggesting that Twitter has a meaningful value, particularly for smaller companies with less access to mainstream media and a desire to break through the clutter (Andrews, 2013). Social media best practices require community brand managers to hone content by utilizing social media metrics and analytics to gauge interaction responses and feed results into future decisions.

GETTING AHEAD OF THE SOCIAL MEDIA PACK

In the past six years, there has been a shifting away from early adopter Twitter top accounts and toward consistently connected influencers within marketing social networks.

Social media best practices require users to go beyond attracting followers and fans, and it can be argued that the quality of interaction is much more important than the numbers over time. Garst (2013) identifies a formula for success, which includes avoiding common mistakes. She prefers offering social media tips, repeating motivational quotes, answering questions, and general conversation over selling. Garst agrees with most successful social media practitioners who lead with valuable content. Second, Garst urges users to remain focused on target demographics in deciding whom to follow, what to say, and when. She clears a lot of social media noise by using tools such as Hootsuite to manage and filter conversations.

Friedman (2013) listed six key trends that emphasize growing social and mobile media use: Among social media and mobile trends was a "meteoric rise in influence" (para. 2). From social videos to amazing photography, best practices continue to

TABLE 11.2 *HubSpot Marketing Ranked Monitoring Tools (2020)*

1. Tweet Deck is a Twitter live conversation interface (tweetdeck.twitter.com)
2. *
3. Tweet Reach is a Union Metrics snapshot (tweetreach.com)
4. Follower Wonk searches Twitter profiles and bios (followerwonk.com)
5. *
6. Mentionmapp is a social network analysis tool (https://analytics.mentionmapp.com/)
7. *
8. Hootsuite dashboard offers a free trial and education license (https://hootsuite.com/)
9. Board Reader is a forum search engine (https://boardreader.com.cutestat.com/)
10. BuzzSumo offers content insights (https://buzzsumo.com/)

Source: Whalley, B. (2019). The 13 Best Free Social Media Monitoring Tools For Every Marketing Team. *HubSpot.* https://blog.hubspot.com/blog/tabid/6307/bid/29,437/20-free-social-media-and-brand-monitoring-tools-that-rock.aspx

Note: * 2. BrandWatch (formerly Social Mention) now has large paid clients; * 5. SumAll could not be reached in early 2020; and * 7. Khoros (formerly Lithium and Klout) is a marketing customer care program.

redefine the nature of online social media storytelling and influence. Snapchat revolutionized social networking by extending "photo-messaging" into media storytelling (Manjoo, 2016). Its $30 billion initial public offering partially came from Spectacles sunglasses that "can record video clips" and are "sought-after gadgets" (para. 2), but that failure (and competition from Instagram and TikTok) sharply reduced its stock price.

Social media are fast and sometimes prone to quick viral sharing of content. Mobility and location drive social networking toward authentic real-time engagement, but social media branding and marketing rely heavily upon the features of entertainment. As was the case before social media, entertainment interest is likely to divide along traditional demographic group differences.

Experts focus on tips that utilize top tools to animate text and images, measure impact, stand out with slideshow content, target audiences for growth, improve audio and video quality, optimize video, use multiple cameras and switching for live streaming, track LinkedIn content engagement, and sustain Instagram follower growth (Jenkins, 2016). Snapchat's snap filters were popular – these have become part of other apps, such as ride-sharing service Uber (Hawkins, 2016). With so much social media noise, there is a need to stand out from others.

Organizations continue to struggle with writing an effective social media policy that assists employees in their use of Facebook, Twitter, LinkedIn, Instagram, and Pinterest – the big five US social media sites. Schiff (2015) suggested key organizational steps: 1. Involve all departments; 2. Use a (web) filter; 3. Set aside times each day for social media use; 4. Have a written social media policy; 5. Don't be draconian – The company owns its social media accounts, not employees; Employees have the right to communicate with other employees, and talk about the company on social media; and employees must disclose when they are posting on behalf of the company (pp. 1–2).

PERILS

Social media communication may backfire on a user. Some consider social media a sword with two edges that when combined with snarky comments may lead a user to be suspended or fired from work, or worse (Nathanson, 2013). For example, Twitter blocked the use of animated PNGs – images similar to GIFs – after trolls misused the innovation by posting "potentially seizure-inducing images to epileptic and photo-sensitive individuals" (Bonifacic, 2019, para. 1). A programming bug allowed hackers to post multiple-animation files that bypassed restricted auto-play content. Twitter added that, "APNGs were fun, but they don't respect auto-play settings, so we're removing the ability to add them. This is for the safety of people with sensitivity to motion and flashing imagery, including those with epilepsy" (para. 2).

In general, one of the social media perils is that trust for anything considered an advertisement is very low. Consumers, however, listen to friends for most recommendations. Marketers, for example, try to appeal to and even reward potential influencers. They also use social media sharing and collaborative game-like experiences. They hope to remain authentic rather than having the public turn on them with negative sentiment.

Social media branding, re-branding, and community building typically link messages to research findings used to create strategic media campaigns. While it is not that difficult to generate interest and buzz through a hashtag, it is impossible to completely control users, including those who may try to hijack the campaign for their own purposes. Still, the best practices involve building relationships – the kind that may lead some followers, fans, or friends to come to your defense amid a social media crisis. In this sense, social media best practices align with traditional media relations that use the power of celebrities and the excitement of events.

For business owners, it makes sense to start slow with social media and seek advice from those with experience. Social media consume time, and they are an expense. Best practices suggest that businesses may benefit from having a Facebook page, which then generates weekly insights data. Individuals should create a LinkedIn profile, monitor key Twitter sources, and consider the value of YouTube videos. The list of social media sites will continue to grow, which means that it is problematic to enter these spaces without a clear plan, strategies, goals, objectives, and tactics. It also is a problem to jump into social media spaces without first considering the value of creating a website or blog. By doing this, users really must begin to have an understanding of SEO and analytics before creating value from online relationships. By using social media to communicate with people and businesses, it is possible to raise awareness and interest in relationships. As has been the case with email for more than two decades, online interaction must be timely and relevant to avoid being ignored.

IT, COLLABORATION, VIRTUAL TEAMS, AND OTHER TRENDS

Information Technology (IT) offers new ways to explore technological capabilities, best practices, and learning through the use of shared mental models and other perspectives. Much of the quality work in social media is a function of teamwork, and these collaborative teams can also help personal and organizational brands avoid making mistakes caused by decisions made without thought. Collaboration happens when groups work toward common purposes, which typically take into account stakeholders. The field of collaboration science is emerging through engineering the ways in which people think and work (Morgeson, Reider, & Campion, 2005). Collaboration is concerned, then, with the composition of group members within a social media team, as well as the ways that leadership may promote creativity and encourage individuals to act in the interest of the larger good (Day, Gronn, & Salas, 2004). Collaborative communication within social media seeks to foster mutual understanding through co-orientation (Lin & Cheng-His, 2006). As individuals seek agreement and understanding, there may be perceived performance, financial, physical, convenience, social, and/or psychological risks that deter potential group success (p. 1208). Co-orientation within a team would allow leaders to measure whether or not the group can accurately predict orientations of other group members (Christen, 2005). Creativity may be "inspired and steered by great leadership" that understands the process and generates innovative ideas (Mallia, 2019, pp. 13–15). Abernathy and Sciarrino (2019) identify "creative destruction" as frequently driven by "disrupting innovation" that "attacks the cost of structure of an established industry"

(p. 93). In higher education, for example, online degree specialization may focus on areas, such as digital and social media, public relations leadership, data marketing, and creative strategies. From a communication perspective, these areas require teamwork in order to be successful.

Hollingshead and Contractor (2006) found that adding new communication media to existing capabilities can, in fact, enhance communication and interaction in small groups: "Collaboration among group members entails cognitive as well as emotional and motivational aspects of communication" (Hollingshead & Contractor, 2006, p. 115). Technologies may enhance within-group communication, provide additional information to the group, or alter tasks. Theoretical concerns include the degree of media richness and potential effects. Mediation may increase anonymity, increase task centeredness, make communication less personal or even have an effect on the consensus-building process.

Snapchat's monthly trends are one way to keep pace with rapid change. For example, in November of 2019, trending topics included Thanksgiving, the Baby Yoda viral meme, and historical humor (Forbes, 2019). From Black Friday to the 24th Arabian Gulf Cup, some topics focused upon regional events. For example, Disney's Frozen II movie was released during this month and received a notable number of Snaps. Celebrities tended to come from a particular sport or type of music. The viral slang phrase "OK Boomer" surfaced on Snapchat as a way for young people to call out or dismiss out-of-date baby boomer generation ideas.

Social media communication for older and new media are becoming products of mobile media platforms and apps. An entrepreneur must be strategic in leveraging team knowledge and skills to test ideas, focus on innovative disruption, and pivot toward the most promising social and digital outcomes. The development and refinement of best practices requires team collaboration and constant learning about new tools and ideas.

DISCUSSION QUESTIONS: STRATEGIES AND TACTICS

1. How do mobile media devices and mobile-friendly platforms impact social media communication? What are the major changes and trends?

2. How do newspapers, radio, and television journalists need to change to adapt to a social media environment? What are the potential rewards and risks?

3. What role may collaboration and teamwork play in improving the quality of social media and refining best practices?

REFERENCES

Abernathy, P. M., & Sciarrino, J. (2019). *The Strategic Digital Media Entrepreneur*. Medoford, MA: John Wiley & Sons.

Andrews, E. L. (2013, April 1). The Bottom Line on Corporate Tweeting. Graduate School of Stanford Business. www.gsb.stanford.edu/news/research/bottom-line-corporate-tweeting

Bonifacic, I. (2019, December 28). Twitter Blocks Animated PNGs to Keep Trolls from Using Them to Trigger Seizures (Updated). *Engadget.* www.engadget.com/2019/12/23/twitter-blocks-apng-stop-seizures/

Buttry, S. (2013, December). Better Journalism Through Engagement. *Slideshare.* www.slideshare.net/stevebuttry

Campbell, S. W., & Ling, R. (2011). Conclusion: Connecting and Disconnecting through Mobile Media. In S. W. Campbell and R. Ling (Eds.), *Mobile Communication,* pp. 323–330. New Brunswick, NJ: Transaction.

ChicagoNow (2013). ChicagoNow's Blogapalooza 3.0. *Storify.* http://storify.com/ChicagoNow/chicagonow-s-blogapalooza–3–0

Christen, C. T. (2005). The Utility of Coorientational Variables as Predictors of Willingness to Negotiate. *Journalism & Mass Communication Quarterly 82*(1), 7–24.

Day, D., Gronn, P., & Salas, E. (2004). Leadership Capacity in Teams. *Leadership Quarterly 15*(6), 857–880.

Forbes (2019, November). Business: Snap Chatter – November 2019: Thanksgiving, Black Friday, Baby Yoda, and 'Gonna Tell My Kids.' https://forbusiness.snapchat.com/blog/snap-chatter-november–2019

Friedman, P. (2013, December 19). 6 Social Media Trends of 2013 and What They Mean for the Future. *The Huffington Post.* www.huffingtonpost.com/peter-friedman/social-media-trends-of-2013_b_4463802.html

Gardner, H., & Davis, K. (2013). *The App Generation.* New Haven, CT: Yale University Press.

Garst, K. (2013, August 15). Twitter "Business Killers" to Avoid. http://kimgarst.com/twitter-business-killers

Gleason, R. (2013, December 18). Personal email, WBBM Newsradio 780 news director.

Hawkins, A. J. (2016, December 21). Uber Just Added Snapchat Filters and Friend Locators to Its App. *The Verge.* www.theverge.com/2016/12/21/14024192/uber-snapchat-filter-friend-locator-app-update

Hollingshead, A. B., & Contractor, N. S. (2006). New Media and Small Group Organizing. In L. A. Lievrouw and S. Livingstone (Eds.), *The Handbook of New Media,* pp. 114–133. London: Sage.

Hunsinger, J. (2014). Interface and Infrastructure of Social Media. In J. Hunsinger and T. Senft (Eds.), *The Social Media Handbook,* pp. 5–17. New York, NY: Routledge.

Jenkins, L. D. (2016, September 8). 20 Social Media Tools and Tips from the Experts. *Social Media Examiner.* www.socialmediaexaminer.com/20-social-media-tools-and-tips-from-the-experts/

Lane, E. (2013, December 9). Social Media Alive with *The Sound of Music* on NBC. www.huffingtonpost.com/eden-lane/social-media-alive-with-t_b_4401085.html

Lin, T. M. Y., & Cheng-His, F. (2006). The Effects of Perceived Risk on the Word-of-Mouth Communication Dyad. *Social Behavior & Personality 34*(10), 1207–1216.

Mallia, K. L. (2019). *Leadership in the Creative Industries, Principles and Practices.* Medford, MA: Wiley Blackwell.

Manjoo, F. (2016, November 30). While We Weren't Looking, Snapchat Revolutionized Social Networks. *The New York Times.* www.nytimes.com/2016/11/30/technology/while-we-werent-looking-snapchat-revolutionized-social-networks.html

Morgeson, F., Reider, M., & Campion, M. (2005). Selecting Individuals in Team Settings: The Importance of Social Skills, Personality Characteristics, and Teamwork Knowledge. *Personnel Psychology 58*(3), 583–611.

Nathanson, R. (2013, December 9). Social Media: Perils and Payoffs for Public Officials. *Albuquerque Journal.* www.abqjournal.com/316631/news/social-media-perils-and-payoffs.html

Patel, N. (2016, June 22). 6 New Social Media Marketing Tools the Experts Use. You Should, Too. *Entrepreneur*. www.entrepreneur.com/article/277510

Quesenberry, K. (2019). *Social Media Strategy: Marketing, Advertising, and Public Relations in the Consumer Revolution*. Lanham, MD: Rowman & Littlefield.

RTT News. (2013, December 16). *The Sound of Music Live!* Ratings Higher Than First Reported. www.rttnews.com/2239727/the-sound-of-music-live-ratings-higher-than-first-reported.aspx

Schiff, J. L. (2015, September 29). How to Craft an Effective Social Media Policy. *CIO*. www.cio.com/article/2987244/social-networking/how-to-craft-an-effective-social-media-policy.html

Sherblom, J. (2020). *Computer-Mediated Communication, Approaches and Perspectives*. San Diego, CA: Cognella.

Future of Social Media and Information Literacy

What is also needed is a critical approach to the nature of information and debate more generally, which seeks to build on and enhance people's understanding of the complexities of social media interaction.
  – Philip Seargent & Caroline Tagg (@philipseargent & @Carotagg, 2018, p. 187)

A fake news story led to threats of nuclear war between Pakistan and Israel on Christmas Eve … Pakistan Defense Minister Khawaja Asif responded to a fake news article on his official Twitter as if it were real.
  – Ben Westcott, CNN (@Ben_Westcott, 2016)

In many ways I consider my Twitter activities a giant, distributed, never-ending media literacy project.
  – Andy Carvin (@acarvin, 2013)

The rapid adoption of social media use – from just 5% of Americans in 2005 to 69% by early 2017 – helped us to understand why Facebook and other sites represent so much opportunity and challenge (Pew Research Center, 2017). The share of US adults remained about the same, as growth in India, China, and other parts of the world continued to surge (Pew Research Center, 2019).

In the 24/7, real-time world of social media, users need the ability to quickly make good decisions. Media literacy is the skill of deconstructing messages and understanding context. In fast-paced Twitter conversation, even world leaders sometimes are "duped" by "fake news" – responding in potentially dangerous ways (Westcott, 2016, paras. 1–3). This is important for social media novices, as well as communication professionals, who may become caught up in a social media moment. The pressure to measure social media business impact continues to offer hope and concern (Li & Stacks, 2015). As Webster (2014) observed in his book, *The Marketplace of Attention: How*

Audiences Take Shape in a Digital Age: "The forces of cultural production and consumption conspire to produce an environment that is at once diverse and concentrated" (p. 3). For example, as the Consumer Electronics Show (#ces2020, #ces) launched an array of new technologies, a social network analysis identified the focus of hashtags within Twitter posts: #ai, #iot, #robotics, #tech, #5g, #vr, #infographic, and #innovation (NodeXL, 2020). These reflect a direction in technologies that target the consumer market. Social media communication will be influenced by and also contribute to social and technological change.

At any moment, our collective and limited attention span may be captured. Digital literacy has been viewed as a function of cultural change, social networking, collaboration, and complex interaction (Seargent & Tagg, 2018). Justine Sacco was a public relations professional, but she said something on Twitter that cost her a very good job. She was in London getting ready to board a long flight to Africa when she tweeted:

> @JustineSacco: Going to Africa. Hope I don't get AIDS. Just kidding. I'm white! (December 20, 2013).

Those 12 words caused a global uproar on social media while she was in the air for more than ten hours. There were parody accounts and critical tweets with #HasJustine-LandedYet on Twitter. By the time her flight landed in Cape Town, South Africa, her name had been removed from the InterActiveCorp website – a PR firm with many large clients. IACA issued an apology, calling the tweet offensive and outrageous. At first, Sacco deleted the tweet, but it had already been captured in screenshots and virally spread across the Internet. Her initial action drew more criticism, and she took down the Twitter account. Sacco was fired from her executive job as communications director for the racist remark, and many found it difficult to understand how a professional could make such a huge mistake. Her apology even called it "a huge stupidity" (Dimitrova, 2013, para. 1). Sacco should have had better media literacy skills, but she also had a previous history of questionable tweets. The case is also noteworthy because the tweet sparked a social media "mob" reaction likened to "trial by social media," which is similar to the more traditional notion of "pillory of the press" (Bowcott, 2011). It is understood that media exposure – traditional or social – may generate an immediate penalty of mass public ridicule. Years later, the case continued to reverberate. Biddle (2014) apparently was the first to post the tweet for (the now-defunct) Gawker and its Valleywag tech blog, but months later met for dinner and apologized:

> I said I was sorry posting her tweet had teleported her into a world of media scrutiny and misery … "I was so naïve," she said. She had never expected the tweet would be interpreted the way it was … Her tweet was supposed to mimic – and mock – what an actual racist, ignorant person would say … Not knowing anything about her, I had taken its cluelessness at face value, and hundreds of thousands of people had done the same – instantly hating her because it's easy and thrilling to hate a stranger online.
> (paras. 15, 18, 23)

Two years after the tweet, Sacco continued to try to rebuild her career in an interview with *The New York Times* (Ronson, 2015):

> "I cried out my body weight in the first 24 hours ... it was incredibly traumatic. You don't sleep. You wake up in the middle of the night forgetting where you are." She released an apology statement and cut short her vacation. Workers were threatening to strike at the hotels she had booked if she showed up. She was told no one could guarantee her safety.
>
> (para. 30)

Sacco's extended family in South Africa had been supporters of Nelson Mandela, but the damage of the tweet was done. "I had a great career, and I loved my job, and it was taken from me, and there was a lot of glory in that," she told Ronson. "Everybody else was very happy about that" (para. 50). He concluded that social media are "so perfectly designed to manipulate our desire for approval ... Her tormenters were instantly congratulated as they took Sacco down ... Their motivation was much the same as Sacco's own – a bid for the attention of strangers..." (para. 60). Sacco's name in a Google search continued to be linked to the offensive tweet, and connected to stories about others losing their jobs over poor choices in social media, as well as concern about how to stop online shaming (Leon, 2020; Nark, 2016). For example, Emily "The Pistachio Girl" Youcis was fired by the Philadelphia Phillies' Citizens Bank Park vendor Aramark for involvement in "white identity politics" (para. 4). Mandkur (2016) has linked the reaction to inappropriate social media content to the psychology of mob behavior: "They are irrational, emotional and irresponsible just like mobs in the real world" (para. 9).

One way to view social media is through the metaphor of "the stream," which reflects the idea that information flows and may even crest (Madrigaldec, 2013, para. 1). The idea of a stream emphasizes real-time data, such as that on Twitter, which has no beginning or end. A premium is placed on the sharing of current information, and the conversation is *"permanently unfinished"* (para. 13). Such a stream may not lend itself to quality content or media that remain fresh for very long. In a media literacy sense, users and fans must understand these characteristics, deconstruct what they are viewing, and make conscious decisions about how to spend time.

The lure of the social media stream is also a problem within schools. Teachers, who can be seen using their cellphones, do so even though this activity by students often may be prohibited during the school day: "It turns out that this is a hotly debated issue" (Dobrow, 2013, para. 4). A media literacy approach would be to develop good teacher and student use habits, rather than restricting access to the devices, because prohibition misses learning opportunities. A #DeleteFacebook Twitter hashtag reflected frustration in recent years with the abusive power by the largest social media company serving nearly one-third of the estimated 3.5 billion users of the most popular sites. The strong appeal of social media use, including Facebook and Instagram, may be grounded in a desire to know about our friends, maintain relationships, and stay connected with social networks that share relevant information (McEwan, 2019).

In this book, social media have been explored from a variety of perspectives and within different contexts. From computer-mediated communication concepts to the applied fields of journalism, public relations, advertising, and marketing, we can identify motivation for online engagement and influence. In this chapter, we look at how social media may be important in driving social change. Media and information literacy address what we know and how we know it. It is a perspective that urges us to become smarter social media users.

🏹 BOX 12.1

Thought Leader Sammi He

The most significant change in the PR industry is due to widely adopted social media usage. Public relations practitioners get substantially shorter periods of time to react to an issue or crisis. The general public, journalists, investors, employees, and other related parties can follow the development of any event online through various social media tools, such as Snapchat, Instagram, Twitter, YouTube, and Facebook.

Public Relations and social media have been intimately linked for quite a long time. Social media platforms are taking on larger roles in PR agencies, as they can be utilized to not only draw atten-

FIGURE 12.1 *@SammiHe.*
Courtesy of Sammi He

tion to stories, but even drive or shape the narrative. The increasing popularity and significance of social media pressure PR professionals to change the way they think and operate, and agencies need to adapt quickly or risk losing to competitors.

In the next five years, we should continue to see more of the so-called "influencers," who have a significant number of followers on their Instagram, YouTube, or blog accounts. Those individuals usually build audiences with like minds and interests, which give PR professionals an advantage in more productively reaching consumers on a variety of channels. Influencers have their own virtual circle, which allows the messages to be circulated without too much promotion, and outreach becomes a crucial part of PR strategy at the same level of importance as media relations. However, many of those individuals do not belong to a specific agency or company, which makes it more difficult for PR professionals to pitch stories and also require us to be more diligent in terms of finding the most suitable influencer for a certain brand.

In addition, the changes in how people consume information require brands to adopt more visual content. Social media have already adapted to this with the successes of Snapchat and Instagram Stories, and Facebook Live. This growing trend in visual content means that PR professionals will not only develop a new type of content but also engineer a new format for effectively delivering brand messages. For example, more press releases ditch the old boring word style and instead include videos, images, and interactive links. By utilizing visual elements, brands may directly engage with audiences. As a result, PR agencies also need to hire people with new skill sets and be able to film and edit visual content. Social media sites provide PR professionals with the opportunity to craft communication plans that enable brands to engage with consumers 24/7. Done right, social media also may help clients reduce the cost of a campaign, and yet generate more positive and effective results.

Sammi He is a communications specialist in New York City. She is previously a member of the Corporate/Financial Practice of BCW (formerly Burson-Marsteller). Sammi has nearly a decade of experience in communication, with an emphasis on media relations, financial communications, strategy development, and executive positioning. She has worked closely with many Fortune 500 brands, including TIAA, Coca-Cola, SAP, HP, and Bank of America, among others. Sammi has also helped many of her Chinese clients establish and increase awareness in the US through various activities.

MEDIA LITERACY

Literacy skills are a fundamental requirement of an elementary and secondary education, yet media literacy may not be emphasized within traditional early education. Further, life-long learning by adults about the nature of global media corporations; framing of media messages; potential effects on children and adults; and application of this knowledge in the role of active, deliberative citizenship is crucial (Tewksbury & Rittenberg, 2012). George Takei, for example, went from being known as Sulu on the *Star Trek* television show to a social media star. More importantly, he used his connection to fans to attack negative stereotypes about Asians and LGBTQ+. Takei told *The Daily Beast*:

> Ours is a people's democracy, and it can be as great as a people can be, but it's also as fallible as people are. So, this democracy is vitally dependent on good people to be actively engaged in the process.
>
> (Stern, 2014, para. 17)

Through his website, Oh My! memes and a play about his life, Takei blended entertainment and political activism that was powered by social media communication. His content may be seen as a form of social media literacy education in response to the ignorance that also is spread online in the social media marketplace of ideas. Hobbs (2016) noted:

> All our understandings of media, literacy, technology, and culture are inevitably situated in the particularities of a certain time and place ... (Scholars) helped us see digital and media literacy as a process of heightened awareness of form, content, and context ... probing the deeply social nature of representation and interpretation ... we experience as users, consumers, and creators of media and technology.
>
> (p. 234)

Social media photographs, for example, are stored "in an overflowing file cabinet of images in my brain, a virtual repository of personal scenes and faces alongside visual notations from the public sphere" (Hobbs, 2016, p. 222). Social media users also *participate* in "the grassroots creative production that constitutes the dominant content of YouTube, that forms the basis of exchanges through social media, that generates millions of Wikipedia entries, or that yields the stories housed in the top fan-fiction archives" (Jenkins, 2016, p. 149). Critical and cultural theories need to take into account the complex nature of the interaction.

The social media environment presents a challenge that young, middle-aged, and older people alike have not faced in the history of civilization – to exercise personal responsibility in an unprecedented era of open communication and access to a global audience. Whether we know it or not, we all have the power to be publishers, yet few of us are formally trained to do so. Consider high school students in the United States who find the freedom the Internet offers as an attractive method of expression. However, mass media are full of accounts of the dangers of predators using this information (Coronado, 2006). In the years during social media development, the problem of inappropriate and illegal online communication has become widespread. The general issue led the state of Massachusetts in the early days of social media to urge MySpace.com, a website devoted to personal pages and groups, to raise the minimum age of users from 14 to 18. Age restrictions imply that teens do not or cannot be *taught* to exercise sophisticated media and information literacy skills. The soaring popularity of personal websites is only one part of the larger social media literacy issue.

☐ BOX 12.2

MySpace Online Communities

MySpace Describes Its Definition of an Online Community

One of the earliest social media sites, MySpace, never grew to the size of Facebook, but maintained its focus on music and other communities:

> MySpace is an online community that lets you meet your friends' friends. Create a private community on MySpace and you can share photos, journals and interests with your growing network of mutual friends! See who knows who, or how you are connected. Find out if you really are six people away from Kevin Bacon.

MySpace is for everyone:

- Friends who want to talk Online
- Single people who want to meet other Singles
- Matchmakers who want to connect their friends with other friends
- Families who want to keep in touch – map your Family Tree
- Business people and co-workers interested in networking
- Classmates and study partners

Anyone looking for long lost friends! This MySpace online community description falls short of taking a media literacy approach, but it does suggest the creation of "a private community" for photograph sharing. Too often, the marketing and business interests of social network sites emphasize use and encourage it without development of users' critical thinking skills. A social responsibility perspective would offer specific examples of private and public communication.

Source: Techterms (March 6, 2007). MySpace. www.techterms.com/definition/myspace

---

The reach of Facebook and its popular Instagram site raised concerns from critics who worry that they control too much of global audience attention. A Yale computer science professor suggested that a solution might be found within blockchain. "Revolution Populi" was created as, "a social media that's collectively owned by its users, where terms of use are determined democratically and privacy is guaranteed by blockchain-based encryption" (Holmes, 2019, para. 2). "It may seem far-fetched, but they're counting on the general public becoming so fed up with Facebook – but still craving a social media outlet – that Revolution Populi becomes a global movement" (para. 4). Similarly, a Twitter team was creating project Bluesky, that "will take inspiration from email, an open 'protocol' that anyone can implement," and "the aim is for Twitter to be ultimately rearchitected on top of it, in what would be an unprecedented demonstration of the viability of a decentralized social media protocol's viability" (Price, 2019, paras. 3–4). The move could be an acknowledgment of the current difficulties Twitter faces in trying to moderate offensive content.

It is unfair to see social media sites as only powerful and potentially harmful to young people. Clearly, they also provide socialization and interaction opportunities. When a missing person report is posted on Facebook, for example, it can assist law enforcement in an investigation. The key is how social networking is used. A media literacy perspective allows us to examine content and technology from a variety of angles, not just one.

From a computer-mediated communication perspective, Huffaker and Calvert (2005) examined issues of online identity and language among teenage blog users. They found that a majority of teen bloggers presented extensive personal data, including first names, age, and contact information. One in five teens revealed a full name. The integration of media and information literacy produces an emphasis on schools and education, library usage, intercultural communication, and global media. Culture and stereotypes have been found to exist within social media, as they do in society.

Developments in social media presented new questions about how the public processes information and entertainment. Peter Levine, Deputy Director of The Center for Information and Research on Civic Learning and Engagement (CIRCLE), discussed the proliferation of unreliable information and the challenges posed by it: "Some prominent individuals and institutions are calling for schools to prepare young people to identify reliable information online" (Levine, 2005, p. 1). In this context, there is a call for formalized information literacy education in the schools, but US K-16 education has been slow to respond. One important issue for schools is the examination of media use in different environments, such as during social free time and within different cultural contexts (Hart, 2001; Lealand, 2001; Vered, 2001). Educators need to respond to the larger framework of student media and social media use in a global and multimedia environment. In such a world, media and information literacy must be placed within an emerging multicultural education framework. Public and private elementary and secondary school teachers appear to support the goals and values of media education, but the constraints of curricula, time, and resources limit their willingness to expand instruction and include media education. While media literacy education has spread throughout the United States, it has not been fully adopted by educators (Yates, 2004). Media and information literacy education have yet to reach a mature status as an integral and essential part of school curricula. Schools present one set of concerns for those wishing to understand media and information literacy, but libraries are a different context. The role of media librarianship has been transformed by technological and social change. Librarians and library patrons are increasingly likely to be in interaction with one another, likely to be utilizing technology, and likely to approximate pedagogical structure. This blending of classroom, library online, and social media contexts will continue to evolve, as online interaction grows in popularity.

LIFE-LONG LEARNING AND MEDIA LITERACY

Social media and information literacy is a dynamic field of study, which is being dramatically influenced by social and technological change (Briggs, 2020). For example, the introduction and diffusion of the video iPod made it possible for people to download media content and take it for viewing anywhere. Thus, such portable media messages competed for attention with ubiquitous place-based television (i.e., TV screens in supermarkets, schools, doctor's offices, gas stations, etc.) and traditional print media. The rapid diffusion of mobile smartphones, tablets, and other devices followed, and created a media-rich environment. Everyone is challenged to exercise more sophisticated media literacy skills. Increasingly, it is not enough to be able to read and understand text-based messages. The prevalence of multi-media requires people to exercise advanced visual literacy skills.

Media literacy also includes asking critical questions about data. LinkedIn, for example, can be a very useful professional tool, but it also can be abused by marketers. Matney (2019) used the #DeleteLinkedIn hashtag because of the site's collection of data commonly found in **customer relationship management (CRM)** software designed to track sales and potential customer leads:

"LinkedIn is just a CRM where the customers all populate their own cells of the spreadsheet. It gives users spam and pop-ups that seem designed to help them find where the notifications settings on their phones are" (para. 5). Matney (@lucasmtny) expressed the concern that LinkedIn "has monetized itself by going out of its way to obfuscate this data for the majority of its users" (para. 9). Too often, social media companies maintain data that belong to users in all age groups, but they are not offered free and easy access.

Aging baby boomers – those born between 1946 and 1964 – were a key group facing their retirement years. Interesting issues emerged about whether this group, raised on television, would behave as their parents did in terms of traditional media usage. In fact, this group quickly embraced social media sites, such as Facebook, as well as online media usage on sites such as Twitter. Newspapers and television remain important sources for boomers, yet inexpensive tablets encouraged the shift away from traditional media uses. Awash in new media choices, boomers are set to make lifestyle choices that break the mold of previous generations. From a global media literacy perspective, boomers can be thought of as users and fans that critically examine consumer content (Hilt & Lipschultz, 2005). In this sense, the media literacy approach directly challenges critical theorists who argue that consumers are passive and easily manipulated – especially when users have the tools at their fingertips (Mathison, 2009).

The Internet led some authors to emphasize the importance of digital literacy skills, information literacy skills, technology literacy, and visual literacy as significant elements in understanding media literacy. Shapiro and Hughes (1996) asked what individuals would need to know to be considered competent and literate in an information society:

As we witness not only the saturation of our daily lives with information organized and transmitted via information technology, by the way in which public issues and social life increasingly are affected by information-technology issues – from intellectual property to privacy and the structure of work to entertainment, art and fantasy life – the issue of what it means to be information-literate becomes more acute for our whole society.

(p. 1)

The stream of social media content makes it difficult to precisely define literacy, much less social media literacy. Silverblatt (1995) organized media literacy around four prime aspects of message interpretation: process, context, framework, and production values. He builds upon this through a definition of media literacy that has five elements – awareness of the impact on individuals and society; understanding media processes; message analysis strategy development; content as cultural indicators; and enhancement of media enjoyment and appreciation. Silverblatt's framework may work for social media users in allowing them to step back from the social stream and understand cultural significance of the communication in a way that he describes as critical awareness (Silverblatt & Zlobin, 2004). Within social and mobile media, messages vary in form and content. Instead of following narrow professional content rules, any user may produce content using any set of production rules. The optimistic view is that social media promote citizen decision-making, collaboration, and compromise, yet there also continues to be anecdotal evidence that users tend to retreat to conversations with like-minded individuals and organizations.

GLOBAL MEDIA CORPORATIONS

One concern has been that traditional media ownership is increasingly highly concentrated in the hands of a few major global corporations (Bagdikian, 2000). Beyond the homogenous messages distributed by these large corporations, most users have been educated without the media literacy tools to challenge media values of violence and blind consumerism. McChesney (1999) saw media literacy as a movement designed to increase education, skepticism, and knowledge:

It is fueled by the large public discontent with the hypercommercialism, banality, and asininity of corporate media fare, as well as the commercialization of education and every possible facet of social life. Media literacy has considerable potential as long as it involves explaining how the media system actually works and does not posit that the existing system is by definition good, democratic, and immutable.

(p. 301)

Social media seem in one sense to liberate individuals from corporate control by offering new communication options. Still, large corporate social media sites, such as Facebook and Google continue to dominate much of the landscape (Ng, 2016). For example, Facebook purchased the WhatsApp messenger program, a popular tool that helped about 63 billion messages ring in the 2017 New Year (Novet, 2017). Facebook also owns Instagram – a quickly growing mobile app leader that is incorporating photo shopping tags (Constine, 2016), "Stories" that copy Snapchat's success (Hunter, 2016), and make it easy for brands to offer free products and pay to Instagram influencers (Chafkin, 2016). Facebook Live vaulted into video streaming leadership (Spayd, 2016), as an anti-social side of streaming (Dewey, 2016) included a live attack by teens (Johnson & Babwin, 2017). Police now consider social media monitoring essential to their law enforcement efforts (Bostick, 2017).

Instagram and Snapchat have become important social and business tools. The attraction of a Snapchat from Mount Everest is easy to see (CBS News, 2016), so brands seek to use it. The majority of early Snapchat advertising was for specific products, such as activewear and consumer electronics advertising (Heine, 2016b). Meanwhile, social media managers sought to measure specific metrics: unique views, story completions, and screenshots (Wright, 2016). Users must learn to understand that they are being observed on social media, and data are monetized. Social media offer a paradox of freedom and control – users are free to communicate, but they do so within systems designed by large media industries (Albarran, 2013). Amazon, for example, became a dominant retailer that also launched a popular streaming video service.

FRAMING OF MEDIA MESSAGES

Relatively little structured education exists to prepare viewers to deconstruct and critically examine complex media messages. One example would be the innovative undergraduate program at Webster University. This field of study views media literacy as "a critical thinking skill that focuses on the source of much of our information: the media." Programs such as this address media literacy through:

- awareness of media impact on individuals and society;
- understanding of mass communication processes;
- developing critical approaches to analyze media messages;
- media content awareness of text, sound, and images; and,
- exploration of cultural and social constructions, depictions, and presentations of diverse groups by media.

Further, some campuses use information literacy in education curricula to address issues related to instructional design, web page development, and website evaluation. Educational institutions reflect dramatic and relevant changes in society.

Traditional media, such as radio and television, also are adapting to this new environment. Where once the nightly network newscast was king, the lines have blurred between news and entertainment. For example, cable television programs like *The Colbert Report* employ satire and actual news video to make fun of the political and social landscape at the same time as they critique it.

At its core, media literacy (Media Literacy, 2003) is the ability to pay close attention to content (including the visual) and make sense of a wide range of media messages and presentations (Green et al., 2012). The critical examination of text, photographs, audio, and video requires awareness, education, and practice.

In one example, a tourist photo was altered to include what appears to be a jet heading toward the World Trade Center. The image was widely distributed in the weeks following September 11, 2001. In fact, a close examination of the lighting, color, clothing, sky, and angles reveals it is a fake. Likewise, the email stories disseminated about the image did not withstand critical scrutiny. The **Snopes** website is dedicated to debunking false Internet information, and this content is widely shared via social media. One great advantage of the emerging social media world is that each shared item can be scrutinized by participants within social networks to assist a user in discovering whether or not content is authentic.

POTENTIAL EFFECTS FROM APPLIED MEDIA LITERACY

In order to understand the emerging field of media and information literacy, attention must be paid to a wide range of interdisciplinary studies. Media research frequently addresses literacy concerns as they relate to dynamic news construction, audience perception of stories, and cultivation of long-term beliefs (Dominick, 2009). At the same time, library studies have been at the heart of questions related to how people seek, find, process, and use new information. Thus, media and information literacy draw from traditional disciplines, but it forges a new way of looking at how people use media (Baran & Davis, 2000; Barnes, 2003). Social media literacy urges users to reflect upon content ownership, privacy invasion, and other issues addressed in this book. It may be attractive, for example, to use a private business messaging app for office communication. However, journalists using Slack found out that their messages can be subpoenaed for use in civil and criminal court cases (Torres, 2017). Likewise, LinkedIn is a popular personal branding site, but is also is populated by marketers interested in collecting and using personal data (Von Rosen, 2017).

As people adopt new and different media, including social media through SNS platforms, studies will need to be grounded in what we already know about the development of visual and computer literacy skills (Kupianen, 2013). Media audiences are known to possess complex schemas – ordered information that offers cognitive explanations (Graber, 2006). Potter (2008) aligned media literacy as a perspective related to media exposure and meaning making from messages. Meaning making is cognitive and affective – capable of generating emotional response (Rodman, 2001).

Media and information literacy matter because people of all walks of life need to be able to deconstruct media messages and critique the quality of information sources. For example, many days after 9/11 there came a moment when morning network TV shows left coverage and returned to the mundane: cooking recipes, review of the latest popular music artist CD, and the following of sensational murder cases. Likewise, we could have predicted the shift away from Hurricane Katrina coverage. While some light has been shed on the ebb and flow of news cycles, viewers armed with media and information literacy knowledge and skills would immediately recognize what is happening and why. From organizational routines to individual behaviors, news and information are important. Media tactics help explain content from a political and economic perspective. This level of understanding about media behavior needs to diffuse into media and information literacy education for all ages. From WikiLeaks (Beckett, with Ball, 2012) to virtual relationships (Brown, 2011) and political change (Garrett & Danziger, 2011), social media present literacy challenges and opportunities.

Media and information literacy remain in most places outside the definition of what elementary and secondary school age students *need* to know. This is even the case in most higher education requirements. If everyone seems to agree that we live in a media and information age, why have educators been so slow to respond? Is it because of politics, economics, or some other macro explanations? Most disciplines must and will make media and information literacy central following the 2020 Covid-19 Coronavirus global pandemic. Globalization is likely to place increasing importance on cultural theory, democratic theory, and development of new social movements. This may be related to development of new media as technological tools for social change. As individuals are empowered by their media and information literacy skills, it is possible that these abilities will be harnessed as cultural tools in grassroots battles to maintain local and national identities.

Social media literacy extends to policy questions and issues. When a University of Kansas media professor spoke out following the Navy Yard 2013 shootings in Washington, DC, he received death threats and personal attacks. The university placed the professor on leave and revamped its disciplinary policies to include social media. The following social media policy amendments were made by the Regents in the weeks following the event. However, the policies were later revised to reflect First Amendment values.

☐ BOX 12.3

University of Kansas Social Media Policy

The Kansas Board of Regents in 2013 added controversial social media language to a section of their suspension, termination, and dismissal policies, but then revised it in 2018 with a governance statement.

CHAPTER II: GOVERNANCE – STATE UNIVERSITIES

6 USE OF SOCIAL MEDIA BY FACULTY AND STAFF

1. a Commitment to Academic Freedom and First Amendment
   The Kansas Board of Regents strongly supports principles of academic freedom. It highly values the work of state university faculty members. Academic freedom protects their work and enhances the valuable service they provide to the people of Kansas.

   The Board also supports this statement from the 1940 Statement of Principles of the American Association of University Professors:

   College and university teachers are citizens, members of a learned profession, and officers of an educational institution. When they speak or write as citizens,

---

they should be free from institutional censorship or discipline, but their special position in the community imposes special obligations. As scholars and educational officers, they should remember that the public may judge their profession and their institution by their utterances. Hence they should at all times be accurate, should exercise appropriate restraint, should show respect for the opinions of others, and should make every effort to indicate that they are not speaking for the institution.

Further, the Kansas Board of Regents recognizes the First Amendment rights as well as the responsibilities of all employees, including faculty and staff, to speak on matters of public concern as private citizens, if they choose to do so, including through social media. In general, for both faculty and staff, any communication via social media that is protected by the First Amendment and that is otherwise permissible under the law is not precluded by this policy.

This policy shall be construed and applied in a manner that is consistent with the First Amendment and academic freedom principles.

2. **b** Social Media Policy
In keeping with the Kansas Board of Regents' commitment to the First Amendment and principles of academic freedom, the Board supports the responsible use of existing and emerging communications technologies, including social media, to serve the teaching, research, and public service missions of the state universities. These communications technologies are powerful tools for advancing state university missions, but at the same time pose risks of substantial harm to personal reputations and to the efficient operation of the higher education system. The Board therefore believes it is prudent to adopt this policy on the proper – and improper – use of social media.

1. For purposes of this policy: "Social media" means any online tool or service through which virtual communities are created allowing users to publish commentary and other content, including but not limited to blogs, wikis, and social networking sites such as Facebook, LinkedIn, Twitter, Flickr, and YouTube; "social media" does not include e-mail sent to a known and finite number of individuals, or non-social sharing or networking platforms such as Listserv and group or team collaboration worksites.

2. Authorship of content on social media in accordance with commonly accepted professional standards and in compliance with all applicable laws and university and Board policies shall not be considered an improper use of social media in the following contexts:
   i. academic research or other scholarly activity;
   ii. academic instruction within the instructor's area of expertise; and

          iii. statements, debate, or expressions made as part of shared governance and in accordance with university policies and processes, whether made by a group or individual employee.

3. The United States Supreme Court has held that public employers generally have authority to discipline their employees for speech in a number of circumstances, including but not limited to speech that:

          i. is directed to inciting or producing imminent violence or other breach of the peace and is likely to incite or produce such action;

          ii. when made pursuant to (i.e., in furtherance of) the employee's official duties, is contrary to the best interests of the employer;

          iii. discloses without lawful authority any confidential student information, protected health care information, personnel records, personal financial information, or confidential research data; or

          iv. subject to the balancing analysis required by the following paragraph, impairs discipline by superiors or harmony among co-workers, has a detrimental impact on close working relationships for which personal loyalty and confidence are necessary, impedes the performance of the speaker's official duties, interferes with the regular operation of the employer, or otherwise adversely affects the employer's ability to efficiently provide services.

In determining whether an employee's communication is actionable under subparagraph iv, the interest of the employer in promoting the efficiency of the public services it performs through its employees must be balanced against the employee's right as a citizen to speak on matters of public concern.

4. When determining whether a particular use of social media constitutes an improper use, the following shall be considered: academic freedom principles referenced in subsection b.2., the employee's position within the university, whether the employee used or publicized the university name, brands, website, official title or school/department/college or otherwise created the appearance of the communication being endorsed, approved or connected to the university in a manner that discredits the university, whether the communication was made during the employee's working hours and/or whether the communication was transmitted utilizing university systems or equipment.

5. The chief executive officer of a state university, or the chief executive officer's delegate, has the authority to make use of progressive discipline measures pursuant to Board or university policy, up to and including

suspension, dismissal and termination, with respect to any faculty or non-student staff member who is found to have made an improper use of social media. Existing university grievance and review processes shall apply to any such action.

6. **c** Application of Policy
This policy on the use of social media shall be construed and applied in a manner that is consistent with the First Amendment and academic freedom principles and shall apply prospectively from the date of its original adoption by the Kansas Board of Regents on December 18, 2013.

Kansas Board of Regents 98 Policy Manual (Rev. 06/20/18) (pp. 98–99)

The revision scaled back the initial tone of the language that connected termination to "improper use of social media on social networking sites such as Facebook, LinkedIn, Twitter, Flickr, and YouTube." The revised policy grants the university "authority to make use of progressive discipline measures," including "up to and including suspension, dismissal and termination" for "any faculty or non-student staff member who is found to have made an improper use of social media." While the 2013 policy led to a faculty member suspension without a hearing, the current rules require the use of "university grievance and review processes."

Sources: Kansas Board of Regents, Current Social Media Policy (2018). https://governance.ku.edu/kansas-board-regents-current-social-media-policy

Social media literacy skills might have led the professor to pause and reflect on the need to inject into a Twitter controversy, or at least the manner of the communication. Likewise, a social media literacy perspective should have kept the Kansas Board of Regents from revising their policy so quickly after an incident. Rather than focusing on communication restrictions and punishment, the board might have been able from the outset to generate a statement that respected free expression and balanced it against the need for public safety.

Global social media literacy will continue to generate new questions (Lipschultz & Hilt, 2005). Computer and visual literacy skills must evolve with constant technological change (Potter, 2001/2008). Individuals, for example, using mobile and social media, face literacy issues in the interaction between people, messages, sounds, and visual images (Hobbs, 1997). Social media literacy needs to be connected and understood as social activity (Vered, 2001), cultural experience, and knowledge (Hart, 2001). Beyond simple access and use (Lealand, 2001), social media users will face critical multicultural challenges (Haynes Writer & Chávez Chávez, 2001; Yates, 2004). Social media literacy experts will need to keep up on issues and educate users (Widzinski, 2001), as few people have adequate time to devote to the fluid environment that has political significance (Best, 2005). Old and new media alike present information and other content in a variety of forms. Mass media and information literacy is a way of thinking about theories, skills and practices utilized to make better judgments. The field is one approach that assists consumers of social media.

✿ BOX 12.4

Thought Leader Carol Fowler

Social media platforms have given unprecedented access to the tools of mass communication once only held by journalists, as well as brands through advertising. This has had a profound impact on the influence and profitability of traditional news media, and the change is ongoing. The largest shift has taken place, and now the lords of traditional media understand that there is no "putting the genie back in the bottle." Anyone with a Twitter account can be a reporter. Social media also created an environment in which it is permissible, and even encouraged, for journalists to share personal opinions about politics and religion. Objectivity, while ideal, is no longer essential. There are a handful of examples of reporters

FIGURE 12.2 *@carolfowler.*
Photograph by David Klobucar, courtesy of Carol Fowler

getting fired for what they have shared in social media, but usually it is because they crossed the line of good taste, rather than because they let their personal feelings about an issue they're covering be known. It's a gray area that has made the job of running a news operation even more challenging. The smartest, most forward-looking media companies have clear social media guidelines for employees – both journalists and non-journalists – so that the boundaries of self-expression are clear.

The credibility of information is in question, in ways such as never before. Can you believe what you read? Those trained in the principles of journalism follow a code of ethics, but what's the code of ethics in sharing news and content on Facebook? It's up to the public to be more discerning than ever. The rise of social media has created a demand for education in media literacy. I hope that in the next five years, parents and educators take a more active role in teaching young people what sources of information they should trust. As I write this in 2020, Facebook is viewed with more skepticism, having been at the epicenter of a foreign government's interference in the 2016 presidential election.

Social media has also tipped the scale by creating a powerful mechanism for consumers to hold brands accountable, whether that be a restaurant, auto dealer, appliance maker, or mortgage lender. The idea of calling a lawyer or taking your complaint to the Better Business Bureau? How old-fashioned!

As of this writing, about 70% of people read consumer reviews before making an important purchase. Those reviews have real value, and brands are more respectfully and strategically reaching out to individual customers in the social space. In its highest use, social media should be a conversation, not a one-way rant. I am most excited about coming up with new ways to facilitate greater understanding on all sides. Transparency is becoming the norm, and brands and media companies who engage in it less will suffer the consequences of social shaming.

Carol Fowler is a nationally recognized content strategist with more than 30 years of broadcast and digital management experience. She has held senior leadership roles at four Chicago newsrooms and is currently Director of Content at KSDK (NBC), St. Louis. Fowler graduated from the University of Missouri-Columbia with a Bachelor of Journalism degree and a minor in Political Science. In 2014, she founded a social media management agency, KloboMedia, and until her move to St. Louis in 2019, Carol taught at Northwestern University's Medill School of Journalism about media innovation and Chicago's start-up culture.

Social media literacy skills empower users to examine the technology values that exist within much of what is shared and discussed. There are corporate benefits when we buy and use the latest technologies. Wearables, technologies that are connected to various parts of a user's body, opened sharing data across social networks. Clearly, there are issues that go beyond personal privacy, yet social media messages tended to focus on "cool" new technologies, instead of concerns about impact of usage. The Microsoft Project Oxford has gone further in research on facial expression within photographs – a window into "emotion recognition" that could be used for good or ill.

At the same time as the wealthy developing world uses the latest social media technologies, the poor have little or no access, may be exploited in the manufacturing processes, and may be the victims of environmental disasters caused by unrestrained development. If we reduce social media to consumer satisfaction, then this postmodernism may be a "hedonistic" search for needs that will never be fully met (Stevenson, 1995, p. 149). Such issues force us to consider the largest social media literacy question of all: Are we making progress?

ENGAGEMENT, NETWORKED COMMUNICATORS, TRUST, AND INFLUENCE

This book began by exploring how the entrepreneur business culture promotes social media change. The evolution of social media communication involves intense competition over fragmented audiences. Sometimes, we see this in rather immature ways. For example, Facebook CEO Mark Zuckerberg had not used his Twitter account in about eight years. Twitter CEO Jack Dorsey, immersed in a controversy with Facebook over filtering political advertising, publicly unfollowed Zuckerberg's dormant account (Morse, 2019). Small online spats happen within a larger technological context of dramatic change.

By recognizing the challenges of big data privacy, media organization power, and control, user best practices must be informed by knowledge about the networked world. We can learn to critically examine data, platforms, and policies. We can effectively use social media without being forced to surrender our identities, interactions, and communities. The increased use of **natural language generation (NLG)** of content may or may not simplify content accuracy and trust. Artificial intelligence within stories could lead to better verification of facts, or it may obscure authentic sources of news and information. At the same time, there is a tendency to inflate the success of AI, chatbots, and other computer processing. Marcus (2019) concluded that researchers and news media repeatedly "have fanned the flames of hype," and general AI "still seems like it might be a couple of decades away ..." (paras. 7–8). At a time when email open rates dipped below 30%, some marketers turned to invasive SMS text messages that promise very high access to engaged consumers – some initially identified as social media fans through click for more buttons (Baer, 2019). AI uses machine learning to target consumers responding within marketing probes. Customer service may begin with a chatbot, but it could lead to a deeper relationship. The touchpoint of an email address or mobile number offers an opportunity to collect narrative data (Moeller, 2016).

AI-generated photos have been found in fake accounts (Anderson, 2019). Facebook claimed that one set of pro-Trump accounts pushed conspiracy theories (Collins, 2019). The power of AI can clearly be abused (Coddington, 2019). Still, machine learning offers some promise through "generative AI" to become an important component within the creative process (Miller, 2019, para. 3). Experiential environments – "a series of immersive, interactive, and multisensory journeys" – hold a promise of enlightenment, engagement, and collaborative opportunities that might "ultimately foster greater empathy and understanding" through "a sense of presence" (Pavlik, 2019,

p. 226). Algorithms originate with human developers, and it remains possible to retain "agency in – and responsibility for – how these systems ultimately operate and influence the media" (Diakopoulos, 2019, p. 242). The "coevolution of technology, people, and society" through AI could be informed by human values and norms, and may benefit from "hybrid" processes that favor "precision" and "authenticity" (pp. 241–251). That said, an opposing view suggests:

> This will never be sleek and mathematically precise; it is messy, just like life. It is clear from decades of research in communication, sociology, and science and technology studies that technological systems do not erase social problems but merely shift and obscure them. Every technological system reflects the conscious and unconscious bias of its makers; AI is no different.
>
> (Broussard, 2019, p. 678)

Amazon Alexa, Apple Siri, and other voice command devices offer hands-free navigation. On its face, these technologies make online access simple and convenient. However, the introduction of a microphone into private homes also is a serious privacy challenge. For example, Amazon Echo Dot audio was used by police investigating a Florida woman's death (Francis & Henault, 2019). The company responded that, "Amazon does not disclose customer information in response to government demands unless we're required to do so to comply with a legally valid and binding order," and "audio is not streamed to the Cloud or recorded unless it detects a wake word" (paras. 13–14).

Trust should be earned over time. Social media offer the opportunity for users to evaluate the influencers rather than accept media agenda setting. Responsible social media conversation takes ownership of communication. Users should be able to tell their own stories and judge those of others. Rather than a reflex, social media sharing should be a thoughtful activity. From professional strategies and tactics to simple user interaction, a media literacy approach offers the potential to use social media in promoting a better society.

Newer sites, such as TikTok, emphasize entertainment value. The competition to achieve celebrity status combined with marketing exploitation may spark new global issues. The Influence Grid (2019) ranks top TikTok influencers by use of tags, number of followers, average number of views, favorites, and engagement. Individuals and brands rushed to the swarm of the Chinese app downloads and potential for access to large audiences (Malnik, 2019). In light of the potential, some sports brands were quick to embrace TikTok as a fresh way to reach fans (Moran, 2019).

From Dubai to Shanghai, social networking has become a normal behavior for individual users desiring to present a version of the self by interacting through online communication and cultivating a sense of community – sometimes across great distances. At the same time, global social media communication features commercial marketing and advertising that is very similar to what developed in the United States.

Among the social media trends to watch: the popularity of messaging, the desire to authenticate users and content, the increased development of augmented and virtual reality, and the proliferation of **chatbots** – "a kind of artificial intelligence that can have a conversation with someone" (Rohampton, 2017, para. 13); **blockchain** Internet of Things (IoT) "ecosystems" (Dickson, 2016, para. 1); and sophisticated content marketing action based upon millions of social media users (Ciotti, 2016). Marketers want to optimize sites and conversion rates to increase online consumer purchasing, and social media strategies will be a part of these efforts (Rouke, 2017). Although these marketing forces are real, a part of social media communication remains driven by individuals' fundamental motivation for interactivity, interpersonal communication, self-expression, and entertainment (Hunt, Atkin, & Krishnan, 2012).

The future of social media communication is likely to feature continued improvement of smaller and lighter hardware driven by advances in software programming. The key questions must focus on how people, organizations, and businesses will use these new technologies to communicate across SNS and other social online spaces. For journalists, public relations professionals, advertisers, and marketers, social media communication defines what Microsoft's Bill Gates once called "The Road Ahead." The challenges and opportunities involve understanding key concepts, defining best practices, examining data, operating within a legal framework, and striving to be ethical. For those willing to take the time to master social media communication, individual and professional rewards are likely to follow.

FIGURE 12.3 *College students browsed Apple laptop computers on a city campus in Hangzhou, China, where mobile smartphones became very popular by 2012. The technology spread across the globe. India and dozens of countries experienced huge growth in Internet and social media use in recent years.*

From Instagram Stories skippable advertising (Constine, 2017) to the optimization of Twitter bios (Mullin, 2014), individual users and large brands have tried to capture the interests of millennials, Gen Z and other age groups – no wonder Snapchat and Instagram continue to battle for mobile leadership (Heine, 2016a). Snapchat bested Google Glass with its innovative company-sponsored lenses (Jacobson, 2016). The fluid environment offers spirited debate about the need for new features, such as a Twitter edit button (Oremus, 2016), as well as concern when it and other sites violate social norms (Flynn, 2016). We seem to be too far down the social media road to simply leave a social media site when we are unhappy about content and questionable behavior, such as trolling (Gibson, 2017). Twitter may have a competitive disadvantage to Instagram, for example, where there are efforts to combat online harassment (Peyser, 2016). Instagram continues to rapidly innovate the app. A lot of recent focus is on paid advertising tools, such as a checkout feature, donation stickers, and tagging of products and services (Julian, 2019).

Social marketers were nearly drowning in predictions over key trends that help define the future of social media communication. Among the most intriguing in the years ahead:

- A return to personal conversation with a focus on media storytelling content quality, and noise reduction

- Understanding appropriate uses for chatbots, machine learning, and computer-generated writing and editing

- Strategic paid promotion within a larger advertising budget context

- Targeted use of video on key channels that offer a return on investment

- Emphasis on measurement analytics that demonstrate increased business revenue and strategic outcomes

- Branding through the ethical use of social media influence.

(Stahl, 2019)

Social media marketing strategies frequently involve moving from an existing site and using previously proven tactics on new platforms that may communicate in fresh ways. At the same time, efforts to include corporate social responsibility (CSR) campaigns may not feel authentic to younger audiences. Change is difficult and frequently challenges existing social norms. The use of memes by millennials, for example, has been identified as a vehicle to speak "truth to power," and "resist, comment on, and point out the failings" of race, gender, or age in coming from "a space of creative resistance" (Maddox, 2019, p. 153). Social media developments may suggest a set of marketing trends:

- Social media scams and scammers disappoint audiences and lead to fatigue.

- Facebook responded to public criticism by paying more attention to user privacy, and also moved to hide public "likes" data.

- Instagram Checkout was an early step within the integration of shopping within social media posts.

- Instagram focused on special creator accounts for public figures.

- Google updated its verification system for YouTube creators and other content.

- Regulators appeared ready to respond to TikTok and other social media threats.

(Sehl, 2019)

With about 3.5 billion estimated social media communication users, it is clear that most heavily rely upon popular sites (Patel, 2019). As social media managers reject vanity metrics in favor of goals, strategies, and tactics, some users responded by exercising more personal privacy. It is not that consumers have rejected social selling. Rather, they appear to demand "authentic" and "meaningful connections" that "nurture trust" (paras. 22–30).

It is not that social media communication offers a utopia, for there are clearly important concerns about data privacy, socially responsible behavior, and media literacy. Users have become more aware of the dangers of data privacy loss within social media. While crowdfunding opens possibilities for innovation, some social media communications in this area are scams. From disinformation to promotion of user narcissism, social media represent a paradox of good and bad. Online videos, photos, and other rich media content have become increasingly important and compete with traditional media for attention. Technological advancement had few boundaries. Facebook, for example, was said to be working on a way to read brain waves, and social media communication of the future could be physiological. In the end, though, it is not possible to reverse the technological momentum of the last four decades. The most we may hope for is to harness capabilities, think about best uses, and make reasoned decisions about the future.

DISCUSSION QUESTIONS: STRATEGIES AND TACTICS

1. How would social media literacy improve the quality of communication within your social network? Crowdsource your friends or followers, and ask: What is important to you about social media? What concerns you about the future?

2. Is there a balance between free expression and responsible social media communication? How does media literacy promote user understanding?

3. In what ways are social media promoting social change or the status quo? How do you think this might be different going forward?

4. How can an organization use social media to drive specific positive outcomes without sacrificing ethics?

REFERENCES

Albarran, A. B. (Ed.) (2013). *The Social Media Industries*. New York, NY: Routledge.

Anderson, M. (2019, December 21). Twitter, Facebook Ban Fake Users; Some Had AI-Created Photos. *Associated Press*. https://apnews.com/7c9fd798212cac63925d205142e811ea

Baer, J. (2019, January 6). 5 Ways to Get More Customers and Improve Customer Experience with SMS. *Convince and Convert*. Email; Your 2019 Content Strategy: 5 Trends You Can't Ignore. www.convinceandconvert.com/content-marketing/content-trends-2019/

Bagdikian, B. H. (2000). *The Media Monopoly*, sixth edition, pp. 239, 241. Boston, MA: Beacon Press.

Baran, S. J., & Davis, D. K. (2000). *Mass Communication Theory: Foundations, Ferment, and Future*. Belmont, CA: Wadsworth/Thomson.

Barnes, S. B. (2003). *Computer-Mediated Communication, Human-to-Human Communication Across the Internet*. Boston, MA: Allyn and Bacon.

Beckett, C., with Ball, J. (2012). *Wikileaks, News in the Networked Era*. Cambridge, UK: Polity Press.

Best, K. (2005). Rethinking the Globalization Movement: Toward a Cultural Theory of Contemporary Democracy and Communication. *Communication and Critical/Cultural Studies 2*, 214–237.

Biddle, S. (2014, December 20). Justine Sacco Is Good at Her Job, and How I Came to Peace with Her. *Gawker*. http://gawker.com/justine-sacco-is-good-at-her-job-and-how-i-came-to-pea-1653022326

Bostick, C. (2017, January 4). Social Media Extends Long Arm of Law. *Observer-Dispatch*. www.uticaod.com/news/20170104/social-media-extends-long-arm-of-law

Bowcott, O. (2011, July 5). Contempt of Court Rules are Designed to Avoid Trial by Media. *The Guardian*. www.theguardian.com/law/2011/jul/05/contempt-court-rules-trial-media

Briggs, M. (2020). *Journalism Next, A Practical Guide to Digital Reporting and Publishing*, fourth Edition. Los Angeles: SAGE.

Broussard, M. (2019, Autumn). Center Humans, Not Machines, in AI for Journalism. *Journalism & Mass Communication Quarterly 96*(3), 678.

Brown, A. (2011, March-April). Relationships, Community, and Identity in the New Virtual Society. *The Futurist*, 29–31, 34.

CBS News (2016, May 24). Mount Everest Climber on Snapchat Accomplishes Rare Feat. *CBS News*. www.cbsnews.com/news/cory-richards-mount-everest-climber-documenting-summit-on-snapchat-reaches-the-top/

Chafkin, M. (2016, November 30). Confessions of an Instagram Influencer. *Bloomberg*. www.bloomberg.com/news/features/2016-11-30/confessions-of-an-instagram-influencer

Ciotti, G. (2016, May 21). What 3 Million Visitors Taught us about Content Marketing. *Growth Hackers*. https://growthhackers.com/articles/what-3-million-visitors-taught-us-about-content-marketing

Coddington, M. (2019). *Aggregating the News, Secondhand Knowledge and the Erosion of Journalistic Authority*. New York: Columbia University Press.

Collins, B. (2019, December 20). Facebook Says Pro-Trump Media Outlet used Artificial Intelligence to Create Fake People and Push Conspiracies. *NBS News*. www.nbcnews.com/tech/tech-news/facebook-says-pro-trump-media-outlet-used-artificial-intelligence-create-n1105951

Constine, J. (2016, November 1). Instagram Tests Shoppable Photo Tags. *TechCrunch*. https://techcrunch.com/2016/11/01/instagram-shoppable-photos/

Constine, J. (2017, January 11). Instagram Stories Hits 150M Daily Users, Launches Skippable Ads. *TechCrunch*. https://techcrunch.com/2017/01/11/instagram-stories-hits-150m-daily-users-launches-skippable-ads/

Coronado, R. (2006, April 27). Man Pleads No Contest to Molesting Girl, *Sacramento Bee*, p. B2.

Dewey, C. (2016, May 26). The (Very) Dark Side of Live Streaming that No One Seems Able to Stop. *The Washington Post*. www.washingtonpost.com/news/the-intersect/wp/2016/05/26/the-very-dark-side-of-live-streaming-that-no-one-seems-able-to-stop/

Diakopoulos, N. (2019). *Automating the News, How Algorithms are Rewriting the Media.* Cambridge, MA: Harvard University Press.

Dickson, B. (2016, December 27). How Blockchain Can Create the World's Biggest Supercomputer. *TechCrunch.* https://techcrunch.com/2016/12/27/how-blockchain-can-create-the-worlds-biggest-supercomputer/

Dimitrova, K. (2013, December 21). Tweet on AIDS in Africa Sparks Internet Outrage. *ABC News.* http://abcnews.go.com/International/tweet-aids-africa-sparks-internet-outrage/

Dobrow, J. (2013, December 4). Do as I Say, Not as I Do: Teachers, Cellphones and Media Literacy. *The Huffington Post.* www.huffingtonpost.com/julie-dobrow/do-as-i-say-not-as-i-do-t_b_4379085.html

Dominick, J. R. (2009). *The Dynamics of Mass Communication,* tenth edition. New York, NY: McGraw-Hill.

Flynn, K. (2016, November 17). Twitter CEO Apologizes for White Supremacy Ad. *Mashable.* http://mashable.com/2016/11/17/twitter-white-supremacist-ad

Francis, E., & Henault, R. (2019, November 1). Audio from Amazon Echo Dot Could Sway Investigation into Woman Killed by Spear. *ABC News.* https://abcnews.go.com/US/audio-amazon-echo-dot-sway-investigation-woman-killed/story?id=66700090

Garrett, R. K., & Danziger, J. N. (2011, March). The Internet Electorate. *Communications of the ACM 54*(3), 117–123.

Gibson, C. (2017, January 10). Will Leaving Twitter Make Life Better for These Outspoken Liberals? *The Washington Post.* www.washingtonpost.com/lifestyle/style/will-leaving-twitter-make-life-better-for-these-outspoken-liberals/2017/01/10/4255836c-d42a-11e6-945a-76f69a399dd5_story.html

Graber, D. A. (2006). *Mass Media & American Politics,* seventh edition, p. 196. Washington, DC: CQ Press.

Green, S. C., Lodato, M. J., Schwalbe, C. B., & Silcock, B. W. (2012). *News Now, Visual Storytelling in the Digital Age.* Boston, MA: Pearson.

Hart, A. (2001). Researching Media Education in Schools in the United Kingdom. *Studies in Media & Information Literacy Education 1,* 1–5. www.utpjournals.com/simile

Haynes Writer, J., & Chávez Chávez, R. (2001). Storied Lives, Dialog – Retro-reflections: Melding Critical Multicultural Education and Critical Race Theory for Pedagogical Transformation. *Studies in Media & Information Literacy Education 1,* 1–4. www.utpjournals.com/simile

Heine, C. (2016a, October 30). Here's What Gen Z and Millenials Love and Hate about Instagram and Snapchat. *AdWeek.* www.adweek.com/news/technology/heres-what-gen-z-and-millennials-love-and-hate-about-instagram-and-snapchat-174318

Heine, C. (2016b, May 19). Snapchat Advertising Data Reveals What Kinds of Brands Have Bought into the App. *AdWeek.* www.adweek.com/news/technology/snapchat-advertising-data-reveals-what-kinds-brands-have-bought-171562

Hilt, M. L., & Lipschultz, J. H. (2005). *Mass Media, an Aging Population, and the Baby Boomers.* Mahwah, NJ: Lawrence Erlbaum.

Hobbs, R. (1997). Expanding the Concept of Literacy. In R. Kubey (Ed.), *Media Literacy in the Information Age,* pp. 163–183. New Brunswick, NJ: Transaction Publishers.

Hobbs, R. (2016). Epilogue. In R. Hobbs (Ed.), *Exploring the Roots of Digital and Media Literacy through Personal Narrative,* pp. 233–236. Philadelphia, PA: Temple University Press.

Holmes, A. (2019, October 22). A Yale Professor and Goldman Sachs Veteran are Teaming up on an Eccentric New Blockchain-powered Social Network to Try to Make Facebook Irrelevant. *Business Insider.* www.businessinsider.com/david-gelernter-revolution-populi-social-network-trying-to-disrupt-facebook-2019-10

Huffaker, D. A., & Calvert, S. L. (2005). Gender, Identity, and Language Use in Teenage Blogs. *Journal of Computer-Mediated Communication 10*(1). http://jcmc.indiana.edu/vol10/issue2/huffaker.html

Hunt, D., Atkin, D., & Krishnan, A. (2012). The Influence of Computer-Mediated Communication Apprehension on Motives for Facebook Use. *Journal of Broadcasting & Electronic Media 56*(2), 187–202.

Hunter, M. (2016, August 2). Instagram Launches 'Stories.' A Product to Take on Snapchat. www.cnbc.com/2016/08/02/instagram-launches-stories-a-product-to-take-on-snapchat.htmlCNBC

Influence Grid (2019). Find the Best TikTok Influencers. www.influencegrid.com/

Jacobson, R. (2016, October 24). Snapchat's Sponsored Lenses are Making the Company A Lot of Money. *Business Insider.* www.businessinsider.com/snapchats-sponsored-lenses-are-making-the-company-a-lot-of-money-2016-10

Jenkins, H. (2016). Henry Jenkins on John Fiske. In R. Hobbs (Ed.), *Exploring the Roots of Digital and Media Literacy through Personal Narrative*, pp. 138–152. Philadelphia, PA: Temple University Press.

Johnson, C. K., & Babwin, D. (2017, January 6). Police: 4 Charged in Facebook Live Attack to Appear in Court. *AP.* https://apnews.com/7474fef837284608be0aa6cd5a92b698

Julian, J. (2019, October 25). 12 Key Instagram Updates from 2019 that You Need to Know About. *Social Media Today.* www.socialmediatoday.com/news/12-key-instagram-updates-from-2019-that-you-need-to-know-about/565607/

Kupianen, R. (2013). *Media and Digital Literacies in Secondary School.* New York, NY: Peter Lang.

Lealand, G. (2001). Some Things Change, Some Things Remain the Same: New Zealand Children and Media Use. *Studies in Media & Information Literacy Education 1*, 1–4. www.utpjournals.com/simile

Leon, H. (2020, January 21). Elon Musk's Advice to Jack Dorsey on Fixing Twitter Seems Trifling at Best. *Observer.* https://observer.com/2020/01/elon-musk-jack-dorsey-twitter-advice/

Levine, P. (2005). The Problem of Online Misinformation and the Role of Schools. *Studies in Media & Information Literacy Education 5*(1), 1–11. www.utpress.utoronto.ca/journal/ejournals/simile

Li, C., & Stacks, D. (2015). *Measuring the Impact of Social Media on Business Profit & Success, A Fortune 500 Perspective.* New York: Peter Lang.

Lipschultz, J. H., & Hilt, M. L. (2005). Media & Information Literacy Theory and Research: Thoughts from the Co-Editors. *Studies in Media & Information Literacy Education 5*, 1. www.utpress.utoronto.ca/journal/ejournals/simile

Maddox, J. (2019). Calling Out Racism for What It Is: Memes, BBQ Becky and the Oppositional Gaze. In L. S. Coleman and C. P. Campbell (Eds.), *Media, Myth, and Millennials*, pp. 139–155. Lanham, MD: Lexington Books.

Madrigaldec, A. C. (2013, December). 2013: The Year 'The Stream' Crested. *The Atlantic.* www.theatlantic.com/technology/archive/2013/12/2013-the-year-the-stream-crested/282202/

Malnik, J. (2019, October 9). How to Get Started with TikTok: A Guide for Marketers. *Social Media Examiner.* www.socialmediaexaminer.com/how-to-get-started-with-tiktok-guide-marketers/

Mandkur, P. (2016, December 26). #taimur: Social Media & the Mob Mentality. *LinkedIn Pulse.* www.linkedin.com/pulse/taimur-social-media-mob-mentality-prabhakar-mundkur

Marcus, G. (2019, November 30). An Epidemic of AI Misinformation. *The Gradient.* https://thegradient.pub/an-epidemic-of-ai-misinformation/

Mathison, D. (2009). *Be the Media*. New Hyde Park, NY: Natural E Creative Group.

Matney, L. (2019, November 3). Week in Review: #DeleteLinkedIn. *TechCrunch*. https://techcrunch.com/2019/11/03/week-in-review-deletelinkedin/

McChesney, R. W. (1999). *Rich Media, Poor Democracy, Communication Politics in Dubious Times*, p. 301. Urbana, IL: University of Illinois Press.

McEwan, B. (2019, December 19). Can't Delete: Why We Stay On Social Media. *Psychology Today*. www.psychologytoday.com/us/blog/the-networked-relationship/201912/cant-delete-why-we-stay-social-media

Media Literacy (2003). Center for Media Literacy. www.medialit.org/reading_room/article37.html

Miller, R. (2019, December 2). AWS Announces DeepComposer, A Machine-Learning Keyboard for Developers. *TechCrunch*. https://techcrunch.com/2019/12/02/aws-announces-deepcomposer-a-machine-learning-keyboard-for-developers/

Moeller, S. (2016). Susan Moeller on Roland Barthes. In R. Hobbs (Ed.), *Exploring the Roots of Digital and Media Literacy through Personal Narrative*, pp. 222–232. Philadelphia, PA: Temple University Press.

Moran, E. (2019, December 4). Sports Media Brands Using TikTok to Advance Digital Growth. *Front Office Sports*. https://frntofficesport.com/tiktok-sports-media-brands/

Morse, J. (2019, December 17). Jack Dorsey Just Unfollowed Mark Zuckerberg on Twitter in Spectacular Fashion. *Mashable*. https://mashable.com/article/jack-dorsey-unfollowed-mark-zuckerberg-twitter/

Mullin, B. (2014, December 17). 7 Journalist Twitter Bios We Love (And Why We Love Them). *Poynter*. www.poynter.org/2014/7-journalist-twitter-bios-we-love-and-why-we-love-them/308831/

Nark, J. (2016, December 7). When Free Speech Comes at a Cost. *The Inquirer*. www.philly.com/philly/news/405131696.html

Ng, A. (2016, December 28). Facebook, Google Top Out Most Popular Apps in 2016. *CNet*. www.cnet.com/news/facebook-google-top-out-uss-most-popular-apps-in-2016/

NodeXL (2020, January 1). #CES2020. http://nodexlgraphgallery.org/Pages/Graph.aspx?graphID=219736

Novet, J. (2017, January 6). Facebook Says People Sent 63 Billion WhatsApp Messages on New Year's Eve. *VentureBeat*. http://venturebeat.com/2017/01/06/facebook-says-people-sent-63-billion-whatsapp-messages-on-new-years-eve/

Oremus, W. (2016, July 12). Why Twitter Won't Give Us an Edit Button. *Slate*. www.slate.com/blogs/future_tense/2016/07/12/twitter_needs_an_edit_button_here_s_why_it_doesn_t_have_one.html

Patel, D. (2019, December 20). 12 Social Media Trends to Watch in 2020. *Entrepreneur*. www.entrepreneur.com/article/343863

Pavlik, J. (2019). *Journalism and Virtual Reality, How Experiential Media are Transforming News*. New York: Columbia University Press.

Pew Research Center. (2017, January 12). Social Media Fact Sheet. www.pewinternet.org/fact-sheet/social-media/

Pew Research Center. (2019, April 10). Share of U.S. Adults Using Social Media, Including Facebook, Is Mostly Unchanged since 2018. www.pewresearch.org/fact-tank/2019/04/10/share-of-u-s-adults-using-social-media-including-facebook-is-mostly-unchanged-since-2018/

Peyser, E. (2016, July 30). Why Instagram's Plans to Combat Online Harassment Won't Work on Twitter. *Gizmodo*. http://gizmodo.com/why-instagrams-plans-to-combat-online-harassment-wont-w-1784582206

Potter, J. W. (2001/2008). *Media Literacy*, second edition and fourth edition. Thousand Oaks, CA: Sage.

Price, R. (2019, December 11). Twitter Is Trying to Build A Decentralized Social Media Service that Could Transform Its Business – Or Present New Kinds of Headaches. *Business Insider.* www.businessinsider.com/bluesky-twitter-team-decentralised-social-media-2019-12.

Rodman, G. (2001). *Making Sense of Media.* Needham Heights, MA: Allyn and Bacon.

Rohampton, J., (2017, January 3). 5 Social Media Trends That Will Dominate 2017. *Forbes.* www.forbes.com/sites/jimmyrohampton/2017/01/03/5-social-media-trends-that-will-dominate-2017/#1c6180fa141f

Ronson, J. (2015, February 12). How One Stupid Tweet Blew Up Justine Sacco's Life. *The New York Times.* www.nytimes.com/2015/02/15/magazine/how-one-stupid-tweet-ruined-justine-saccos-life.html

Rouke, P. (2017, January 6). Five Predictions for Conversion Rate Optimisation (CRO) in 2017. *eConsultancy.* https://econsultancy.com/blog/68648-five-predictions-for-conversion-rate-optimisation-cro-in-2017/

Seargent, P., & Tagg, C. (2018). Critical Digital Literacy Education in the 'Fake News' Era. In K. Reedy and J. Parker (Eds.), *Digital Literacy Unpacked*, pp. 179–189. London: Facet Publishing.

Sehl, K. (2019, December 17). 8 of the Biggest Social Media Moments in 2019. *Hootsuite.* https://blog.hootsuite.com/biggest-social-media-moments-2019/

Shapiro, J. J., & Hughes, S. K. (1996, March/April). Information Literacy as a Liberal Art, Enlightenment Proposals for a New Curriculum, *Educom Review 31*, 1. www.educause.edu/pub/er/review/reviewArticles/31231.html (June 19, 2006).

Silverblatt, A. (1995). *Media Literacy, Keys to Interpreting Media Messages*, pp. 2–3, 128–131, 303. Westport, CT: Praeger.

Silverblatt, A., & Zlobin, N. (2004). *International Communications: A Media Literacy Approach.* Armonk, NY: M.E. Sharpe.

Spayd, L. (2016, August 20). Facebook Live: Too Much, Too Soon. *The New York Times.* www.nytimes.com/2016/08/21/public-editor/facebook-live-too-much-too-soon.html

Stahl, S. (2019, December 10). Back to the Future? 90 Content Marketing Predictions for 2020. *Content Marketing Institute.* https://contentmarketinginstitute.com/2019/12/content-marketing-predictions-2020/

Stern, M. (2014, January 22). "To Be Takei" Traces George Takei's Journey from Japanese Internment Camp to Cultural Icon. *The Daily Beast.* www.thedailybeast.com/articles/2014/01/22/to-be-takei-traces-george-takei-s-journey-from-japanese-internment-camps-to-culturalicon.html

Stevenson, N. (1995). *Understanding Media Cultures.* London: Sage.

Tewksbury, D., & Rittenberg, J. (2012). *News on the Internet, Information and Citizenship in the 21st Century.* Oxford, UK: Oxford University Press.

Torres, C. (2017, January 4). Innovation: Don't Want the Public to See Your Newsroom Gossip? Don't Put It on Slack. *Poynter.* www.poynter.org/2017/dont-want-the-public-to-see-your-newsrooms-gossip-dont-put-it-on-slack/444202/

University of Kansas, Board of Regents (2013). Suspensions, Terminations and Dismissals (6)(b) Other. www.kansasregents.org/policy_chapter_ii_c_suspensions

Vered, K. O. (2001). Intermediary Space and Media Competency: Children's Media Play in "Out of School Hours Care" Facilities in Australia. *Studies in Media & Information Literacy Education 1*, 1–4. www.utpjournals.com/simile

Von Rosen, V. (2017, January 2). LinkedIn Changes: What Marketers Need to Know. *Social Media Examiner.* www.socialmediaexaminer.com/linkedin-changes-what-marketers-need-to-know/

Webster, J. G. (2014). *The Marketplace of Attention, How Audiences Take Shape in a Digital Age.* Cambridge, MA: The MIT Press.

Westcott, B. (2016, December 26). Duped by Fake News Story, Pakistan Minister Threatens Nuclear War with Israel. *CNN*. www.cnn.com/2016/12/26/middleeast/israel-pakistan-fake-news-nuclear/

Widzinski, L. (2001). The Evolution of Media Librarianship: A Tangled History of Change and Constancy. *Studies in Media & Information Literacy Education 1*, 1–4. www.utpjournals.com/simile

Wright, I. J. (2016, April 28). 4 Metrics to Measure on Snapchat. *PR News Online*. www.prnewsonline.com/4-snapchat-metrics

Yates, B. L. (2004). Applying Diffusion Theory: Adoption of Media Literacy Programs in Schools. *Studies in Media & Information Literacy Education 4*, 1–4. www.utpress.utoronto.ca/journal/ejournals/simile

Glossary

Advertising—paid and commercial messages purchased by an advertiser or agency representative. Sponsored content or "native advertising" mimics the look and feel of editorial or news content.

Advertising Value Equivalency (AVE)—is a largely discredited model of placing a dollar figure on the value of earned media, such as a news story, and relating it to advertising rates. It was used as a way for PR people to claim ROI for their media relations work.

Adoption—in the diffusion model refers to people who use a new product, service, process or idea.

Algorithm—computer code that filters and organizes social media content based upon a set of goals and objectives.

Analytics—measurement of social media behavior through a variety of metrics. A stream of new tools has been developed to present real-time and near real-time data on social media dashboards, such as Google Analytics.

Apps—short for *applications*, an app is software, for use on a desktop, laptop, tablet or smartphone, that allows the user to apply the power of system software for a particular purpose.

Augmented reality (AR)—use of geographic data and mobile smartphone data and images to augment physical spaces with vast amounts of computer data.

Authority—the presence of links and backlinks builds SEO authority and tends to improve page rank.

Benchmark data—use of foundational data within a social media campaign. By benchmarking, a social media entity may set and track longer-term goals and objectives, as well as effectiveness of tactics.

Best practices—standard practices of an industry, developed gradually, that are the processes and social media content that have worked well over time.

Big data—huge and complex data collection over time that typically requires cloud computing and sophisticated algorithms designed to interpret it.

Blockchain—connection of big data computing, part of the Internet of Things (IoT).

Blog—these are online sites, often owned media, in which somewhat formal and regular posts (information and commentary) are published. Early blogs were characterized by authenticity, which is the idea that the author presents a more "real" and unfiltered identity.

Board—Pinterest uses the term "board" to reflect the online space where users "pin" content to a virtual message board.

Bounce rate—percentage of sessions with a single user interaction on a website.

Brand ambassadors—support brands by sharing their stories and broadening reach.

Brand evangelists—tend to be fans of products or services with a desire to spread enthusiasm.

Brand storytellers—narrative influencers promoting a specific brand.

Branding—the marketing technique of emphasizing a brand for a product, service, organization or individual. A logo, face or even a song may reinforce the brand for consumers.

Breaking news—real-time events and news that happen as developing news stories. Traditional media emphasize breaking news, and this content frequently is spread on social networks.

Business-to-business (B2B)—business between two businesses rather than between a business and consumer.

Buzz—the aggregate social network activity from a word, term, phrase or other content. On Twitter, for example, we can track #BreakingNews buzz on a graph of time (X) and total number of tweets (Y).

C-suite—top-level corporate executives making key decisions that may include social media policies.

Chatbots—artificial intelligence that generates an automatic response to a social media user each time she or he responds.

Citizen journalism—individuals use online platforms to distribute news created as non-professional citizen journalists. This content may be "hyperlocal," with a neighborhood focus that does not attract large enough audiences to interest mainstream media.

Click-through rates (CTR)—a measure of user clicks on sponsored results.

Community—a core CMC concept that describes how individuals create groups, including interest groups, by sharing information within social networks.

Computer-mediated communication (CMC)—a social and research construct that begins to explain the nature of social network and social media behavior and culture.

Convergence—an early description of the merging of previously separate media, such as print (newspapers and magazines), broadcasting (radio and television), advertising, public relations and marketing. So-called "convergence newsrooms" were developed to allow content producers to work across online media platforms.

Conversation monitoring—the process of monitoring online activity, emphasizing engagement through responding to comments, reactions and posts by others.

Conversion—marketers convert social media activity to sales.

Cost of Ignoring (COI)—a newer metric developed in response to criticism of the lack of social media ROI; it emphasizes the need for online engagement.

Cost Per Click (CPC)—a social media alternative advertising measure to the traditional cost per thousand mainstream method for pricing commercial messages. CPC charges advertisers for every audience user click.

Cost Per Thousand (CPM)—a traditional advertising price method estimating how much to charge for every 1,000 audience members who will see the ad. For example, one online national video service charges about $25 CPM. The Super Bowl, which has the largest national audience, has increased over the years from $5 to $27 CPM, while a popular primetime show may cost $35 CPM.

Credibility—is related to trust and believability. In media research, we talk about source and message credibility. The more content has both, the more likely audience members will be to trust it.

Crowdfunding—raising money by making online appeals that leverage social networking and social sharing.

Crowdsourcing—social networks allow individuals to interact in real time. Crowdsourcing is defined as a method for gathering, filtering, generating and distributing information within a social network. On Twitter, for example, crowdsourcing is used during breaking news to separate facts from rumors.

Customer relationship management (CRM)—organizes engagement around customer satisfaction, loyalty and retention. The software is used to track customers and potential sales leads.

Digital Rights Management (DRM)—systems of control over content access to seek user payments.

Diffusion—the spread of new ideas, new practices, new processes and new products. Diffusion research identifies the earliest innovators (2.5%), early adopters (13.5%), early majority (34%), late majority (34%), and laggards (16%). The percentage of adopters (Y) is graphed using an S-shaped curve over time (X).

Direct Message (DM)—In Twitter, followers may send private messages that are not broadcast on the larger network.

Early adopters—in a diffusion cycle, the first to adopt new technologies and/or ideas.

Earned exposure—customer reviewer expressions of positive feelings about products or services.

Earned media—public relations professionals work to receive positive attention for their clients through content that is not paid advertising. Earned media may be the product of media relations, a campaign, real-time engagement or other activities.

eCommerce—online sales and business.

Electronic Frontier Foundation (EFF)—organization promoting free and open Internet.

Electronic Word of Mouth (eWOM)—an extension of face-to-face communication applied to social media marketing.

Emoji—small, colorful images used to express feelings, these grew from text emoticons developed in the 1990s.

Engaged Journalism—newsroom use of social media engagement tactics, such as chats, events, and other opportunities to interact with audience members in a community.

Engagement—the term that describes strengthening social network interaction from passive to more active. It goes beyond passive viewing to clicking on a link, liking content, sharing content and responding to content in some way that can be seen by social media users.

Entrepreneurs—social media sites have been created and developed by the technology sector, which values an innovative culture. Personal computer hardware and software were first developed by young entrepreneurs, such as Bill Gates and Steve Jobs, and the current industry features inventors and their start-ups.

Facebook Insights—a dashboard showing social media managers' performance over time of fan page posts.

Facebook Live—a real-time streaming video app within Facebook that allows for viewing, commenting, and use of like, love, sad and angry emoji.

Fake news—a term applied to propaganda, distortion, and manipulation or lies shared with an intent to deceive readers.

Fan—a Facebook user may like a page and become a fan. By doing this, the posts on this page appear on the user's news feed.

Fremium—sites may offer a free trial to advance the diffusion process in the marketing funnel toward purchase.

Gatekeepers—those who perform a traditional news editorial function of story selection.

General Data Protection Regulation (GDPR)—a European Union (EU) legal privacy framework applied to personal data that U.S. sites adopted in 2018.

Hardware—the physical computing equipment, such as a desktop, laptop, tablet or smartphone. We also speak of components – keyboard, mouse, monitor, router, modem, etc. – as hardware.

Hashflag—a paid emoji that automatically appears when a promoted hashtag is used.

Hashjacking—hijacking a hashtag already in use on Twitter for an event.

Hashtag (#)—the number sign is used on Twitter and, more recently, Facebook as a filtering device. By searching for and using hashtags, subsets of the larger feed can be seen and used.

Human-computer-interaction (HCI)—early research into how humans engaged with computer hardware and software.

Hybrid media—new media that incorporate some older media rules, such as news editorial practices.

Hyperlinks—Web links to other content via an Internet URL address.

Idea starter—a type of user identified by Edelmen TweetLevel as someone who begins discussion or is an early participant. Specifically, these users on Twitter are rewarded with a high score for "originating detailed opinion and thought leadership."

Identity—what we present online through the use of words, photographs, sounds, videos, emoticons, avatar or other means. Each time we decide to communicate (and even when we do not) we suggest an identity to social network site users.

Impressions—awareness of information, such as from seeing it during a search.

Influence—users with a lot of fans, followers or connections tend to be considered influencers. Celebrities' large reach affords them monetized influence, but micro-influencers with 1,000 to 100,000 followers also may be influential due to higher engagement with fans.

Innovation—a business culture favoring change over stability.

Integrated Marketing Communication (IMC)—planning and strategies that integrate traditional advertising, marketing and PR approaches.

Interaction—each engagement with another SNS account reflects a decision to interact. Interaction and engagement are a key foundation for social media use.

Internet of Things (IoT)—increasing use of online commands to control home and business devices.

Internet Protocol (IP)—an address number attached to a user computer or location.

Key Performance Indicators (KPI)—continuous monitoring of important business variables.

Keywords—words used within SEO to move page placement higher in a search by relating to common user language.

LinkedIn—professional business network site purchased by Microsoft.

Live tweeting—during an event or breaking news, eyewitnesses and commentators may tweet in real time with updates on any new information.

Location-based services (LBS)—designed to allow users to check in at locations.

Marketing—promoting and selling products and services targeted at a specific market. Research is usually utilized to focus marketing, which may involve use of advertising and social media marketing.

Measurement error—all measurement has error, and researchers estimate amounts.

Media cloverleaf—Edelman PR divides the media environment into four overlapping parts: traditional media, owned media, hybrid media and social media.

Media communication—a theoretical perspective that moves away from mass communication and mass audiences toward fragmentation.

Media literacy—is a way to describe the need for media audience members to possess skills that allow them to deconstruct and understand media content. For example, an information literacy approach would emphasize knowledge and learning. Media literacy scholars suggest that children need to be taught to realize when they are being sold products and services through sophisticated advertising and marketing campaigns.

Meme—social media content that features cultural imitation. Production typically uses easily identifiable characters, iterations and humor. For example, there is a persistent use of an image from the 1971 *Willy Wonka and the Chocolate Factory* movie because of an early meme generator site.

Metrics—the measurement of behavior within social media. A variety of social media "dashboards," such as Google Analytics, Sprout, Chartbeat, Hootsuite, Cision, Tweetdeck, Sprout Social are in use.

Microblog—short, or limited space, blogging began with Twitter and its 140, and later 280-character limit. Micro-blogging became a genre to comment through without taking the time and energy to publish a more formal blog site. Even for those blogging, microblogs are used to push out links and drive traffic back to the site.

Micro-influencers—on Instagram and other popular social media sites tend to have about 1,000 followers. Brands offer free products or payments to reach individual social networks.

Mobile communication—smartphones and tablets connected through WiFi or cellphone data. Mobile Internet connections allow for the use of a wide variety of social media apps.

Natural language generation (NLG)—uses automated software to turn data into language, such as for a chatbot or simple news stories. The organization, structure and compilation of content is accomplished by applying AI computer code to a goal.

Narrative—use of storytelling techniques, such as a story arc.

Network visualization—social networks generate large amounts of data that may be viewed as a series of network maps of communication hubs and spokes. Visualization depicts through graphs the social space between SNS accounts.

Non-Governmental Organization (NGO)—entities operating in the non-profit sector rather than government or commercial for-profit businesses.

Objectivity—a norm within journalism placing value and emphasis on balance, fairness and telling at least two sides to every story. In the second half of the 20th century, journalists strived for objectivity. Recent scholars see it as an unachievable ideal. Social media users of social networks frequently emphasize subjectivity and opinion.

Opportunity costs—the cost of using money on one expense and not having it available for other possibilities.

Organic—is a way to describe naturally evolving social media content. Facebook contrasts content that organically circulates on the social network with paid content that is then boosted to the top of feeds, or given more prominent placement.

Owned media—typically company-owned media, such as a website.

Packet switching—the method of moving Internet data in packet chunks and re-assembling content upon arrival.

Paid search—search engines charge advertisers for top placement within search results.

Pandora—a streaming music service.

Pay-per-click (PPC)—an advertising model that monetizes website clicks.

Paywall—a system requiring registration and payment by users.

Pins—Pinterest describes any posting on a user board as a pin, which is the online metaphor for placing a scrap of paper on a bulletin board.

Platforms—online sites that offer various social media services.

Posting—is the act of uploading media content to a social media site. Beyond organic content, the text, photographs or video distributed through a posting may receive wider distribution by paying for a promoted post or sponsored content on a site.

Promoted posts—social media sites charge advertisers to appear in prominent positions that are likely to be seen.

Privacy—a concept first suggested in the late 19th century that calls for legal protection of intimate details of life, especially when a person seeks to protect these from public view.

Propaganda—information designed to promote or advance a view, cause, person, product or idea. Before World War II, propaganda was simply considered persuasion. However, World War II propaganda caused people to associate the term with a pejorative meaning such that now it suggests the spread of false information.

Public relations (PR)—seeks through professional best practices to present, maintain and manage public images and reputations. Ongoing campaigns use media relations tactics to present perceived positives. Reputation management efforts may be in response to a crisis from perceived negative information.

Reach—a traditional mass media measure of distribution, social media are also interested in measuring the broad distribution of content.

Real-time social engagement—current PR best practices include nearly immediate response to conversation monitoring of social media. Within a relatively short time, sometimes a matter of minutes, a brand engages on a social network about a trending topic, issue or person.

Redditors—these active regular users of the Reddit site drive conversation.

Reliability—social scientific measures of consistency or reproducibility of results.

Return on Investment (ROI)—calculation of a financial gain minus the cost of an investment. ROI is expressed as a percentage or ratio and is sometimes considered a measure of efficiency.

Retweet—re-distributing a previous tweet with the letters RT in front of it, this allows Twitter users to easily share content to their social network. Twitter users also post MT for modified tweets and PRT, if an item is a partial retweet.

Rich media—photographs, video, info-graphics or other visual elements.

Right to be forgotten (RTBF)—European law empowering users to have personal information removed from the Internet and disconnected from search engines, such as Google.

Roles—individuals adopt roles, much as an actor might. A social media professional, for example, may perceive and express the role of an innovator or entrepreneur.

RPIE—the Public Relations Society of America PR process of research, planning, implementation and evaluation.

Search Engine Optimization (SEO)—Google algorithms produce a system for pushing some Internet content to the top of any specific search.

Search Engine Result Placements (SERP)—using SEO techniques to drive high placement during keyword searches.

Sentiment analysis—computer and human coding for positive, neutral and negative comments.

Smartphones—mobile telephones connected on cellular networks that provide an Internet connection through devices that have personal computer capabilities.

Snaps—Snapchat user postings to the site.

Social business—application of business strategy, goals and tactics within social media marketing campaigns.

Social graph—on Facebook, this is a user's complete social network.

Social media dashboard—measurement tools that organize data for efficient analysis.

Social networks—an array of online platforms used to connect with others.

Social Network Site (SNS)—any online platform that enables communication between site accounts.

Software—computer code that allows hardware to be used via an operating system, programs and applications.

Sponsored content—paid media content that may appear near editorial media content and free social media content.

Start-ups—new business ventures, sometimes with the funding help of "angel investors," launch social media sites and apps. An innovation culture, annual events such as "South By Southwest" (#SXSW) and the tech journalism community drive interest and activity in the diffusion of new ideas and products.

Stories—mobile apps Instagram and Snapchat offer users Stories as a tool to string together a series of postings into a larger narrative.

Storytelling—a fundamental concept in journalism and media communication. People have told stories since the development of language and oral tradition. Storytelling techniques, including the use of narrative, drive interest in content.

Tactics—strategic PR campaigns devise a set of tactics used to achieve communication goals. For example, if a campaign is designed to raise awareness about an issue, a tactic may be to create a YouTube video that can be shared by bloggers.

Tagging—On Facebook, a person can be tagged in a photograph. In doing so, a name is associated with a face and perhaps a place, and these data can be shared across the social network. More generally, geotagging is use of a computer software code that identifies location. A smartphone photograph may be geotagged with the location, and this data can be presented or used within the context of an application.

Terms of Service (ToS)—contract law that users click and agree to use software, apps or websites.

Thought leader—in each area of the social media communication industry, leaders emerge who can communicate as influencers of the field. These thought leaders may be very active in social media and are asked to speak at conferences and meetings. They frequently blog and publish articles and books.

Transparency—the social media approach of disclosing all relevant interests and not having a hidden agenda.

Trending—on Twitter, different words and hashtags trend at any given time. These are the most talked-about items. These can be organic or "promoted" as advertising.

Trust—is considered an important and fundamental characteristic for a lot of influential social media content. Trust is related to credibility and believability, which frequently is assessed by judging previous behavior, including communication.

Tweet—Twitter originally limited each individual message to no more than 140 characters, but this was relaxed. Twitter Limits also include: 1,000 Direct Messages and 2,400 tweets per day; 1,000 follows per day; and ratio limits after 5,000 follows.

Twitter Analytics—a dashboard for social media managers to track real-time account data.

User-generated content (UGC)—created content by users, often not sponsored by traditional professional media organizations.

User profiles—online descriptions of user identities.

Uses and gratifications—a research perspective emphasizing active audience participation.

Validity—in social science, the determination that measurement is conceptually what it was planned to be.

Vanity metrics—measures that do not go beyond popularity, such as number of followers, when these data are not related to strategies and tactics.

Verification and verified accounts—authenticity of identity is an important online concern. Twitter created a blue checkmark to identify those accounts that have been verified through its internal process, and this also appears on some Facebook pages. Additionally, Facebook users may take advantage of a two-step verification for login that includes a text message code to a mobile phone for account security.

Viral—content that is shared quickly and widely because of high interest. Social media enables individuals to post viral videos on YouTube and rise to almost-instant fame.

Virtual communities—online spaces creating a community experience among users.

Vlog—video bloggers use video posts instead of text. Vlogs are regular commentary in a video medium.

Word clouds—a word visualization of frequently used social media language.

Word of mouth (WOM)—personal influence is spread through word of mouth communication. In the past, this was mostly done face-to-face. Now, CMC allows for mediated WOM through social media communication.

Index

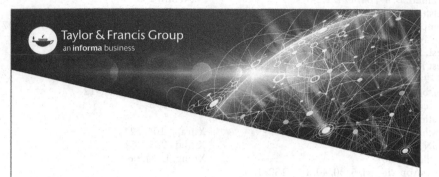

Taylor & Francis eBooks

www.taylorfrancis.com

A single destination for eBooks from Taylor & Francis
with increased functionality and an improved user
experience to meet the needs of our customers.

90,000+ eBooks of award-winning academic content in
Humanities, Social Science, Science, Technology, Engineering,
and Medical written by a global network of editors and authors.

TAYLOR & FRANCIS EBOOKS OFFERS:

A streamlined
experience for
our library
customers

A single point
of discovery
for all of our
eBook content

Improved
search and
discovery of
content at both
book and
chapter level

REQUEST A FREE TRIAL
support@taylorfrancis.com

 Routledge
Taylor & Francis Group

 CRC Press
Taylor & Francis Group

Printed in the United States
by Baker & Taylor Publisher Services

Printed in the United States
By Bookmasters